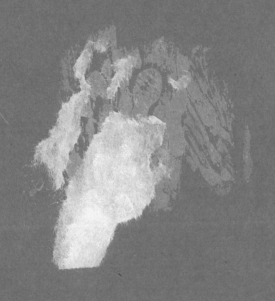

MARRIAGE, LOVE, SEX AND DIVORCE

by Jonathan Gathorne-Hardy

SUMMIT BOOKS

NEW YORK

Published by SUMMIT BOOKS
A Simon & Schuster Division of Gulf & Western Corporation
Simon & Schuster Building
Rockefeller Center
1230 Avenue of the Americas
New York, New York   10020

SUMMIT BOOKS and colophon are trademarks of Simon & Schuster
Designed by Irving Perkins Associates
Manufactured in the United States of America
10 9 8 7 6 5 4 3 2 1

Library of Congress Cataloging in Publication Data

Gathorne-Hardy, Jonathan.
    Marriage, love, sex and divorce.
    Includes bibliographical references and index.
    1. Sex customs. 2. Sex in marriage. 3. Marriage. 4. Divorce.
I. Title.
HQ32.G37   306.8   81-13517
                             AACR2
ISBN 0-671-40103-3

ACKNOWLEDGMENTS

IN THE course of researching and writing this book I interviewed and asked advice and help from a great many people, both in Britain and America. Many of these appear in the text (not always, at their own request, identifiable) and to all of them I owe a considerable debt of gratitude.

Amongst these, there are some I would like to single out; and there are others not mentioned but whom I should also like to thank. There is Jenny Scott, who typed the bulky manuscript when the book was a third as long again as it is now; Scott Supplee who did invaluable research for me; I had several very valuable conversations with Philip Hodson, Editor of *Forum* in Britain, and his assistant Anne Hooper; Meg Goodman and Toni Bellfield of the Family Planning Association were infinitely helpful. Peter Laslett and the Cambridge Group for the History of Population and Social Structure gave me much valuable information, some of which I was reluctantly compelled to jettison. Among the writers in this field I talked to, I am particularly grateful—even though I did not always agree with them—to Rhona and Robert Rapoport in London, and in New York to George and Nena O'Neill, and especially to Mildred Newman and Bernard Berkowitz for finding time in their crowded schedules for some stimulating discussion. Jenny Render, Sean O'Connell and Brian Davies all rendered extremely important services whose worth they are best qualified to know. I would like to thank Summit Books, and in particular Tom Maschler and Jonathan Cape for the generosity and flexibility that enabled me to write the book. Finally I would like to thank Xandra Hardie, Jill Sutcliffe and Jonathan Segal who performed miracles of careful and intelligent editing quite unprecedented in my experience of either English or American publishers.

The many books, papers and journals I consulted appear either in the text or among the references. But it is not always possible, without clumsiness, to convey how strongly a particular book has helped and influenced a passage or chapter. Two instances of this are Brenda Maddox's *The Half Parent—Living With Other People's Children,* and more especially the excellent study by Morton Hunt, *The World of the Formerly Married.* I would also like to thank A. M. Heath & Company Ltd, McGraw-Hill Book Company and the author for permission to quote from this. And I should like to acknowledge the permission of the Forum Press Ltd to quote from *The Best of Forum 1978.* My thanks are due, also, to Victor Gollancz Ltd (London) and Taplinger Publishing Co., Inc. (New York) for permission to quote from Sheila Kitzinger's *Giving Birth: The Parents' Emotions in Childbirth,* copyright © 1971 by Sheila Kitzinger.

May 1981   J.G-H.

CONTENTS

1

INTRODUCTION

TWELVE YEARS ago, when I was thirty-six, I got divorced after ten years of marriage. Five years after that an affair, which had been turbulent but, to me, very important, ended abruptly and painfully.

It was during the anguish, despair, loneliness and expense following these events that I increasingly found myself wondering: what was I doing to myself, what was being done to me? What was happening to marriage, and why? Was it breaking down and, if it was, would society break down as well? *What in fact were we as a society doing to ourselves?*

I started to read about marriage. Over the last thirty years, the subject has been wrung almost dry. Every form of marriage has been investigated and written about: there are books about companionate marriage, symmetrical marriage, open marriage, closed marriage, group marriage, gay marriage, serial marriage, non-marriage, marriage just to have children, marriage without children. And certainly I learnt a good deal.

Depending on how you define 'breakdown', of course, it was arguable that that was indeed what was happening to marriage—in Britain at the moment it looks as though eventually one quarter of all marriages will end in divorce, in America that one third will. In that respect, I found that my ten years wasn't bad by American standards—the average length of a divorced marriage there is about six and a half years. Not too good by British stan-

dards, however. In Britain it is thirteen years, but steadily short-
ening. Perhaps I was just ahead of my time.

I still found myself little nearer to answering those questions
which spread out from my divorce and the break-up of my affair.
And the reason is simply that writers on this subject invariably
concentrate on a single aspect—marriage breakdown, divorce,
creative divorce, *How to Save Your Marriage, Open Marriage,* and
so on. So much is this assumed that whenever I mentioned I was
writing a book about marriage, I was always asked what 'angle' I
was taking. No one, it seemed to me, had tried to get to grips with
the subject as a whole. As a result, as regards the general picture—all was confusion.

I thought there might be scope for a book which didn't take an
'angle', which stood back and, however roughly, tried to grasp the
subject entire—causes, distant and contemporary, consequences,
what it was *like* now, to be subject to whatever it was we were
subject to, to see what would happen in the future.

And yet—grasp the entire subject! What would that involve, or
rather was there anything it would not involve? And consider the
complexity, the difficulty of some of the topics I would have to
discuss, the strong feelings they aroused: child-upbringing, the effect of the feminist movement, of women working, the changing
roles of men and women, divorce, its effect on children, sex—initially it seemed to involve grasping a truly enormous amount of
sex. This has been written about even more than marriage. There
is virtually nothing left to discover—unless it be why men can't
have proper multiple orgasms like some women, a rippling flow of
fifteen or twenty in a row. (In fact I later found out that there are
men who claim to have them. And also explain how they can be
achieved; though the instructions are rather baffling and my own
efforts at following them—squeezing of sphincters and so on—
met with less than total success.)

But even here, where I began my researches, there is confusion.
It seemed to me obvious that what we call the 'sexual revolution'—the liberalising of sexual behaviour over the last thirty
years—was absolutely fundamental to the subject. There did not

appear any need to go too deeply into it—surely we all knew
roughly what had been going on—but it was important to see how
far it had gone, what areas it had affected, whether it was continuing or if a reaction had set in.

To my surprise I found that a good many commentators, sociologists, historians thought there hadn't really been a sexual revolution at all: some thought behaviour hadn't changed decisively, or
it had only changed among a minority, or there had been changes
but you couldn't call it a revolution. This was one of the first
questions that had to be answered.

Because of the size and complexity of this book, the large number of other books and articles I had to read, the number of people
I spoke to, the research and the writing had often to take place at
the same time. Sometimes I would be two-thirds through both,
and then come upon some book which appeared to disprove completely what I had already decided. At least once—as when I suddenly read Steven Goldberg when I had almost finished the chapter on feminism—the shock was more than I could contain. It
means that, though my book may be more discursive than it
should be, the writing was—and so the reading will be—to a certain degree a process of discovery. And when I say we shall discuss
or explore this or that it is, to a larger extent than the usual conventional pretence, the truth.

But there is more to it. As I progressed further and further into
the book, I found that I began to understand what had happened
to me, about a number of things I had done, or had done to me, in
quite a different way. As a result, I felt better about them. Now it
had been no part of my purpose to cheer people up. On the
whole, I find books of that sort—*How to Brighten Your Life and
Wife, How to Live More*—maddening; the aim spurious, the tone
false. I felt my life had gone wrong; I suspected therefore our society was going wrong—and secretly looked for some satisfaction
in involving society in my own disaster. Yet, instead of gloom or
even secret satisfaction, I just began to feel slightly but steadily
better—my head clearer, my understanding greater.

It was partly finding out things I didn't know—discovering, for

instance, that the apparently chaotic period following divorce or
the break-up of an affair was not without pattern; or some of the
facts about oral sex. But in fact it wasn't so much a series of individual illuminations as a *process*. I think the best way of explaining it is by analogy with analysis—with my experience of analysis,
that is.

After the events I referred to at the beginning of the chapter, I
had three years of analysis. The effects of this are rather strange.
Although of course you do recall incidents you had forgotten or
not thought about for years, there are not many recoveries of this
sort, nor are they often dramatic. On the whole, one knows the
shape of one's life and what went on. What does happen, however, is that the relative importance, the significance of events
and people start to alter. Innocuous figures at the corner of your
memory—a nanny, a dead sister—turn out to be crucial; two or
three unconnected memories, retained for no apparent reason,
fall into a pattern you are still repeating. In slowly working this
out, you quite often have to face parts of yourself, and events,
about which you feel strongly—feelings of fear or disgust or rage
or anxiety or excitement or desire or guilt. But it is the *process* of
all this, over time, which steadily, if with long gaps, does the work
so that, even after three years, the internal landscape has star-
tlingly changed. Of course three years is not enough. Perhaps only
six or seven major shifts take place. But even in three years a fair
amount can be accomplished.

I think the best way to regard this book is as an analysis of love,
marriage, sex and divorce in the West today. It does not 'grasp the
entire subject'. I have no doubt there is scope for such a book—
but the idea is absurd. You might as well write a book called *Life*.
This is, as it were, a three-year analysis. But that does not mean it
is necessarily easier. The six or seven areas which I found to be
significant will be looked at in depth. It will sometimes be difficult for another reason. I don't want to push the analogy too
far—it is after all marriage and so on that is being analysed, not
you—nevertheless there must be an element of self-analysis involved because many of the subjects we shall look at are those

about which people feel strongly; subjects like women working, the relative unfairness of divorce to men and women, emotions about stepchildren, sexual appetite or inadequacy, child-upbringing and child suffering and many others; and these feelings are, precisely, ones of fear, disgust, rage, anxiety, excitement, desire, guilt. Since I put my views with as much force and clarity as I can we shall often disagree. Not that this matters, provided I provoke you into seeing more clearly what you think or feel about that particular subject. When the whole field has been traversed you will, I hope, understand what is happening and why.

There remains the question: does it have any particular significance, beyond the ordinary personal significance such matters automatically have in our lives?

By the time I had finished the book it seemed to me that something very important might be happening in Western society, a watershed comparable with the advent of Christianity (though quite different). In fact, I think we all know approximately what is happening; it stares us in the face at every turn. But for some reason the extraordinary significance of the development has not been grasped—perhaps just because the events themselves are so obvious.

I have put this realisation at the end because it was the final part in my process of understanding what was going on. But in fact I also began with the same question, since if marriage generally was breaking down as mine had individually, and if there was a distinct possibility that society was in danger, as many distinguished commentators assumed, then I should know it early. It would dictate the shape of my research and of the book. I wondered first, if anything like it had happened before—and if it had, was it happening now for the same reasons, in the same way, and would it have the same outcome?

We must begin, that is, like any sensible analyst does with a patient, by looking into the past.

2

SAXON SEXUALITY AND THE RAGE TO DIVORCE IN ANCIENT ROME

IN THE past, Babylonian, Greek and Hebraic law all recognised divorce as a solution to marital breakdown and made provision for it. But the scale in no way approached that pertaining in the West today, nor was there the same pattern of rapidly increasing divorce, which would make comparison more fruitful.

Few records survive from the first centuries of English history, but it is likely that up to the eleventh century divorce was easy, and casual sleeping around and affairs were common. Most of the evidence comes from the Celtic civilisations in the first centuries after Christ. This reveals not immorality so much as a completely different sexual and marital morality—one which to a certain extent echoes some developments today. Marriage was not expected to last for life—or anything like it. It could be a trial marriage. So Fionn marries Sgathach 'for one year'; and one year's trial marriage was allowed in Scotland till the Reformation. The tenth-century Ordinances of Howel the Good allowed seven years, and until late in the Middle Ages—a circumstance that makes Henry VIII more understandable—frequent changes of partner were quite usual. Sexuality in those early centuries was uninhibited and frequent. Virginity was not prized, lovers were expected. Queen

Medb boasts to her husband that she always had a secret lover in addition to him and her Official Lover (i.e., three men). When Princess Findahair mentions to her mother that she fancies the messenger who has been sent from the opposite camp, the Queen replies, 'If you love him then sleep with him tonight'. These attitudes of the past survived in remote areas. In the mid-fifteenth century, an Italian cleric, later to be Pope Pius II, spent the night in a Scottish border village. After supper, the men and children withdrew to a fortified tower, leaving the Italian and the women to the mercies of the Scottish bandits. They justified the exclusion of the women on the grounds that all that would happen to them was rape—which they didn't think wrong and which the women didn't mind. When the future Pope went to his room, two young women came in and offered to sleep with him—which was customary behaviour to a guest. He refused, fearing the bandits might cut his throat while he was in a state of mortal sin.

As in all periods of unrestrained sexuality, women were perfectly frank about their desires. Deirdre seizes Naoise by the ears and tells him she is a young cow and wants him for her bull. That these attitudes were prevalent in England, too, is suggested by contemporary comment. Boniface on the eighth-century English: '[they] utterly despise matrimony . . . utterly refuse to have legitimate wives and continue to live in lechery and adultery after the manner of neighing horses and braying asses.' Similarly free behaviour has continually reappeared right up to and including today; but after the tenth century it was done with appeals to the customs of the past; above all, it is shown by the continual and fruitless attempts of the church at repression and control. You don't need to control something that isn't there.

Nevertheless, I don't think it is much help to use this beguiling period as an example to set against our own. For one thing, we have no clear picture of the society. The evidence, although it exists, is scanty, and frequently interfered with by the Church. For example, there is a charming mediaeval tale of Blancheflor visiting Perceval in his bedroom one night to seek help. It is freezing cold and the gallant knight invites her to lie chastely in bed with him to warm herself. In the original Celtic version the invitation, and its immediate acceptance, were anything but chaste. But the main reason these Celtic civilisations are of little help to us is that they represent a settled pattern which had existed for several centuries and was either inherited from the Roman or, more likely, was indigenous. You do not get that sudden onslaught of divorcing marriages which recently has become, and still is, our pattern.

1 The rage to divorce in ancient Rome

The only other society that has ever remotely duplicated our experience—and that is the measure of our uniqueness, a uniqueness not often appreciated—is exactly that Roman culture which may have influenced the Celts and early Britons. Some of these duplications are trivial—though it is extraordinary how minute customs have lasted unchanged for 2,000 years. The Roman bride wore a veil (orange not white). She would have had a golden ring placed on the same finger as brides do now; a ritual founded on the Egyptian discovery of a delicate nerve starting at this finger and ending at the heart. After the bridal procession the bride was taken to her new home and lifted over the threshold by the bridegroom.

The archetypal Roman marriage of the two centuries before Christ in the stern days of the Republic was totally male dominated. Women were forced to marry whomever their fathers wanted them to, or were chosen by husbands—who immediately had absolute power. A father could summarily execute a child for disobedience, or a husband kill his wife for adultery. But during the first half of the first century A.D. a change began to take place. Women (supported by men) gradually approached equality with their husbands, until there emerged the proud, independent, dignified Roman matron, companion, lover and helpmate, often celebrated by Pliny the Younger. Marriages became close and enduring. There are numerous stories of wives who would rather die with their husbands than live after them. Pliny tells of Arria, wife of Caecina Paetus. He was condemned to death by Claudius after a revolt in A.D. 42. When the time came, she took a dagger from her robe and plunged it into her breast. Then she pulled it out again and handed it to her husband with words which still have a ring after all these centuries: 'It does not hurt, Paetus'.

More usual were long, devoted, companionate unions, like the wife of Pliny's friend Macrinus who 'lived with her husband 39 years without a quarrel, or fit of the sulks, in unclouded happiness and mutual respect'.

But I know of no stories of a husband killing himself when his wife died. It was still the man's life that was central, but with the woman helping in a more equal situation than before. Pliny, who sets down several accounts of married bliss, also gave his own wife as an example: yet the only real reason he seems pleased with her was because she admired his writing. He didn't sleep with her and had his secretary (*notaria*) as a mistress. Marriage then was usually an arrangement, not so much of strong feeling, as of a degree of character compatibility joined to economic suitability, under a fairly mild male dominance. It resembled the better marriages of the nineteenth century.

It was during the end of the first century A.D. and the second century that there took place a series of developments which resemble those of the last forty years in an uncanny way and which, in that society at least, were both symptom and cause of very profound effects indeed.

Child-upbringing in the first and second centuries A.D. became much more permissive. The decline in the authority of the father, described by both Pliny and Martial, meant ferocity gave way to tenderness and love, love to overindulgence. In all ages, a more permissive upbringing is a prelude to sexual freedom.

This happened in Rome. The search for sexual pleasure became increasingly free and increasingly pursued. Experiments in love-making—group orgies, three men to one woman and so on—and instructions in love-making—positions, methods of stimulation, oral sex—became common. Nor were they as ludicrously mechanical or heavy-handedly culinary as they are sometimes today. Ovid's *Ars Amatoria* is a delightful guide to seduction. The Romans knew something of romantic love, but it was rare; they regarded it as unbalancing, and also thought that it interfered with freedom of choice in sexual partner. However, it is from Ovid that we derive, via European poetry, especially Shakespeare, the idea that sexual seduction—a delicate, charming, elaborate, and all-important pursuit—should be combined with romantic love. In Rome, there was chiefly sex. And as the appetite became more obsessive, adultery became more and more common. Special courts had to be set up; ferocious laws were enacted against it, and then instantly ignored. Augustus in particular tried desperately to discipline his increasingly dissolute capital—although his daughter and granddaughter had to be sent into exile for notoriously scandalous behaviour.

There was an equally powerful feminist movement. Women now entered traditional male spheres, legal work, politics, and so on. They wrestled and hunted. Juvenal's satires are full of them, women like Meria who 'with spear in hand and breasts exposed, takes to pig sticking'. This extended to gluttony and drinking. And sex.

If two people in a marriage instead of one demand, and have the power to insist on, personal happiness and satisfaction, then clearly the chances of marriage's breaking are doubled—probably more than doubled. Unhappy marriages became innumerable. Juvenal has the figure of the unhappy husband urged to try and forget at dinner the despair caused by the shamelessness of his young wife who 'is wont', in Juvenal's evocative words, 'to go forth at dawn and to come home at night with crumpled hair and flushed face and ears'.

> 'Caeli', cried Catullus, 'Lesbia nostra, Lesbia illa,
> Illa Lesbia, quam Catullus imam
> Plus quam se atque suos amavit omnes,
> Nunc in quadriviis et angiportis
> Glubit magnamini Reni nepotes'.

'O Caelus—my Lesbia, that Lesbia, that same Lesbia
whom Catullus loved more than himself and all his dear
ones, now at the cross-roads and in the alleys tosses
off the spawn of lordly-minded Remus'.

By the end of the second century, equality, freedom, and feminism had produced an almost contemporary response. Here is a
familiarly one-sided open marriage. 'We agreed long ago', says a
lady in Quintilian, 'that you were to go your way and I mine. You
may confound sea and sky with your bellowing. I am a human
being after all.'

In the middle of that century adultery suddenly diminishes.
The Romans had been compelled by the stress placed on marriage
to choose another solution: divorce.

The pattern they followed was almost precisely the one we
have followed so far, and may well follow further. Divorce was
first arranged by the husband as and when he liked. Next, some
form of marital wrong, usually infidelity, became necessary. Gradually this became more and more a formality, and the more common divorce the more trumpery or false the pretext. Cicero, at
fifty-seven, dropped his wife of thirty years and mother of his
children, to replenish his bank account and revive his bed with
young, rich Pubilia. (Not that his wife, Terentia, seemed to mind.
She was tough. She married twice more—first Sallust, then Mer-
sala Corvinus—and did not die until she was a hundred.) The Emperors' lives were scandalous. Aging Sulla took a young divorcee
as his fifth wife. Caesar divorced Poppeia for no reason at all. In-
nocence was not sufficient. 'Caesar's wife must be above suspicion.'

Then it was enough if the couple agreed the marriage had broken down. They had to state their wish to divorce in front of seven
witnesses, and a message to this effect was delivered to the court.
Divorce, then as now, fuelled itself. It became ever more common, the dignity and importance of marriage correspondingly
less, and finally either partner could end the marriage at will. This
is more or less the position today in Britain and America, though

there are still some legal forms and a period of time has to pass to prove 'irretrievable' breakdown. The Romans, always efficient, dispensed even with this. Either one of the couple would simply tell the other to go. The form of words has been preserved. The one whose house it was: *'Tuas res tibi agito'*—'Take your belongings away'. And the reply (showing how mercenary the whole thing had become): 'Keep your belongings to yourself'! (*'Tuas res tibi habeto'.*)

During the last century of the Roman Empire, as a great civilisation collapsed, a raging epidemic of divorces roared unchecked. Juvenal talks of it, describing women with eight husbands in five years. Martial talks of Telesilla 'now marrying her tenth husband'. Divorce became so common, we learn from Jurists, that it was not unusual for a bride, after many intermediate stages, to return at length to her first husband. The reasons given were trifling and often, as when a soldier husband went to war, reasons which in the early days of Rome would have been those for remaining faithful. As Martial said, such marriage was really a misuse of terms. 'She who marries so often does not marry; she is an adultress by form of law.'

Now the Emperors panicked and began to set standards of strict monogamy. Trajan and Plotina, Hadrian and Sabina, Antonius and Faustinia were all imperial couples faithful for life. But it was too late. The fever raged unstoppable.

2   *Sexual indulgence with slaves, and other factors*

The Roman breakdown took place over some 200–250 years. The major elements which have given rise to our situation today can mostly be traced back 100–200 years. Who can say what will happen over the next 100–150?

Human societies are kept together by learnt patterns. And the learning and transmission of these is vital because they can be forgotten or unlearnt—and if this happens society collapses. The family, however constituted, is the most important single area where these patterns are taught. If it collapses, therefore, society

is in grave danger. Professor Edmund Leach, Provost of King's
College, Cambridge, assumed in a recent Reith Lecture that the
value of a secure and stable family for the efficient transmission of
values and customs was simply axiomatic. Dr Jack Dominian,
Director of the Marriage Research Centre at the Middlesex Hospital, London, assumes, without going into it further, that 'the
welfare of societies and nations depends on the well-being of the
individual marriage and family'.

But although we can learn from Rome, I don't think that we are
following the same pattern as that tremendous collapse. The
Roman breakdown was due at least in part to the ferocity of its
outside enemies, the Goths and the Visi-Goths, the Vandals and
Huns, pouring in upon an Empire which had grown dispropor-
tionately large. It suffered a series of military defeats which might
in the end have brought it down however Puritan its rulers and
people. This was compounded by another very powerful external
enemy: the plague.

It was an age of quite unparalleled coarseness and brutality, to
which the few muggings and murders we worry about, the 'violence' on our TV screens are peccadilloes. Murder and assassina-
tion were as common as car accidents are now. The games were
incessant and of appalling savagery. Gladiators fought to death in
front of crowds as large as the largest modern football crowds.
A major 'event' could last 117 days in the second century, with
4,941 *pairs* of gladiators fighting until one or other died, the field
strewn with corpses. Criminals were butchered to death in front
of crowds and, later, torn to pieces by wild animals. Gambling
was also feverish at these events. This went on for two centuries,
completely eroding any value in life itself—and if life does not
matter, why should it matter how you live it?

The divorce and sexual phenomena took place among no more
than some debauched thousands. The middle class, the equestrian
order, and the lower middle class were all much closer to the pau-
perised masses than to the relatively few fantastically wealthy
landowners and capitalist business men—who were in today's
terms nearly all millionaires or extremely rich.

And the temptations were considerable. It is moderately easy in many Western countries today to have sex before marriage, sex without marriage, or sex outside marriage. Successful film or pop stars no doubt have opportunities greater than others. But the sexual opportunities open to the Romans were of a completely different order. Their Empire is an example of how a society based on a vast number of slaves nearly always ends up by destroying or completely corrupting the institution of marriage.

The victories of Trajan had sent a great flood of men and women pouring on to the Roman slave market from Dacia, Arabia, from the distant shores of the Tigris and the Euphrates. They filled the houses of the rich, and many of them were young, beautiful or handsome, cultivated even—and a great deal more manageable. Respectable households swiftly gave way to the temptation in such numbers that they filled the pages of the satirists. Martial mocks the master who brings to stay the highly sexed little slave mistress he cannot bear to be without; or attributes Marulla's many children, not to her husband Curia, but to Curia's cook, his bailiff, his baker, his flautist, his wrestler and finally his buffoon.

But this was discreet, responsible. Some, greedy only for pleasure, indifferent to scandal, became impatient not just of marriage, but of the lightest regular slave mistress or slave lover or two; they ruled as pashas over great slave harems. When Larcius Marcedo, a senator and colleague of Pliny, was assassinated, a vast swarm of his slave girl concubines was seen rushing to the body, howling with grief. Even the few respectable households where normal love affairs were forbidden succumbed to the laxity of slave love. Slaves were considered as less than human, so adultery with them wasn't 'real' adultery, and the atmosphere of irresponsibility and licentiousness which this created was the final blow to marriage.

The aims of Roman freedom were quite different from those in the West today. Their culture was too superficial, too desultory, to withstand the temptations that beset it; those temptations themselves, the product of huge wealth and unending slave opportunity, too strong. The result was a moral collapse which we not only do not approach but can barely envisage.

3   *The invention of anxiety*

'In our days', continued Vera—mentioning 'our days' as people of limited intelligence are fond of doing, imagining they have discovered and appraised the peculiarities of 'our days' and that human characteristics change with the times.

LEO TOLSTOY,
War and Peace

Since Rousseau's ideas on Natural Man, but in particular today, most people have assumed that there exists a deep, spontaneous 'normal' impulse upon which culture or religion has laid a sort of gloss, an 'idea of how to behave', which may distort or suppress but cannot alter the reality. Reality can be 'rescued' as it were. At the crudest level this may be true—everyone needs food, libido always exists, as does the potentiality of orgasm in a woman. But at every other level these 'ideas' themselves *become* the reality— they dictate the food we eat, when we eat it, how much and where and by what methods. Our libido, the potentiality for orgasm, are part of our genetic inheritance—anything from 50,000 to 4 million years old. But the way we feel and want love and sex, the fact that we marry and what we expect from marriage, the very goals of life itself, are part of our cultural inheritance—from the immediate past back four, five, six thousand years. And the forces at work here are just as important. To call them 'ideas', in fact, is altogether to miss their tremendous surging power. They are a jumble of pagan customs long forgotten, of dead religions and dead societies, themselves sometimes expressing and containing yet deeper impulses. We ignore these forces at our peril, because they contain imperatives which we work out regardless. Thus it is not institutions that matter—the history of the last thousand years shows these can change and accommodate or even vanish—it is states of mind. We transmit systems of irrational anxiety or desire which, however much they seem to change, always make it impossible to approach our problems with detachment, in a new way. In this sense, as Ibanez said, we are ruled by the dead.

For instance we are all aware that though it is frequently at the core of the initial impulse to marry, romantic love is not just unrealistic, it is actually destructive as a basis for this strenuous state. This is because its origins lie 700 years back in a semi-religious code whose aims were explicitly anti-marriage (anti-sex, too). Over the centuries sex and marriage and children (and soon I suspect 'individual growth') all gradually joined together with romantic love and the resulting jumble has diffused down from élite and court circles until it has spread through every stratum in our culture.

But there is another more superficial but more obviously useful level of historical awareness. Take industrial society in the last quarter of the twentieth century. The complexity and competitiveness of modern life, the speed of change, its pace, the isolation and strain and polluted environment of the huge urban conglomerations in which we live, and their growing violence, throw ever increasing pressure on the individual. This is compounded by complete spiritual desolation, a hectic consumerism, a ceaseless appetite for material possessions. This is an age, uniquely, of anxiety and stress. You find this obvious—a cliché even? A cliché it certainly is. I don't for one moment think it is true.

Every age imagines it is unique, and usually that it is uniquely lewd. Lynn Linton, a writer in the middle of the Victorian age, was convinced she was alive in a time of appalling licence, and urged her readers to 'wait patiently until the national madness has passed, and our women come back to the old English ideal, once the most beautiful, the most modest, the most essentially womanly in the world'. It is a form of conceit.

As regards anxiety, one can make a case for almost any period, plucked at random, to refute the stress-of-modern-living cliché. The Age of Anxiety—England 1450–1500. Civil War has been raging. You expect death, your own and your loved ones', from appalling diseases all the time. Your teeth are in agony, your gall bladder about to be pulled out by tongs. If, being female, you are about to have a child (and women are practically always pregnant) there is a 60–40 chance of dying; your child (your love, *pace*

Stone, no less) far more likely to die than live. Murder, violence, robbery are daily occurrences. Taxation is vicious and your short and painful life is almost certainly lived in chronic poverty, than which nothing is more anxious-making. And high above, but all-pervading, is a vengeful God, spitting out guilt and terror.

Once again, the idea in human affairs is all important. We *invented* anxiety. Because we think we live in a time of great change and turbulence, of marriage breakdown and personal stress, we actually increasingly bring this about and increase its effect. Anxiety feeds on itself. Even quite general knowledge about the past can have a calming effect. It is the only way to acquire perspective, to find out what is important and what is not. Nowhere is this more true, and more necessary, than in America.

To Europeans, Americans frequently seem to have no sense of history at all, profound or superficial, general or particular. (Talk-show host to ex-Premier Cao Ky of South Vietnam, who now runs a liquor store in California: 'We still have a minute left, could you tell us what went wrong?') Nor is this surprising. In Europe, vast numbers of families have been in their present countries four or five hundred years, a thousand years. Even in 1970 one-third of the people in the United States were still either born abroad or were the children of foreign-born parents. It is a nation still as it were molten, still violently spinning, still forming its history as it goes along. Nowhere is 'the age of anxiety' anxiety so intense as it is in America. Often one can refute their anxieties in the particular. For instance, the population of America is intensely mobile. Mobility is indeed the major indicator used to demonstrate the unsettled restless nature of that society. Americans are partly rather proud of this. There is something forceful, rootless, pioneering, adaptable about it. A refusal to stagnate and be bound by history, a willingness to seize opportunity. But it is also a source of strain and anxiety. It was indeed seen as a major source of pressure on the family—and therefore as a cause of marital breakdown—in an article by that brilliant *Village Voice* commentator, Alexander Cockburn.

Yet are Americans historically 'intensely mobile'? The volatility of a society is calculated by change of addresses, usually taken over one, five, ten or twenty-year periods. Certainly, American mobility is quite high by contemporary standards. Over one-year periods (around the 1960s) one-fifth of the population in the U.S. moved, almost double the figure in the U.K. and more than double that of Japan. Over five-year periods the difference is not so great; though half of all Americans move, over a third of the British do. The idea behind the stress of mobility—the sense of impermanence and superficiality it gives as communities continually form and dissolve, new faces appearing, old ones vanishing, the sense of a quick-changing society and, by extension, quick-changing marriage—is that it is different from some much more stable society in the past. The vision, unspoken but implicit, is usually vaguely pastoral and small scale—some rural community in that seventeenth-century Stuart England from which the first immigrants sailed. A cottage, a village of cottages, smoke curling in the spring air; a calm, traditional, settled community where marriages, too, were settled and enduring.

Yet the curious thing is if you look closely at those very Stuart villages the actual picture is completely different. Far from being stable, the turnover in 'traditional' England was far higher than it is in America today. At Clayworth, a typical village in the English Midlands, at the height of political and social stability between 1676 and 1688, the change of population was nearly two-thirds. In another ordinary rural Stuart village between 1618 and 1628, the turnover was of the same order. Similar figures exist for France, though these are from the late-eighteenth century and are not quite so high. Death played a major part, but 30 per cent or more was due to migration. And to move in those centuries was far more absolute than today when telephone, letter, car and plane have squeezed countries until the whole of Europe, the whole of Europe and America together are in many respects smaller than England was before the railway came in the nineteenth century.

Societies have often before been subject to the stress of migration, of transient communities. That does not mean migration does not impose stress, of course, a feeling of impermanence; only that it is not new.

History can calm; it can disquiet; it can suggest the future; it can interest and amuse. And one sphere where it does all these things is the one we call the sexual revolution—if indeed there has been any such thing.

3

SEXUAL REVOLUTIONS

Sixteen-year-old girl: *'Parents should acknowledge that peo-*
ple do fuck, which was hard for me to realize because my
mother didn't acknowledge this. And just because you have
to be home by one doesn't mean you can't fuck from eleven
to one . . . Well, I really hope I'll be a lot closer to my
daughter than my mother and I were.'
> ROBERT SORENSON, *Adolescent*
> *Sexuality in Contemporary*
> *America*, 1972

Thank heaven for having given me the love of women. To
many she gives not the noble passion of lust.
> JOHN WILKES, *Essay*
> *on Women*, 1763

IT MAY seem obvious to you that behaviour *has* altered over the
last thirty years. Certainly, there has been a great change in what
we say and how we say it. Fuck entered the *Oxford English Dic-*
tionary (in a supplement) for the first time in 1972. But that does
not prove anything. The Victorians were quite aware that the important point was what you were or were not allowed to say. Reality remained the same. Victorian novelists often found this irritating and reacted against it in secret. Here is Thackeray in
Vanity Fair:

> . . . people remember Lady O'Dowd performing a jig at
> Government House, where she danced down two Aides-

de-Camp, a Major of Madras Cavalry, and two gentle-
men of the Civil Service; and, persuaded by Major Dob-
bin, C.B., to retire to the supper room, 'cassata nondum
satiata recessit' 'she retired, weary but still ready for
more'.

Harmless enough, except that the phrase is actually Juvenal's on
Messalina when she'd had a bet with another woman as to which
of them could have the most men in succession before becoming
exhausted. In literature, in the media, in manners, appearance is
everything, reality nothing. Bertrand Russell, lecturing on marriage and morals in America in 1929, was not allowed to give his
talk in front of women. Then he found the lecture was going out
on radio. 'It didn't matter ladies hearing it if they were not *seen*
hearing it.'

Part of the trouble is the word 'revolution', a word conceived to
describe political and economic events where change can be
swift. Literary taste and media interest can change in a revolutionary way, as well. But attitudes and behaviour in such fundamental areas as family, marriage and sex do not change in a whole
society anything like fast enough, it is argued, to call it revolutionary.

We have retained many of our old attitudes towards social behaviour, often quite openly, as surveys about the death penalty or
the dive back into the prefeminist 1950s, made by followers of
Marabel Morgan, show. Sometimes those attitudes are disguised
or even unnoticed. The stigma, or feeling of failure, on divorce
remains very strong—despite the numbers of people getting divorced. In Britain, the Church, acting against the advice of two of
its own committees, still refuses to marry divorced couples. People will admit what is appropriate, but many still *feel* quite different. At the moment in New York or Los Angeles it is not appropriate to admit guilt over homosexuality; though some psychiatrists
find that many of their patients do in fact still feel guilty. The
same is true of divorce.

We think and express ourselves, and often judge our world, in literary and media terms; we don't necessarily behave in the same way. We would all probably say we were a child-loving society. Yet it is perfectly clear that a very large and growing number of people regard their own happiness, their individual 'growth', as a great deal more important than the happiness of their children.

Behaviour is so slow to alter because it is least amenable to change in its most fundamental area—that of child-upbringing. On the whole, people bring up their children in the same way they were brought up themselves. They do this to a considerable extent unconsciously, even against their will. Battered babies grow up to become battering mothers or fathers—*and can't control themselves.* Some long-term studies of infant care show how by 1940 a modified fun morality had entered American child-upbringing. But it had to be clean fun. Playing with genitals could be diverted by a toy. By the 1960s, libidinal pleasure had become an end, but mothers who had been babies in the 1940s often found they were made uneasy by genital touching and would covertly distract, expressing smothered but strong disapproval.

A great many commentators think that the changes of the last thirty years are essentially ones of expression. So argued Nicky Hart, Lecturer in Sociology at the University of Salford, in a recent study of divorce—though some people might well think that her deeply depressed sample was locked into gloom of such exceptional blackness as to be impervious to all but the most violent of contemporary events. The sales of romantic fiction, read chiefly by married women of twenty-five or over, are by far the largest of any single category of book. These sales indicate an intense desire for romantic love, but of a safe and conventional sort—without sex before marriage, without wild affairs, and ending, after some small impediments which comprise the plot, in a happy, life-long marriage. The 'permissive revolution' is not general. Over the last ten years there has been absolutely no change in the type or severity of problems which come into the British edition of the magazine *Forum*—the same guilts, anxieties and ignorance pour through the letter box and in the same number. Indeed, far from increasing sexual health, the picture sometimes seems one of sexual chaos. At some time a quarter to a half of all marriages will suffer from sexual dysfunction; clinics continue to spring up all over America and are now (as usual, five years or so behind) starting in Britain. And the enormous erotico/porn market is evidence of the extent of sexual deprivation and dissatisfaction.

The distinguished sociologist and anthropologist, Geoffrey Gorer, thought it was clear in 1970 that people were greatly exaggerating the spread of permissiveness in Britain. He felt it mostly took place in London—largely, the impression was, on top of or under the desks of the media. His survey at least partly confirmed this. Britain appeared, at the height of the permissive revolution, to be a nation of virgins—26 per cent of men and 63 per cent of women were so at marriage; 46 per cent of men and 88 per cent of women married the first person they slept with.

A rather curious picture of the successive sexual and moral revolutions could be derived from Gorer's survey. He asked one ingenious question: 'Do you think a man and a woman can have a real friendship without sex playing a part?' In this way he hoped to isolate the censorious because they would feel such a friendship *should* not take place, and the licentious because they would feel it *could* not. This would leave the calm and comradely. These turned out to be 70 per cent of the population. Gorer now further analysed other answers the remaining 30 per cent had given—such as number of and attitude to orgasms, numerous partners, shooting homosexuals and so on—and found that 10 per cent of them were licentious (three-quarters men, one-quarter women) and 20 per cent were censorious. 'Since these groups feel so intensely about sex, it is understandable that their voices are heard much more frequently than those of the majority whose imaginations are less heated.' Thus the picture is of constant turmoil among this 'overheated' 30 per cent. At the end of the sixteenth century, during the Restoration, in the eighteenth century and again today, the licentious dominate; during some of the seventeenth century and nineteenth century and perhaps again in the future, the probably repressed high libido censorious take over. All the time, largely unaffected, the mass of the people, the calm 70 per cent, go on behaving much as they have always done.

1   *'Sexual intercourse began in 1963'*

Philip Larkin

At the same time, it would be rather odd to find that nothing had altered except the way we express ourselves—and the behaviour of some magazine staff and the populations of New York, London and a few of the big provincial capitals. Erotic instruction, incitement and stimulation have been available to whole populations for twenty or thirty years on a scale and of a vividness never known before. Some attitudes must have changed, and if attitudes change, *ultimately* behaviour does. What makes the last thirty years extraordinary is that we are seeing the result of historical trends and social movements—some long term, others less so; some interacting, others independent—all culminating or coming together at approximately the same time. The revolution in behaviour may have been rapid; the causes are far more profound.

For example, although the long-term infant studies showed how old attitudes do persist in child-upbringing, the main conclusion was how much things have changed over the last seventy years. In 1914 a baby was allowed to cry for a legitimate need—if ill, hungry, thirsty or in pain. Then a parent could pick it up and deal with the problem. But there could be no question of its crying because it felt bored, say, or because it wanted to be cuddled. That was intolerable. It should be left to cry so as to learn that crying will not get what it wants—'one of the worst habits it can learn'. Pleasure was not a goal, least of all sexual pleasure. During the 1920s and 1930s this gradually altered until by the 1940s 'fun' and pleasure were goals; pure libidinal pleasure was not to be punished but diverted. Spock's *Baby and Child Care* came in 1946 (two and a quarter million copies sold to date) and by the 1960s and 1970s mothers were urged to behave with great tolerance towards all auto-erotic impulses and babies were encouraged to suck, soil and wet and touch their genitals. Some mothers found this hard, it is true, but the evidence is that parents built on the basis of their own permissive childhood to be even more permissive towards their own children and that this development has been going on for the past seventy or eighty years.

It is often said that we love our children more than past societies did, and that this is shown in our liberal method of child-upbringing. It has even been said that this is the only clear trend of the last 300 years. No doubt we are different; but it seems to me very difficult to prove we are more compassionate or caring than parents of the past. In some ways we are more selfish, in others less so. What happens is that goals change or do not change, new 'discoveries' are made or refuted. Thus it has been found that overpermissive upbringing appears to a child to be indifference. Children of overpermissive parents often show the same symptoms—insecurity, delinquency, aggression and so on—as those suffering from parental neglect and deprivation. The goal of relaxed toilet-training, touching genitals, and so on, was quite specifically based on analytic and behavioural studies over many years showing that it would liberate adult sexuality. This goal has not altered, nor has this aspect of upbringing.

In the 1970s the age of onset of puberty, which had been steadily arriving earlier for about 100 years, appears to have come to rest. The menarche in girls is now around twelve-and-a-half to thirteen, compared to a probable fourteen to fifteen or an even later onset in the past. The same development of puberty, though it is harder to pinpoint precisely, took place with boys. Clearly this is biological pressure for a change in sexual customs.

It is a mistake to suppose there was no birth control in the past. Since the beginning of time there has been *coitus interruptus*, and in a crude way it was extremely effective, being responsible for most large scale fluctuations in population. (It is still quite common; 700,000 people were relying on it in England in 1978.) But syphilis provoked the first move which eventually led to contraception as we know it today. Syphilis may have been brought to Portugal from Haiti by Columbus's sailors in 1494, and it reached France, Germany and Switzerland a year later. Racing through Europe on the wings of love, it arrived in Scotland in 1497, and Hungary and Russia in 1499, carried by the dispersing armies of Charles VIII. Vasco da Gama took it to India in 1498, and it reached China in 1505. In 1506 we find the Bishop of Crete dying of it. In ten years the little bacillus had conquered the world.

Response was swift. In 1564 the Italian anatomist Gabrielle Fallopia recommended a linen sheath, moistened with a lotion, to be worn as a protection. It was not until the eighteenth century that these had developed so that they could also be used as a contraceptive. They were great cumbersome things made of sheep's gut and—a pleasant touch—were tied on with a red ribbon which went round the scrotum. They were, however, still worn largely for protection, which explains Madame de Sévigné's well-known but usually misunderstood remark that they were gossamer against infection, steel against love. Boswell hated his and left it off whenever he dared, swearing he'd support any child that resulted. The nineteenth century saw the breakthrough. Vulcanisation of rubber by Goodyear and Hancock in 1843 led to a far more effective sheath, which grew more and more efficient, and thinner, becoming in the 1930s gossamer for love too. But the most efficient use of rubber was popularised by a Dutch physician, Dr Aletta Jacobs, in 1883: a domed cap attached to a circular watchspring, which covered the cervix and upper vagina. The Dutch cap gave women complete control over their own fertility for the first time in history. It is highly significant that its invention accompanied the first positive moves towards feminine political and sexual emancipation.

Until contraceptives, the practical base of the double standard remained. There were even laws against the dissemination of contraceptive information in the nineteenth century. The Dutch cap only spread slowly among the middle and upper classes (prostitutes in Paddington were still using sponges soaked in antiseptic jelly at the end of the 1930s). Not until the development of the pill, the intra-uterine device and male and female sterilisation (all of which themselves have long histories) was the whole population of women finally potentially free. Once again, here is a vital 400-year-old movement culminating in the 1960s and 1970s.

As these various movements began to converge during the 1920s and 1930s there were increasingly expressions of opinion and developments like those of today. The publication of sex manuals in vast numbers was a prewar, not a postwar development. *The Hygiene of Marriage*, published in 1923 by Dr Isabel Emalie Hutton, went into eight editions by 1947, with dozens of impressions and hundreds of thousands of copies. In some ways, it still carried Victorian overtones. The title for instance—as though marriage somehow needed cleaning up. She was against masturbation and sex before marriage, and said that too much intercourse was debilitating. She advocated twice a week, a suggestion she said Luther also made (odd source). The diagram of the female reproductive organs is absolutely terrifying—like the entrance to Hades surrounded by flames. But she considered the object of sex to be pleasure, and central to marriage. She advised stimulating the clitoris to give a woman an orgasm if she has not had it by the end of intercourse. She knew that many people thought sex should end after women have the menopause, but said it can and should go on into old age.

I would deduce from all this something one might call the catastrophe theory of history. Catastrophe theory states something we all know, that things alter under pressure, that pressure builds up and up and then things alter suddenly—*catastrophically.* A bridge (or a camel) withstands increasing weights until it breaks *suddenly*; a row brews in a marriage and then breaks out *in a flash.* Where catastrophe theory becomes interesting is that it says a great many, if not all, situations are like this—wars, student revolts, decisions to divorce; that you can construct graphs which explain and demonstrate this mathematically; and that if you know the significant factors you can foretell the catastrophe. I cannot begin to understand the mathematics. They may be totally incorrect. But it does seem as though, given a sufficient number of strong social forces all coming together and acting together at the same time, behaviour in fundamental areas such as marriage and sex *can* change relatively quickly.

Sexual behaviour for the majority has altered decisively and dramatically over the last thirty to forty years. It has altered for very large populations indeed (something like a quarter of the world's population would seem to be affected). Premarital sex and pregnancy, amount and type of sexual activity, number of orgasms, old age and sex, adultery—these are all well-defined areas where changes have been isolated and measured. (See Appendix A.)

But if it can be so clearly demonstrated that what most people think has happened has indeed happened, it might be wondered why so many people deny it. The reason is that if it is a shallow, media change we have witnessed, with small groups of vocal 'overheated' people apparently going slightly off their heads, then it can change back. This I suspect is what most proponents of the idea want. But if it isn't, then it is less likely to do so; at least the change back will have to be the product of equally powerful forces and will take as long.

Although on the whole the innumerable surveys and studies are careful to make allowances for biased samples and other anomalies, occasionally they slip up. One minor fact of the sexual revolution is that people appear to have become more inventive sexually. To Americans, the great indicator is oral sex. There seems to have been some sort of explosion of oral sex in America—of cunnilingus (a man giving it to a woman) and fellatio (a woman giving it to a man). Here's Hunt, American author of *Sexual Behavior in the 1970s*, comparing the youth of today with those at the time Kinsey was writing (1940s and early 1950s).

	Kinsey (Adolescent to 25) %	*Hunt* (18–21) %
Fellatio	33	72
Cunnilingus	14	69

Every single survey reports the same thing—and with peculiar satisfaction. Americans seem particularly pleased, even obsessed, with this development. Some writers appear to think it has never happened before, that it represents the final triumph of sexual freedom over puritanism, shows how amazingly 'comfortable' they are with their sexuality; it is even, perhaps paradoxically, represented as an especially highly sexed activity.

No doubt some of this is true, but Dr Albert Ellis, the distinguished if eccentric American sexologist, considers that it is low-sexed women who require endless new positions and variations while highly sexed women are perfectly satisfied with less elaboration. A study carried out recently in Melanesia among a people noted for the importance they attached to pleasurable and successful sexual relations and the vigour with which they pursued them, found that they used only one position and showed complete indifference when other positions and activities were described to them.

Fashion operates to some extent in sex as elsewhere. Feminine beauty changes—women shaped like lutes in the thirteenth century, the great wenches bulging and flopping out of Rubens's canvases, the double and triple chins of the eighteenth century, girls like English public school boys in the 1920s. But there are fashions in sexual practice too. France resembles America in attitude and behaviour as regards oral sex; but oral sex is not fashionable in England. It is conceivable that this has an historical base to do with the lack of personal and public hygiene in the seventeenth and eighteenth centuries. Men and women then lived in the constant sight, smell and even sound of human faeces and urine. Pepys (obsessional about the subject and always describing his own faeces) opened the door of a dining room and found the wife of his patron on her pot. He himself, waking in the night at Oxford and finding there wasn't a pot, relieved himself in the fireplace—twice. People scarcely washed (Pepys never had a bath). Upper-class women in England seem to have been peculiarly careless of hygiene. It is true that the body smells of women can be extremely important in sex, but these women seemed to have gone beyond some barrier. Those interested in sex complained a good deal. John Wilmot, Earl of Rochester, wrote in the 1670s:

> Fair hasty nymph, be clean and kind
> And all my joys restore
> By using paper still behind
> And sponges for before.

In the mid-eighteenth century the rake Wilkes noted, 'The nobler parts are never in this island washed by women; they are left to be lathered by the men'. Similar comments, and the use of the bagnio (baths) as places of assignation suggest that Englishmen in the seventeenth and eighteenth centuries would have found some rudimentary and occasional cleanliness an aid to sexual pleasure. France was the same (Versailles was famous for the piles of human excrement heaped behind doors and in corners) except in one respect. It was in France that oral intercourse became fashionable during the eighteenth century, and the reason would seem to be the invention of the bidet, which began to appear in upper-class French houses at the start of the century (the original meaning was 'little horse'). That this was known to have made the change of fashion possible is supported by the fact that English opposition to the bidet, when the country became prudish again, was on moral grounds.

2   *The libidinous eighteenth century*

Life can little else supply
But a few good fucks and then we die.
                        JOHN WILKES, 1763

It is here, with the eighteenth century, that history once again provides some fascinating parallels. It is not, in general terms, possible to say if 'sexual revolutions' have taken place among entire national populations. Some historians use illegitimacy figures to prove they have, and one might suppose that if over a fairly short period a great many illegitimate children are born, then it must show that premarital and/or extramarital sex are increasing and so attitudes to sex and marriage are changing. Oddly enough it does neither.

But we can certainly find such revolutions, if not among whole societies, then in very large sections of them. The most recent of these took place among the aristocracy and certain sections of the upper and urban middle classes in the eighteenth century.

The foundation was child-upbringing. This, under various influences (Rousseau, Locke, the decline of religious enthusiasm) gradually became more and more indulgent until it reached a degree of permissiveness that has no known historical parallel until mid-twentieth-century America. Henry, Lord Holland, father of Charles James Fox, is an example. 'Let nothing be done to break the boy's spirit,' he said. 'The world will do that business fast enough.' Nothing was done, and little Charles smashed his way through childhood in happy abandon. His father gave a huge dinner party for the foreign ministers of Europe. At the dessert, the children came tripping in. Charles, then in petticoats, spied an immense bowl of cream in the middle of the table and expressed a wish to climb inside it. Lord Holland insisted that he should be gratified and, despite Lady Holland's remonstrances, had it placed on the carpet. Charles clambered in and sploshed about sending cream flying over foreign ministers, ambassadors and the carpet.

Oral, genital and toilet training were all indulgent. Infants were breast-fed on demand and slowly weaned after about eighteen months. At first fed by wet nurses (partly to preserve upper-class breasts, partly because it was thought you couldn't make love while breast-feeding), by the end of the century mothers were feeding their own babies. In the unsavoury sanitary conditions, toilet-training was of little concern. Swaddling bands were a nightmare to clean, so children were left to wallow in their own excrement as long as possible.

The architecture became conducive to sexuality. Bedrooms increased in number and became private, instead of part of a long corridor. (One might note that only over the last forty years has this essential privacy become generally available. An interesting extension of this to youth took place, principally in America, during the 1950s and 1960s, when the car became a mobile or instantly available bed—as in *Saturday Night Fever* for instance. As and where *mores* changed, adolescents were able to return to their own rooms.)

Sex became increasingly important both as an end in itself and as an essential ingredient in, indeed reason for, extramarital liaisons. The process had begun during the Restoration at the Court, where the sexual atmosphere was totally free. Marriage, as Rochester put it, was regarded as 'the clog of pleasure, the luggage of life'. Just as we say 'affair', so they softened the crude word adultery into 'gallantry', and during the eighteenth century it swiftly spread through the aristocracy and sections of the upper and middle classes. Their great houses were indeed often like little courts with young people, close confined, sent far from their homes. It became customary for upper-class men of rank to keep a mistress, or more usually a succession of mistresses. These girls were from well-to-do professional and merchant backgrounds, not lower-class scrubs. Between 1781–84, the mistress of the Earl of Surrey was the daughter of a bankrupt attorney; the Earl of Aldeburgh kept the daughter of a lieutenant killed in America; the fifth Duke of Bedford the daughter of a bankrupt physician; all this from *Town & Country Magazine* which told its readers such things. In circles such as these the double standard began to disappear; at the end of the eighteenth century, with the bluestocking movement and associated figures, the first notes of feminism were heard. Some mistresses were clearly in a bad way financially at first, but they would, and did, jettison their lovers if they were unsatisfactory; and they could become rich. Married ladies of the aristocracy behaved with equal freedom, producing large numbers of bastards—the Countess of Oxford, the Duchess of Devonshire and Lady Elizabeth Foster produced together something like a small school of mixed parentage. Lady Mary Wortley Montagu said in 1724 that wives were committing adultery so often that 'the appellation of rake is as genteel in a woman as in a man of quality'. As always in liberal ages, female sexuality became the measure of pleasure—and, as today, women became spokeswomen for it. Aphra Behn, the seventeenth-century woman dramatist, referred to the vagina as:

> That fountain where delight still flows
> And gives the universal world repose.

John Cleland's delightful hard-core novel *Memoirs of a Woman of Pleasure* was (and is) such a success because it was written from the point of view of Fanny Hill, the heroine. People seem to have been at least as concerned as we are with the importance of the female orgasm and the role of the clitoris, and even if some of the very minutest reactions had eluded them, many had not. De Mandeville noted in 1724 that 'all our late discoveries in anatomy can find no other use for the clitoris but to whet the female desire by its frequent erections'.

Boswell's sexual life was not untypical of the sort it was possible to lead towards the last third of the eighteenth century. Apart from some sixty prostitutes with whom he had relations in Edinburgh, London, Berlin, Dresden, Geneva, Turin, Naples, Rome, Florence, Venice, Marseilles, Paris and Dublin, Boswell's sex life between the ages of twenty and twenty-nine, summed up in purely quantitative terms, reads like this: he unsuccessfully tried to seduce more than a dozen ladies of quality—Scots, English, Dutch, German and Italian; he made mistresses of three ladies of quality, had liaisons of various lengths with four actresses, a brief but passionate affair with the lifelong mistress and attendant of Rousseau; he kept three lower-class mistresses and had two illegitimate children, one in 1762, one in 1767; and he made a short but successful assault one morning on the pregnant wife of one of the King of Prussia's guards at Potsdam. Boswell possessed an urgent sex drive—and incidentally a very large penis, of which he was proud—but the point is that the fairly promiscuous pattern and ease of satisfaction are, except for whores, like a good many sections of society today. So is the free way in which Boswell talked about his escapades and shocked no one. And, like today, this movement was a European one (the record for promiscuity was probably European. Augustus the Strong, Elector of Hanover and King of Poland, had 354 acknowledged bastards).

There were yet other parallels, often down to quite bizarre details. We share an interest in incest. In repressive periods homosexuality often becomes the focus of powerful attention (it was rife at the Court of James I as the Puritan wave gathered itself

higher and higher; again in the nineteenth century). Incest manifests itself in permissive periods, usually quite late in their development, perhaps because where passion, sex and love are important, then its rare forms are cherished. Or perhaps, as a realisation
of just how much is permitted sinks in, so the deepest and most
forbidden desires of all begin to stir. Whatever the cause, it sur-
faced towards the end of the eighteenth century and the start of
the nineteenth; with Byron and his half-sister, with Chateau-
briand in *Atala*; it was a major theme of the Romantics, and Poe's
lovers are usually related (Poe married his cousin). It has emerged
again in the last few years, suddenly becoming much more common than anyone realised. Wardell Pomeroy, Kinsey's colleague,
recently advocated it in *Forum*, provided no one involved objected. It was the subject of a major novel, *Ada*, by Nabokov. And
as I write, incest films stream from the studios: Bertolucci's *La
Luna*, Louis Malle's *Souffle au Coeur*, Visconti's *The Damned*.

There are coarser similarities. Consumption of drink increased
a great deal in the eighteenth century, particularly of cheap spir-
its like rum and gin. Boswell ended up virtually an alcoholic. V.D.
was probably as common in the great cities as it is today. Boswell
caught gonorrhoea seventeen times in nine years; syphilis was
rare. The cure was grisly and could last weeks or months; a strict
diet without drink, chastity, the ingestion of mercury, itself a dangerous poison, and hours spent sweating in a sweating tub. As sex
became more important, so a rudimentary technology emerged to
serve it, such as the sheaths with their cheerful ribbons gathered
round the scrotum. Dildoes were first available in London around
1660. They were imported from Italy, and were sold, according to
Rochester in his poem *Signor Dildo*, at the inappropriately named
Sign of the Cross in St James's Street and were bought and used by
the randy aristocratic ladies of the court. A hundred years later
they were still being imported. They embarrassed customs officials, since they were neither listed as dutiable, nor prohibited.
Nevertheless, one consignment was burnt. It was said, probably
rather wildly, that 'scarce a lady comes from abroad without
being in possession of one or two'. By 1782 respectable London

papers like *The Herald* were publishing advertisements by men openly 'soliciting female friendship'. Nor was it just men. An advertisement from a provincial journal at the start of the nineteenth century reads: 'Minnie, a sweet pretty girl, rather short and stout with fair hair, musical and accomplished, would like to hear from a nice gentleman wanting a sweet little wife.' Call girls and women of easy virtue advertised too. *Harris's List of Covent Garden Ladies*, the issue of 1786, contained 105 of them. This extract, clearly written by a skilled copywriter, is designed to attract to one well practised, yet in whom 'the coral-lipped clitoris still forms the powerful erection . . . nor has the sphincter vagina been robbed of any of its contractive powers; the propelling labia still make the close fissure'.

Exactly the same growth of erotic/pornographic literature and magazines took place. This too began in earnest at the court of Charles II. There were a number of good writers—John Wilmot, Earl of Rochester and Sir George Etherege—but on the whole it was written in rather weak doggerel. The subjects were frankly pornographic, using four-letter words and giving explicit descriptions of various sexual activities. Great emphasis was put on female masturbation with dildoes; also on anal penetration, though it seems likely that the harping on this had more to do with the fact that the word commonly used for penis—'tarse'—rhymed with arse. These verses were avidly read and preserved, passing in manuscript from hand to hand—a sort of sexual samizdat.

Increasing quantities of printed pornography and erotic literature poured out in the next century. Cleland's novel, *Fanny Hill*, appeared in 1748. This was one of the few works which succeeds in being erotic without using four-letter words—indeed, like Nabokov, it is erotic for this reason. Though the author and publisher were prosecuted, nothing serious happened to them and the book was defended by the *Monthly Review* as 'not offensive to decency'.

By the end of the eighteenth century a market existed for regular pornographic magazines to be successful, forerunners in some respects of our *Forum*, *Playboy* and so on. (Though hard-core sex-

ual violence and other perversions do not appear until the nineteenth century.) For instance, *The Covent Garden Magazine or
Amorous Repository* of 1773 had sexually provocative stories using
exactly the same formula—'real life' accounts of sexual incidents
and adventures—upon which *Forum, Playboy* and other magazines now rely. In 1756 John Shebbeare remarked how 'every
print shop has its windows stuck full with indecent prints to in-
flame desire through the eye'.

It might seem from this that the permissive 'revolution' of the
eighteenth century was not just an élitist movement. Some historians would argue it was far more general. They point, for instance,
to the enormous numbers of whores in London at the end of the
eighteenth century and early nineteenth century—7,000 of them,
with 900 brothels and 850 'houses of ill-fame' (that is, no staff, just
beds)—far more than was required by the exploiting middle class.
Among the girls themselves it is not so much sexuality, as despair
and poverty that is in evidence; but it does suggest a fairly easy
attitude to sex among the array of 20,000–30,000 working-class
apprentices in their adolescence and early manhood whom the
whores existed to serve as much or more. But this view has come
recently under some attack. On the whole, the evidence for the
'revolution' is drawn from memoirs, diaries, letters, novels, biog-
raphies and autobiographies and similar contemporary accounts.
These are not sufficient to say precisely or conclusively what was
going on among the vast mass of society which left no record.
Nevertheless, what is clear is that from 1660 until about 1810
there took place in England and over most of Europe, among
some of the aristocracy and also extensive sections of the upper
and middle classes, a movement in most essential respects like our
own. A similar movement among the same sort of group took
place during the sixteenth century.

A perfectly sufficient explanation of what we have seen, and are
seeing today, is this. From time to time élitist circles throughout
the last 400 years have enjoyed sexual and moral relaxations of
this sort. They require, above all, sufficient wealth, privacy, time
and the generation of an appropriate ideology. Our century, par-

ticularly the last thirty-five years, has seen the mass become the élite. All we are seeing, though on a large scale, is a perfectly familiar development.

3 *Why and how and when will the sexual revolution end?*

These movements seem to last from 80 to 120 years. They then come to an end and go into some form of reverse. In the end sexual permissiveness (and sexual repression) generate extreme features which set in motion anti-movements that finally swing the pendulum back. The highly permissive child-rearing of the late eighteenth century bred a large number of ill-disciplined and poorly socialised children demanding instant gratification, which in turn led to social costs: the wasted, dissipated lives of the rakes, the appalling scourges of drink and venereal disease, the illegitimate births and the desperate thousands of wretches who became prostitutes. Anxiety about these extreme developments frequently allies itself with anxiety about outside events. In the sixteenth century, it was the growing social and political crisis, the collapse of the mediaeval church order, the growing religious turmoil; in the late eighteenth century, fear of social chaos became inflamed to white heat by the French Revolution. Instinctively, society seems to seek to impose order on the outside world and on itself. The third, and decisive force, which arises partly in response to these conditions, but still more from its own internal logic and pattern, is religion. It is this which effectively brought about the reaction both in the sixteenth century and the eighteenth.

At the end of the 1950s and during the 1960s permissive upbringing certainly reached some sort of height, particularly in America. Since then, there has been a mild reaction. The drug situation, venereal disease, teenage abortion are often labelled as 'extreme features'. We are intensely anxious about crime, terrorist chaos, the inability of capitalism to generate growth, and if it does, the effects of that growth in pollution and despoilation. Although there is no clear indication of a widespread religious revival, there is a great deal of 'religious type' enthusiasm—ecology (clearly at bottom a movement towards asceticism and purity), astrology, Eastern religions, psychiatric religion, and so on. Quite often all these and others held in a huge disorderly lump at the same time. And we are nearly at the end of our time. 1880 has been suggested as the beginning of the current liberal development. We are at, or have just passed, the apogee. The swing back has begun, or is about to begin. But one characteristic of our revolution shows no sign of reaction. In 1963, Betty Friedan wrote: 'The sex-glutted novels (of the 1950s) became increasingly explicit and increasingly dull; the sex kick of the women's magazines has a sickly sadness; the endless flow of manuals describing new sex techniques hint at an endless lack of excitement.'

Well, I know the feeling; but Betty Friedan put it down to the frustration of bored women: stop the frustration and you'd stop the flow.

Variations of the idea that there is something wrong with the flow/flood/torrent (the nouns are always rather highly coloured) are almost universal. The feeling is that if we could get it right, achieve a balanced attitude to sex, then all this writing about it would wither away. Alex Comfort, in one of his countless books on these topics, says that erotic literature is usually a substitute for sex itself. *Playboy, Forum* and the rest usually say in private that their frankly inciting pages are read by people who want fantasies to fuel their masturbation. How do they know? They produce no evidence. It certainly doesn't show up in their surveys or readers' letters.

Leaving aside gross violence, or obviously depraved sex—with consenting two-year-olds and so on—to which different considerations apply, I think these strictures are really an expression of hidden puritanism, a disapproval and contempt still felt at some level even by the magazine practitioners themselves. Publication of erotic and pornographic material (and in essentials there is no difference. The aims and subjects are the same. If it is done well we call it erotic; if coarsely and badly, pornographic), the production of books and prints and objects of this sort, did not diminish during the eighteenth century; it continued to grow. The same is true today. It is more sensible to see this, not as a substitute for experience, but, for a good number of people, part of the expression of it. We take this for granted with other major drives and concerns. No one is surprised at the 'flood' of popular knowledge books, or the torrents of *Self-help* . . . books (about one quarter of the U.S. best-seller list—far more than books about sex), or the endless flow of cookery books and articles. We should not be surprised that sex attracts the same sort of interest.

4

IDEOLOGY OF THE
SEXUAL REVOLUTION
AND THE GENESIS OF
OBSESSION

OUR IDEOLOGY of sex contains three very Victorian ideas. The first is *Laissez-faire.*

We see the seeds of this in the novelist Charles Kingsley who believed that sexual union (in marriage, naturally) was the greatest bliss on earth. There was heavenly bliss, of course. But although Kingsley secretly felt that sin against God was a mistake, sin against sex was a crime.

That sexual expression should be allowed because it was highly pleasurable was elaborated by several other writers, Grant Allen and Olive Schreiner for instance, but by far the most interesting and influential was Havelock Ellis. Ellis never ceased to marvel at the wonderful manifestations of sex. His intensity and earnestness, his passionate adoration almost, of the *function* of sex, did not just survive thirty years continuously writing sexual histories but seemed to grow with each succeeding case. His willingness to tolerate any sexual activity or fantasy was probably reinforced considerably by the fact he was affected all his life by 'urolagnia'. That is, he experienced sexual pleasure from urinating, and intense sexual stimulation from the sight or even the idea of a woman urinating. He wrote at length and lyrically on this theme and considered it a subject for serious art. He was of the opinion that a masterpiece of Renoir's had treated it and been altered and ruined by prudish overpainting. Ellis's chief complaint was that the Victorians had denied women sexuality. He had a deep, in fact reverent, attitude to women's sexuality—a respect tested more acutely than most since his wife was a passionate and extremely active lesbian. Ellis was equal to the task: 'In what the special beauty of that night lay it was not for her to tell or for me to ask, or to divine, but I know she always recalled the anniversary of it as one of the sacred days of her life.'

'Sacred'—that is the clue. Ellis took two other powerful Victorian elements—religious preoccupation and reverence for the purity of women—and transferred the first to sex generally and the second to a near-worship of women's exquisite sexual sensations. But his holiness, his sex-as-a-religion, blurred the distinction between the sexes. Another figure added the authority of a great artist to sex-as-religion, and became a towering literary influence, serving to intensify the difference. Indeed the difference was at the centre of his religion. To D. H. Lawrence the relations between the sexes were deep, mysterious, holy; in particular the sex of women was deeply mysterious and awesome. Tom Brangwen in *Women in Love*: 'When he approached her, he came to such a terrible painful unknown. How could he embrace it and fathom it? How could he close his arms round all this darkness and hold it to his breast and give himself to it? What might not happen to him?'

One strong current in our contemporary way of writing and thinking about sex has come from a mishmash of Lawrence/Ellis/Grant Allen/Schreiner—a brew in which the religious importance of sex, sexual freedom, tolerance of the unusual, and sexual hedonism bubble confusedly together, manifesting themselves in attitudes as apparently different as the sex-as-sacrament-in-marriage of the Mother's Union and various Anglican persuasions, to sex as prose poetry, of which Nabokov and Updike have probably been the most elegant practitioners.

It would be a mistake to suppose that, without Kinsey, this mishmash would have continued unchanged until today. We are a scientific, technical, number-obsessed culture and it was probably inevitable that sex would be subjected to scientific, technical and statistical enquiry. Ellis himself, and the Austrian Krafft-Ebing, discoverer of sexual psychopathology, pioneered the use of large numbers of case histories; the American Robert Latou Dickinson (1861–1950), with books like *Atlas of Human Sex Anatomy* (1933) had begun, so far as he was able, detailed physiological studies (though he sometimes reminds one of some early version of the car, banging and backfiring, peering up vaginas with a primitive glass penis through which a dim light could glimmer, precursor of that far more sophisticated and scientifically elegant plastic phallus later to be wielded to such effect by Masters and Johnson). And very seldom are one or two books alone responsible for major shifts in direction. What seems to happen is that a huge slow change takes place among a good number of readers. But the writer has changed first and it is his *timing* that is important. He crystallises, makes explicit. More readers and yet more are influenced. Once the majority of readers have changed, *then* the book becomes influential in a much more clearly defined way. Rousseau was this kind of writer. So was Betty Friedan in the America of the early 1960s. Kinsey's success was a classic of this sort.

1 Character and crusade of Alfred Kinsey

Kinsey's influence—still not fully appreciated—was decisive to the second revolution. He enormously and specifically reinforced the mishmash that sexual activity was a good thing in itself, and that no particular sexual activity was wrong. It followed that the more sexual activity you had the better. His insistence on physical fact, on number, led directly to the narrowly physiological, the mechanical and functional, which has underlain all research into sex and much of the writing about it in book, magazine and for film over the last twenty-five years. Finally the simplicity, even crudeness of his approach, the fact that it could be easily grasped, combined with his success, turned sexual freedom from being a trend among the élite and literate, into a mass movement, possibly for the first time in history.

Kinsey and his supporters and colleagues always fiercely denied he had any desire to promote sexual activity. As to being mechanistic, his aim was scientific knowledge and since it is much easier to apply scientific method to number, and to the physical elements (perhaps only these aspects are susceptible to science) the bias, in a pioneering work, would inevitably be to them. In fact his denials, perhaps only necessary in the context of his day, were demonstrably untrue, even then.

His colleague and biographer, Wardell Pomeroy, thinks that Kinsey's basic drive was that of a collector. As a boy, he collected stamps. By the time he was a young assistant professor of zoology at Indiana the drive had become obsessional. His target was the gall wasp. Kinsey collected more gall wasps than anyone had done before, far more than were necessary for an effective scientific study. He sought gall wasps all over America and Mexico. In the end he'd collected not only every species, but several examples of each kind. When he finally handed them all over to the American Museum of Natural History in New York, crate after crate, it was the largest collection ever given to that institution—four million different gall wasps. He was equally obsessive, or competitive, about his library of sex and erotica, striving to make it the largest in the world, larger than the British Museum or (typically of legendary size) the Vatican collection. He was obsessive about his interviews. The aim was to find out objectively, by means of interviews, with no moral bias, what people did sexually. Kinsey hoped to get 100,000. In the end he and his team collected 18,000.

Any collector is interested in the rare and unusual. If you are collecting sexual case histories, these are the ones that will stand out. Pomeroy and Kinsey were fascinated by their absorbing subject. To preserve secrecy, the histories were written in code, which was learnt and whose rules were never written down. They chatted together in code. 'I might say to Kinsey while we were going up in a public elevator, "My last history liked Z better than CM, although 00 in CX made him very ER". Translated: "My last history liked intercourse with animals better than with his wife, but mouth-genital contact with an extramarital partner was very arousing".'

The more interesting case histories will be active ones. There is a natural bias, both in the *Reports* and in the other writings of Kinsey and Pomeroy, for the prose to rise, the attention to concentrate on these active and unusual cases—and some of them were extremely, irresistibly active and unusual:

> The longest history we ever took was done thus, cojointly by Kinsey and me. We had heard through Dr. Dickinson of a man who had kept an accurate record of a lifetime's sexual behavior. When we got the record after a long drive to take his history, it astounded even us, who had heard everything. This man had had homosexual relations with 600 pre-adolescent males, heterosexual relations with 200 pre-adolescent females, intercourse with countless adults of both sexes, with animals of many species, and besides had employed elaborate techniques of masturbation. He had set down a family tree going back to his grandparents, and of 33 family members he had had sexual contacts with 17. His grandmother introduced him to heterosexual intercourse, and his first homosexual experience was with his father. If that sounds like *Tobacco Road* or *God's Little Acre*, I will add [a typical *Report* touch, this] that he was a college graduate who held a responsible government job. We had traveled from Indiana to the Southwest to get this single extraordinary history and felt that it had been worth every mile. At the time we saw him, this man was 63 years old, quiet, soft-spoken, self-effacing—a rather unobtrusive fellow. It took us 17 hours to get his history . . . At one point . . . he said he was able to masturbate to

ejaculation in 10 seconds from a flaccid start. Kinsey and
I, knowing how much longer it took everyone else, expressed our disbelief, whereupon our subject calmly
demonstrated it to us.

They observed an equally responsive woman, whom Pomeroy
still remembered vividly after twenty years when contributing an
essay to one of the excellent glosses on Masters and Johnson. She
was able to have from fifteen to twenty orgasms in twenty minutes. Kinsey and Pomeroy watched her in intercourse and masturbation. With intercourse she had her first orgasm between two
and five seconds after entry. She was sixty when they observed
her, and she did not have her first orgasm until she was forty; also,
her satisfaction depended on, was responsive to, that of her partner, and she would relax, her sex drive stilled, as easily after three
orgasms as after thirty if her companion had also come. Comforting.

Kinsey insisted on his status as a zoologist, and, whether to emphasise the scientific (or hide the human) nature of his enquiry he
always signed himself Alfred C. Kinsey, Professor of Zoology. But
sexual activity itself had to be made respectable—the more active
the more respectable. Time and again in the *Reports* a lawyer
who has masturbated forty times a week will be 'distinguished in
his profession'. Women masturbated more often without fantasy
than men. But these 'were among the socially most significant,
most efficient and energetic women' in all his sample. 'Many of
them were professionally trained in medicine or psychiatry or
some other field.' And this emphasis was apparent in their other
writings. The exceptional man in the case I quoted was not just
quiet-spoken but 'a graduate'. Of one of the very few films Pomeroy and Kinsey took of a couple having intercourse, Pomeroy
notes: 'Both of them were (and still are) regularly employed in utterly respectable jobs; they have five children; they are regular
church-goers and Sunday School attendants . . .' This need to be
respectable was reinforced because, as a culture, the West ap-
proves of activity—and therefore active people tend to be happy

and successful. If we were a meditative culture other human facets would become uppermost. Kinsey's samples confirmed this. He found reason to believe that early adolescent males, who began engaging in intercourse and masturbating early, were often more 'alert, energetic, vivacious, spontaneous, physically active, socially extrovert and/or aggressive individuals in the population', than the late adolescents, who were inclined to be 'slow, quiet, mild in manner, without force, reserved, timid, taciturn, introvert and/or socially inept'. In the U.S. particularly this must have struck with force.

But Kinsey was far more polemical than this, and more than he has been given credit for (and he deserves great credit). Not that he claimed it. He and Pomeroy repeatedly and vehemently denied that it was any part of his purpose to alter behaviour. This is rubbish.

It is just not *possible* to enter fields of this sort 'objectively', to enter them and not affect behaviour. One of Kinsey's repeated assertions was that 'there is no right or wrong biologically'. Nothing can harm you—except as a result of guilt imposed by an outside morality. He said, 'Biologically there is no form of outlet which I will admit is unnatural.' He had a film of some bluntness which he would show to emphasise this—a bull mounting another bull, achieving full anal penetration and ejaculating as it withdrew. If a course of action which you feel impelled to follow, or even curious about, is not biologically harmful, if any wrong attached to it is 'imposed', the implicit inference is, why not follow it? Even revealing the realities of how people behave, as opposed to confronting the moral goal head-on, may compel the moral goal to shift if it is shown to be completely unrealistic, or to do damage. One of Kinsey's main contributions was to demonstrate the extraordinary range not just of sexual behaviour but of appetite. Professor J. Haldane, the distinguished British biologist, commented, 'It was as if some people ate thirty times as much or slept thirty times as much as others.' Actually, it's far more as though some people could subsist on an orange pip a day and others required a roasted ox. Furthermore the range of behaviour evolves and increases gradually as an increasing range is shown to be possible—you find this with monkeys and termites extending the range of their nutritional intake for instance.

That Kinsey *would* alter behaviour was inevitable, therefore, and since these observations are partly zoological, one can assume he was aware of this. But he also wanted in a much more overt way to influence how people behaved. He admitted freely that he wanted to alter attitude—he realised, said Pomeroy, that 'the world can be a more comfortable place for everybody if we get to the bottom of these things'—but then made it plain that by attitude he meant behaviour. He saw how useful his studies would be to marriage counselling and to the way prisoners were allowed to behave.

The Boy Scouts wrote and asked his advice on masturbation and sexual restraint. Kinsey was unequivocal. 'Our years of research have failed to disclose any clear-cut cases of harm resulting from masturbation, although we have thousands of cases of boys who have had years of their lives ruined by worry over masturbation.' As for restraint: 'We have many histories of athletes whose performance was definitely improved by regular sexual outlet. We have specific records on athletic performance that were lost because the men had worked themselves into a nervous disturbance through sexual restraint.'

Kinsey had an extremely dominant and combative character. Pomeroy never knew anyone get the better of him in an argument—'I doubt if anyone could.' But this aggressive element expressed itself in an intense urge to teach and persuade. He would lecture his staff on all sorts of things. It is this which one can feel driving beneath the surface of the *Reports*. And his passion—which called forth a ferocious energy, making him work eighteen hours a day—occasionally burst out in his language and behaviour. Outlets—his rather ugly word for a means to orgasm—were not just important, they were vital; as necessary, he wrote, 'as the tying off of an artery that has been cut, the provision of air for a suffocating man, or food for a starving man . . .'. The very word 'outlet' is revealing—the sense is of something dammed up, pent, explosive. And such was his identification and sympathy with sexual suffering that he openly wept when told some particularly harrowing story of frustration or guilt.

Such forces are not released by the collector's instinct. Indeed, the first question one would ask of such an interpretation would be—why sex? The answer to both questions—the drive and its aim—lies in a childhood and youth of total sexual ignorance and appalling frustration. His father in particular was cold and repressive. Kinsey became intense, 'zealous', and lonely. His first publication, written at the age of seventeen, after spending many hours of patient observation standing alone in woods while it poured with rain, has a lugubrious, almost Thurber-like ring: 'What Do Birds Do when It Rains?' He was known, in the dating-conscious society of South Orange High School, as the boy who never had a girl. It seems inevitable he should have become obsessed with masturbation. He spent long hours of his adolescence playing the piano. A friend at college came to him saying he was terribly worried by a very serious problem—masturbation. Kinsey, although deeply shocked, knew at once what had to be done: they must both kneel down, there and then in the dormitory, and pray together that his friend have the strength to stop masturbating. Many years later he spoke of the strict morality of his father, 'which', he said, 'he could neither forgive nor forget'.

After twenty-five years of such suppression, sexual freedom would never lose its delight, the crusade never diminish in importance. And Kinsey—despite becoming a workaholic, remaining obsessively clean, and also for many years frightened of psychiatrists—flowered in unexpected directions. He developed enormous charm and warmth, particularly when conducting interviews. Mildred Newman, a very early interviewee, remembered him vividly. 'It was in a hotel bedroom,' she said. 'He was terribly nice. Really sympathetic. I wasn't a bit frightened or offended. I told him everything.' (Her friend, not married, was interviewed by Pomeroy and 'didn't tell all the truth'.) Kinsey also grew into a brilliant platform speaker, never needing notes.

And he was phenomenally successful. The *Male Report* slightly more so than the *Female*. But even the *Female* was translated into Hebrew, French, Portuguese, German, Spanish, Norwegian, Finnish, Italian and Dutch. The English edition went to eighty-six countries. Both *Reports* sold continuously and colossally, and have continued to sell ever since. Kinsey had the whole treatment with which we are so familiar today—TV, cover of *Time*, the media obsessed for years on end; but for the late 1940s and early 1950s it marked a new record. It was this enormous surge of continuous popular acclaim, still more violent attack and popular exposition which contributed largely to making sexual freedom a mass movement.

2 *Number fever; orgasm obsession; sexual engineering and Masters and Johnson*

If sex is such a good and important activity, then to be unable to have it, or to have it unsatisfactorily, becomes increasingly disastrous. Impotence, which is certainly depressing but from time to time to be expected, becomes virtually a crime: '. . . in our culture,' wrote Albert Ellis (using italics) in a book recently reprinted, 'impotence is conceived of as being such a *horrible*, such a *heinous* symptom . . .'; America cannot laugh about this. Woody Allen may be maladroit, but he always gets his girls and the impression is he's got what it takes. Even when he's had by a machine one feels the machine at least had a pretty good time. It is impossible to imagine a good American novel about impotence. Kingsley Amis's brilliant *Jake's Thing* was a best-seller in America, partly because the ghastly fear could be faced vicariously. By the 1970s enormous books were being written entirely about the female orgasm; essentially, that is what the *Hite Report* is. Today there is not just anxiety about having one orgasm, but considerable anxiety about not having, or envy of those that do have, several orgasms.

In the eighteenth century the language of sex was pleasure. Today, in America at least, it is number. This shows up clearly in surveys done among their readers by the American magazine *Redbook* in 1975 and 1978. Satisfaction is not the goal. More than half the men and 40 per cent of the women reported that they were not having enough sex, and this among those who were having intercourse at least five times a week. Clearly, they felt they *ought to have more sex.* The pressure is on. A feverishness is noticeable, not just in the magazines and films, but in novels. Heroines, and perhaps particularly heroes (I think of Kepesh in Roth's *The Professor of Desire*) have to know what the positions are, the angles of penetration, the orifices, above all *how many times?* Throughout history men have boasted of their conquests, and in liberated ages women too, as in Messalina's competition; this is the first time conqueror and conquest worry about how and how often they both come.

Although there is a certain amount of feverishness, the British seem moderately calm about number. (See Appendix B.) The vast majority—75 per cent—in Gorer's 1970 survey of British sexual behaviour and attitudes were at ease with their sexual performance. It will be interesting to see if anything, in particular the progress of feminism, has altered this (a massive three-year survey is in progress from Glasgow). My guess is that attitudes are changing, and that Gorer was being overcomplacent about a finding which probably owed a good deal to women's ignorance and lack of feminist militancy at the time. The editor of the magazine *Parents* said in an interview recently that the most frequent question mothers wrote and asked was, 'Why can't we have orgasms?'

Kinsey did not just make Masters and Johnson possible—as they freely admit—he made some such enquiry as theirs inevitable and dictated the form of it. Where sex and orgasms are so important, 'dysfunction' as Masters and Johnson call it, is a disaster.

'Dysfunction', 'outlet'—the language is bleakly mechanical (it is interesting, incidentally, that Kinsey's father was a professor of engineering). This engineering view and a developing engineering vocabulary—perfectly appropriate for the purposes of Kinsey and Masters and Johnson—has thoroughly invaded other literary

treatment and exposition of sex. Others have suffered. There is no
need to describe the growing sense of despair, a feeling of gasping
in an erotic vacuum, as, in the way of duty, I clawed my way
through the joyless *Joys of Sex,* and then down (that was a peak!)
through heavier and yet heavier manuals. Suddenly I remembered Alexander Cockburn. He had been planning to write a review of about ten of these books for *The New York Review of
Books.* Could I borrow it? His letter in reply said he too had nearly
gone under. He couldn't complete them, or write the review. He
was full of sympathy. How was I? 'Still capable of The Act?'

Yet the engineering style is not totally unerotic—if it were,
many magazines would fold. But it is completely un-individual.
Because it concentrates on sex-as-object, it is the physical organ
that feels, not the person it belongs to. (Jake, in Amis's words,
gloomily flipping the pages of the porn magazine *Mezzanine,* describes a photograph of the female sex organ: 'In itself it had an
exotic appearance, like the inside of a giraffe's ear or a tropical
fruit not much prized even by the locals.') In *Forum* (which relies,
as did eighteenth-century magazines, on the vignette) the letters
are genuine, but they all seem to come, to use the jargon, from the
same quivering, sopping, convulsively orgasmic pen.

Here is an example from a recent *Forum* collection. It is a good,
but by no means extreme, example of the idiom.

Sleeping Vaginas

A few months ago my husband started bringing home
Forum. I have been fascinated by the letters you publish
from so many unhappy, bored housewives. Since I have
solved this problem for myself, I decided to write an
open letter to these women and to those middle-aged
widows who are sexually frustrated and bored with life.
What my friend and I have done may be an inspiration
and may possibly help a few of them to discover the joys
of youth through sexual freedom and expression among
our own sex.

First, I want to point out that we are not kooks. We are all college graduates. I have a degree in English literature and I taught high school up until a few years ago. Our standards of living are average to moderately well-to-do. Our ages vary from fifty-three to sixty-one and all of us have grown children. Our bridge club was a dull event because we were bored with ourselves, with each other, and especially with our husbands whom we constantly griped at and about. All this, we now realize, was due to our sexual frustration with husbands who had lost most of their interest in us.

Since Marge and I are apartment neighbours as well as bridge partners, we met for coffee each morning after our husbands left for work. One morning nearly three years ago, while she was complaining about her dull sex life with her husband, I blurted out that I had solved a similar situation by masturbating. This broke the ice between us and soon we were discussing the subject quite openly. By the time she left my pants were soaked, so I hurried into the bedroom and lay down to fantasize about her masturbating herself, in no time I had a terrific orgasm. On the spur of the moment, I reached for the bedside phone and called to ask Marge what she was doing. When she hesitated, I said I knew she was doing herself! I then proceeded to tell her of my fantasy about her and my powerful climax. She then also admitted to fantasizing about me with the same results. I suggested she return so we could do it together. In moments she entered wearing a terry cloth jump-suit. I met her at the door in the nude and her eyes went right to my vagina, which I was stroking, as she quickly stepped out of her jump-suit. Instantly she raced to sprawl on the sofa, one leg on the floor and the other raised up over the back of the sofa which spread her thighs wide. There, in all its hairy glory, was the beautiful vagina I had been fantasizing about. I dropped into a chair across the room, leaned back and spread my legs over its arms. Soon we were going at ourselves in total abandon, each with eyes glued on the action of the other's cunt. Needless to say, we climaxed almost simultaneously in orgasms that jarred every bone in our bodies, leaving us momentarily exhausted.

Never had I experienced anything as erotic or as sexually exciting, and even today it is a constant thrill to watch another woman bring herself to the point of no return and explode. Each of us, I believe, has a little voyeurism in us as well as a little exhibitionism. I find it just as much a thrill to know Marge was on fire from seeing me do myself as I was at watching her. This combination, plus the excitement of four-letter words of encouragement, seeing the passion build in her body, hearing her moans of ecstasy and listening to the erotic squishy sounds of her fingers whipping her juices into a lather, was absolutely devastating in effect.

After we rested, we had coffee and talked about our first experiences at masturbation as young girls while enjoying the view of each other's cunt through the glass topped breakfast table. Soon we were horny again and returned to our former positions where we spent nearly three hours. Afterwards we agreed that each of us must have had twenty orgasms.

Although I feared I would be sore and tender, I found myself wet and horny while awaiting her the next day. She entered, stepped out of her jump-suit and asked if I was as wet and horny as she was. With this she felt my cunt and instinctively I reached for hers. I found it as soaking wet as mine and a total delight to feel. We ended up standing just inside the door, our nude bodies pressed together with our tits rubbing, as we furiously brought each other off so hard that our knees buckled. We ended up in a laughing heap on the floor.

This delightful relationship continued each morning.

We would rush through our housework becoming hornier by the minute in anticipation, take a quick bath and be ready for each other by ten.

There is no way to explain how this activity has improved our lives. We are no longer bored with life, irritable and continually nagging our husbands. Our marriages have improved as a result and even our husbands' sex lives have improved because they find us once more responsive to them sexually. My own husband can't figure out why but he swears I'm a better fuck now than when we married. Our bodies, especially our tits and bellies, have firmed up. I've gone from 162 to 144 pounds by switching my former sweet tooth to a sexual outlet.

My husband retired in June, so my coffee sessions with Marge have been somewhat curtailed, although his golf games allow us about three mornings a week together. This plus our Thursday 'bridge club' which has become something more than a bunch of middle-aged women playing cards, keeps me happy and content. I've never felt better, younger or more alive in my life.

So come on you middle-aged gals who feel life is passing you by. Your cunts aren't dead. They're just asleep. All of you may not be lucky enough to find a neighbour or a bridge club like mine, but certainly each of you has a close friend who is as bored and as sexually frustrated as you are. Open up! Confide your secret desires to her and you may be surprised at how quickly she accepts your invitation. You'll find life has just begun.

3   *The sexual revolution and women as sex objects, promiscuity, romantic love, marriage and divorce*

Many people find the idea of someone being 'a sex object' distasteful. Margaret Mead, along with thousands of others, said that Kinsey would take love out of sex. The same criticism has reappeared for years. Feminists become particularly furious. They regard it as degrading and humiliating. An aspect of sadism is to degrade the partner to pure object. In sadistic fantasies the binding of the partner and cool watching of their reaction is usually the centre. In order to treat people in this way you have to reduce them to units, numbers. The cruelty of ancient Rome had an element of this in it. Behind the eyes of the man watching Miss World lurks the potential Camp Guard at Belsen. In view of the fairly widespread reaction against such degradation, in particular of women, it is odd that the most extreme demonstration of woman-as-sex-object, one so stark, so concentrated, apparently so unaware of its true nature that it takes one's breath away, should be found in the *Hite Report*, a book that purports to come from the heart of the feminist movement itself. The most convincing proof of how far the physiological objectifying of sexual behaviour has been taken by the media is here, where all woman's attributes and dreams and reactions are sliced away until she is left with just one thing—her clitoris. A clitoris grown gigantic, it is true, and the naked concentration supposedly hidden by some cursory glances elsewhere; but that, in essence, is the heroic scale of the reduction.

Rage about women as sex objects often has that semi-hysterical note which suggests it is the result of automatic prejudice. In this it resembles attacks on advertising. Both are so *obviously* bad, that thought becomes redundant; attacks on them become lightning conductors for every sort of guilt, rage, fear or desire. The advertising/media element of degradation seems to me comparatively trivial on its own. For expression in the mass some sort of stereotyping is unavoidable. The treatment of men is just as 'degrading'—it has simply had less attention directed on to it: the vacuous male models, the randy old lecher in the soap opera, the mindless male chauvinist, the helpless 'baby' man.

The kernel of the matter is: does objectifying of this sort, in advertising or anywhere else, affect how people feel about themselves, about the opposite sex, and how they behave towards each other? It is true that to destroy people in concentration camps you must reduce them to units. It does not follow that sexual objectifying will lead automatically to such an extreme expression of it—or even that they are related.

In fact, it seems likely that the opposite is true—that a good deal of such objectifying is essential. It is becoming increasingly clear that the readiness to fantasise, the desire to do so, are as much a female drive as male. It is just another part of that huge slow process whereby women are at last licensed to do as they please. Sexual objectifying plays a large role in many feminine fantasies. It is part of the mechanism. Pure sex-object relationships—perfectly possible for both sexes—are rare and short-lived. In most partnerships both elements exist in desire: lover as person—sex subject; and lover as embodiment of sex—sex object. Objectivity is necessary in a more general way to every relationship. In love, identification, intoxication and objectivity all play parts. Without objectivity, a relationship can become chaotic and dangerous. In divorce: 'He/she's changed. I don't recognise who it is. It's a different person.' These disasters and surprises happen in relationships which neglect objectivity.

People fear that more and earlier premarital sex will lead to a sort of mindless pulp of adolescent promiscuity. It rather depends what you mean by promiscuity. Gorer seems to define it as more than three partners before marriage—which seems to me quite absurd. But if promiscuity is defined as absence of love or affection, little discrimination, ten to twenty partners over a period of six months to one year, and quite often running them concurrently—then nothing approaching this is happening. All surveys and studies agree on the enormous importance of love. (See Appendix B.)

In some ways this primacy of emotion is surprising. When obstructions to love and sex are removed one might expect intense feeling, which thrives on obstruction, indeed finds it essential, to decline. This happened among the French aristocracy in the eighteenth century, where love became bad taste and was replaced by sensuality and intelligence. It became the practice to talk of *passionettes*—little passions. The God of Love became a cherub.

That this has not happened to us is a tribute to the overwhelming power of romantic love in our culture. This power goes on appearing throughout adult surveys too, particularly in America.

No one knows the full effect of the whole movement on marriage. The removal of guilt and anxiety, the solution to severe sexual problems and terrible frustrations, are very great benefits which do show up in the studies of marriage. (See Appendix B.) However tedious those endless books of mechanical engineering are to read, they seem to have performed a service. Traditional areas of anxiety have diminished; women have less guilt; men don't worry so much about the size of their penises. In Britain in 1969, 17 per cent did worry; and in the Hunt 1974 survey for *Playboy* 67 per cent said it made a difference. Kinsey's studies showed the vast range of penis size. From 4,000 measurements in the survey and a further 1,200 from the records, he found they ranged from as small as one inch when erect to the largest recorded ten and one-half inches; the average when erect was six and one-half inches. Size made no difference to sexual pleasure or ability. Masters and Johnson confirmed this, noting also that size bore no relation to the size of the skeleton; big men had small penises and vice versa. Size makes no difference to sexual pleasure because the vagina involuntarily closes firmly on whatever penis is there. But the difference is subjective, affecting men and women. And one can see how one inch, however adroit, might worry—even if without cause; just as Boswell, unjustifiably, gained comfort from his huge member, though this must, when ready for action, enveloped in sheep's gut, his testicles festooned with red ribbons, have presented a formidable sight.

No one is certain how the current sexual atmosphere has affected marriage. There has not been a great upsurge of extramarital sex. But then adultery declined at the end of the Roman Empire, to be replaced by divorce. So our rising divorce figures may be a straightforward product of the sexual revolution.

It would seem an obvious conclusion. More sexual freedom has meant a far more 'free-wheeling' society in which sexual partners can be changed and divorce is part of the pattern. But whether this really leads to more divorce depends on whether sexual dissatisfaction is a cause or symptom of marital breakdown. Practically every study of marriage breakdown and divorce is quite clear that sexual difficulty or dissatisfaction is not a cause; it is almost invariably a symptom that other things are wrong.

Marriage can be looked at as a partnership (sometimes battleground) involving endless negotiation and exchange. Each partner has particular demands and interests, infinitely varied in force and type, in exchange for which he/she will satisfy the demands and interests of the other. This negotiating, this balancing, is continually shifting and altering. It is this that gives marriage, or any long relationship, that peculiar quality of incessant change, from year to year, month to month, sometimes it seems almost minute to minute. As in all negotiations, if things are going badly for one or both sides, they will tend to bring more powerful cards into play. A breakdown, if it comes, will most likely be expressed in terms of those powerful interests. The culture dictates what these powerful interests are. So if sex is considered an extremely important goal of relationships, then ultimately many difficulties in the negotiation will be expressed sexually. Once this happens the marriage or relationship is in increasing danger—sex, from symptom, becomes cause.

Conversely, if the main point in a negotiation is being gained, minor difficulties can be ignored; but if the main one is not gained, the minor difficulties become maddening. If sex does go wrong, it will be expressed in irritations, in disruptions of the balance, that appear to have nothing to do with sex at all.

This is a sociological model. The problem may simply be one of semantics. If being married to someone or living with them and loving them are seen as intimately and inevitably related, which they are, and if having sex with someone and loving them are also seen as intimately and inevitably related—as we've seen them to be—then to say a marriage breaks down because it breaks down sexually is really the same as saying a marriage breaks down because a marriage breaks down. This amalgam and interdependence is one of the central developments of romantic love.

Sex is central, but also extremely elusive. This elusiveness means that it can frequently disguise itself—and I suspect that it does this quite often in medium term or longer marriages (say after six or seven years). By the time these marriages reach the psychiatrists or therapists who write studies of divorce, the initial sexual and romantic restlessness (of which the husband or wife may be ashamed or frightened) has already raised up that complex of reasons and reactions which precipitate breakdown and divorce. Certainly Eleanor Alter, a penetrating New York divorce lawyer, has noticed this as a new element among her older clients, especially among women: 'They expect the bells to ring every time, and after 25 years that just isn't going to happen.'

5

FEMINISM: ASPECTS OF WOMEN'S POWER AND WOMEN'S FREEDOM

The admission of women to complete equality with men would be the most certain mark of civilisation: it would double the intellectual forces of the human race and its probabilities of happiness.

STENDHAL in *Rome, Naples, Florence,* 1817

'Ah! but women have no sphere, Mr. Mason.' 'They have minds equal to those of men and ought to be able to make themselves careers as brilliant.'

LUCIUS MASON in *Orley Farm* by Anthony Trollope, 1862

We are becoming the men we wanted to marry.

GLORIA STEINEM, 1978

ONE OF Chaucer's most penetrating and highly flavoured portraits is that of the wife of Bath: a figure at once coarse, brilliant, greedy, and lecherous as a man. Her tale, too, is psychologically sharp. A young knight is to be banished from the court for rape, but is saved by the intervention of the Queen and her ladies. He can only regain his place in life by setting out upon a perilous journey to find the answer to the question: 'What is it women most desire?' After the usual torments and trials, he finally discovers the true answer: women desire to have mastery over their husbands. Many marriages are about power.

1 *Betty Friedan and the subjection of women*

The genesis of women's liberation over the last thirty years is best described by Betty Friedan in her book *The Feminine Mystique*. Almost universally known in America, she has not been nearly as much read in Britain as she deserves. In recent years she has been to some extent thought old-fashioned and superseded by more strident voices, but in my view she is still by far the most intelligent and sympathetic of the feminists. She also writes much better. Her thesis—which sometimes seems almost single-handedly to have started the movement in America—was quite simple. In the late 1940s and 1950s, home and children became the only and overwhelming centre of women's lives. Housework and child-upbringing were elevated into religions. This was *the feminine mystique*. These goals, especially the first, were neither enough nor what they seemed. The result was appalling and increasing frustration: 'I, like other women,' wrote Betty Friedan, 'thought there was something wrong with me because I didn't have an orgasm waxing the kitchen floor.' The solution: women must break out, live for themselves, have jobs, careers. This would also liberate men, freeing them from burdens and responsibilities.

The causes of this concentration were varied. Betty Friedan lays weight on the Second World War. There was a need (or a felt need) to replenish the population with babies. A shortage of jobs for returning troops meant women had to find work at home. Men took over the editing of women's magazines, and since they didn't want women to take jobs, the whole thrust of these periodicals of enormous circulation was put into exalting housework, and the role of mother and wife. The result was a pulp fiction as ludicrous in its way as that found in Victorian magazines. This was compounded by the vast housewife/child/mother industry and accompanying advertising complex which grew at this time.

I do not think these causes were as powerful as they have been made out. There was no real need to have babies after the war. There was a far greater death toll in the First World War, yet no such reaction took place. If a need was imagined (felt), then why? And in Britain, women's magazines were not edited chiefly by men, yet the same development of a feminine mystique took place. Media, and industrial and advertising exploitation always increase the force of social movements, but cannot cause them; they depend on existing states of mind, existing markets to allow them to come into being at all.

Sociologists, who are meant to do no more than study and explain society as it is, *cannot* in fact write about behaviour without in some way affecting it. The very area a sociologist chooses, the fact that he tries to crystallise and make clear, the fact that he, too, needs to sell or win acceptance, quite apart from almost inevitable personal bias, all bring this about. The popular effect of most sociologists is much weakened by the appalling way they write; but very occasionally they are not thus handicapped.

In a series of articles and books between 1942–64, one sociologist, Talcott Parsons, constructed by far the most persuasive model for the 1950s ideal family. In any group there are two types of leader: those who deal with the outside world, who are instruments of the group, and therefore 'instrumental'; those who deal with events within the group who express its needs, and are 'expressive'. Parsons said that this happened in families and the division was biologically based. Men were more dominant and tougher and so were instrumental; whereas women were less dominant but more perceptive and therefore 'expressive'. The resulting set-up was ideal for society because it meant men could concentrate on work, could become mobile or not as labour needs demanded. And it was ideal for individuals in general because dividing labour on biological grounds prevents competition. In particular, it satisfied man's nature, while providing him with emotional care and help. It satisfied women's nature, since she was naturally expressive; it also provided her with a home, economic security and social status (she could tinker with outside occupation—hobbies, part-time work—but it must not interfere with her central position). Lastly, it was ideal for children since they could identify with those role models, internalise them and finally repeat them. They were satisfied and, once again, society would be as well.

This solid, precise piece of sociologist's engineering, which I have much simplified, was really the most subtle expression of a male-dominated society which also valued women. It is, I suspect, still the most widely accepted model pattern. *Strictly,* however, it is no longer what exists. In America, more than half of family groupings in fact don't consist of wife/husband/children; and during the 1950s millions of women in Britain and America confined to this role began to go fairly mad. Millions still do.

Central to the 1950s onwards, and still very powerful, was the child-care ideology which successfully nailed women to the home. The cardinal figures were three men: Bowlby, Winnicott and Spock, accompanied by hosts of elaborators, popularisers and commentators. To each, the mother had to be a permanent full-time nonstop presence; her work in the home was crucial to society and her child, the effects of the first five years were absolutely irreversible. Fathers were almost ignored. Dr John Bowlby, Consultant Psychiatrist to the Tavistock Clinic in London, emphasised the appalling results of mother not doing her job: *'Loss'*, *'Separation'*, the very titles rang with a thrilling guilt into the tender heart. Dr D. W. Winnicott, a brilliant child psychologist, raised the mother's role, especially the role of her breast, to lyrical heights which recall the mishmash. It seems possible that Winnicott wanted to *be* a nursing mother.

All these writers, Spock especially, also wrote much good sense—but what is interesting is how people seem able to interpret child-care books according to their own aims (again, especially Spock). One odd but well-known result was the overpermissive parent–spoilt child—more common in America than Britain.

One boy had infantile temper tantrums in his 11th year when his mother refused to butter his bread for him. He still demanded her help in dressing . . . He summed up his requirements in life very neatly by saying that his mother would butter his bread for him until he married, after which his wife would do so.

'I used to let them turn over all the furniture and build houses in the living room that would stay up for days, so there was no place for me to sit and read. I couldn't bear to make them do what they didn't want to do, even take medicine when they were sick. I couldn't bear for them to be unhappy, or fight, or be angry at me . . . I felt guilty even leaving them for an afternoon.' (U.S. mother)

This intense and pitiful devotion and concentration of attention—induced, or at least raised to fever pitch by Bowlby/Spock *et al*—was only matched by the intense concentration on housework. The main, indeed only, point about housework is that for large numbers of people it is awful. The more you have to do and the longer you do it, the more awful it becomes. It has been shown to be far worse than the worst monotonous factory work. (See Appendix C.)

Yet in an attempt to fill empty days, women did more and more of this monotonous, fragmented work. In America, day-care centres for children virtually vanished. The more labour-saving devices women bought the more work they did. A survey done at Bryn Mawr showed that farm workers' wives did 60.55 hours of housework a week; women in cities of under 100,000—78.35 hours; in cities over 100,000 (where labour-saving devices were most common) they spent 80.57 hours cleaning and cooking. Time-and-motion studies, like one by the Michigan Heart Association of Wayne University, showed 'Women were working more than twice as hard as they should', squandering energy through habit and tradition in wasted motions and pointless steps.

The frustration, boredom, sense of futility and waste, showed up more and more in studies of depression, alcoholism and mental breakdown, and in the very magazines that were partly instrumental in creating the women's role. By the late 1950s housewives identified completely with victims of blindness, deafness, physical maiming, cerebral palsy, paralysis, cancer or approaching death. Articles and stories about people who couldn't see or speak became a staple of women's magazines at this time.

This situation came to a head when the implications of another, utterly fundamental development finally dawned. People, especially women, were living longer than they had ever done before. (See Appendix C.) Fewer children were being born and whereas fifty to one hundred years earlier child-bearing continued into the mid-forties, now it ended in the mid-thirties. One half to one third of a woman's life was free of children, so she had to have an occupation—or spend thirty-five or forty years of her life dusting.

2   The false triumph of the feminists

The result we all know: that great thrust of feeling and action spearheaded and made vocal by the feminists, but in fact a gathering upsurge of female consciousness, spurred on by economic necessity, against the injustices and disadvantages of women's conditions. And it is fascinating to see, as the vast flock started to wheel in a new direction, how all the sociologists and psychologists and therapists and anthropologists and conductors of seminars and studies and surveys started, slightly *en retard*, to wheel too.

It was suddenly realised that most of Bowlby's work was done with children suffering the most extreme deprivation, in institutions for instance. It was quite unlikely, indeed hysterical, to suppose such harrowing effects would follow a holiday away from the children or a part-time job. Specific studies showed that the family wasn't a solid block, but individuals. And once individuals became important, so did their needs, their reactions. Seen in this way, mothers took on quite a different aspect. They might not necessarily love their babies. Dr Jolly, paediatrician of *The Times*: 'It is now becoming more accepted that not all mothers feel instant love for their newborn babies.' A mother might not want to breast-feed—it was not essential. A woman might not want to have any children at all: 'The experience of parenthood is not essential for the successful growth and development of an individual to maturity,' reported GAP, a psychiatric organisation, in 1973. Books appeared showing that mothers could go out to work without harming their children. Women became less and less important as *mothers* (and so more important as people) until finally their role was diminished in the sanctum itself. Behavioural scientists were 'surprised' to find that peer group and social play were more important than mothering for developing sexuality and sexual adjustment. Lack of peer group experience left ineradicable incapacities, whereas deficient mothering could be overcome by helpful companions, especially with girls.

As the ideology of the 1950s was dismantled and a new one erected to allow women to work, someone had to take the mother's place in the family. Father. From 1963 onwards books and studies appeared analysing and promoting the role of father, until in 1974 Michael Rutter, Professor of Child Psychiatry at the University of London, could write:

> The sixth myth is that parenting means mothering. For many years books and articles on parental care were exclusively concerned with mothers. That is no longer acceptable today and any scheme to produce better parents must be concerned with fathers (or future fathers) just as much as with mothers (or future mothers).

Spock's only major revision in eighteen years, which also came in 1974, was that fathers should share far more in upbringing; in some ways they became more important:

> Children who reported that their parents were away from home for long periods of time rated significantly lower on such characteristics as responsibility and leadership. Perhaps because it was more pronounced, ab-

sence of the father was more critical than that of the mother, particularly in its effect on boys.

Thus it is that sociologists and other specialists always confirm the *Zeitgeist.* In the 1950s research was addressed to women, the data were drawn from them, the questions were asked from within a particular conventional framework. If you see women as part of a Talcott Parsonian block, you'll ask one set of questions and get one set of answers; if you see them as individuals with perhaps widely differing needs, you'll ask another set. Sociologists, psychologists (historians as well) are starlings like the rest of us; they are 'true' precisely according to the degree with which their findings conform to the direction and way the flock is wheeling; if they see truth in the opposite direction and fly there they are, as we shall see, ignored.

The result of the movement among women has been paradoxical; it has been at once an enormous success and at the same time an almost total failure. Women in enormous numbers, married and unmarried, with or without children, now work; the most important positions in practically every important sphere are still held by men; women are concentrated overwhelmingly in the lower paid sectors; and even when they do identical jobs, women are usually paid less. (See Appendix C.)

3   Can a feminist revolution ever succeed?

Perhaps the essential things to try and get clear are whether women can do the same jobs as men, if they can do them as well, and whether they should do them.

It is hardly too much to say that an entire and major theoretical pillar, certainly of the feminist movement, but also of the far more general upsurge of women freeing themselves to work, rests on a handful of tiny tribes—most, but not all, described by Margaret Mead and then infinitely repeated. Margaret Mead showed that, although there was a pattern of sex differentiation in the tasks women and men did, there were in fact virtually no tasks or roles which women hadn't done in one society or another—whether it was hunting, farming, or bearing heavy burdens. And where women in one culture did the tasks performed by men in another, they did them just as well. The anthropologist I. Kon found that though on the whole the more primitive the society the more sharply defined the sex roles, this was not always so. The Mbuti pygmies have few formal rules for division of labour by sex. Men and women hunt together without ridicule or social disapproval; roles of father and mother are not sharply differentiated and the tribe, including its youth of either sex, are all responsible for child care. Odder still, sex roles could be completely reversed, depending on the culture. Where we expect males to be assertive and females gentle, the Tchamuli of New Guinea expect males to be gentle and females assertive, while the Mundugumur of the same area expected both males and females to be assertive (there are quite a number of societies where women are sexually assertive). The Arepesh Indians, however, expected both sexes to be gentle.

The conclusion drawn from all this material has been that the culture plays an extremely important part in determining what women shall do and how they view themselves and are viewed by society. To the feminist it is *totally* important. All roles and qualities are interchangeable—only society's attitude must be altered. But most people, while vaguely allowing some biological biases (women better with children, men more logical) would probably agree the social importance is crucial. Indeed, it is only on this basis that the flock could try and wheel in the direction it has. But this often leads feminists and other writers into logical inconsistencies. They find that women are slowly being released from the status of a depressed caste. However, they are adopting uncritically all the values of the dominant men who have kept them like that—that is, the 'masculine' values of competitiveness, achievement, striving for power and material gain. This is a common argument. We are a matrist age dominated by patrist values. Women's clothes approximate to men's and not vice versa, and so on. Dr Jessie Barnard, Emeritus Professor of Sociology at Penn

State University, urged women to use their people-oriented feminine powers—intuition, gentleness and so on. But if these 'feminine/masculine' attitudes are culture-role based, then as someone changes role so will they change attitude. The qualities are dictated by the role. The quality of dominance and toughness is *inherent* in most executive positions. You cannot have a gentle, intuitive executive. Anthropologists find that when women take on 'male' roles they assume 'male' qualities. Reports sometimes appear in the papers of women executives starting to grow facial hair and becoming oversexed. I can find no reliable evidence of this.

Cultural impositions, once received, have the force of instinct. A West European or American man feels *instinctively* emasculated if forced to urinate squatting—as Eastern men do quite naturally. And societies have always regarded sex role changes as extremely dangerous. In France in the eighteenth century men who did women's work, or who allowed tough wives to beat them, were exposed to the charivari—that is, the hooting and tin-banging torment of the whole community howling round the house. Societies may have been right. In the last sixteen years there has been a sharply falling suicide rate in England and Wales, compared to eighteen other countries of Europe, where it has on the whole been rising (the extremes are a fall of 34 per cent in England, a rise of 48 per cent in Switzerland). A recent report by the World Health Organisation found that high among significant factors was the changing role of women. Where their role had changed most, the suicide rate was high, where least, low. The rate for both sexes was affected, but it was clear that most suicide-rate changes were among women. An increase in the number of women in further education or the proportion of births to women over thirty—both crucial indicators of women seeking *careers,* as opposed to just work—were closely related to an increase in their suicide rate.

The role attitude, imposed, but with the force of instinct, is difficult for either sex to alter, particularly for women. When Reza Shah abolished the Chador (veil) in Iran in 1935, resistance among women was so strong that soldiers were ordered into the streets to tear the Chadors from their faces. Some older women did not leave their houses between 1935 and 1941, when the Shah was deposed. There were no baths in the houses and to get these women to public baths they had to be put into sacks and carried there by their men.

A very common 'career' for female characters in contemporary films is that of photographer. A photographer is not part of the crowd, and has no role in it. A photographer is a spectator. Perhaps the most poignant example of the difficulty of role change is Simone de Beauvoir—a figure revered by feminists throughout the world for thirty years. Yet the central relationship of her life—with Sartre—has been instinctively dominated by the sexual double standard. He decided at the beginning that each would be free to follow 'contingent' loves, and immediately, and for the next forty years, took full advantage of this. The list of his mistresses is long. But Beauvoir has only had two publicised affairs, and that with Nelson Algren foundered, largely, because of her inability to prefer him to Sartre. It seems likely that she would have been faithful to Sartre if Sartre had been faithful to her. Of her feminism, Sartre says, 'It is her private world, in which I have never set foot.'

The reaction against feminism has always come far more violently from women than from men. Betty Friedan noticed this after her book came out. In fact a great many men were sympathetic to the movement and often gave her book to their wives. A recent *McCalls* survey (a conservative readership it is true) found that one-third of the women asked deeply resented the way the feminist movement had downgraded the housewife and mother role.

What might seem an extreme demonstration of this is the crusade associated with Marabel Morgan, which started in 1973 with her book *The Total Woman*. She advocated doing two things to have a successful marriage. First, realise marriage is about power and the *ultimate* power is the husband. Mutual adaptation does not work. Second, the marriage must jump right back into the early 1950s. The husband is for work, the wife will return to 'those long baths and then powder, perfume and pizazz . . . Take a few extra moments for that bubble bath tonight . . . Remove all prickly hair and be squeaky clean from head to toe. Be touchable and kissable. . . . Waltzing to the door in a cloud of powder and cologne is a great confidence builder.' Ring him up at the office and say 'I crave your body'. Your reward will be like Marabel's. 'One afternoon he (husband Charlie) called to find out if I'd be home at 3 o'clock. I couldn't imagine what was coming and I was stunned to see a truck pull up with a new refrigerator-freezer.'

You can laugh at Marabel and her *Stepford Wives* vision; you can't dismiss her. It is quite clear that her method works. Husbands, after getting over the initial shock, exist in a state of bemused bliss—and marriages become tranquil. Wives may have to grit their teeth a good deal. Marabel Morgan agrees it's hard—she herself found God indispensable ('the power source')—but it works for millions of people. Her book has sold over four million copies since 1973 and is selling still. There are over seventy Marabel Morgan Centers, not just in every state of America but in Japan, South America, Germany, Puerto Rico and France (though not, significantly, in England. She had what she described as 'an excellent response', but no one actually wanted to start a centre.)

It requires extremely exceptional couples, but in particular exceptional women, to lead full family and career lives at once. Just how exceptional is shown by a long dense study specifically made of this situation (dual-career families) by Rhona and Robert Rapoport.

'I'm sure you're going to find,' said the husband of one of such couples, 'that the whole business of women working is dependent on other responsible women who deal with children.' Without a fairly substantial army of nannies, au-pair girls, daily helpers, and private boarding schools (all the families in the Rapoport study had children) these dual-career families would have found life impossible. Dual-career depends on wealth. The Rapoports were criticised when their book first appeared because their couples, especially the women, were superenergetic and efficient. In reply, they quoted an American study into dual-*working* (as opposed to career) couples which found that they, especially the women, were also exceptionally resourceful and energetic. I don't see how this helps the Rapoports. It simply confirms that in today's circumstances that sort of life—'work' or 'career'—is for the exceptional.

Women especially had to be superefficient and energetic (wife: 'I feel that I even have to sleep fast to get through the housework'). The husbands were invariably supportive, helpful, encouraged their wives to work, and did *some* housework—but this was the tricky area. Here they reached limits, running up against what the Rapoports call the *'identity tension line'*.

Finally, they found all their couples had a number of extremely significant characteristics in common. The wives were often a first child or only child; that is, one might suspect, their family's 'son'. They were the product of higher education. (Both these observations were confirmed by other, much larger surveys in America and Norway.) Their mothers had worked. The tension in their families was high—not disturbing, but higher than normal. Among the men, the chief characteristic was a close relationship with their mothers which allowed them to support their wives and view their success without jealousy. These last two are very interesting. Increased divorce means anxious home backgrounds are probably more common. Girls seem to react by wanting to have their own earning capacity. Boys will be thrown still closer on their mothers. Families with these various 'exceptional' characteristics would probably constitute about 10 per cent of any Western population. In America, the feeling is that women have only got to make an effort for the top positions and top occupations and they will get them.

It would be possible to deduce from the facts and arguments in this section the following conclusion: Western society will probably stay in much the same position as it is now. A limit has been reached. It is clear that a large number of women (perhaps 30 per cent) want to remain mothers and housewives—some even want to return to the 1950s. Probably about double that number cannot manage, or do not want, any radical role reversal or real careers.

They like to work and do minimum housework before marriage and especially before children; they want occupation again when the children have grown up. What remains (it is proving hard enough) is to remove the obvious injustices like unequal pay and unequal chances to get the same job; and to fight prejudice against, and alleviate female guilt amongst, the exceptional 5–10 per cent.

This argument is almost certainly that of a large number of people, particularly a large number of men. And it is sustainable just considering the reaction of *women*. We haven't looked at men themselves. They also find the change of roles, the challenge of occupation hard. In particular they find housework hard. Men appear to have serious lapses of memory, even delusions about housework. A survey by the sociologist Audrey Hunt in 1975 found that 75 per cent said they did about a quarter of the housework. But nearly half the women in the survey said their husbands gave them no help *at all*. Audrey Hunt commented evenly, 'it seems more probably that the husbands were exaggerating, since if the wives were minimising they would be more likely to underestimate than say husbands did not do it at all'. It is sometimes suggested this is a sort of family version of Western capitalist exploitation of labour. This is rubbish. Research in Sweden, Finland and the Soviet Union shows that in those countries too there have only been 'lip-service' changes as regards men helping women in the home.

But the main male complaint was that their work was not being altered—housework was just being added. Their wives, on the other hand, were altering their working lives in a direction of their choosing. The wives could argue that they were bringing in money and so 'paying' their husbands. But it is true that, despite Betty Friedan's hopes, neither the feminist movement nor the larger one of women working have brought men any benefit in the fundamental area of altering their working lives.

Finally—Total Men. In 1978 John Fenton, a U.S. publisher, produced a new magazine called *Male Chauvinist*. It contained articles with subtle titles such as 'How to Cheat Your Wife', 'Why Women are Emotional', 'How to Sleep with your Secretary' and

'Chauvinist of the Month'. Fenton, twice divorced, was quoted as saying, 'I acquiesced in the new male role-playing and it cost me financially, emotionally and physically. Women should be kept in submission. We've had enough of this liberation bullshit.'

In 1979, David Stone, ex-RAF pilot, founded The Campaign for the Feminine Woman in England. 'Women's Lib is a dangerous cancer and perversion which must be eliminated.'

4 Men become mothers

In 1978, *Woman's Own* did a survey among its 6 million British readers to find out how much fathers were helping with the children: five out of six husbands had looked after the children on their own, two out of three had read to them, three out of four had put them to bed. But, and this is the measure of how expectations have changed, the editors of *Woman's Own* were surprised how *little* the men were helping with the children.

By the 1920s anthropologists such as Edward Westermarck had observed that parental love was just as strong among fathers as among mothers in many primitive cultures. In fact parental feelings are stimulated by anything small and helpless—but as far as his own children went, the father's love was stronger the closer he was to the helpless being *from the start*. This love was an instinct, operating automatically and with uncontrollable force, bringing into play every fibre of the being. This bonding mechanism in fathers—sprung by sight and touch—has been confirmed by modern research.

Since the end of the 1950s fathers seem to be loving their children more. In a book on unmarried fathers, Dulian Barber found that many of them longed to be more intimately involved as parents with their often accidentally conceived children; while Dorothy Burlingham, the distinguished analyst and colleague of Anna Freud, found that men were marrying women who had low maternal drive so that they could fully express their paternal feelings.

Sometimes this seems to get slightly out of hand. Robert Feiss found that in America men were collapsing after labour, complaining of not receiving enough 'emotional support'; they became furious that they could not feed their babies and spoke of 'breast envy'. But the most extreme case I found came from a 1973 study by Sheila Kitzinger, prenatal teacher with the National Childbirth Trust of Great Britain. All the fathers had been brainwashed first in her ante-natal classes. After the birth, each couple had to report. Here is an example.

'I was awakened at approximately 3.00 a.m. by my wife in the bathroom. She told me she felt labour was beginning. I propped her up in bed. It took us all of half an hour to establish reasonable harmony of breathing with contractions. I breathed with her through all levels. I insisted that she breathe properly and relax; otherwise it would hurt. I did not remain a logical adviser, but rather a catalyst, acting through the spontaneity of love rather than logical detachment.' After establishing harmony, he leaves to call the mid-wife. Then quickly returns and gets Pippa on her side, 'rubbing her back and breathing simultaneously with her when the mid-wife arrived. I was by this time wholly involved in the labour and her breath was my breath.' The labour proceeds until 'Now came the bearing down stage and the most painfully beautiful experience I have ever had. My wife was in a sitting position now. I had my right arm around her back with my hand under her arm supporting her, while her left arm was around my back.

'I knew there was no point in saying, "relax honey", I had to feel it with her. The perspiration was running down my back. I said, "Come on honey, deep breath— now, bear down!! Hold on, hold on!! Now breathe." I could see a tiny portion of the baby's head . . . My wife and I took a breath and bore down. "Bear down, honey, it's coming! Bear down, bear down, hold on, hold on." The baby's head popped out . . .

'The perspiration was rolling off my head. Then the glorious moment when the little being was wholly released from the vagina. The nurses turned the baby round. "It's a girl, honey!" I shouted. "It's a girl honey, honey!" I was beside myself with joy! I had given birth along with my wife. I was exhausted. It was glorious, just glorious . . . ecstasy . . .'

The wife's account, somewhat swamped by all this, is much shorter, barely five lines, carrying a sense almost of redundancy: 'It was very much a joint effort. Without John I'm afraid I never would have made it. He played the most important part.'

These may be extreme examples. The phenomenon itself is widespread, important, and often moving. It is also highly relevant to our discussion of divorce later on, when it becomes tragic.

The change in emotional temperature from earlier attitudes, those before the war for instance, is most extreme among British middle and upper middle classes—and here, oddly enough, it has affected both mothers and fathers. This is because up to 1939 these classes did not bring up their own children, but left it to nannies. After the war, this stopped. One can see evidence of the growth of love in their increasing guilt and reluctance to send their little children to prep schools, and in their much closer involvement in the boarding public schools when finally they do send them.

Drawing attention to this change among fathers has in fact been an oblique start to attacking the possible conclusion we reached at the end of the last section—the conclusion that the limit to female emancipation has been reached. I now want to make the attack a great deal sharper.

5   *What to do with the children*

The crux of the problem for working women is children. Women have worked before. Up to the eleventh century, until developments in the plough made the work too hard (deeper furrows), women did most of the essential agricultural work in Europe. Their position was no better as a result. The work was drudgery. Men didn't want to do it—any more than they want to type now. Until women hold a far larger share of top jobs, and jobs in prestige occupations, there has been and will be no fundamental change. But women also want families—which they can hardly be denied. If they have children early, they jettison the career. If they have them late, they may not have them at all. Couples married between twenty-five and twenty-nine have a 14 per cent infertility risk; thirty to thirty-four, 23 per cent; after thirty-five, 40 per cent. The infertility clinics are swarming with desperate women who have used contraceptives for years because they put their careers first. Le Masters, author of *Parents in Modern America,* in 1970, found that all career mothers suffered a severe and extensive crisis with their first child, because it meant giving up an occupation of deep significance to them.

A similar picture of frustration is found among vast numbers of ordinary working women. In America, women are having fewer children and having them later; there are indications of the same happening in Britain. This almost certainly reflects the number of women working. But the unsatisfactory nature of this work attempt is shown by the housewives aged thirty or older who continue by the million to show the same symptoms as at the end of the 1950s: depression, suicide attempts, stress symptoms like palpitations and sleeplessness. Tons of valium are crunched down daily. In the 1976 *McCalls* survey, housework was still what most readers (31 per cent) hated most. And there are still millions who would work if they could—a quarter of the 6 million *Woman's Own* survey, and an estimated 1.8 million women in a recent Equal Opportunities Commission document. A further 3.8 million have low-paid part-time jobs they dislike. And all these women are under the same constraint—how to look after the children.

The first solution is to let someone else look after them; and it is obviously essential here to find out what effects child-minding, day-care centres and the rest have on children. Over the last thirty years an enormous amount of research has been done on this. The result—exhaustively analysed in 1960 by Lois Meek Stolz, Emeritus Professor of Psychology at Stanford University, and the Rapoports in 1977—is extraordinary: no definite conclusion can be reached in any major area. It is possible to say *anything* about the children of working mothers and support it by some research or other. It was found the children of working mothers were more delinquent; but a closer look at the sample found that these mothers had themselves been delinquent, and were in any case poor. Another study showed that working wives were more content, they were able to have a closer relationship with their children and their children were more stable. The Swede, Gunnel Lindblom, said in 1978: 'Women in Sweden are in a better situation than anywhere else, but it is the children who pay the price . . . the results of this can be seen in drop-out children.' I was also told that in Sweden the long hours of day care were producing a Kibbutz-style reaction—remote children, incapable of deep relationships. Another study found that even good nursery care produced children who were 'diffuse' in attachment. This is interesting because it could be one way of adjusting to divorce and freer sexual liaisons. (See Appendix C4.)

In part this reflects the enormous diversity in types of care, of child reaction, of mother, but I think there is a more fundamental way of looking at it. Both in America and Britain day-care centres have in fact declined over the last five years. This is usually explained by the economic recession; yet, despite that, women have managed to increase their share of something they really want— work. It is a picture of desperate need, combined with deep reluctance. There is something inherently despairing about a day-care centre. Here is a description of a typically 'good' one in America.

> Basement spacious but dark, stale air. Semicircle of small chairs set in rows before huge TV. Ominous. 2-hour after dinner naptime! Too much talk from JD about money, keeping charges down to $3.50 a day. Depressing sights—dark unfurnished windowless 'isolation

area' for sick or hurt kids incarcerated until parents pick up . . . weeping 3-year-old girl clutching father, begging him not to leave (JD: 'he has custody') . . . Half of all children who have attended this center over its four years are from divorced parents. Children who spend longest days at center, 7 am to 5 pm are the young ones. Staff of six.

In England mothers have voted with their feet by preferring parent participation play-groups (numerically few) or child-minders (estimates vary—perhaps half a million, of whom 330,000 are illegal). They grope for something of the closeness which you find in the only two successful examples of nonmother child-care—the elderly relative or joint-upbringing of many primitive cultures or the nanny system of the British middle classes between 1840–1939. It is for this reason—the desire of mothers for their children—that the Kibbutz system in Israel is gradually breaking down.

It is clear, surely, that little children of two, three or four should not spend ten hours away from home. What is the point? What is the point of having children if as soon as it is humanly possible you send them away? Why have them? The day-care/child-minder solution is spurious because mothers don't really want to do that, nor should they be expected to; yet children are the crucial element preventing them having careers and making even work (as opposed to career) exceptionally difficult or low grade.

6   Solution of the shared society

It has long struck me as odd that hardly any feminist, however radical, can see that logically equality should mean just that—or it will mean inequality. Men and women must be equally responsible for looking after the children and home and earning the family wage. Otherwise, although no doubt some amelioration, perhaps total removal, of current working inequalities can be obtained, there will be no fundamental change. No matter if it takes decades, that must be the ultimate goal: an economic and social revolution of apparently some magnitude.

In one sense, the move to part-time work (and that is what this change entails—a very wide adoption of part-time or shared-time work) has been proceeding for about a century and a half. In 1820, labourers could work twelve or fifteen hours a day. In Britain, negotiations are now in progress over a thirty-five-hour week and suggestions started for a thirty-hour one; the three-day weekend is commonplace in America. Once you have a twenty-hour or three-day week—not difficult to imagine over the next thirty years—you have the practical base for shared home and work responsibility. Given the addition to the labour force of the women who do not at present work but want to, it could, in practical terms, come much sooner.

In Britain there is virtually no experiment along these lines (or conversely, a great deal, if you regard strikes and low productivity as a primitive form of work sharing). But in most other European countries and in America a good many companies successfully run flexitime, the method whereby, provided certain key hours are manned, you can work when you like. In Switzerland 60 per cent of all employment is run in this way. In Germany *flexiyear* contracts are becoming popular: you contract to work for varying numbers of months a year. Similar schemes exist in America: in Santa Clara, California, for instance, 18 per cent of the county's employees recently exchanged less pay for much longer holidays. Again, it is not difficult to envisage these practices extending and converging with the move to less work over the next three decades.

The benefits that would result for career or working women are the reverse of the difficulties and frustrations. In fact the entire sample in one of the largest studies of successful working women, the study by sociologist Erik Grönseth, consisted of both partners working part-time. Grönseth also chose partners who shared housework equally (he was interested in the effect on their sex lives). As has been shown, husbands are taking to the children; they are not taking to housework. With part-time work there would at least be some fair exchange. Men, as far as work stress goes, have derived no benefits from women's liberation whatsoever. On the contrary. They now die relatively even earlier than they did in 1920. For example, in America men died at 53.6 to women's 54.6 in 1920; in 1975 the figures were 68.7 to 76.5. (People point to the figures for depressive illness to illustrate the stress on women. But depression isn't 'manly'. Men get drunk instead. Figures for alcoholism are always far higher for men than women.) One could expect some alleviation of this unfair state of affairs. And there would be clear benefits to children. Unable to decide whether leaving a two-year old for ten hours a day in day care is harmful or beneficial, 'research' at this point speaks clearly. Where both parents work outside and inside the home, children develop the capacity for both assertiveness and tenderness; they see themselves as possessing the desirable characteristics of both parents and both sexes.

But the important question is: Is role-sharing possible? I don't mean by this, could it be organised, or could the work get done. It does not seem likely, given say thirty years, that the ever more technologically expert West would find the organisation beyond it. As to the amount of work—when the entire industrial base of Britain went on to a three-day week in 1974 it effortlessly achieved the same output it does on full time today. All work studies of business executives, however 'busy', invariably show— as they did with housewives—that anything up to half the work is unnecessary. It was studies like these, and similar ones in industry, that allowed two distinguished American economists to prove that the same GNP could be maintained with far less work per capita—and that was with the *same* work force. Here, we would be augmenting the work force by many millions.

There is no doubt such an economic and social revolution is possible. But the obvious stumbling block is this—we have already seen that some large but unknown proportion of women (perhaps 30 per cent) don't want to work or alter their roles. A larger proportion of men don't want to change, though many of these might be impelled by time and vigorous wives. But this revolution would give an enormous advantage—of promotion and so on—to those who continued full time. In the face of this, how can we expect decisive change?

Unemployment in the European Economic Community as of May 1979 was running at 16 million. Add to that figures in the other countries who are sharing in the vast social movements we have been discussing and the number becomes 26 million. (See Appendix C.) It is notoriously difficult to make economic forecasts, but as far as I can ascertain the consensus of expert opinion is that high unemployment will probably dominate the 1980s. That is to say, the 'Western' countries are already condemning the equivalent of a small European nation to one of the most self-destroying, morale-disintegrating conditions that exists. It is a strong argument that we should already have worked out a more equitable way of sharing work.

There is a powerful case that soon it won't be *should*, but *must*. Once again, the effects of the accelerating microelectronics revolution—the silicon chip—have become highly controversial. Americans tend to be optimistic. The trouble with their optimism is that it is entirely unspecific. Their argument, in effect, is that it's been all right before; it will be again. Dr George Champine, director of Advanced Systems for Sperry Univac, points out how the mechanical reaper, the spinning jenny, the cotton gin didn't in the end cause unemployment. The comparison is ludicrous. The old industrial revolution was spread over 130 years at the least; it moved in a series of unrelated, and often unrelating discoveries, sometimes affecting quite small areas. The microelectronic revolution, if even half of what I read is accurate, cannot properly be compared even to the computer developments of the last two decades. So much so that the American sociologist, Seymour Martin Lipset, believes chips will be able to do everything, and carols blithely on about how society will return to the equality of ancient Athens—all work done by 'slaves'. The chips are even going to do the housework.

However, whenever any detailed or specific study is done, the picture becomes quite different. The area which always seems least likely to manage the sort of sex-role and economic revolution I have in mind is the industrial base. Yet oddly enough, this appears to be the area which will be most radically affected by the microelectronic changes. Professor Stonier of Bradford University has calculated that eventually 10 per cent of the current labour force will provide *all* that we need in, he estimates, thirty years. Not everyone agrees with his calculation, but even if we halve or quarter the figure, a reduction in the industrial labour force of something like 60 per cent would be staggering. The great upsurge in new jobs is supposed to come in the service industries where most women work, and would thus create an ideal battleground in which to introduce the shared society. But when these too are looked at carefully, a different picture emerges. The British Government commissioned just such a study. The results were so frightening they refused to publish it, though eventually they agreed to let the authors, Ray Curnow and Iann Barron, do so. The bulk of the service industries are in the information sector, which in fact comprises 65 per cent of the working population. This was the focus of their study and they found microelectronics would bring about reductions of up to 20 per cent, equivalent to an increase of 13 per cent in general unemployment.

It is very probable that over the next thirty years the force dictating a total move to part-time work will become as overwhelming as that dictating the rationing of food in Britain in wartime—and for the same reason: there won't be enough to go round.

Even if it does not happen on this scale, the argument remains. A great many women are dissatisfied with their lives: some because they are in unsatisfactory jobs, some because they are not in jobs at all, some because job and home is too demanding, some because they are not advancing their careers, or are about to give up careers to have children. The reason in all cases, is, practically and because of psychological orientation, their children. The daycare solution is inherently unsatisfactory and women don't really want it. The only logical solution I see is a dual sharing of work and home with men. A move towards this, already foreshadowed to some extent by changing attitudes in men, may be helped by the economic developments just outlined. But whether it is or not, dual sharing will have to be fought for. It won't just arrive. On the contrary, the less work there is, the more men will seek it for themselves. But for the first time in history the *possibility* of a shared society is *arriving*. This, and only this, should be the goal of feminists over the next thirty years. Without it, their rhetoric, their arguments about the family, their radicalism are entirely frivolous.

That then, was the position I had reached at this stage of the book. I was therefore somewhat shattered, because I did not hear of it until I had written thus far, to read *The Inevitability of Patriarchy* by Steven Goldberg. Goldberg seems to prove that not only should women not take on male roles in society to any large degree, it is actually *impossible* for them to do so. There are fundamental physiological differences which lead 'inevitably' to male dominance in all societies and in all important roles except mothering. His book ends with a warning. If woman wants and gets the right to meet men on equal terms—'She will lose'.

The example of Goldberg is typical of what happens when an anthropologist or sociobiologist flies in the opposite direction to the flock. His views are argued with—and then ignored. In a BBC TV documentary on the subject on May 21, 1979, he wasn't even mentioned. However, Goldberg won't just go away. His arguments have far-reaching implications. In the English edition of his book he answers his American critics effortlessly, convincingly and, in the case of the feminists, often contemptuously.

I embarked, therefore, on a week's hard reading, resolved either to demolish Goldberg or so to reduce him that he no longer posed a threat to the position I had reached—or else I would capitulate. In the end of a finally exhilarating struggle I had reduced him. But his is a closely, often fiercely reasoned book, the arguments densely packed. (I have accordingly relegated the battle to Appendix C, where you can read it and return; or continue, confident that he does *not* undermine that attempt at a far more open and equal society which is the only solution to feminist—and many other—problems.)

7   *The feminist revolution and its effect on marriage*

The woman's movement is, along with the sexual revolution, clearly one of the most important influences on marriage today. Many commentators think it is a major cause of divorce. It is not as simple as that.

At one extreme, the connection between the movement among women and marriage breakdown is obvious. The women who come to hate men under the first surge of feminist belief often deliberately break their marriages, or suggest changes so radical and swift that the result is the same. This phenomenon is an early and usually temporary stage. Betty Friedan and the Rapoports both told me it is now more common in Britain than in America. In Britain you sometimes find it in the Gingerbread Groups, set up to help husbands and wives who are on their own, where for the women it is exacerbated because the husbands have vanished or refuse to pay maintenance. Sometimes these women become champions of lesbianism; a course to some degree imposed because they often condemn heterosexual romantic love as irrational and therefore limiting feminine choice, and also sexual intercourse with men because it is so delicious it may become a necessity (this is an argument of Beauvoir's also—perhaps easier to advance as you approach your seventies).

It is clear too what is happening in the middle ground. In America, where once only women went to marriage counsellors, now 50 per cent of the clients are men. Claude Stein, a transactional analyst in San Francisco, says the nuclear family demands a top dog and a bottom dog: 'No matter how bad things are for both, top dog is more comfortable than bottom dog. As long as the man is the top dog, it's going to be the woman who cracks. But when bottom dog suddenly turns around and says "Go make your own dinner and masturbate with a paperback," it is going to be hard on the husband. He's going to look for a therapist.'

There is a Japanese TV programme which specialises in getting back missing people. Twenty years ago, it was 70 per cent men running away; now it has reversed—70 per cent women clear off.

In Britain, said David Barkla of the Marriage Guidance Council, it used to be entirely women who asked for advice; now the trend is for both partners to attend. He also said that most counsellors were women who were feminist-inclined and it was impossible for some elements of their own attitudes not to enter their counselling (and so to the degree that divorce is due to feminist friction the Marriage Guidance Council is probably fomenting it).

Sometimes the struggle to obtain a new balance in an individual marriage does not begin for years. There was a couple married sixteen years; call them Jim and Doreen. Doreen was naturally untidy, Jim fanatical—always polishing, for every cup, every saucepan lid a hook, and 'Woe betide anyone who mixed them up'. But by devoting herself full time to house and children, Doreen preserved a semblance of order and the marriage was successful. Then the children went to secondary school. Doreen took a job. Gradually the household slid downhill, hooks got muddled, then ignored, floors went unscrubbed, washing-up piled in tottering towers—finally it was a shambles, 'chaotic'. Jim didn't see why he should take to housework. The atmosphere, following the descent to chaos, became at first 'oppressive', then explosive. Finally Jim walked out and set up with a new woman.

But to the extent (unmeasurable) that divorce rates are pushed up by women's demands and by the slowness of society and men to adapt to them, then, as the demands are met, as men and society do adapt, to the same extent will divorce rates sink back. We are in a transitional stage, and when the movement has been adapted to it, it will cease to be an area of friction.

It will even become a force for increased stability; is indeed sometimes already that. Betty Friedan quotes several studies showing that marriages where women work are happier, in particular sexually more successful, than where they confine themselves to the home. And Grönseth's Norwegian men who survived the supposedly castrating role-change to half-housewife found it actually enhanced—a quarter said their sex lives improved.

6

THE PRIVILEGE BULGE

BETTY FRIEDAN'S explanation for the abject subjection of women to home and children after the war and during the 1950s was largely the war itself—the need for babies, the women's magazines edited by men. I've already said I found that odd. It was not nearly so true of Britain, nor of other countries where a similar move took place. Her argument also seems insufficient.

I then noticed that some of her most telling illustrations were quite early—sometimes earlier than she knew. The Bryn Mawr Survey which showed women working harder and harder the more labour-saving devices they had, which she quoted in relation to the 1960s, was in fact done in 1938. The boy who said his mother would butter his bread until he married, when his wife would do it, came from a 1943 study. I think there is, not an alternative (they reinforce each other), but a different way of looking at it.

1 An explanation of the phenomenon

The parents of the 1950s and early 1960s were born in the late 1920s, the 1930s and early 1940s. The great movement that had been growing from the beginning of the century, but which at last began to spread out with more and more popular and persuasive power during these years, was the psychoanalytic one started by

Freud. The influences at work on those born in the late 1920s, the 1930s and 1940s became increasingly permeated by psychoanalytic ideas as they grew older. In America, during the 1950s there was, with the growth of clinics and therapists, what amounted to a psychoanalytic explosion. This did not happen nearly so fast in Britain—except in the sphere of child care. All the influential child-care books in Britain, the 'experts' in the media, the vast pamphlet literature disseminated by the local authorities through the baby clinics, were resolutely based on the findings of psychoanalytic theory by the mid-1940s.

During this period, despite wide differences, two fundamentals remained central to the movement. Freud, in his deep search for the source of individual ills, had located them in baby and childhood—in the conflicts and traumas starting there and in the repressions resulting. But if the source was there, so was the cure. That is to say, psychoanalytic theory was a hopeful one. I think people tend to forget how exciting this was. For the first time perhaps in history it seemed possible, in the late 1940s and 1950s, that you could be *certain* of creating happy children, happy adults. You could change the world. This, in those optimistic years of burgeoning wealth, was the exhilarating crusade of the child-care writers—and the crusade of the parents who followed them.

But Freud was concerned with curing adults. The second fundamental of the psychoanalytic movement was that it was possible, in varying degrees, to do this; but a corollary was, since everyone was subject more or less to the same factors causing mental distress, that everyone could lead lives of greater happiness if they took similar steps—to release repressions, resolve conflicts, and so on. It is a truism that parents lead their lives through their children. They reveal what they themselves want by the way they bring them up. But this was particularly true at this time when the focus on child-upbringing, the belief in it, was so intense. A therapist during this period had a nine-year-old patient who stole. 'She'll outgrow it,' said the protective mother, her permissiveness born of a need for vicarious satisfaction. At one point the nine-year-old asked the therapist, 'When is my mother going to do her own stealing?'

The developments of the 1950s should be viewed as the expression of a generation—the Privilege Bulge Generation—brought up under the ever-growing influence of psychoanalytic ideas and in search, therefore, of personal happiness and fulfilment—and the way they brought up their children was but one aspect of this. This explains (indeed nothing else can) the success of writers like Kinsey and Friedan. It is not until a vast number of people have already changed, that books of this sort, crystallising, expressing and later influencing a general mood, can be successful. People bought and read Kinsey because they wanted a freer life, in this case sexually freer; indeed they had begun to live it. Half Kinsey's force came from saying, look, a great many people do these things. They are normal. The same was true of Betty Friedan. Her clarion call to women to work, not to be subjected by home and children, came in 1963, about six years after the movement was well underway. By the late 1950s, over 30 per cent of American married women were *already* working.

Here, too, lies the significance of the 1960s. The emphasis should not be on the youth of that decade, as it usually is. What is interesting about developments then is that they took place because of the generation born in the late 1920s, the 1930s and 1940s. Not only among them, but among their children, because they allowed and wanted it. If they hadn't, it wouldn't have happened. In America, this tends to get obscured because of panic about excesses and lack of control. It can be most clearly and precisely demonstrated in Britain; the medium is her public schools.

The only really significant influence on these ancient institutions has always been the people who pay the bills—the parents. Time and again they have demonstrated an astounding ability *not* to change. Between 1800 and 1825 they tolerated appalling sexual licence, ferocious bullying and savage flogging in the face of universal press and often Parliamentary attack. Then, as the parents started to react, numbers plummeted. Within ten years the schools were transformed. The same thing happened at the end of the nineteenth century; it happened again in the 1960s. At that time the schools were still fairly rigid, highly disciplined, uniformed little communities, with traditions, methods of punishment, biases in the curriculum going back decades and sometimes centuries. Once again, these accretions vanished over ten short years, and the *only* reason they could do so was that the middle-class fathers and mothers who supported the schools wanted them to change.

But people don't easily give up privileges won, pleasures tasted, freedoms enjoyed. The generation born in the late 1920s, the 1930s and early 1940s are now in their thirties, forties and fifties. As they progress through society they hold to what they've gained. Just as they did earlier, they widen and expand the view of society towards their age group, indeed all age groups, as they advance, forcing it to expand and widen itself, to change—hence my expression 'the Privilege Bulge'. Several results of the Privilege Bulge powering its way forward will be looked at. Here is one. Since the 1960s commentators have continued to repeat automatically that we are a 'youth-dominated culture'. But this is simply not true. Of course there *is* a youth culture—the vast pop industry, special films, *Grease* (significantly set in Privilege Bulge country). But a high proportion, I would say a major proportion, of novels, films and TV serials are not to do with young people at all. They are to do with those between 30 and 50. And this as far as love goes is historically new. Love has hitherto on the whole been reserved for youth. *Seduction* of youth by middle age was a theme (*Chéri, The Edwardians*). But late-flowering passion was, in women, either disgusting (Gertrude in *Hamlet*), wicked (*Phèdre*) or, if in a man, ludicrous (Baron Ochs in the *Rosenkavalier*). No longer. The theme of Privilege Bulge love is very common. It is the subject of some of Updike's best books. Age is often the defining factor—'Pitying, he took her hand, but the contact was damp and made them self-conscious; they were too old to hold hands' (Jerry in *Marry Me*)—but it does not restrict the passion. This can have a hectic quality equal in intensity to the strong flame of youth. The Privilege Bulge makes most films, acts in them and writes them—and is therefore their subject. I think as I write of *An Unmarried Woman* or *Same Time Next Year*. I think of a recent musical about forty-year-old love called *Ballroom* which played in New York last autumn.

As the Privilege Bulge advances still further, its power will increase, especially in economic and political terms. (See Appendix D.)

To make the metaphor somewhat inelegantly explicit, once the intestine of society has been thus widened, it will not easily close again. It is not in the interests of those who follow that it should. The Rapoports quote studies to show that children reared in the style of the 1960s and 1970s (which essentially persist) *continue* to need, among other things, a lot of praise, new experiences, and recognition. They know they too will soon be in the position of the Privilege Bulge. They look likely, say the Rapoports, to cope far better with any transition to middle age because they are actively and cunningly planning ahead. They too will not supinely let slip those sweets of media concentration, the freedoms they enjoyed when young.

2   *Second echo from Rome—the new gods*

Dr Albert Ellis was giving me half an hour in his Manhattan consulting room. He had been a distinguished sexologist in the late 1950s; but his name, almost fame, came from many years' practice of 'Rational psychotherapy'. He looked rather as Woody Allen may at sixty-eight—shrivelled, tanned. It was a large wood-panelled room, with black leather banquettes. Old Woody was lying back when I came in; he did not get up but simply stretched out a wiry forefinger and snapped on a tape recorder (I learnt later there had been some acrimony over misquotes). He was in an open-necked shirt and pullover. I, with vague ideas of Harley Street, had overdressed. I had been reading about Rational psychotherapy and, though it was not what I wanted to talk about, one thing had struck me. I asked: Surely it was true people learnt *emotions* when young, which they then repeated?

He instantly became quite violent. You didn't learn *anything*. That was a lot of crap, a lot of horseshit. You taught *yourself* things. You taught yourself responses to these pressures. It was like walking. It was a lot of crap to say you 'learnt' to walk. You taught yourself. Tie a baby up for two years and then let it loose, it'd teach itself (I wondered if this had ever been done).

But Ellis, thoroughly invigorated, was now leaping irrelevantly on. Had I read his latest book? Mankind was biologically screwed up. There was no God. No one cared for us. That was a lot of horseshit. But all over the world, always, people had believed in God and gods. Why? We were a lot of babies.

I didn't reply—though I understood the forcefulness of his response. As far as I had read, the root of Rational psychotherapy lay in your attitude to yourself. This attitude almost invariably depends on events in early childhood to which you have responded by teaching yourself to think in a certain way, to have certain ideas about yourself—that this is 'terrible', that you will 'fail'. But since these are 'ideas', they can be changed. They can be shown to be illogical, and you can teach yourself new 'ideas' in their place. The role of the therapist is not passive. On the contrary. The role of the therapist, in this case Ellis, was extremely active and pugnacious, to point out, with great thumps and thwacks of his personality, the illogicality of the false 'ideas', and get the patient to teach himself new ones. 'After a month of steadily pounding away at this patient's fears of failure . . . I then kept analyzing, attacking, ridiculing and challenging these beliefs . . .' 'As is not unusual in my handling of this type of case, I attacked this patient's anti-sexual attitudes full blast.'

Clearly, it was important they should be 'ideas' and not 'emotions' since the first could be 'changed', the second less obviously so in a learning sense; it was also important you had 'taught' yourself and had not 'learnt' it, so that you could 'teach' yourself something else and not have to be taught by someone else. It seemed to me entirely a matter of semantics—quite unprovable either way. As for 'teaching yourself', the repeated biffs of Ellis's not inconsiderable character seemed a classic, almost crude, example of being taught.

As I say, I only had half an hour, and we proceeded with the interview. Walking back afterwards, I thought about Ellis. I thought how all the therapists I saw had the same indefinable quality of being used, a prostitute feeling. Tired. Overknowing. They are seen for a space like prostitutes, then paid. We are all paid, of course; but only prostitutes and psychiatrists/therapists/analysts are paid for such *personal* services.

However, two things had especially interested me: the powerful waves of personality coming from the wizened figure, and the fact he was successful. Rational psychotherapy was an extremely effective, long-tested, highly thought of form of treatment. It worked. Yet, it is directly contrary to what is still probably the most common method of psychotherapy, which derives from Freudian analytic technique. The patient must find out for *himself* what is wrong; the value lies in self-discovery, in slowly working through his fears, angers and so on. The range within this is enormous—thus, no guidance can be given, or very active help. But that is broadly the idea—and it works too.

When you get therapies which are essentially opposite in their base, method and aim, and both are successful, then you are not in the realm of science but of religion. It is a matter of belief. And there are dozens of different treatments, therapies, methods. We are today—and once again there is that mysterious echo from the Roman world which is in one respect our only parallel—in the same situation that existed for two or three hundred years around A.D. 1. Then, too, dozens of different religions flourished, until finally one, Christ's, slowly triumphed. That is why the successful contenders today—Jung, Freud and hosts of others—have had to have, often do have, such powerful, charismatic personalities. Ellis's brief, rather aggressive, diatribe against religion, God and gods, was quite relevant really.

3   *The rage to 'grow'*

How, as they advance, are the Privilege Bulge yet further expanding society, yet further exploiting their position? The answer is they are *growing*.

The concept of individual 'growth' is to some degree inherent in the goals of psychoanalytic theory. It is a short step from curing, 'integrating', releasing neurotic or otherwise handicapped personalities, to developing them to their fullest. And if them, why not everyone? It also owes something to the existentialism, deriving from Sartre, which was popular in the 1950s and 1960s. The essence of this, unless I misunderstand it, is that our lives are something we can make and remake for ourselves day by day. The mid-life crisis—the couple of forty to fifty, the children gone, the wife therefore out of a job, the husband unlikely to advance further in his, both fearful of waning attractiveness, both reverberating to the sight and sound of adolescent vigour and adolescent love, has long been recognised. Margaret Mead was writing about it in 1948. Even before that Jung had postulated a second adolescence in middle age.

But it has been the needs and demands and desires of the Privilege Bulge which have inflated this out of all measure. Now the idea is of perpetual 'growth', infinite expansion. Adolescence is not over at eighteen or twenty, it is permanent; or, put another way, not one adolescence but dozens. Books appear describing, apparently with reason, in fact quite arbitrarily, when the next spurt will come—every five years, every seven. I say perpetual, and this is true. Growth, as the Privilege Bulge stretches for the infinite, goes on up to the second you die. 'It is a mistake,' write the Rapoports, 'to think one does not participate in one's death.' It, too, can be 'a fulfilling experience', though the final savouring of it must, one supposes, be only momentary. Flooding out from America, this is becoming a mighty movement, a crusade; it's boom time in the Yoga, Zen and Aikido classes, the encounter and consciousness-expanding groups and transactional analyst courses, the human potential and crotch-eyeballing sessions: the biggest growth industry at the moment is growth itself.

I certainly don't deny that human beings have enormous potential for development in all sorts of directions at all ages. Some of this movement is valuable and has affected our main areas of concern—love, marriage, sex—beneficially. But it has also in many respects got quite out of hand, and looks like getting more

so. People become gripped by fantasies of secret talents and un-
discovered gifts, of huge reservoirs of untapped power, and these
fantasies induce a rage to discover 'the true self', their lives in the
present, the people they are with, the people they in fact *are*, become maddening or frustrating.

Look at this 'growth' for a moment. How do you do it? If you
are a woman, it means getting a job. This is axiomatic. Any book
anywhere near the subject of 'growth' assumes it without question. The O'Neills, the American authors of the best-selling *Open
Marriage*, in their book *Shifting Gears*, to choose one out of about
150,000 possible examples, talk muzzily about women 'realising
themselves', 'growing', 'enriching' themselves in a job. The fact is
80 per cent of jobs today, men's and women's, don't enrich anyone
except the firm, the shareholder or the government. The trouble is
a lack of definition. How are women (or men, for that matter)
supposed to be 'enriched', what is it that 'grows'?

Take the case of Jessica Davidson, aged forty-two, who had a
Cambridge B.A. and a talent for getting on with people. She became appointments secretary and receptionist at a nearby child
guidance clinic. She welcomed the mothers and children, put
them at their ease (her talent), checked their appointment,
alerted the therapist or psychologist or whomever they were seeing, saw they set off down the corridor, greeted the next arrivals,
checked their appointment, sent them along, greeted . . .

Certainly, for a while the job had been interesting enough,
though it had mainly been the relief from housework, getting out,
company, gossip, and of course money. But as for 'realising herself'—after five, or was it six, years, she said it was pure routine.
She had mastered the mechanics of the job in half an hour; the
contact with the clients was on the whole brief and extremely superficial; only the gossip remained.

How can anyone in any meaningful way be said to 'grow' in this
situation? The point is most jobs are repetitive, unchallenging,
trivial and boring—if they do anything, they diminish people.
This is true, to an extent, of sizeable chunks of 'interesting' jobs. It
is even more true at the level of job women are compelled to take

(90 per cent of typists, 60 per cent of clerks and packers). It is partly the fault of the feminist movement. Betty Friedan acknowledged that 30 per cent of married women were working by the end of the 1950s, but said it was not 'real' work, not 'self-realising' work; it was low-level drudgery. It still is. All that has happened is that the feminine mystique has been replaced by the *feminist* mystique—and these same jobs are supposed to be 'fulfilling'. So women rush out, in a fever of expectation, into some demeaning occupation, far below their worth, paid too little money—or stick in such jobs for years for the same reason. I suspect that one of the vaunted cures for feminine dissatisfaction is probably often a major cause of it. A cause to some extent restricted to women since on the whole men don't go into their jobs to 'grow'.

4   *The* Self-help *books fallacy*

The phenomenon of the *Self-help* books derives from three forces fundamental to American society. The first is Protestant. The authority for the Reformation was founded directly on the Bible; the resultant obsession of the Puritan with the power of words has lasted till today. It was the Puritans who for the first time in English history (if one excludes the rather limited Catholic *Index Librorum Prohibitorum* of banned books) created a comprehensive censorship. Their belief in the power of the word took deep root in America and was one factor in the choice of a written constitution; which itself, of course, increased the belief.

Self-help books have elements of this deep origin which they sometimes reveal in curious ways. As regards 'growth', the idea is often to be, freely and spontaneously, 'yourself'. To do this, little rules are given, diagrams, catch phrases: 'Say what you see and tell what you feel without criticising the other.' Often the rigmaroles seem deliberately unpleasant. In crotch eyeballing you get rid of hang-ups by having large groups of people stare at your genitals. The apparent paradox of 'spontaneity' through a series of rules, of having the behaviour of 'yourself' imposed by someone else, the elements of reward and punishment in the books, are all resolved when it is seen they are really descendants of the Methodist/Puritan self-*improvement* books. And this particular religious stream is of course the reverse of spontaneous.

The religious origin is shown, too, by the enormous element of faith in these books. If you *believe*, the Kingdom of Heaven is yours (usually on earth as well, as it was for the Puritans, proving you are favoured by the Lord). 'Say "I'm great"—and you will be!' 'You are a great person to be!' (each soul is important to God). It is not just interesting, it is essential these books should be bestsellers; just as mass fervour was an essential ingredient in the evangelical movement which produced the great flow of self-improvement books.

America is a new nation (one third *still* either born abroad or children of foreign-born parents in 1970). But this fact has enormous historical impetus behind it. Americans have wished their children to be better than them, but also to be different, to be 'American'. They deliberately withhold themselves as models to facilitate this, and as a result rely on experts (this is a further explanation of why the 1950s upbringing developments went further in America than elsewhere). But this withdrawal and reliance on experts—book-writing experts—are passed on. That is to say, the *Self-help* books are also (though they don't realise it) 'How to Help Yourself Become American' books. That is why their instructions are often so active—they can be demonstrated to, and shared with neighbours: 'We're American!' 'I'm American!' That is why America is swept *overnight* by bio-diets or vampire films or crotch-eyeballing circles. Hence the smile on the face of the jogger; the glint in the eye of the father as his son, with 100 million others, slides down the sidewalk at 50 m.p.h. on a pair of six-foot wheeled motorised stilts.

The third reason is a cause/effect one. What you believe to be powerful *is* powerful. The belief in the word in America has made it powerful, which makes it more powerful. Revolting food is eaten because of the way it is described. Novelists and writers have a far higher status than in Britain—closer to that in France. The press plays the powerful role there that television does in Britain. Journalists of even medium rank have status equal to that of M.P.s in Britain.

Among the most powerful of the writers, by far the largest single category, those whose major topics are precisely the ones we are discussing, are the authors (frequently a man/woman team) of the *Self-help* books. They are invariably intelligent and rich. Occasionally charming. Busy (usually with another self-help book). Fairly bitchy about each other: 'When X married for the second time, that first year a Christmas card came. It had a list of *all* his publications to date—name, publisher, *price!* She was just allowed her name.'

It is interesting (another echo of their Protestant and Puritan forerunners) how often the books are the result of personal revelation—a divine experience to be shared with the millions. Marabel Morgan wasn't reacting to feminism at all, however much her followers are. She was reacting to a marriage on the rocks. With an almost supreme effort she compelled herself to behave as though she were in love with Charlie. Eight months' suspicion—*'then he fell in love with me again'*. It was he who suggested she tell the world.

At one, rather limited end of the scale, and in certain defined areas, these books serve a purpose and do good. There are those which are designed to be read in conjunction with therapy. Masters and Johnson stress this side to their treatment of dysfunction for instance. Dr Ellis said his *Guide to a Successful Marriage* was really an adjunct to Rational psychotherapy. It's a pity you can't gather this from the book itself.

You can make a cabinet from a self-help book. Where the advice on behaviour is extremely specific, it can help. The only area this applies to is sex.

There is a branch of the literature which is not so much *Self-help* as 'what like'. I think, for instance, of *The Half-Parent* by Brenda Maddox or *The World of the Formerly Married* by Morton Hunt. The first describes what it's like to be a stepparent, the second to be divorced. It is always comforting and helpful to find that others have felt and feel as you do in similar circumstances.

A *Self-help* book can crystallise and give shape to ideas and impulses already there. That is to say, it won't initiate anything or change anyone, but it may assist them in some limited degree upon a path already contemplated or embarked on.

And most endeavour depends on confidence. 'You can do it Duffy Moon', says Duffy Moon each morning to his mirror—and feels a momentary glow. Constant repetition, mild self-hypnosis, and he may be able to 'go for that new job, stand up for himself'.

But, one might think, responsive to such simple remedies and other little tricks of the same sort, there probably wasn't all that much wrong with Duffy's confidence in the first place. It is for those whose confidence has been severely damaged, who suffer from anxiety or depression or neurotic flaws or compulsions, those who need the solutions promised by the books most, by whom they are most eagerly bought, it is for these—the opposite end of the scale—that such books are not just useless but extremely harmful. Severe personal problems having their roots deeply hidden in unsatisfactory relationships of childhood almost invariably require the help of someone skilled from outside. The *Self-help* books—bearing, to adopt a phrase of David Caute's, as much relation to psychiatry as domestic plumbing does to physics—promising you that you can help yourself, allow people to avoid facing up to the sources of their problems and temporarily bury themselves in reassurance, continuing as anxious or compelled as ever, or until they are overwhelmed. One author couple I talked to said a regular correspondent had been about to commit suicide. He read their book and hadn't. Since then every time he felt anxious, he read a few pages. He took their book like a pill. Oddly enough, they hadn't heard from him for several months, a year.

The fact is, the world is full of advice, the press, friends, books rising kilometres high. If a writer can give someone advice, the likelihood is they've had it before. The question is—why have they not changed?

My own view is that the bulk of these books is more or less useless. And their authors know they are useless. They reveal this by the way the books are written, often hiding under turgid images of virtually contentless prose:

> A static life plan, such as the one dictated by the maturity myth, insists that we *follow* rules set down by others in accordance with the *external* demands of society; a dynamic life strategy allows us to *lead* our own lives in accordance with our *internal* needs. A static life plan creates a situation in which *stagnation* and *loss of self* become inevitable; a dynamic life strategy makes it possible for us to achieve an ongoing *growth* that will bring a continuing *discovery of self.*
>
> From a condensation,
> by the authors, of *Shifting
> Gears* (their italics)

Or else, like some copywriters, and for the same reason, they write every sentence or even word on a separate line, to make you think you are getting
emphasis.
And
clarity.
And above all
Insight.
See?

They reveal it by their extraordinarily superficial idea of growth (because of course growth remains the aim. Remove the lack of confidence, the anxiety, and you can start to 'grow'). It is really a materialist fallacy. All experiences are like bank notes of roughly the same value. Any experience 'enriches' you, like any note does. There is no attempt to evaluate the experience, or explain the enrichment. Whatever you do, particularly if it is something new, you in some way get bigger, there is more of you, a sort of automatic accretion of psychic 'wealth'.

What all these books principally amount to, therefore—exploiting and coasting in on America's deep reverence for the written word—is a very considerable branch of escapist/wish-fulfilment literature. Clearly, if everyone who read 'How I became Chairman—And How You Can Too' did succeed, there would be a good deal of chaos in a lot of businesses. But they don't. They read about the author doing it, identify, and have a blissful week fantasising their rise to power. The pleasure *Self-help* books give—as opposed to the harm they do those in real need, and the disappointment they bring those who hopefully follow them—derives from the fact that they are really 'Have a Fantasy This is Going to Happen' books.

Perhaps this wouldn't really matter all that much, were it not that they throw all their considerable weight and influence—along with several other factors—behind the final direction of Privilege Bulge growth.

5 'Growth' is a new person

> *'I look at you boring yourself stupid around the house*
> *and I felt I caught a bird in an art school and put her*
> *in a cage. All I'm saying is, the door is open.'*
> *'You're not saying that. You're saying you want me*
> *out.'*
> *'I'm NOT. I'm saying I want you to live. It's too easy for*
> *both of us. We're protecting each other from living.'*
> JOHN UPDIKE, *Marry Me*

It may seem a truism to you that we 'grow' through relationships. In a sense, of course, it is inevitable. Nearly all pursuits involve other people, and the interaction with them, our relationship with them, their criticism and praise of us, validate the activity and to varying degrees constitute it. From this the jump has been made that *all* relationships can and if possible should contribute to growth, and that marriage, as the most important, should contribute most.

How widely assumed it is that marriage must lead to growth,

can be shown clearly by the converse; if marriage does not lead to growth—dump it. The O'Neills in their book *Open Marriage*, along with most *Self-help* books, don't even argue the point. If growth, 'identity', are threatened by marriage, then get divorced. An article in *Psychology Today* noted recently that young people viewed any infringement or even postponement of their 'personal fulfilment as a source of serious conflict'.

This is a totally new burden to lay on marriage. And the strain is increased once again because of the fuzziness of the concept. What, after all, do you do after five, six, ten years of marriage? The suggestions are: get some new 'interests' in common, or separately, the wife gets that 'job' again, new friends. Such things do indeed keep marriages alive and interesting. But they are accompanied by—and in comparison the results seem so remote from—the usual inflated and supercharged verbs and adjectives: 'enrichment', 'deep potential', 'satisfying growth and fulfilment'. 'You can see these pointless divorces,' said Eleanor Alter of her practice, talking of later Privilege Bulge tragedies. 'You hear the details. You can see the marriage hasn't been too bad; it's been O.K. This unrealistic attempt to change their whole lives; you see it especially in men, but in women too.'

As a result of this over-inflation, there develops a second unconscious pressure. If growth is through relationships, then the closer and more intense and deep the relationship, the deeper and stronger the growth. In the West, one relationship above all qualifies for this—the passion of romantic sexual love.

Love is often the theme of Privilege Bulge novels and films—but it is new love, the person leaving marriage, or being left, to 'find' themselves with a new lover. One can see the logic at work in *Open Marriage*. This is composed entirely in growth jargon—so, if one partner meets a new person, he or she comes back enriched and automatically enriches the other, presumably by some kind of osmosis. Therefore the *more* enriched we are, the more we enrich our partner, and the O'Neills' conclusion is that this may lead to new loves. In fact the logic is it *should* lead to new loves. That is how the book was taken, correctly, by its hundreds of thousands of readers, and it caused a certain amount of havoc.

Yet, how much of an illusion is the growth, which seems so integral, so dizzying a part of romantic love—those moments when one seems to unfold, seen through the entranced eyes of another, in a series of intoxicating and almost unbelievable revelations. This is one of the ambiguities at the heart of Updike's *Couples*. Foxy, in the years during which she has 'grown numb to his handsomeness', feels herself 'dying' beside her husband. New love feels like life itself. This, the fountain of the new, like the ceaselessness of a spring, is what carries Piet Hanema in his progress through the couples.

> But by daylight he had discovered on her rapt Roman face an expression of peace deeper than an infant's sleep, that the darkness of night had never disclosed on the face of his wife. Furtive husbandly visitant, he had never known Angela as he had often known his lovely easy matter-of-fact morning lay. The line of her narrow high-bridge nose and double arabesque. Her white hairs belying her body's youth.

The book is full of the sensation of growth—of learning, discovering, living more intensely, of terror, of desire. Yet at the end— what is left? Has Piet, have any of them, grown? I don't think so. Love is a state not a process. As the emotion subsides, or turns sour, the 'discoveries' evaporate and vanish. The intensity is real enough, but Piet remains unchanged. He is described at one moment as a man growing older without growing wiser. Perhaps in the end all he has learnt, if he has learnt even that, is how better, more adroitly, to commit adultery.

The logical mush and frenzy of expectation surrounding growth, increases the strain on marriage and leads to unconscious pressure towards a new partner. This is considerably augmented by the mush having to a large extent invaded the whole colossal edifice of life-support systems surrounding marriage, relationships and growth.

For example, it is a fact that, though ending marriages is not actually a declared aim of psychiatrists or psychoanalysts—the aim of analysis is to free a patient from neurotic suffering and help him or her to develop and lead a meaningful life—nevertheless analysis very frequently does end in divorce. I think quite often the aim is there but undeclared. The patient is virtually by definition neurotic and therefore the choice of partner is highly likely to have been wrong. The analyst will certainly find 'growth' is being smothered. Besides, to remove the partner is something tangible that can be achieved. There is a comfortable sense of clearing the decks. It removes a rival. And, in so far as the old relationship was proof of neurosis, so the proof of the new, 'cured' patient is in a new relationship.

If this is true of expensively trained and extremely expensive analysts and psychiatrists, how much greater is the temptation to those less well trained and less scrupulous. The growth of therapists, counsellors, sex clinics and the rest is only second to the growth industry generally. In their book, *The Marriage Savers,* Joanna and Lew Koch have a handy appendix of thirty closely printed pages listing people and organisations under the most general headings (to give an idea of number, there are at present 10,000 members of the Transactional Analysis Association alone. Thousands more practise, but are not members). Edna Barrabee, a member of the American Association of Marriage Counsellors, talking to writer Benjamin de Mott, said: 'In this field anyone can do anything. Anyone from any walk of life . . . This new commercial counseling center is openly a superservice agency . . . Boy, are they smart. The next thing you know they'll be opening like those income tax places, one on every corner.'

De Mott visited a superservice agency. It had been 'created in January 1974 in answer to an urgent need for help to marriages on a positive preventive basis'. (Preventing divorce presumably, not preventing marriage.) But with its emphasis on speed of turnover and quick results, advocating the quick sharp smash, rather than the difficult and slow mending and reconstruction, saving a marriage was not really the aim. The president was Maxine Schnall, mid-forties, divorced. 'On overall objectives, whether to "save" marriages or junk them, Maxine,' said De Mott cautiously, 'is clearly a little left of center, headed towards the creative split school.' Maxine was more forthright. 'Sustaining the marriage—oftentimes that's not what you want to do. It's not best. Divorce could be the most creative thing to do.'

6   *The Privilege Bulge and sex*

In 1952 Kinsey was asked to speak on old age and sex in New York. He declined: 'The problem of sexual adjustment for the aged is much less pressing than the problem of sexual adjustment for any other part of the population.'

Not for the Privilege Bulge it isn't. For them it looms bleakly as the next, what was once near-sexless stage. By 1970, the position had reversed. Dr William H. Masters wrote this: 'If someone asked me what the single most important statement is in *Human Sexual Inadequacy*, I would pick this material on the ageing male.'

What Masters, a central figure of advance Bulge (he is now sixty-three), and Virginia Johnson had discovered, or rather rediscovered, was this. Around fifty, men take longer to obtain an erection. They become nervous, probably try drink which aggravates the problem, try again and again, repeat and set up a pattern—and soon give up, too fearful to try again, too angry and humiliated to discuss it. Impotence sets in. A doctor will tell them (Masters and Johnson cite such a case) that it is a natural result of ageing.

This is not so. Age means that it takes longer to get an erection but the potential for getting an erection *remains exactly the same*. It is just a question of being patient. Of caressing for five or ten minutes. Sometimes the erection will not at first be so hard. The man (and woman) must learn the simple skills of inserting a rather limp penis, because then (provided love-making in the past ten years has been a regular twice a week or so—this is very important) then like some valiant old warhorse responding to the trumpet, it will become erect again.

The erection soon becomes as hard as ever. And it is at this stage that the man around fifty has a considerable advantage over his younger counterpart (or rival). His ejaculatory control is far greater, he can therefore hold his erection for longer and at what M. & J. call a high pleasurable state of tension. (The multi-orgasmic woman has greater pleasure—indeed it is at this age many first discover they are multi-orgasmic.)

But it was the second discovery that was most important. The male in his fifties has *less need to ejaculate.* He can enjoy sex just as much without ejaculating. If he doesn't ejaculate, then he will find he can have an erection again and again with his usual regularity—even with more than usual regularity. M. & J., their sober prose usually free from such embellishment, put it in italics:

> *This factor of reduced ejaculatory demand for the ageing male is the entire basis for effective prolongation of sexual functioning in the ageing population.*

It is when husband and wife believe orgasm is all (a further deleterious result of Kinsey's obsession with 'outlets') and compel the husband to have one when he doesn't need to that his erective powers diminish.

Similar considerations apply to women. They too will take longer to arouse, and patience will be needed here. They may lubricate less, and their orgasms become less intense. Intercourse may also become painful through thinning of the vaginal walls. These problems are easily and swiftly corrected by hormonal replacement therapy. Thereafter, sex can continue with immense satisfaction more or less indefinitely.

Masters and Johnson *rediscovered* these facts. It is fascinating to find the Taoist physician Lun S'su-Mo giving precisely the same instructions 1,300 years ago. A modern account of this Chinese philosophy and its sexual practices has recently been published. The philosophic and medical base is different. Taoists believe there is a fundamental harmony between all things on earth mas-

culine (*yin*) and things feminine (*yang*), and it is in their joining
that harmony is created. Ejaculatory control means longer and
more frequent intercourse, which means a greater mingling of the
vital *yin* and *yang* essences of man and woman. Furthermore,
man is born with only a limited amount of semen (a very long-
lasting fallacy) and so the less he uses the better. The book has
nothing to do with separating orgasm from ejaculation, as some
commentators have suggested.

Some of the aims are the same as ours today: the greater satisfaction of women, the continuing of sexual love into old age for
instance. The instructions, particularly to the Privilege Bulge, are
even more precise: a man of sixty should make love twice a day,
but he should only ejaculate once a week. A man of fifty can ejaculate twice a week. To insert the limp penis, he should make a
ring round its base with his fingers and thrust and manoeuvre
through this.

It is possible that there is a still stranger side to the seldom-
ejaculatory passion now opening up before the men of the advancing Bulge. The Chinese Taoists have by no means been the
only group to follow this path.

In 1864, an American, John Humphrey Noyes, published a book
called *Male Continence* setting down in considerable and, for the
period, frank detail, his experiences over the past twenty years.
Mrs Noyes used to have repeated miscarriages, and when she
nearly died they both determined to find some way of making love
without her becoming pregnant. *Coitus interruptus* he rejected,
being intensely religious and not wishing to emulate Onan. Nor
did he approve of contraceptives—'those tricks of the French vo-
luptuaries'.

His view of sex was different from that held generally. 'It is held
in the world,' he wrote, 'that the sexual organs have two distinct
functions—viz the urinary and the propagative. We affirm that
they have three—the urinary, the propagative and the amative.'
It was on this last, the loving aspect of sex, he wished himself and
Mrs Noyes to concentrate. He therefore pursued his sexual analysis more deeply.

The act of intercourse 'has a beginning, a middle and an end. Its beginning and most elementary form is the simple presence of the male organ in the female'. Presence is followed by motion, motion by crisis. Now 'suppose the man chooses to enjoy not only the simple presence, but also the reciprocal motion, and yet stop short of the crisis . . . If you say that this is impossible, I answer that I *know* it is possible—nay, that it is easy'. He knew because he had done it. 'Beginning in 1844 I experimented on the idea and found that the self-control it required is not difficult; also that my enjoyment was increased; also that my wife's experience was very satisfactory, which it had never been before; also that we had escaped the horrors and the fear of involuntary propagation.'

Noyes was thrilled and exalted by his great discovery. He felt he had found not just a source of personal happiness, but a clue to the power which bound together the early Christian communities. A born missionary, he gathered disciples and created a community, first in Vermont, later at Oneida, in upstate New York. The religion was a new, pure Christianity; the morality based on Male Continence and what Noyes called 'Complex Marriage'. Like the founders of all communities, Noyes found exclusive couple attachments interfered with communal solidarity. At Oneida, all were to love all, and the force binding them was the loving force of sexual intercourse. When a couple decided, with the advice and permission of the elders, to make love, Male Continence was practised.

One would, in a single respect, like more detail—did the men *never* have an orgasm? Not one? Noyes's account would suggest not. I can't help suspecting—this may just be my coarse modern sensibility—that there must have been some ejaculating, masturbating or nocturnal emissions; something. But the Oneida community endured for thirty years. All accounts agree that its members were singularly happy and noticeably less neurotic than their Victorian contemporaries. In particular this was true of the ladies, spared, as one put it, 'the miseries of Married Life as it is in the World'. Comments like these and Mrs Noyes's evident pleasure make it clear the women did not restrain from orgasm. On the contrary.

But the results seem to have been more peculiar and more profound than simple community contentment. The men found (and oddly the women too) that self-control practised to that degree led to some extraordinary experiences, part physical, part spiritual—experiences which were very like those described by mystics. There is a good deal of evidence that this is so. Several Indian mysticisms state this, principally the theory and practice of Tantra. It also seems probable that Noyes was correct, at least about some of the communities in the early centuries of Christianity. It was common then for ecclesiastics and pious laymen to have 'spiritual wives', who were called Agapetae, Syneisaktoi or Virgines Subintroductes. Little is known of their exact relationship, but, according to Aldous Huxley, it is likely that in some cases, Male Continence, intercourse without orgasm, was practised as a religious exercise leading to valuable spiritual experiences.

The most emphatic confirmation comes from certain of the Cathars in the early Middle Ages—particularly the Adamites from the thirteenth century on. These, like Noyes, practised sexual communism in order that every member of the group could love every other member; and their method, *Modum specialem coeundi*, was, precisely, Male Continence. They too discovered it to be a method of mystical learning, and so they called it *acclivitas*, the upward path. A Spanish follower of the Adamite heresy declared at his trial that 'after I had first had intercourse with her (the prophetess Francisca Hernandez) for some twenty days, I could say that I had learned more wisdom in Valladolid than if I had studied for twenty years in Paris. For not Paris, but only Paradise could teach such wisdom.'

It seems that if men remove or severely curtail the obvious and universally accepted hedonist aim of intercourse, their orgasm, then some rather curious things will happen. I say *will*, because they appear to happen automatically (Noyes had a quite different aim in view), even if you are not of a mystical or religious bent.

There suddenly opens to the Privilege Bulge, therefore, who are increasingly constrained to do this anyway if they wish to continue making love, an entirely new avenue to that 'growth' they seek so frenziedly and unsatisfactorily everywhere else—and a growth, moreover, of an infinitely more exalted and more 'enriching' character than even the self-help mush has dared promise them.

There is not an enormous amount of evidence that this is yet happening. The pursuit is more down to earth; and as the Bulge proceeds so society widens up far ahead to accommodate it. Writing in 1977, Alex Comfort foretold this increase in extreme old age sex as the Privilege Bulge neared the nineties. 'We won't drop them,' he said belligerently about their full sex lives, 'at the whim of a nursing home administrator.' A survey of 1,163 elderly Danish men showed that 12 per cent of those eighty-six to ninety were sexually active, that 3 per cent of the over-nineties had made love in the last year, and 23 per cent of the over-nineties masturbated. One of the Sleeping Vaginas in the *Forum* extract was in her sixties.

The nursing home administrators are already having to adjust. In one old people's home, the staff were amazed by how much went on—and embarrassed. (Society has begun to come to terms with sex at fifty; not yet at eighty, with all those bags and pouches.) It came to light because the building had not been designed with that in mind. In particular, the beds had not been properly designed. They were too small, and, in their transports, considerable numbers of the inmates were rolling out of them and smashing femurs and pelvises.

As to the effect of sex continuing into extreme old age on Privilege Bulge marriage, it is impossible to be precise. For millions, it will be a blessing. At the same time, once more it imposes new burdens, new expectations. All studies of intercourse show a steady decline the longer a couple are together. This has been a problem for centuries. Balzac, who wrote a marriage advice book, *Physiologie du Mariage*, in 1828, was blunt: 'Think of your mistress.' I suspect *Playboy*, *Penthouse* and *Forum* play a major role here. Some experts are confident. Masters and Johnson say their clients have great success—new positions, sensate focusing sessions and so on. But then, couples who go to them *want* their interest revived. David Barkla of the British Marriage Guidance Council thought it was possible to reawaken interest; he would tell his clients they were privileged to know a great deal about another human being. That is true; indeed the observation is a moving one. At the same time, it is a privilege which might strike someone who has enjoyed it for eight, ten, fifteen years with something like a dull thud. And if one, how about knowing a great deal about a second human being, or even three or four more? Barkla also said: 'Boredom is our greatest problem.'

Middle- and late-aged divorce has risen along with all other divorce rates and, to an incalculable degree, the expectation of continuing sex is, and will increasingly be, a factor. This is unfair to women. Older men are still considered more attractive than older women; their liaisons with younger partners are more common—though no one seems to know why. The reverse has often been far more common than it is now. It may be, to speculate, a function of the Oedipus complex: the son desires the mother, but she is too close and later inhibits attraction to older women. The father is sufficiently close for the daughter to desire him, but not so close as to taboo completely later love of an older man. In which case, as the results of much further father-involvement work through, there may be some alteration here (there are signs of this already in some recent films, for example, the Travolta film, *Moment by Moment*). In which case here is another of those fascinating demonstrations of how society engineers its changes of direction at many different levels at the same time. Less spectacularly, a number of observers have detected a possible trend for older women to experiment with homosexuality. According to Otto Preminger, lesbian relationships are now far more common than adultery in the highly moral community Hollywood has apparently become: 'they don't threaten the marriage'. And of course Sleeping Vaginas again.

What, in a general way, has happened is that, for all ages, growth has joined sex and much else as the point of any relationship, including the most important relationship—marriage. That is to say it has joined the concept of romantic love.

7

ROMANTIC LOVE

Who marrieth for love without money hath good nights and sorry days.

J. RAY, *A Collection of English Proverbs*, 1678

The Unanswered Question, for me, is, do most of us need a passionate central relationship?

NELL DUNN, *Living Like I Do*, 1976

EVERYONE KNOWS roughly what is meant by romantic love. It can be used without ambiguity. This is because most people who marry 'fall in love'. Yet practically all those professionally concerned with divorce agree it plays virtually no part in that event. What has happened to this, at first vital, ingredient in the interim? For now it reappears. It is considered more or less immoral to remarry for other reasons—to provide a father or mother for children, for example, or for security. Even the practical users of a marriage bureau aim to and 'generally do fall in love'. What is this love they fall into? Where does it come from? What is it like, how necessary is it and why and for how long and how often?

1   *Desire dies because every touch consumes the myth and yet, a myth that cannot be consumed becomes a spectre . . .*

W. B. Yeats

122

The twelfth and thirteenth centuries, although the 'Age of Chivalry', were extremely brutal. The knights of the Crusades, for instance, were simply a gang of vicious and often drunken thugs, murderers and fornicators. Jean de Joinville, the lively thirteenth-century French historian, describes Bohemund sending sacks of sliced-off noses and thumbs to the Greek Emperor; when Richard I arrived at Marseilles he found the English knights had spent the funds for the entire campaign on prostitutes.

Their marriages were equally down-to-earth arrangements simply to get land and power. Affection and respect were irrelevant, and if the 'deal' turned out badly, or a better one appeared, the wife was cast out, often on grounds of incest (fourth or fifth cousin relationships were so described).

During the second half of the twelfth century there rose in various courts of Provence in the South of France, but particularly in that of Eleanor of Aquitaine, the idea of 'courtly love'. This was sung and practised by the troubadours, those wandering or resident courtier singers and story tellers. In part a loyalty based solely on love, it was in opposition to the brutality of the time and to marriage as it then was. Marriage and this sort of love were completely incompatible. Here is some of the famous 'Judgement' at Eleanor's Court of Love in 1174.

> We declare and affirm, by the tenair of these presents, that love cannot extend its rights over two married persons. For indeed lovers grant one another all things mutually and freely . . . whereas husband and wife are held by their duty to submit their wills to each other . . .

The love was for, of, an 'ideal'. That is, the woman was idealised, made perfect, and it was her perfection which shamed her lover, contrary to the age, into attempting perfection too.

It was anti-marriage for another reason. What the troubadours were after was intensity of sensation. This is made quite clear in the *Treatise on Love*, written by Andrew, chaplain to Queen Eleanor, in 1186. He recognised that married people could enjoy deep affection—and indeed many of the troubadours were married and had children. But they were not 'in love' with their wives. Such transports could not survive permanence. Andrew also realised that this profound sensation was much increased by frustration. Therefore the love was chaste. It was a cult of nonsexual passion, or rather, unsatisfied passion, for someone they could never marry. The language was that of physical love—what other terms were there to use?—but it was symbolic.

There was also a religious element. During the twelfth century, at the same time and place and among the same people, there also rose one of the great Christian heresies: the heresy of the Cathars, or Albigensian heresy. It involved an exalted and mystic concentration on heavenly love. The Cathars and troubadours were plainly not the same—there were tens, even hundreds of thousands of Cathars and only 500 known troubadours. But some sort of mutual influence and transfusion seems to have taken place—precisely what no one is clear. The élite of the Cathars—'The Pure'—were chaste as well.

The third element was Arabic. It used to be thought the troubadour movement—subjects, verse, form, ideals—sprang more or less from nowhere over twenty years, between about 1160 and 1180. Fairly recently it was discovered that in fact it began in Moslem countries during the ninth century, and it had the same two-pronged root: religious, transforming the Mohammedan religion by ideals of love, and expressing this love in terms of erotic but symbolic metaphors; and also a cult of intensity of sensation, which applied itself to intensity of feeling in chaste (that is, frustrated) love. This movement went to Andalucía in the tenth century and eleventh century and, passing through the adjacent Spanish dominions, to their neighbours Provence and Languedoc, in the twelfth century. As the first, the Arabic was probably the most important element.

Constituents in this love are still relevant today. It must be intense. The loved one is thought more or less perfect—even defects are adored. It is anti-marriage. It is exclusive—and for this reason makes considerable play with jealousy. A new love makes one leave the old. Real jealousy increases the worth of love, and is indeed a sign of it (that is why people often assume a false jealousy to reveal love). Love is suspicious.

The O'Neills and other writers seem to assume that because romantic love makes such play with jealousy it is somehow responsible for it. This is rubbish. Jealousy is universal in animals, who have weapons to use against rivals. In men it is also automatic, and has existed in practically all cultures and at all times, whether they have concepts analogous to romantic love or not. The Botocudos of South America quite frequently exchange wives; but infidelity outside this pattern is punished savagely. Jealousy was and is very common and has roots which often have nothing to do with romantic love (self-love, pride, insecurity). What the troubadours did was to start a process which intensified jealousy by codifying it and also making it one of the chief languages of a particularly intense form of love, until eventually it became possible to write a drama of passionate love, *Othello*, which was *only* about jealousy.

This was made much simpler by the first great development in romantic love: the attraction into its orbit of sexual love. The reversal of one of the main original tenets of romantic love was always likely by virtue of exactly that mystical, religious, Cathar element which had given rise to it. From the earliest times, through the Dionysiac cults, the pagan revivals of the Middle Ages, right up to today, man has found that sex, sexual passion, sexual excess, is one way of engendering certain powerful religious and cathartic experiences he craves. Sex is then a direct route into the deep subconscious where these forces are both generated and where lie the needs they arise to satisfy. We know sex enjoys this route because we cannot control it. You can look at someone and by fantasy or association (or, in the case of women, acquiescence) say 'I will make love to them' and do so. You cannot say 'I will be attracted to them'. That arises, or does not, intuitively from much deeper levels.

Sex is related to certain religious experiences in another way. The aim of mystical exercise is to lose the sense of self in some-

thing higher, more pure. This is founded partly on a desire to escape the self—to escape the body with its ills and pains and desires, the mind with its fears and despair. The sexual experience is
one sure way, in its overwhelming power, of doing this too—even
if only for a short time. It is an appetite; it returns again and
again, bringing each time the promise and then actuality of escape.

In fact the Cathars were not all *that* chaste. Some, as we've
seen, practised intercourse without orgasm. The love of the troubadours too seems to have been sensual. Andrew in his *Treatise*
deals with seducing nuns. Embracing, kissing and desire were allowed; but 'engaging in the work of Venus' or intercourse, was
'the worst of crimes'. Certainly—but not what you'd call exactly
out of sight.

The danger of using language symbolically is that the interpre-
tations will become lost or muddled. To the mystic, 'love', 'desire'
will have elevated, ideal meanings; humanity, in its coarse way,
will return to more mundane usage. The joining of troubadour
'love' and sex was likely. That does not mean it was inevitable.
We have so long associated the two that it seems entirely natural—obvious. But the Greeks and Romans regarded it as absurd,
even mad. The combination of passionate love and sex is no more
'natural' than their separation—indeed, separation is probably
better for the proper cultivation of both.

In any event, quite soon romantic love and sex were inextricably entwined. But sex still remained wrong. In the great myth of
adultery, Tristan and Isolde, which the French writer and philosopher de Rougemont uses in his fascinating unravelling of this
subject, Tristan was clearly guilty of a fault in sleeping with
Isolde. Though this is really a misreading, the 'fault seemed also to
be a *splendid experience more magnificent than morality*'. Adultery became glorified. The prime aim remained intensity. Therefore the love was blocked, thwarted. For the next seven centuries
the tale of romantic love was one of obstruction and frustration.
That is why, according to the proverb, 'The course of true love
never did run smooth.'

Eleanor of Aquitaine left her Court of Love in the south of France to marry Louis VII of France. In 1154 she married Henry of England. Each time she took her troubadours. The persecution of the Cathars in France meant some of the troubadours fled to Italy, taking the concept of love with them. By the fourteenth century, with Petrarch, romantic love became, in the great poetry of his love for Laura, the rhetoric of the human heart; the theme which has dominated Western literature, painting, poetry and drama (and so our magazines, films and television) ever since. Laura is the occasion for his love, his passion, *his love of love.*

> I know to follow while I flee my fire:
> I freeze when present; absent, my desire
> Is hot.

Malory, Dante, Cervantes, Marlowe, Shakespeare, Milton, Sterne . . . one should perhaps pause at Dante.

Dante saw Beatrice only twice, and he fell in love with her *instantly.* People, of course, only 'fall in love at first sight' because they want to, because the ground has been prepared unconsciously beforehand. The fact that Dante could do so (or could write about it—it makes no difference) shows that by his time (Dante's dates are 1265–1321) the ideal of romantic love had become sufficiently strong and sufficiently accepted for this degree of unconscious need to become manifest. It would not be precisely true to say that the literature of romantic love created the phenomenon. Words are not magical. But, as La Rochefoucauld said, few people would fall in love if they had never heard of love. The adoption of a literary convention naturally fosters the use of latent feelings which can be most easily expressed in that way.

Such feelings existed before (there are romantic love poems from ancient Egypt) but they were rare and were regarded as an accident, an illness or a mistake. As such feelings become more and more written about they become a social convention and therefore a psychological necessity. That is the rule: you feel, or want to feel, what you should feel, and then you have to feel it (this all applies with varying force to the topics of feminism, sex, 'growth'). Dr Ellis in his book on marriage says that people believe because their partner loves someone else he or she loves them 'less'. This is a romantic love idea and therefore fake. But that is the point—it is a romantic love idea and therefore people believe it and therefore it is true. Of course, Ellis or anyone else can biff and bang 'full blast' that it is a false 'idea', and that a true idea is that they don't love you less, or you don't 'need' their love—and you change your mind. The process is exactly the same, if cruder. Every time a new literary convention of this kind occurs, neglected potentialities of the human heart become activated. Goethe's novel *Werther*, for example, led to a wave of suicides. Jean-Jacques Rousseau got the whole French Court drinking milk. Philip Roth, for all I know, had the same sort of effect in a minor way with *Portnoy*.

As century followed century, the gravitational force of romantic love grew stronger and stronger, steadily pulling towards itself two more mighty forces.

The next great conjunction started in the seventeenth century. Stories of romantic love started to end happily; even more extraordinary, *they began to end in marriage*. Until then they had ended tragically, a fact of crucial importance to de Rougemont. There arose during the eighteenth century an intense cultivation of strong feelings for their own sake. *Any* feelings would do, even the tiny pleasure of releasing a trapped fly: 'Go, thou little innocent thing. You shall not a moment longer be confined, for perhaps already I have robbed thee of joys which the exertion of my whole life cannot repay.' But the best feelings, the feelings to which one could abandon oneself whole-heartedly, were those of romantic love. There was pride in this. Men and women competed. For this reason Hazlitt wrote his *Liber Amoris*, an account of violent but hopeless passion for his landlord's commonplace daughter. The key phrase is: 'I am in some sense proud that I can feel this dreadful passion—it gives me a kind of rank in the kingdom of love.'

From 1740 on a flood of novels poured on to the market with

romantic love as their theme. By the 1780s there were libraries in
every major town; circulating libraries, laden with passion, carried the books into the countryside. The market was principally
leisured and well-off women, with little to do but dream. As a heroine of one novel said in 1786: 'I subscribed to a circulating library and read, or rather devoured, from 10 to 14 novels a week.'

At last, very gradually, the phenomenon of romantic love began
to spread in life, as it had long done in literature. Until now it had
really been confined, as a form of behaviour, to courts, and to the
great houses of nobles and the very rich—and for exactly that
reason: only the rich could afford books or read; only the rich had
the leisure and relative privacy for such indulgence. Now, for the
first time in history, it began to spread down; among some of the
wealthier classes it became a more or less acceptable reason for
marrying. Or people did marry for that reason, whether accepted
or not. There is a sudden increase in couples fleeing to Gretna
Green. And a totally new pattern appears (in life more than literature as yet): the unhappy and disastrous marriage chosen by people themselves. In 1794 a woman called Dorothea Hart fell
deeply in love with a man who finally left her: 'What could induce the specious rogue to seduce my affections, betray me to lin-
gering torments, and then desert me for ever, is a problem I could
never solve. Ah, my poor heart, what cruelties did it suffer. What
more than Hell born woe when the monster struck his last
blow . . .'

It seems incredible to us—who have all fallen in love, or think
we have, or dream of doing so for the first time or again—that this
form of behaviour is quite new; yet this is true. One can see this in
the astonishment of eighteenth-century figures at their first
sight of it.

In the *Diary of a Surgeon in the Year 1750–51* by John Knyreton, the author, working in a London hospital, had to amputate
the leg of an attractive young girl from Norfolk who'd injured her
knee. She'd 'fallen in love' with a farmer's son, no doubt influenced by novel-reading, and been packed off to London by her
disapproving guardian. One day the farmer's son appeared in the

ward, having discovered where she was. Despite her operation, their passion flared up anew and they were married next day at the bedside. Knyreton was amazed at 'this strange, intoxicating distemper of love, which I have heard described as a disease . . . surely one affection above all others one would pray to be inoculated with' (we would say 'against'). His wondering was at least half-shared by all the other patients in the ward, depending on their attitudes to the new emotion. They watched it 'half of them in tears and the other half unwonted quiet, according to their several temperaments'.

It was noted by contemporaries how much more prevalent this new way of feeling and behaving was in England and America than elsewhere. William Cobbett, the English radical writer and traveller, remarked in 1829 that 'it produces self-destruction in England more frequently than in all other countries put together'. In America it developed in the same way but somewhat later. It did not arrive on the Continent—Stendhal's *De l'Amour* in 1822 was a 'treatise on a type of madness which is very rare in France'—nor come to be associated with marriage until much later. This was partly because the novel of romantic love was far less popular there; in particular, women's magazines, which began to grow from the end of the eighteenth century onwards in England and America, were not nearly so successful. Also arranged marriages remained far more common, especially in France and Italy, right through the nineteenth century and even into the twentieth century. In 1853 Joseph Droz could write in a best-selling French marriage manual that marriage was 'in general a means of increasing one's credit and one's fortune'. As a result, in both countries adultery developed as the normal way of satisfying love, sex and companionship; there grew up a *tradition* of adultery, and, as the concept of romantic love spread on the Continent, it was in this sphere, where one could argue it rightfully belonged, that it found expression. Something of the sort happened among the English aristocracy and for the same reason. (See Appendix E.) Adultery, by its nature, must always be a romantic love vehicle, but in America and Britain it was the gradual relinquishing of parental control over the choice of partner, the dying away of economic considerations in marriage, combined with the moral restrictions of evangelical religion, which allowed, or forced, the new emotion generated by literature slowly to attach itself to marriage as well.

By the end of the nineteenth century, love among the middle classes was a mixture of nervous sentimentality strongly mixed with a regard for dividends, dowries and property. It is our century, and in particular the last forty years or so which have seen—in the tides of pulp novels, films, pop songs, and magazines and comics and TV, tides which cannot be exaggerated—the final degradation and therefore popularisation of romantic love. I say 'therefore' because as romantic love became increasingly easy and sentimental, endings, after a few difficulties, invariably happy, so the emotion became hypnotically, narcotically beckoning and sweet, attractive to millions. Astounded at its appearance in 1750, by 1970, when Gorer did his survey, 74 per cent of the men and 86 per cent of the women considered they had 'really' been in love.

And as this great black hole of the psyche grew ever more massive, and the sharp outlines of romantic intensity and passion blurred and dissolved, so it became able to suck into itself every new development in its path. Many of these were and are in fact totally antithetical to the still powerful (if buried and confused) aims and expectations of romantic love. Some of these contradictions are harmless, if odd. The real aim is the single, all-absorbing object of desire. But such is the pressure and 'selling' of love that by their late teens both boys and girls have been physically and psychologically attracted to and often 'in love' with dozens of film, TV or pop stars or models, as well as with girls and boys in the street or school.

Often the assimilations are more dangerous. This can be simply technical, as with the idea of the simultaneous orgasm. This concept was invented, or at least popularised, by the hugely successful Dutch gynaecologist Theodor Hendrik van de Velde in his best-selling *Ideal Marriage* during the 1920s, and emanated from the roseate wreaths of romantic love with which he garlanded his essentially engineering approach. Simultaneous orgasm is quite unnecessary and often causes couples considerable anxiety as they strive to attain it. Van de Velde can also be criticised for his major advice towards this end, the still prevalent but also erroneous idea that the man should concentrate 'steadfastly' on direct manipulation of the clitoris to ensure arousal ('It seems,' said one of the women writing to Shere Hite, 'like he's trying to *erase* my clitoris!')

During the nineteenth century children joined the romantic dream, a conjunction made universal throughout society in the 1950s. Yet of all things, children, in their exhausting and demanding reality, are surely one of the most inimical to that concentration and exclusivity demanded by romantic love. The strain imposed by this contradiction is certainly one reason why the majority of divorces takes place in the first three years. A study published in 1970 summarising all the work of the last ten years found that 'children tend to detract from rather than contribute to marital happiness'.

It is here, in marriage, that romantic love does most harm, because despite the many accretions over the centuries (sex, happy endings, children, 'growth') the two states are still fundamentally and completely incompatible, as everyone professes to know. Romantic love is still, as it began, a desire—no matter that it is now often slushy, sentimental, largely sensual—for a *sensation*, a *feeling*. People want to feel this thing they've heard and seen so much of—or feel it anew if it has vanished. They do not primarily seek out their partner for his or her qualities, so much as seek (or more usually invent or impose) qualities which will be the excuse for these feelings. These sensations, their intensity, are antithetical to marriage at all points. They are increased by partings, obstacles, difficulty. Marriage is based on closeness, habit, mutual ease. Love is a distant quest, something pursued; marriage is having been caught, love of someone close to you. Above all, love is the exploration of something new (itself a series of obstacles); marriage growing and being accustomed to one another, the known. And so we see the couple of four years becoming desperately fearful of the flatness, the sameness, the jog-trot of married life, desperately trying to disturb the emotional ties which are gradually forming among the smoothness and serenity of their lives, desperately trying to revive the sensation and passion and love again—'To keep,' as Cyril Connolly said, 'the tension up in marriage'. Until finally, they give up and, as de Rougemont puts it, 'thus remedying boredom with a passing fever, he for the second time, she for the fourth', Western couples tear themselves apart and set out on the search again, a search as inevitably doomed as the first or second or third.

It is here that de Rougemont (who expounds the traditional view) becomes original. He regards romantic love as by far the most important cause of marital breakdown—but not for these fairly familiar reasons. In his view, romantic love, like some Trojan horse of the heart, has carried into the mainstream of Western culture and behaviour, without anyone realising it, a strange and terrifying force whose *aim* is destruction.

2   *On the edge of the sea*
    A whale lay sighing.
    And among its sighs it said—
    In love there is always pain.
          Spanish Copla

For the first 500 years of its existence, in art and literature, legend and myth, romantic love was almost invariably entwined with pain. In part this had to do with the intensity of feeling sought—the troubadour's love, as we saw, was a frustrated love; it was, therefore, by definition unhappy. This tradition of obstacles to intensify love was, as a result, accompanied by the despair and desperate desire—the passion—which the obstacles also induced. But there was more to it than this. The tales of desperate romantic love also appeared in myth and legend. Myths arise to express deep forces at work in society. They are often obscure—partly to involve as much as possible in order to increase their power, partly because they arise to express truths which society does not dare face openly, of which it is afraid. De Rougemont therefore takes the myth of Tristan and Isolde to assist him trace this dark element of pain to its source.

There seem to be three elements significant in the myth of Tristan, since they are found in nearly all versions: there is the taking of a love potion; at the end, both die—romantic love is in some way linked with death; and throughout the story Tristan himself frustrates his love—sleeping with a sword between them for instance.

This last artificiality gives us a clue. When an author uses, and readers accept, artificial tricks, we know what an art form is really about. The convention is allowed to satisfy something deeper or stronger. The modern convention in films or TV that murder and violence are routine is not to express a truth that they are that commonplace, but to allow the viewer to satisfy a craving for excitement, fear and cruelty through watching violence. Similarly, blocks and obstacles, in reality easily overcome, are allowed to intensify Tristan and Isolde's love, to the point that they are willing to sacrifice their happiness to it, and even their lives.

The secret and terrifying nature of the myth begins to emerge. De Rougemont then asks, what precisely is the nature of this love that must be so intense? Do Tristan and Isolde like each other? Indeed, has their love anything to do with each other at all? Not really. Certainly, both emphatically deny it. Isolde: 'Lord, by almighty God, he loves me not, nor I him.' It is the *potion* which is responsible. 'It is the poison,' cries Tristan, 'which holds me from leaving her and her leaving me.' 'Love by force dominates you,' says the hermit. Rather than loving each other, they love the anguish, the exquisite height of love, they love love and being in love. To obstruct love increases and consolidates it, until they reach the most absolute obstacle of death—and it is infinitely intensified and consolidated.

Even now, the nature of that love is not quite clear—though the truth is almost out. It is the three significant elements which allow de Rougemont to burst the myth wide open. The fact that they need a love potion to take away responsibility is a clear indication that Tristan and Isolde are guilty about the true aim of their love. The nature of the obstacles and the end of the myth itself finally reveal this aim. Tristan and Isolde impose chastity on themselves; but a self-imposed chastity is anti-life, a symbolical suicide (this explains the significance of the sword between them). Tristan and Isolde really desire a deliberate death, coming at the end of a passion, a suffering, which will have purified them. The end of the myth is its true goal.

This then is the simple but terrible secret. The love of love has concealed a far more awful passion—something that could never be admitted, that had to be hidden and could only be referred to by symbols: the lovers in the innermost recesses of their being were obeying the dictates of a wish for death; they have been, says de Rougemont, in the throes of the *active passion of darkness.*

This is the secret, the longing for death and suffering, that the West has never allowed to be given away. By repressing it, concealed in tales of desperate love, the secret was preserved. In fact, during the eighteenth and nineteenth centuries it did begin to emerge. From the eighteenth-century interest in the macabre and horrible, people began to derive pleasure from terror and pain (it is possibly significant that there are powerful currents of this abroad today). During the nineteenth century it was realised that pain was part of desire. 'It is strange,' wrote Novalis, the German author of philosophical romances, 'that the true source of cruelty should be desire.' To Shelley the two were inseparable. 'Our sweetest songs are those that tell of saddest thought.' The more powerful the pain, the greater the love and the pleasure. The most powerful pain is death, and so throughout the nineteenth century the most ardent lovers are those who die, are dying or cause death. Finally, with certain German Romantic poets the pretence was dropped. It was not love but death they wrote about. Not surprisingly a complete statement was made by Wagner in his opera precisely on the Tristan myth, which openly flaunts the death wish. But by then the terrible secret of romantic passion had too long been buried. No one realised (or realises today) that they meant precisely what they said.

The need for suffering is fundamental because we reach knowledge and self-awareness by testing ourselves—and extreme tests are bound to lead to death and pain. Progress is seen as overcoming and improving deficiencies in whatever area the advance is being made. But we are only aware of the deficiency by the discomfort or pain it causes us (this is the biological function of pain). Suffering and knowledge are entwined here too. The potion is to provide an alibi, to absolve guilt—'I am not responsible'. We have a potion today. It is sex. Sexual drive is the drug which sweeps us into passion and which we exaggerate to remove responsibility.

If de Rougemont has explained that romantic love really conceals a terrible longing to suffer and die, he did not explain *why* this camouflage is necessary. It is, after all, fairly odd. To do this he has to go back to the third century A.D. when in various forms (depending on the indigenous religion) the dualistic ideas of Manes, a Persian, spread from India over Europe to the Atlantic. In fact, the Manichaean religion was really a synthesis of very ancient pagan beliefs, probably Eastern in origin, which were in essence an attempt to explain and then solve the human condition—its pains and sorrows and fears, particularly the fear of death.

The significant elements of these beliefs were very roughly that the physical human condition was a disaster. This nightmare was self-evident; the explanation was that the world was created and ruled over by a god of evil, of night. The solution was that there was another world, the world after death, ruled over by a god of goodness, of light. These two (hence dualistic) gods, these forces, were waging a fatal struggle to attract mankind, and the aim of man must be to escape from the body, the world of night, in fact to die and come into the world of light, the everlasting world of bliss in the afterlife.

In the twelfth century, two streams of this dualistic thought converged in Provence. The Cathars of the Albigensian heresy were in effect a Christian expression of one of the neo-Manichaean sects of Asia Minor. More significantly, since it also created the travelling troubadour system and often the actual language, a religious tradition from a similarly Manichaean background arose in ninth-century Arabia and arrived by a route we have already traced. At last de Rougemont's picture is complete in its awful and extraordinary simplicity. The myths and stories of romantic love ended in death because this was the virulent ingredient—buried and transformed—which was carried into them from much older pagan religious beliefs. This death wish was peculiarly apt since it was not for death as such, but for an active afterlife where bliss—in this case the transports of romantic love—would continue for ever. It is this agent, still vigorous, but still further concealed today by our intense overstimulation of sex, which is finally triumphing now in the destruction of marriage (something which de Rougemont assumes without argument means the destruction of society).

Several times in his argument de Rougemont fiercely and skilfully rejects the obvious idea that it was sexual frustration which created romantic love. This is necessary because he needs to prove that the prior element and strongest (if hidden) was neo-Manichaean religion. But there is a much simpler and less sinister explanation of these antecedents, which involves physical love and its frustration from the start. The most important 'literary' influence on the troubadours was Arabic. By the twelfth century this tradition contained two crucial elements. The first was a cultivation of *intensity for its own sake.* The duty of the extremely numerous poets was to enhance and increase all sensual sensation (including physical love) in elaborate conceits, using slow-moving and voluptuous images. The second was a tenth-century movement, at first practised by individuals like Ibn Haziin, about the suffering and exquisite pains of love; this joined the Sufi movement which was transforming Mohammedanism by ideals of universal love. But this took place and became popular in precisely those countries where the harem system, the strict segregation of the sexes, was also developing, a system which gradually became very strict indeed. It was this artificial separation of the sexes which engendered the frustration and intensity where notions of romantic love could arise and take general and powerful root; and where, since many knew it, it could become a literary form. Since there was also a tradition of cultivating intensity of sensation for its own sake, it is not surprising the two should join.

This seems to me a more likely, if more mundane, historical explanation. From the twelfth century on, the Church became increasingly successful in imposing its ideal of sexual control, monogamy and chastity upon Western Europe. The general spread of romantic love from the mid-eighteenth century into the nineteenth century saw a particular surge of this repression. (That the triumph of romantic love has taken place during a period of unparalleled licence is a paradox but not a contradiction.) Even if the neo-Manichaean elements were present, I do not see how 'a love of death' can be said to survive as an active destructive force. Because an idea or form of behaviour joins other ideas it does not necessarily preserve all its earlier implications intact. If the idea is altered and transformed, that is what happens. It is not in some odd way also not transformed. One of the main purposes of the pagan mid-winter festival was a temporary reversal of the natural order—a safety valve where 'the last shall be first', with a Lord of Misrule. Christianity took over this festival for the birth of Christ. Although a great many people may get drunk, it would be absurd to suppose any vestige of the old aim had somehow survived 'hidden' in the goals of Christianity.

Stories and legends of romantic love ended in death or separation partly as the result of the Arabic/troubadour tradition, and partly because in no other way could the exquisite emotions they were expressing and exploring be preserved intact—suspended as it were—in the mind of the reader.

In the mind of the reader; but also in life. There is a Spanish word *'ilusion'*. This does not mean 'illusion' or something false; it is a sympathetic word for the understandable and natural hopes which keep people going. But from a strict Catholic point of view these are 'false'. This ambiguity gives the word a certain melancholy.

The bitterness and sweetness of romantic love are similar. It is often the hope and dream of people's lives; yet even when experienced we know, from a common sense point of view, it is false—

and that it will eventually depart. Depart—leaving us once again
to dream about it, need it, seek it. That is why there is always
something melancholy, a sadness hovering on the edge of love.

3 *It takes so little time and it causes so much trouble.*
John Barrymore on adultery

Most professional commentators, the sociologists, therapists
and counsellors who deal with marriage breakdown and often go
on to write the books about it, would say that romantic love has
nothing to do with the state of marriage or with its breakdown.

And, leaving aside for the moment any other reason for breakdown, surely this is part of our received wisdom. Marriage begins
with romantic love, but the day-to-day, year-to-year grind of that
condition, the endless proximity, the strain of children, the need
for security, require quite different qualities and feelings from the
supposedly intense fires which started the whole thing off: tolerance, compromise, often self-sacrifice, humour, loyalty, kindness,
stability. Emotionally it demands something that although sexual
is far closer to affection and fondness, to friendship, than to passionate love.

Much shrewd calculation along these lines continues today,
however concealed by the conventions of romantic love. This is
shown by the paradox that the literature or film of fantasy can
often reveal what people don't want as much as what they do, because it portrays events they *prefer* to have in fantasy and don't
want in real life. A survey of women's magazines in 1970 found
two-thirds of the stories ended in happy marriage, the rest in
present and probably future bliss. The heroes were artists, actors
and doctors, and readership studies showed these were the lovers
women liked to read about. They did not—with the exception of
doctors—want to marry their heroes. Far the largest majority of
the thousands of women who went to Heather Jenner's highly successful British Marriage Bureau specifically eschewed actors and
artists as unreliable income providers. The 'ideal couple' glowing

in the imaginations of millions is probably not all that far from the one in whom building societies, when asked to lend the money to buy a house in Britain, will repose total confidence—a school-teacher around twenty-six married to a girl employed in a bank who takes the pill.

Today (as always) intensity of feeling is the major criterion, and since intensity can only be a subjective judgment, this couple will imagine they are 'really' in love; though considerations far removed from that condition led them into marriage. For instance, the desire for possessions, for material things is very powerful. In many people it is as strong as the need for personal relationships. I knew a man who married someone because he wanted a pair of Russian boots she had; and a girl who after the break-up of a long and passionate affair found that in fact the thing she minded most was having left behind her cast-iron frying pan. The basing of marriage in earlier centuries on property and material things was sound. Numbers of people over the last fifty years have tried to have romantic love emotions foreign to them—or, perhaps more usually, thought or pretended they have had them when they haven't.

Nevertheless, although people still choose each other for all sorts of reasons not connected with romantic love, and having embarked on the long journey together romantic love appears to become steadily less involved, it would be as foolish to imagine this love is irrelevant to both marriage and its breakdown as it was mistaken of de Rougemont to transplant pagan beliefs from the third century to the twentieth century. Romantic love may seem to disappear; in fact it remains powerful and all-pervasive.

People still sometimes speculate (it was once a common discussion) as to whether monogamy and/or sexual fidelity is more 'natural' than polygamy and/or some form of sexual variety. But few ways of behaviour are 'natural'. Society imposes forms—and somewhere there is friction. In monogamous societies the strain is seen in one woman or one man; in polygamous ones—'Do you think,' cries an exhausted Iatmul husband, quoted by Margaret Mead, 'that I am made of ironwood that I am able to copulate with you as much as you want?' I talked to a man of forty-two who had two women alternately week by week and he said he had been forced to have two orgasms a night every night for eleven months; his fantasies were entirely about monasteries.

To look at it another way, for some people promiscuity, or at least successive variety, is easier; for others strict fidelity comes most easily and, whether or not either group can live as they wish, the dictates are at least straightforward. But for most of us, even if the balance shifts at different times and ages, *both* paths are almost equally natural at the same time—for a mixture of contradictory social and psycho-physical reasons. The one, for security, for ease of sex without incessant search, because habit and continuity creates a bond it is painful to break, because children benefit, for moral reasons, financial reasons. The other, because desire for other people does not stop arising, habit and a single mate lead to a waning desire, because of things like 'growth'. Such contradictions are the very stuff of the human condition and we all have to struggle through them as best we can, unendingly and incessantly unhappy and then happy, contented and then discontented.

It is the human condition, but the conflicts and contradictions can be reduced. Most cultures have formal systems of monogamous marriage. A good many reduce the strains of this by making any breach formal too. The Angolans used to exchange wives formally for quite lengthy periods, explaining 'they were not able to eat always of the same dish'. The same practice existed for the same reason among Himalayans. Much more common is to allow the desire for change or variety to burst out in those festivals of sanctioned licence which so thrilled the old anthropologists. The *Fasching* balls in Germany are the most famous European survivor. This formality shades off into the dying traditions of condoned mutual but discreet adultery which derived from long-lasting arranged marriage in France, Italy and Greece (even Greece is now beginning to allow the supremacy of 'love' and free choice in marriage). This tradition is less strong in Britain, and virtually nonexistent in America. (See Appendix E.)

Another way of reducing the conflict is to reduce the emotional intensity involved, while allowing the sexual intensity to remain high. Among the Barrow Eskimo, says Professor Westermarck, the Finnish sociologist and lecturer, 'promiscuous sexual intercourse between married or unmarried people or even among children, appears to be looked on simply as a matter of amusement.' (See Appendix C.)

In the West we make the situation as difficult as it could possibly be by increasing the emotional intensity and reducing the canalising formality to a shambles. This is entirely due to romantic love. The jealousy and exclusivity many times intensified in marriage, and analogous relationships, by romantic love do not seem to fade in the same way as the intense love itself; that is why in spite of the fact we have our informal, ad hoc saturnalia (in some cases more or less continuous) they more usually cause chaos than do good. It is also why open marriage very seldom works and why it is quite pointless saying, as *Self-help* writers sometimes do, don't get het up over adultery and infidelity. That is simply the mindless advice of the courtiers of Canute: those roseate rolling romantic waves are *there*.

The saturnalia cannot be formal and the adultery must be secret and discreet, because romantic love remains, as it has always done, the aim and ferocious and continuous spur to adultery and dreams of adultery. It gives to ordinary sexual restlessness a creed, an ideology. Once it glorified the transgression of Tristan; today this glory spills its rays upon some quite unsuitable associations. I was talking to someone about the stigma of divorce. She said, 'What about the stigma of marriage?' Affairs, what sociologists call 'consensual unions', are now becoming significant statistically. Often lasting years, they are forms of marriage (this is quite clear in Sweden) and by that token cannot sustain the intensity from which derives their glory. At the moment there are something like 10,000 'closet marrieds' in California who don't admit to it because of image anxiety.

The energy of romantic love is really concentrated on the affair within marriage (or marriage-like situation). Here, imperatives operate. Take the Hatchetts, an advanced intellectual couple in the 1930s, who had always agreed that each should have affairs if they wanted to. After six years of contented marriage, it suddenly dawned on them—*neither had had an affair.* They began to feel obscurely guilty. Eventually this became so acute they decided to do it deliberately. Desmond was particularly enthusiastic; Mary, when it came to it, was more reluctant and in the end wanted to cancel the idea. However, Desmond having found a partner, insisted. He had to hang fire, as it were, while Mary searched about. It took her some time, but she eventually found someone. Off they went. In the event, Desmond had a wretched time. It didn't work at all and he came back very disgruntled. Mary, on the contrary, had a marvellous time. She came back wildly enthusiastic and wanted to set off again almost at once. Desmond refused. The marriage didn't break up but it entered a prolonged period of considerable difficulty and strain and Mary took to drink.

Nevertheless, one of the needs satisfied by adultery is for adventure—love as the last unknown frontier; it is the need for experience, for danger, for hurt, for *life*, actually for sex itself as a dramatic and mysterious engagement. Traditionally the terrors of adultery were comic, the stuff of farce and *opera buffa*: there was no divorce and adultery didn't threaten anyone or anything. But the moment you allow divorce, adultery threatens marriage and therefore becomes serious; the easier divorce, the greater the threat and the more serious adultery.

The strength of romantic love—its force, its rules, its determination to find expression—is often disguised, or at least unacknowledged. Perhaps people are ashamed of it. Those 'adolescent passions' says Updike at one point in *Couples*; yet it is by looking at Updike a moment that we can perceive the secret power with which, simply because it has been exercised for so long, romantic love can now exercise unnoticed and therefore more powerfully.

The central element in *Couples* and *Marry Me* is marriage. This is made clear on several levels. The goal of an affair (without which it withers) is marriage. Jerry: 'But I don't want you as a mistress; our lives just aren't built for it. Mistresses are for European novels. Here, there's no institution except marriage. Marriage and the Friday night basketball game. You can't take this indefinitely; you think you can, but you can't.'

More importantly, the central morality of the books, their right and wrong, what dictates their ends is the morality of marriage. Offences against marriage are sins; thus divorce is a sin. 'These years had seen the boatyard crowd go from decay to disintegration. Two couples had been divorced.' The final and ultimate sin is when Foxy and Piet are discovered (in fact betrayed) in adultery. This, owing to the character of Foxy's husband, Ken, threatens marriage directly—and the book has to end since it can, morally, go no further. The punishment is divorce (also the final acting out of the sin); ahead lies remarriage and a return to the central morality again.

However, these novels have something far more striking in common. Though the central morality appears to be that of marriage, in these books this position is shared by another morality, unadmitted but equally strong; a morality whose imperatives equally dictate the behaviour of the characters and against which the final sin is committed, bringing the action to a close. This is the morality of romantic love.

Adultery and romantic love have always gone together because, as we know, one way romantic love reaches its full force is through difficulties and secrecy. Once the cover is blown an adulterous affair is either condoned—in which case it can gallop along unopposed and will soon lose its initial intensity, becoming after a while a form of married love. Or else it will not be condoned but stopped. In both cases the ultimate sin against romantic love has been committed—it has been destroyed. That is why Piet, when Georgene starts to become dependent on him (i.e., moves towards a more settled love ultimately inimical to romantic love), calls it a 'sin'. That is why the most important characters in all the books are those whose love is most intense. An ironic twist in *Couples* is that Piet has already sinned before the final catastrophe by allowing his love to fade. The equality of the two moral systems is nicely illustrated in the second of the Updike books. Romantic love is the moral goal, but so is marriage—and the one destroys the other. So the book ends with romantic love and marriage—the contradiction, the mutual destroyers—poised together, frozen and held in perpetual tension. Jerry's last words can only be delivered to a *dream* Sally—'Marry me.'

In fact I think the ethos of romantic love is stronger than that of marriage. I want to take only one example of this which is interesting because it is unconscious, just as the way in which the morality of romantic love dictates the end of *Couples* is unconscious. The example is the curious chastity of Updike's books. I don't just mean the actual chastity of the central event in *Couples*. This is in fact the same chastity as existed among the Cathars, and may have among the troubadours, that is intercourse without orgasm. In this case it is Foxy who does not have an orgasm. 'These barriers are piled high, so my not coming, dear Piet, does not mean I do not go high with you. I go very high.' I mean more that though both books, but particularly *Couples*, are filled with descriptions of sex, they are both completely unerotic. How Updike achieves this is not easy to say. It is partly the highly wrought 'poetic' quality in his prose, but that this is no bar to eroticism was shown by Nabokov, above all in *Ada* and *Lolita*. It may be his attempt to combine poetic description with the feelings/ideas/images engendered by making love. Here is Piet with Georgene Thorne (a fateful coupling, incidentally):

> Her glistening skin gazed. Wounded by winning, he bowed his head and with suppliant lips took a nipple, faintly salt and sour, in. Suddenly she felt to be all circles, circles that could be parted to yield more circles. Birds chirped beyond the rainbow rim of the circular wet tangency holding him secure. Her hand, feathery, established another tangency, located his core. If her touch could be believed, his balls were all velvet, his phallus sheer silver.

Or perhaps one is dazzled by the variety, the skill. There are Foxy's powdery armpits and petalled cleft simpler than a rose . . . Angela's ambrosial, unsearchable. Or Carol 'who came quickly,

with grateful cries and nimble accommodations, who put a pillow
beneath her hips, who let her head hang over the side of the bed,
hair trailing, throat arched, and who wrapped her legs around
him as if his trunk were a stout trapeze by which she was swinging
far out over the abyss of the world.'

Whatever the reason, it is certain he does achieve a more or less
total lack of erotic excitement; and reveals thereby that his real
interest lies, like the troubadours, in the intensity and perhaps
even more the *manoeuvres* of emotion—just as Piet, at the end,
feels 'a nostalgia for adultery itself—its adventures, the acrobat-
ics, its deceptions demand, the tension of its hidden springs, the
new landscapes it makes us master'.

Romantic love, providing a respectable, age-old, glorifying ideology for natural sexual restlessness, attained immeasurable physical gravitational force by drawing into itself things as fundamental as children, marriage and 'growth'. It so saturates our culture,
pervades it so completely that, like air, it passes unnoticed. Professional commentators don't notice it, unaware that most of the
things they observe are, at least, influenced by it and frequently
caused by it. Updike and countless other novelists and film and
TV scriptwriters can act to its morality unaware. And if they do,
to what extent do we, their material?

Many, perhaps most adults see themselves as ill-assorted, disap-
pointed, rebellious, intense, shameless, unfaithful or deceived. If
in love they wonder 'is it love or not? Do I really love or is it just
affection—or am I in love with love?' When married they ask are
we/I as fulfilled/compatible/adventurous or whatever as those
others are. That boredom which British marriage guidance counsellor David Barcla spoke of as his deepest problem, where else
does it spring from but awareness of, experience of, a longing for
more intense feelings, a longing which derives ultimately from
romantic love?

At the heart of many marriages and love affairs is hugged a
vague restless desire for something more, or something else. The
McCalls survey in 1976 found that fourth on the long long list of
what the readers wanted in fantasy was 'a new husband or lover'.

It is this restlessness which finds satisfaction in the vast purchase of romance literature. A great many people can canalise their desire for romantic love into these and other channels of fantasy. But what if this is not enough?

4 *Passion is the element in which we live; without it we but vegetate*

Byron

> *I was not yet in love, but I was in love with love itself; and I sought for something to love, since I loved loving.*
>
> ST AUGUSTINE

There are social and anthropological reasons for the dominance of romantic love today. (See Appendix E.) But the potentialities of the human heart which this great power awakes have profound psychological roots as well that have nothing to do with the cultural stimulus. We know that a strong bond with one or both parents is a prerequisite for romantic love. It is likely, in fact, that this bond actually creates a need to be repeated (a refinement of this is that romantic love is a necessary force to split the psyche from the parent *in order* to repeat the pattern. This would explain why, once the new adult bond is forged, that particular romantic passion can subside. It does not, unfortunately, explain why the desire for another, different romantic passion continues so often as a felt need).

This is related to Freud's idea of the 'Polymorphous Pervert' which implied that adult sexual patterns depended entirely on childhood experiences. The idea has been considerably developed by the distinguished British psychiatrist Dr Gordon Ambrose in his concept of the 'Polymorph Perverse'. He suggests that the patient, due to chronic repression or suppression, is forced, almost against his will, to repeat the same pattern of conduct over and over again, but the pattern includes things he either intensely fears, or badly wants but denies himself. A man had two unsuccessful marriages and numerous affairs, all of which began to go wrong after four years. Analysis revealed that a deeply loved nurse had left when he was four years old—a fact he had repressed. He had developed a pattern of unsuitable liaisons which ended (often precipitated by him) after this period, as a method of expressing his repressed fears at the event, and temporarily lessening them. The pains and sufferings sought in romantic love are often explained in this way (as are some of the heights of masochism).

The specificity of love—the fact we choose one person rather than another—has been explained by saying we perceive complementary psychological needs. That is, people will choose each other to satisfy psychological needs of their own, and be chosen to satisfy those of their partner (the man chooses the nonmaternal woman to satisfy his own love of children; the woman chooses him so that she can have a career). These needs can be 'normal' or they can be neurotic. Neurotic conflict can blow people apart; but it should be remembered that neurotic need can often bind them together more strongly than usual (often despite conflict— or for it). In this context, highly specific neurotic compulsions, often sexual, can create an intensity of desire and passion perfectly adapted for some specific modern patterns of romantic love.

There is a divorcee, for example, who has become addicted to seducing timid professors. She has learnt to sense instinctively what they will find attractive, and then sets out to coax and beguile them in campaigns which sometimes last many months. When at last she has seduced them into conquering her, her sexual excitement is enormous and she gives way so completely that she sometimes almost faints from ecstasy. But now she starts to lose interest and after a while she has to get out of it—no doubt leaving the intellectual more timid than before. She worries about this, about the instability, the let-down, but then the desire starts to rise again, the memory of the ecstasy returns, any doubt or despair pales before its fire, and she cannot resist seeking out her timid wayward prey as it creeps through the academic undergrowth. In nine years of divorce she has had thirty-nine professors, and whole faculties stretch ahead.

We say 'love at first sight', but it is more revealing to see this as love at a given moment. It is a moment when a person has reached a state of 'love readiness', when he or she has decided to find some outside vehicle to represent, to embody a secret ideal or wish. This is often one from childhood and therefore people seek some aspect of their mothers or fathers in the person they fall in love with. Certain physical associations, often very small, trigger passion. Someone singing can arouse love through the nurse or mother who sang us to sleep. People have fallen in love through the shape of an ear, or a knee, or with a name (Tristan married a second Isolde just because of her name). There is even a recorded case of a man who fell desperately in love with a shadow. He never met the woman who cast it.

But the ultimate love is love of ourselves. In the last analysis it is this great love that can find—by projection—expression in romantic love. We love the shape of ourselves we see in (or impose on) someone else, and that is why the passion of romantic love carries with it the exhilarating sensation of self-expansion with none of the boredom or the trapped feeling of ordinary self-obsession. Sociologists have noted that couples are usually similar and 'equal in physical attractiveness' (there is considerable consensus about what is attractive). That this was one of the fundamental sources of love's power has been known from the very beginning. The Arabs had a fable about a lonely maiden awaiting the true seeker on the other side of the Bridge of Suirat. When he appears she says, 'I am thyself'.

There is a last element that the professional commentators ignore, or have perhaps, immersed in their grim confrontations, never experienced, and that is the entrancing delight of romantic love. When deep fantasy seems suddenly to become real, enormous stores of energy are set free. One sees this sometimes in great leaders: with Joan of Arc, or with Winston Churchill when, at the age of sixty-five, he was at last allowed to grasp the mighty task of leading Britain to victory. But when tapped by love, these powerful drives, springing from the very core, have a miraculous effect, transforming the whole world into something ravishing, spring-like and new.

It is not surprising that throughout history men and women have sought this magic. Nor have they been neurotics necessarily (though don't despise the neurotics' power to feel, nearly 'fainting with ecstasy' as they make love), but men and women of common sense, who must on any reasonable ground be admitted mature. People like Bertrand Russell. 'Despite the pain,' wrote his biographer Clark, 'he wanted the romantic ecstasy again. The search for it was to drive him inexorably, as much as the hope of intellectual satisfaction, as much as the desire for sexual relief, for the next half-century.' Russell had four wives, as well as deeply passionate affairs, and his love-life didn't really reach any sort of calm until he was into his eighties.

Who can be blamed for not resisting the almost irresistible? It was indeed an intoxicating draught the Arabs discovered so long ago, a draught which seems heaven-sent and which, as Shelley well knew and put in *Prometheus Unbound*, can make us transcend the turmoil and feel, for a while, healed and whole.

> . . . and Love he sent to bind
> The disunited tendrils of that vine
> Which bears the wine of life, the human heart.

8

THE LASER BEAM OF
CHANGE

*... the apt and cheerful conversation of man with woman,
to comfort and refresh him against the solitary life*
MILTON on the aim of marriage

WHAT 'BREAKS' at divorce is 'the companionate marriage'. This
ideal—that a couple in a marriage should be companions and
friends and support each other through life—became more and
more prevalent during the sixteenth and seventeenth centuries,
and was particularly conscious among Puritans. The idea of divorce is inherent in the ideal of companionate marriage. If the
main aim of marriage is companionship and mutual help, then
once that ceases there is no point in continuing it. It was Milton,
tortured by his own unhappy marriage, who, 300 years ahead of
his time and without a vestige of contemporary support, advocated divorce and remarriage in cases of hopeless incompatibility.

One explanation of what is happening today is that far too
much stress is being laid on the personal side of companionship
and as a result this is cracking up. The argument runs like this.
The emphasis on companionship in marriage has grown steadily
and generally over the last 250 years. But at the same time the nuclear family has become more and more isolated from the community and close kin which was its support and its alleviation,
until now it stands almost entirely alone, feeding itself, in the vast

urban and suburban sprawls where most of us live. 'You get to know your next door neighbour on either side but you don't get much further,' said an anonymous figure in a study done on an Oxford housing estate. 'I did pass the neighbour next door but one and *gave him the opportunity to greet me*, but nothing happened.' This has been increased as sickness, education and old age have been taken from the family and dealt with by hospitals, schools, pensions and old people's homes. Work, once normally centred on the home, now seldom is. This all means that far more weight— too much—is thrown on close personal companionship. Demanding more, people may get more—there is more love in marriage; but the strains of this isolation are considerable, and if people don't get the quality of companionship they expect they move on.

Two aspects of this commonly held view need correcting. The first is that it much exaggerates the degree of isolation. The nuclear family is certainly more private now than it has ever been before in history; and is thus sheltered from community pressure. But it is not more isolated from the family in general. In fact, technology and mobility have been shown to strengthen family bonds, and in an ideal way: *'close, but not too near'*. The point is, once grown up the children control the amount of contact: they can control where they live and work, how often they see their parents, how often they talk and write to them.

Nor do I see how one can possibly make equations as to degrees or amounts of love. The expression may change; the amount is far harder to weigh. Because custom dictated, say, that women should be supreme in the house but overall submit to men, as in Victorian times, it does not mean men or women loved less. The capacity to love has different roots. Nor did the imposition of education, care for the sick and old, even work itself necessarily reduce communication or companionship in the family. Love must have a function and such burdens are the very stuff of union and affection. Conversely, life is not so easy today that most couples find they have too little to help each other with.

In one respect, isolation is a factor. A crucial event in the early years of marriage for all sorts of reasons is the first child. It is arguably more significant than the marriage itself. But as regards the stress it causes, the resulting isolation is clearly a major one. The Rapoports quote horrific figures of couples trapped alone with their first child. For instance, 25 per cent of economic classes 1 and 2 (Registrar General's Categories in Britain), 59 per cent of class 5 and 40 per cent of all classes only go out together *once or less a year*. There is also a suggestion from the Rapoports that this is somehow aggravated by television. They quote studies in the U.S. and Britain which show that nightly TV viewing was correlated with stress.

I get irritated by commentators' insistence on 'communication'. The middle classes conduct their marriages through words; these are not the only medium nor are they necessary for strong feeling. I think of a middle-aged couple near where I live. He worked in the local factory. After twenty-seven years of marriage they came back from the pub after their usual Thursday visit, and as usual he asked for a cup of tea and as usual she made it for him and as usual passed him the milk. Suddenly he put down his cup and said, 'I don't want no tea, and I don't want no milk, and I don't ever want tea or milk or seeing you again in my life.' He got up and walked out and hasn't been back since. She knows it's final because he's been on to the solicitors.

The middle-class insistence on words usually, as with the Rapoports, involves condemning television for preventing 'communication'. This is too strenuous. There are all sorts of ways of communicating. Sex is communication. There is closeness, contact, when two people who are close read books in the same room. The same is true of television. It is a companionable medium. Television (quite aside from its role as nanny) holds together more couples than it keeps apart. Nor is this contradicted by the various studies. As quoted by the Rapoports they seem no more significant than a study showing that people in the Sahara Desert had greater recourse to water than people living in London.

1   *Better be half hang'd than ill wed*
                J. Ray, *A Collection of English Proverbs*, 1678

The fact that married couples can now expect to spend one-third to one-quarter of their lives together after the children have left is clearly of fundamental importance: it is the base from which operate many of the phenomena we have looked at—the feminist drive to work, many Privilege Bulge urges and so on: and some we haven't looked at—divorce after twenty or thirty years of marriage, for instance.

There is also length of marriage. There is some minor disagreement about how long marriages lasted in the past, but an average would seem to be about twenty years for most couples; but it is also clear that at certain, often prolonged times and different places (particularly France) the average duration could be as little as six years. (See Appendix F.)

From the mid-nineteenth century until 1945 the average length of marriage increased rapidly. Some figures are in Appendix F, but as a rough guide, it isn't far wrong to say couples who don't divorce can expect around forty to fifty years of married life together.

A perfectly plausible case can be put that this is not just a long time—for a good number of people it is a great deal too long. The swift decline in the death rate in the nineteenth and twentieth centuries led to a sudden, and absolutely unprecedented lengthening in the time people had to stay together (in particular together as a pair, without children). Many marriages, subject to other strains we know of, couldn't take it, and Western society was finally forced to adopt the institutional escape hatch of divorce.

I don't think it's as clear-cut as this. If the moment grown children leave is so crucial—as this argument would suggest, since the unspoken idea in it is that people can somehow 'take' seventeen or twenty years of marriage, but not thirty, forty or fifty years—then you would expect to see a sudden rise in divorce after that time. But you don't. On the whole there are, excluding the first four years, and especially the first year, no significant peaks in divorce studies or divorce statistics. Barring anomalies that can be explained by changes in the law, the divorce rates steadily decline the longer people are married. Each year you add to the edifice makes it stronger. Also, until people become quite old, they don't expect to die. The average life may be forty-five or fifty; everyone thinks *they* will live to be seventy. In the same way when people get married today, they still think it will be for life.

Nevertheless, there must remain a less simple, a fuzzier element of truth in the argument of longevity. People can hold in their heads completely contradictory ideas and feelings at the same time: love–hate, attraction–repulsion; or here, long life–short life; marriage-for-life–divorce after six years or thirteen. Thus, until fairly recently, although people personally expected to live till they were seventy, they were also at another level aware that they probably would not. Death was incessantly visible as an experience. And that is why it was so often secretly expected to bring release—and even more often invoked. Miss Weston wrote an acid little verse about a discontented husband in 1808:

> Come soon, O Death and Alice take,
> He loudly groaned and cry'd;
> Death came—but made a sad mistake,
> For Richard 'twas that died.

In the same way, no one can marry today, however certain or determined they are to be together for ever, without being aware of divorce. An American millionairess on the eve of her marriage speaking to reporters: 'It's marvellous to be getting married for the first time.'

It is more than just coincidental therefore that during the end of the nineteenth century and first forty years of the twentieth century the thunder of marital gunfire or, equally terrifying, deep ice-cold ten-year silences in some marital no-man's land, start to fill the air; this is in the period of Ruskin's and Carlyle's marriages, the marriages of the Tolstoys, the Merediths, the Hardys, the period of Great Terrible Marriages whose reverberations echo today. 'All happy families are more or less like one another; every unhappy family is unhappy in its own particular way.' That famous sentence, which strikes with such a chill into the hearts of divorcing parents and with which Tolstoy opens *Anna Karenina* was wrung from the bitter experiences of his own agonising marriage.

But it is worth remembering that on the whole, the real, often very terrible pain of broken relationships, even if it takes more years than one would suppose, does ultimately pass; in the past the hell of an unhappy marriage was permanent. At the same time, hell was not the rule. It is impossible to guess, now or in the past, what proportion of marriages were happy. How do you measure 'happiness'? No doubt then, as today, the majority somehow rubbed along together—probably, since the onus was very much on that, more than do so today.

2   *The bedrock of stability*

It is very odd how the way you phrase statistics alters their weight. You can say that 25 per cent of men and women in England are still virgins at marriage; or, alternatively, that 75 per cent of the girls and 77 per cent of the boys have had sex before marriage, and 45 per cent of these with up to five partners. The way a writer or sociologist puts his statistics shows, as it were, which side he is on, how and in what direction he wants to persuade you. But today no matter how you phrase the statistics, one thing is clear—the institution of marriage itself still rests on a bedrock of statistical stability. Even in America, two-thirds of all married couples will remain married for life (in Britain it will be three-quarters); in 1975 84 per cent of all families were still husband and wife families, and in seven-eighths of these the husband was still in his first marriage. Even among those divorcing, from a half to three-quarters would remarry and remain married a second time for life. It is as well to hold on to these figures, a raft to cling to in the turbulent seas ahead.

The majority of these solid marriages are perhaps not all that different from many marriages in the last fifty or hundred years. The grounds of disagreement may alter, the balance of power change—a husband now involves himself with the upbringing of the children, a wife insists she wants a job or an abortion—but the rows and reconciliations, the emotions remain the same. And, as always, 'the wise husband,' in the words of André Maurois, 'never becomes indignant. Like a sailor in a storm he slackens the sails, waits, hopes, and the passing storms do not prevent his loving the sea.' That is, the texture of this bedrock is familiar; it is also elusive.

Jeremy Seaforth, in an interesting book about homosexuality, describes an old male couple together for years:

> . . . the impression is of an extraordinary congruence of personality, a merging that reminded me a little of the fused characteristics of some of my old long-married aunts and uncles who had said the same things to each other almost every day for half a century, and where words are an arbitrary and almost insignificant outcrop of a profound flowing together of experience and character.

One knows the stereotype, but I can't help thinking of other 'stereotypes'. I think of a very old couple—the little living room has only two pictures, large photographs of their wedding day—where time and their economic situation make it quite *inconceivable* they should break up. As a result, the marriage and partner become the focus for practically all irritations (and pleasures—but it seems to be more irritations) of their life. It is one of perpetual and often stimulating warfare: 'I haven't spoken to him for two days. Not a word!' Then they spend a Saturday evening at the pub and have mutual hangovers. Or he nearly severs his finger, and she tends him, the grumbles moderated. And partly kept vigorous because, to her at least, the inconceivable is not just conceivable but frequently planned: 'I tell you Mr Hardy, I shall go to my sister just like that if I have any more of it. The furniture's mine; I shall take it with me.' Seventy-four and seventy-six, they've been together over fifty years. The oddest thing is they are not actually married. The photographs on the bookcase are false.

I remember going to a dinner party of an old friend. I sat next to her. She was sweet with her husband, as always; the only thing I noticed was perhaps an extra vitality and sparkle. Yet her bags were packed, her plans laid. She left next morning at eight. Or the friend that Jilly Cooper, novelist and social commentator, described to me, who was left by his wife. He couldn't understand it. Amazement was his first and chief emotion. 'We were fucking six times a week—right up to the minute of her departure.'

Happy families may resemble each other, but each marriage at the centre of that family is happy in its own particular way. The ties that bind people, the needs they fulfil in each other, are as complex or simple, as deep or shallow, often as unknowable, as the people themselves. The well-meaning friend who is indignant because her friend's husband is so inconsiderate and selfish, interferes at her peril. The wife married him for that selfishness. And this is still more complicated because we are all always both in the stream of becoming, while all the time wanting to be fixed. It can be, it often is, one of the peculiarities of marriage that it uniquely combines these two elements: that is, the essence of its endlessly changing moods, altering reactions, irritations, attractions, fantasies about leaving, thankful to be at rest—sometimes in the space of an afternoon, of an hour. It is at once in a state that is fixed, but which is also in the process of becoming something else.

Nearly all marriages are mysterious, and the two-thirds of marriages that are stable are usually the most mysterious. I shall more and more use individual marriages, case histories of particular affairs, a woman with a permanent group of three lovers, dozens of divorce experiences and so on, to illustrate and explain particular things that are happening and chart patterns developing; but about the texture of modern marriage, what it is like to be married today, you know as much as I do. It is this knowledge— gained from your own marriage, or sensed from that of your friends, or your parents, from reading, from films—this knowledge of the mysteriousness of marriage, and especially of the texture and mystery of lifelong marriage, that you must use as a reference from now on.

So, having constructed this raft (or rather having alerted you to its existence) it is almost time to put out of harbour on it, wondering, as we do, if its ancient logs are going to last the trip.

3   The laser beam of change

Although I think the most important factors are those we have been discussing, I do not underestimate the neurotic factors in divorce. The things we value in relationships almost entirely consist in interrelations of one sort or another—sexual, psychological, familial—between the two people involved; where they go wrong, they will often do so because of the neurotic personality of one or both partners. Professional commentators say this is by far the most important cause. Is it? The question is not just academic. If the break-up of relationships is a bad thing (arguable, but most people would assume it was) then to isolate the main cause might lead to the cure; at least it would put us on the right path—universal childhood psychotherapy for instance, or far more money on nursery-care facilities, or a considerable extension and strengthening of counselling and therapy services. If the causes are those social areas we've looked at, then we can only make sense of them by analysis and, if possible, by finding some pattern of significance here. Obviously, both approaches are involved, but I have emphasized the social and historical ones at this point for three reasons. First, professional counsellors who become commentators are all psychoanalytically orientated. Those who go to them are therefore likely to need that form of assistance. Second, this group—who form the raw material of their books—are a tiny fraction of the whole. Far the largest majority of breaking or divorcing couples see nobody (in Britain in 1970 3 per cent of married couples saw a counsellor). Finally, the companionate marriage developments which have thrown the weight on to personalities of those involved have grown over the last 100 to 200 years; the divorce phenomenon has developed over the last thirty years. The supposition must be, then, that over the whole area of Western culture married couples have suddenly become ten or twenty times as neurotic in thirty years—which is absurd. Or if you don't think it absurd (any argument is advanceable in this field) then you must explain why; and that is likely to lead you back into the stresses which arise from the very factors we have discussed.

There is a final peculiarity. Except perhaps for romantic love, which is almost entirely disruptive, most of these complex changes and developments are like various different beams of light illuminating and bringing into prominence different areas of our development and of our lives together. Each of these areas is, potentially at least, capable of becoming more fruitful under these powerful but differently directed beams: not just women's lives but their marriages can be more satisfactory if they have rewarding work lives; many men enjoy looking after children, the children enjoy it too, the mothers are freer; to enjoy sex together for years after you are fifty is to continue a self-evident pleasure; or if you are happy with someone, then fifty years together is to be preferred to twenty.

But what if you are not happy, or don't like sleeping with your partner any more, or resent your wife working? The peculiarity I want to suggest, to elaborate the metaphor somewhat, is that all these beams of light, although directed upon very different subjects and situations, also, at the same time, shine together on a single area which oddly enough they all have in common. This area, a central one, is that of marriage-for-life as the only way, or best way, of people to live together. The beams over some decades have gradually been converging on this vital place until, during the last thirty years, they have been shining in the *same* direction. They converged until they were parallel with one another, they joined to become one massive shaft of light, a laser beam, not just light but a power, a force—and under this intense force, the great once-solid globe of marriage began to seeth, the myriads of couples composing it writhing and ever more rapidly changing position, huge chunks half breaking away; it even looked, it now looks, as if the globe may split asunder.

9

DIVORCE—FIRST WAVE REACTION—THE PATTERN OF PAIN

Sir, it is so far from being natural for a man and woman to live in a state of marriage, that we find all the motives that they have for remaining in that connection, and the restraints which civilised society imposes to prevent separation, are hardly sufficient to keep them together.

Dr Johnson

In Britain and in America, it is now relatively easy to get a divorce, usually after periods of from six months to two years. 'Marriage breakdown' is the most common reason. This general picture is approximately true, excluding some Catholic countries, for the whole 'Western' culture group with which we are concerned.

As for the statistics, there are only a few certainties that can be glimpsed in those dense and gloomy thickets. (For both the law and statistics see Appendix G.)

Divorce has been increasing swiftly and steadily all over the Western world since the Second World War. It was up three times in Britain between 1965 and 1975, up two and a half times in America over the same period. The current projections are that for those under forty-five who get married, in America one third will divorce, in Britain one quarter. Everyone expects these fig-

ures to start levelling off some time. They show no signs of doing
so. A second clear pattern is that the younger people marry the
more likely they are to get divorced; most marriages break down
in the first few years and probably something like a third start
doing so in the first year. There is always a considerable interval
between a couple separating and the actual legal divorce—anything between two and five years. So though I shall for clarity
usually refer to the 'divorced', I shall quite often also be talking
about those who are technically only 'separated'.

Those are really the only clear patterns it is possible to find in
divorce statistics. There are a good many patterns which *don't*
exist, but which commentators somehow manage to find. One of
these is the mid-life peak, with more divorce after fifteen or
twenty years of marriage. There is absolutely no evidence, as far
as the general figures go, that this is so.

I think a good many commentators *want* to find a mid-life peak.
It fits in with flights of (often plausible) speculation. The Rapoports conjure with a sort of tuning fork effect: adolescents in a las-
civious fever of romantic love experiment, the middle-aged couple slowly starting to vibrate in envious sympathy. Also,
commentators on divorce are Privilege Bulge to a man and
woman. They like to think that they and their Bulge companions
are reaching fresh stores of energy, ready to set out anew. Privilege Bulge aspirations are a powerful reason why divorce among
people of that age has kept up with the general rise. But there is
no good evidence of a peak here.

Yet, surprisingly, at the eye of the storm itself, the one area
where you might think there was no clear picture—the place
which to those pitchforked into it often seems without landmarks
or boundaries, uncharted, a place of total chaos—there are in fact
quite definite patterns which can be foreseen and roughly timed.
But to understand these we have above all to know what divorce
feels like, because it is this which underlies everything that happens.

1   *Divorce—the modern death*

Strangely enough, for some categories of people divorce feels like nothing at all. There are those who divorced very early, very young and having no children—splitting up after a few months of marriage because they became bored or fell in love with someone else or realised they'd made a 'mistake'. By the time they reach their late twenties they cannot even remember the faces of the people they once slept with. These are not marriages in any real sense of the word, but affairs upon which romantic love tossed, like garlands, a few vows—they are really the experimental marriages advocated in the 1920s by Bertrand Russell and others.

Oddly enough, painless divorce can take place in marriages that have lasted forty or fifty years. Here the couple have started leading rather separate lives in their forties and then, over the years, separate more and more, until almost without noticing they find they have gently glided apart.

Mrs June Croxley of Dorking: 'We had been married for 35 years. Then we decided to have our holidays apart. I went on a pilgrimage to Lourdes and my husband took a tour of the Soviet Union. We enjoyed being apart so much that now we are divorced.'

Between these two poles there is sometimes, rather rarely, pure manic elation and delight. Physical ailments vanish almost on the instant: a woman of fifty stopped vomiting, a man who had had difficulty urinating through tension and fury recovered the joyous flow of a boy. Another man, after talking all night, found 'that for weeks I luxuriated in the feeling of being alive again'. A woman of forty-five sold her house, bought masses of clothes, and flew to see her daughter in Australia in a single ecstatic fortnight.

These, however, are infrequent exceptions. Those who think divorce is some modern form of irresponsible pleasure-seeking have not listened to or experienced the suffering which leads people to take this step; nor—even more germane—experienced or been close to the suffering that enormous step almost invariably entails.

Those terrible cries of pain which rip through our late twentieth-century prose and distort the faces on our screens—the furious hostility of the final bust-ups, drunk, ending in casualty wards; or without rows, in taut despair, dammed feelings coming out in insomnia, nausea, migraines, starvation; it seems likely that some of these pains of divorce have a physical cause, a physical base.

Over the years, the subtle and continuous interaction between a couple alters the chemical structure of the brain; both chemical reactions and electrical patterns are set up which depend on, respond to, the other, and which correspond to the myriad responses between them. This process is automatic and applies to all associations, but the longer the association, the deeper the involvement and interaction, the longer-lasting and more extensive it will be.

This idea of a marriage having created a physical structure in the brain, a pattern of itself in the language of the cells—of whatever permanence—cannot be proved, as far as I know. Neurosurgery, research into the structure and behaviour of the brain is still relatively crude. But it is a concept which, even if only metaphorical, helps to explain a number of things. If something of the sort takes place it would help to explain a phenomenon noticed by American sociologist Jessie Barnard, that the greater the number of specialised roles a man or a woman had in a marriage, the greater the disturbance at separation. A wife who is a mother doesn't just miss her husband's approval, she will specifically miss his immediate approval of her when she's handling the children well; or he will miss his role of handyman to feminine appliances. Functions, actual areas of the brain have been disturbed and broken. It would help to explain the peculiar and devastating quality of the loneliness ensuing upon divorce—that quality of amputation, of having been ripped apart, of internal bleeding.

This physical aspect is nearly always an ingredient, no matter what the confusion and mixture of reactions. As the thirty-two-year-old wife of a banker said: 'When he first left, I felt a rather cautious exhilaration. I kept saying to myself, "I'm free". But at the same time, and increasingly, I felt a heaviness, an emptiness, that came over me like an actual pain. I remember realising one day that it was like an invisible sobbing, underneath, inside my chest. Or sometimes after a spell of feeling gay I would for no reason feel like a balloon with a pinprick, and the air very slowly seeping out.'

Even though one partner initiates the parting—and feels completely justified—both feel rejected, feel guilty, feel they have failed. A woman may be frigid and a husband want to leave, but he feels her lack of response was because she disliked him, found him disgusting. The man depends on her, won't support her—she knows she wanted to dominate him, to have him as her child.

This is compounded by the acute almost physical pain the ripping apart can cause, which attacks those leaving and being left indiscriminately and automatically. A woman medical technician finally, and after planning it, separated from a chronically unfaithful husband after fourteen years.

> I felt worthless, no good, unwanted, rejected, failed. I was in a state of complete and devastating depression. Driving a car, I would often forget where I was, and where I was going. It was terrifying. I had my first accident, and got my first speeding ticket. I also had a severe rash on my wrist that doctors couldn't clear up for months.

As many studies have shown, people *don't know this will happen. It is completely unexpected.* One showed that even those marriages which went through a series of worsening crises, with separations—as it were practising divorce—never found that it in the least prepared them adequately for what was to come. In the study by Hart, Lecturer in Sociology at Salford University, 17 per cent had anticipated and then initiated the parting (a further 33 per cent had forced their partner to leave, which comes to the same thing). They all found the reality was totally different, far more devastating than what they had imagined. And if for them, how much worse was it (and it *is* worse) for those who did not expect it. 'I never dreamt it would happen to me.'

There are what one might call technical aspects of this pain which sociologists tend to spend time on because they can be split up and (apparently) measured. These are usually rather obvious. In the loneliness that descends, there are class differences. The lower classes tend to have independent networks of friends—pub/work or kin/next-door-neighbour—and these can continue to operate after the separation. The middle classes work as a couple, and friend networks can collapse, particularly for the wife. However, among the middle classes the wife can go back to her family; while the husband often can't because of his job. Conversely, the lower-class man can go home to his mother; his wife can't because of the children. Long marriages, unless they have reached the gliding apart stage, where the shared memories, the friends in common and so on have gathered and gathered, these can be the worst to break.

Above all it is the terrible desolation of parting, the texture of loneliness, that—in Hart for instance—suddenly leaps from the dull pages of obvious and unilluminating sociologists' analysis. That sense of being completely alone, no one in the house. 'Nobody in the world to share my worries with.'

Our perception of ourselves is often so bound up with our partner that when he or she goes we can for a while lose all sense of identity, and with that our sense of reality itself. It is a state that sociologists call 'anomie'.

> It was the most ghastly thing that ever happened to me in all of my life. I went upstairs and I was putting the blankets on the cot. It was a yellow cellular blanket, I can see it now, and I was just tucking it inside and I stood there and thought 'I don't know how to tuck in this blanket; how on earth am I going to make this cot?' And I stood up and I looked round the bedroom and I thought, 'My God, however do I get through the days? However do I get my work done?' I had forgotten how to do everything; I felt as though someone had put a glass tube all round me and I was on the inside, and everyone else was outside and far away. And I could not

get to anyone, I was just shut away and I couldn't do a single thing like making a cot. I had forgotten how just to sort of function. I had lost all pattern of all that I could remember and I did not know how to do anything. It was really weird.

Said a man of forty-five:

You had this awful feeling that you were in another world, and you could see yourself and hear your voice from over there [gesturing]. Well I thought I was going round the bend. Everything was slightly unreal, and it made me feel afraid; there was nothing familiar. I felt a complete lack of security. There was nothing familiar to cling on to. I'd be sitting up there in the crane, and suddenly I would burst into tears. . . .

Those who have not experienced or been close to divorce might suppose this was exaggerated or at least, exceptional; that those who suffer in this way might well be expected to commit suicide. Of course, every degree of pain and unhappiness is found, from none to a great deal; but in fact such experiences are neither extreme nor uncommon—and suicide is precisely what you do find. Exact figures are difficult to pin down. One study found that in America the suicide rate among divorced women is three times, among men four times, higher than among their married opposites. I suspect it is often higher; this is likely in Britain at least, where the suicide rates can rise as high as ten times that for the married rate at certain periods. Divorce resembles a curious kind of artificial death which we have decided to impose on ourselves in other ways. The figures for mortality show this. (See Appendix G.)

The pain of divorce underlies all other reactions, which are often caused by it, or become themselves constituents of it. The shock of divorce nearly always reduces sexual desire or removes it altogether for several months: men are impotent more often; women find orgasm much harder or impossible. All this in itself is painful and upsetting. There is also the self-disapproval which

often accompanies divorce, itself a product of social disapproval—the so-called stigma of divorce.

2   Shame—the stigma of divorce

It will never be possible to remove some sense of failure at divorce since it is true—both parties have, at some personal level,
failed. But there is no necessary shame in failure. Failure is a normal part of growth and change. If you fail a driving test, it can
depress you, but you don't feel *shame*. You try again. Equally, to
fail at something very difficult—the ascent of Everest—is disap-
pointing. It is not shaming.

A failed marriage is not a lost driving test, nor is it (quite) a
failed assault on Everest. We are a success-orientated culture and
there will probably always be *some* sense of shame at our failure.
But the shame at divorce is often out of all proportion. And unnecessary social shame can add enormously to difficult situations.

All the same, if our marriage customs now are breaking some
universally valid anthropological pattern then at least the shame
has a sound base. It is a sensible reaction. The family does quite
often break down—in war or famine or revolution—but 'so far',
wrote Margaret Mead, 'in all known history human societies have
always re-established the forms they temporarily lost'. The only
constant in this universal 'family pattern' is that the men support
and protect and feed the females and their young. However, the
forms which this can take are so enormously varied that they embrace without difficulty the Western divorced pattern, and any
exaggeration of it one cares to imagine. In the Trobriand Islands
each man fills the yam house of his sister, not his wife. On the Island of Mentaric the mother's father adopts her children and his
sons feed them. Our adaptation—where the divorced husband
does not see his wife, sees his children at stated times, but supports them or helps to with the next husband—seems comparatively uneccentric. The new pattern breaks no anthropological
rule.

The stigma of divorce derives from unnecessary (anthropologically speaking) fear that the family as an institution is being threatened and from nineteenth/twentieth-century religious condemnation (the Church of England still refuses to marry a divorced person, though you can take elaborate vows and hear elaborate blessings which sound almost indistinguishable). The stigma has diminished, and will do so further, to an appreciable if immeasurable degree. The *McCalls* survey found 19 per cent had divorced and accepted it as completely necessary. I discussed this with an American sociologist, now married for the third time, who said he could admit to his two other wives without shame. To get a proper idea of what it can be like to divorce, it is important to emphasise how slow the diminution is, how frequently disguised, how tangible the stigma, particularly in Britain.

Take two views: that the divorced are not sinners, but those who have made a bad mistake, are suffering and deserve pity; or, an orthodox psychoanalytic one, that divorce is a neurotic way out of a neurotic conflict. The first is modified stigma—the wicked are suffering, as they should; the liberal speaks not of their sin but of their pain. The second is the usual medical trick of turning sin into an illness, a form of condemnation. Bernard Berkowitz and Mildred Newman made the shrewd point that while fashion might dictate that homosexuality or divorce was 'all right', analysis still revealed strong guilt. It can even be revealed by simple conversation. I found later that the American sociologist had in fact had two further wives about whom he apparently hadn't quite felt able to talk.

In her study of divorces, Nicky Hart was frequently told of slights and insults. An electrician described being sacked. His boss 'said that, with all the financial burdens that I would have to face, he would not feel safe, leaving me with access to the till.' She thought these stories were exaggerated, paranoic revelations of guilt. But then she went with some of them to try and find a new club room. Eventually they got one in a pub. When it was all arranged, the publican asked 'What's it for?' She answered without thinking—a club for divorced and separated. At once he turned red and began to yammer about how he'd forgotten, in fact the room was already let. Nicky Hart was shocked at such blatant prejudice; but she was also shocked at herself—she suddenly, violently, wanted to dissociate herself from the label, from her new friends. Outside, no one was surprised: 'That sort of thing happens all the time.'

The stigma reveals itself in all sorts of hidden ways, some no less humiliating because there are elements of truth in them. Where separated men are supposed to be having masses of sex, divorced women are supposed to be desperate for it and are persecuted. 'I was shocked,' said one woman, 'and very angry at the men who immediately made passes at me—colleagues, my neighbours, mostly married men; they were crude enough to assume that I'd be glad to take whatever I could get.'

Married friends tend to drop away. One reason they give, disguised stigma, is that the children are unruly because the mother can't control them, which is somehow part of her selfishness in breaking up the marriage and not sticking it out.

Hart had several among her rather lower economic status, depressed and depressing sample who were so anxious about their parents' shocked reaction that by fantastic tales and mechanisms 'scarcely credible' they pretended, often for years, they were still together. Their anxiety was justified. She had some whose parents were so ashamed they refused to see them. One woman hadn't seen her parents for two years. At the moment they most need love, support, advice and approval, when they are already shattered by loneliness, the divorced and separated sometimes find themselves deprived of the most important source of all—the family they were born into.

Social shame will clearly differ enormously. It is probably greatest among the lower middle class, though nowhere is it totally absent (not even, though it may be repressed, within the divorced themselves). It complicates and intensifies the many practical difficulties of divorce. It can even cause them hardship, as with the dehumanising and often insulting processes of social security in Britain, or the different way the state treats divorced people compared to those widowed.

3 *'How long will it take? When will I recover?'*
                              Divorced woman, thirty-nine. Interview

Some people can't divorce emotionally. That structure in the head, if it exists, is indestructible. They never separate, however far apart they may be physically, however deeply or how often their former partner may have remarried. But—except for the gliders-apart—the emotional, psychological separation is always far harder and takes far longer than anyone getting divorced conceives possible.

The older the couple, the longer the marriage, the less expected the divorce, the harder it is. In Hart's sample, some of these didn't believe their spouses had gone. They reported them to the police as accident victims or missing persons. Thereafter, some of them simply went on thinking of themselves as married. Two of the women in her sample had even bought new wedding rings. One had lost hers when she'd flung it at her husband in a row; the other when her husband, in the closing period of their married life, had pawned it and put the proceeds on a horse.

The refusal to accept reality at all is rare, but the persistence of hope, and after hope involvement and commitment at some level, and after involvement then the presence, suddenly revealed, of strong emotion—all this lasting for many years, is very common. One man after six years still 'vaguely hopeful'. Stanley Spencer's marriage to Hilda Carline, whom he fell in love with in 1919, was the central event of his life. They married in 1925 and were divorced twelve years later; yet their marriage really lasted until they died, she in 1950, he in 1959. On the very first night of his new marriage to Patricia Preece, Stanley in fact slept with Hilda; and thereafter he saw her, thought about her and pursued her continually. He was the last person to see her alive in hospital in 1950, and when she died he 'talked about her as if she were still alive'. His flow of love letters to her continued until his own death nine years later.

Six years after the rupture with his wife, Bertrand Russell suddenly saw her in the street outside Covent Garden. 'Our eyes met before I knew she was there. She has a terrible hold over me still.

Her power of making me suffer irritates me against her, but it persists all the same. There is something that never dies if one has cared deeply for a person. . . .'

It is this sort of thing—continuing sorrow, pity, worry about ex-husbands and wives, suddenly dreaming about them, the surprise recrudescence of strong feeling—that reveals the continuing existence, deeply buried, of the emotional bond.

> A note of congratulation to him and his new wife came to me by mistake—that's how I learnt he had remarried. I felt great anger, and was sick clear to my soul. Yet as far as I knew I had had no intention or even the slightest wish to go back to him after what had happened between us.

Another pattern is that of spasms—oscillating between love and hate, with efforts at reconciliation, followed by furious leave takings. These can involve sudden surges of desire, of passion even, and then, after a short period, realising nothing has changed, the couple sadly part again. An odd phenomenon here is that the pattern of events which occurred over years, through which they have slowly worked their way, now plays itself out at high speed—taking a week or just a few days.

These spasms, too, can continue for years. Hunt describes a wife, long remarried, who is the one her alcoholic ex-husband calls on in extremes—and how she creeps out to feed him, and tidy his disordered and stinking room. Several unremarried women told me they called on their ex-husbands for help, often because, in our still male-dominated society, they needed help getting credit or some such service; sometimes because they were anxious about the emotional life of their children.

With children there enters another of the decisive elements in divorce. Children many times intensify the emotional difficulty of divorce. They provide, particularly for the partner who least wanted to break, the excuse for endless ringing up with small questions or details relayed. It isn't always an excuse; the children need their help, both want to give it. The parents communicate through the children; they collect (fairly crudely sometimes) information about the other's love-life or expenditure. With many couples the man or the woman are prevented from forming deep attachments because they are trying to preserve a sort of psychic family round their children. Nell Dunn, in her excellent study of alternative life-styles, found that two of the lesbian couples she talked to had turned to bisexuality in order to keep intact their emotional tie with their divorced or split husbands. In so far as both parents want to co-operate in supporting their children, and to the degree that children need their parents all their lives, a marriage which has produced a child never ends.

Even without children, this untangling, this destruction of the structure in the head takes anything from one to fifteen years. But it always takes longer than the divorced imagines, and strong emotional ties are usually there buried long after they seem to have gone.

'One can't,' wrote Bertrand Russell, 'transfer love to another person as if it were a piece of luggage to be taken from one train to another. It takes me nine years to recover the freshness of feeling that is wanted for love.' (It is interesting, incidentally, that it takes nine years for the death rate of widowed men to return to that of their married opposites.) In fact, as Hunt notes, there are people who do treat their love as luggage. Unable to take the loneliness, the anguish, they rush into a new relationship at once, often waiting till it is set up before leaving—'chain lovers' who light the tip of the new from the embers of the old before stamping it out. The two to five-year gap between separation and divorce is not primarily a legal gap, though of course legal quibbles and discussions are often its substance. It is largely a result of the reactions we have been looking at. That is its significance.

Some couples start back in horror at the suffering opening up before them, and turn to reconciliation. One quarter of all divorces filed are withdrawn. Of those who go through with it, one out of ten would remarry their ex-spouse (if they have not already remarried); one out of fifteen do so, having been apart an average of three years. Perhaps they should not; it is not easy to rebuild that half-destroyed structure. Hunt quotes a study by Dr Paul Popenoe of two hundred such marriages; he found less than 50 per cent were happy. (But how many marriages are happy? Oddly enough, I can find no statistic.)

4   *'Divorce is marriage carried on by other means, with a bond of hostility replacing the erotic bond'*
Psychiatrist talking to Brenda Maddox

People who study divorce often notice how initially the partners about to separate will feel and express affection, will plan to act 'reasonably'. But gradually, as they plunge deeper, rage, resentment and hate boil to the surface.

In each divorce each partner is part rejected, part rejector. Each is bound by remorse, pain, and residual love. Anger and cruelty set them free from these bonds: force their spouse to leave them, consume the stubborn stumps of their love, make guilt vanish. Hunt describes a young woman who'd never committed a crime in her life, even at school, who suddenly telephoned her husband's stockbroker when her husband, from whom she had been informally separated for some time, was out of town. She ordered the entire portfolio to be sold at once and the cheque to be sent to her. She then put the money—all their savings—into a secret account. One girl described how, just before they separated, she had gone with her husband, and rather in the spirit of the couple who have a baby in a desperate attempt to save a marriage, bought a new three-piece suite. One evening she'd come back to the flat to find her husband had been in and emptied fifteen tins of treacle over it.

The man, guilty at leaving his wife for another woman, is so furious at her outrageous financial demands he has no other feeling. A woman, still in love with her husband, is revolted at his stinginess over child support, the way he never sees his son, and is glad to be rid of him. Anger fuels these reactions, and from anger grows hate.

If unresolved, hate can go on for years—the obverse of love, evidence of the inability to break away. Here is a salesman still grinding his teeth after seven years: 'I hate her more than ever now, because what with maintenance and child support I can't lead a decent life. Meanwhile she's screwing around having a fine time, on my money. She's a leech. She's living off me and enjoying it all the more because it makes my life miserable.'

On the whole, rage and hatred do usually achieve their object. They last longest in those who have not remarried and those forced into the divorce. For the rest, passions gradually become calmer over the first three years. Some ex-husbands and wives, or long-standing ex-lovers, even become close platonic friends. This is rather rare, however, and, apart from understanding and secure new partners, can only happen, in my view, when both have become strongly involved with someone else.

Hate—or at least anger—also helps rehabilitation. Nothing binds the new couple like a common enemy, and soon, myths created together in long talks at night, wild figures stalk the joint memories of each other's past: 'She was hallucinating; they lived in filth.' 'He was alcoholic, out of the picture for long stretches.' 'She was into Women's Lib and deteriorating rapidly.' It is the desire to preserve the common enemy as long as possible with these accretions, as much as it is fear, that stops people meeting their ex-partner. A common extension of this is that people re-write the entire history of their marriages to justify what they have been through. 'We were never really happy,' said a woman who had been married ten years. They are sad, often, these bonfires of the past—holidays, children, Christmases, memories of making love, marriages which were, as you probe, clearly for many years happy enough; it is sad to see it all consumed as you might see a photograph album burnt up.

Sociologists can make the whole subject of divorce and separation oddly unreal, even the practical side which is that most amenable to their discipline. The aim of sociology is to extract facts about social behaviour and generalise from them. Facts about people. People are facts—and so they are dehumanised; the people in the case histories have hair without colour or length, their faces have no features, their voices no accent or tone. I would read an account, endless accounts, of these creatures unstirred, almost unnoticing, until suddenly, by a sort of double-take, a human being would frantically signal to me, trying to escape the bleak statement of 'fact'. Take Nicky Hart's Mrs Murphy, married twenty-four years, aged fifty, who'd given rather a vague account of her husband's leaving (he had a 'fiery love affair' with a publican's wife, then 'lit off' for Malta on his own). 'She was', went on Nicky Hart, 'evicted from her house and spent four months living in a Jaguar motor car with three dependent children until, at the point where her children had to be taken into care, she managed to find her present house. By this time . . .' At which point, comprehension following a little behind the eye, I thought—*four months in a Jaguar motor car with three dependent children!* The cooking, the washing, the sleeping . . .

It is not really possible to separate the practical from the emotional, any more than separating the particular emotional strands alters the fact that they are all inextricably entwined in anyone going through this experience. But to do both is a way of bringing some rough order into a complex subject—and also reveals the underlying 'structure' of divorce. In the practical side of this structure, obviously enough (and yet often unexpected), the first and indeed overwhelming factor is always, as in the vignette above, money.

5 *'I don't like money but it calms my nerves.'*

Joe Louis

All matters of the heart cost money. Marriage does. Affairs do. Divorce costs most of all.

The basic situation is obvious—two households, and possibly after a time two families, have to live on the same income which supported one. The most general, most concrete and one of the most painful results of divorce is an immediate crash in the standard of living.

This is particularly true of the middle classes. The bottom economic stratum, the lowest paid, simply exchange one form of poverty for another (though some of the poorer middle class at once enter this stratum). As far as the middle and lower middle classes go, the two issues are property and maintenance.

The principles of English law, as set out in The Matrimonial Proceedings and Property Act of 1971, provide for a fair division of conjugal property on the basis of equality. In practice this means more or less what it says, property is divided 50–50. If there is only one small house, and it is awarded to the wife because she has custody of the children, then her maintenance will be drastically reduced to compensate the husband. If it is a valuable house, then it will be sold and the money shared. As regards maintenance, the formula is that the wife's income must be brought to reach one-third of their joint income. Thus, if a man earned £5,000 ($12,000) and his wife nothing, he would pay her £1,666 ($3,998.40); if she earned £1,000 ($2,400) a year, he would pay her £1,000 (maintenance is allowed as a charge against income tax). If a wife remarries, her personal maintenance stops; maintenance for the children usually continues until they are seventeen. If she does not remarry, maintenance can continue for life. If a man has several ex-wives, he must support them all, but the one-third rule will not apply, and each will get gradually less as more of them accumulate. The law allows for wealthy women to maintain their ex-husbands, but it is very rare in Britain and rare in America and need not really enter the discussion. (In Russia, on the other hand, it is not unusual.)

In America, the situation as regards property is complicated by differences in individual states. Most divide more or less on the lines of equality. California for instance shares 50–50. (But 'marital property' definitions differ from state to state.) In five states, however, the law is still biased against women. In New York, for example, a property is not shared. It belongs to the person whose name it is in, and this is usually the man. (It is likely these state laws will change fairly soon.)

As far as maintenance goes, or alimony, the situation is roughly what it is in Britain, with the following differences: there are no formal rules as to percentage amount and the law is more flexible. Women under fifty, with no children and who have job skills, are getting smaller and smaller alimony; older women, unskilled and long out of the job market, still get support. In some states, long-term cohabitation as well as remarriage ends personal alimony. As regards tax, personal alimony is deductible by the payer and is included in the income of the receiver. Neither of these applies to child support.

Whether or not this situation is unfair to either sex it contains a good deal of prejudice. For instance, it is supposed in Britain that men can endlessly harass their wives by not paying maintenance. It takes three weeks to get a court order to pay, and at any point the husband can pay the arrears and nullify the proceedings; meanwhile the wife has had financial embarrassment and humiliation. In fact the Finer Commission, in their masterly and much neglected Report on One-Parent Families in Britain, showed quite clearly that the vast majority of men don't pay, not because they won't, but because they can't. 'Neither in the divorce court, nor in the magistrate's court . . . has the law found the method of extracting more than a pint from a pint pot,' said the Report. Those who can and won't are made to. Every year magistrates threaten about 3,000 men with prison for not paying their wives. Ninety per cent pay up.

And there are, of course, areas of unfairness. At a certain medium low level on the economic scale, men suffer most, sometimes appallingly. Nicky Hart says they gain most from marriage and therefore lose most. They lose the services of an unpaid housekeeper. It is not this exactly (I never understand that 'unpaid housekeeper'. In what sense unpaid?). Council house tenants in Britain splitting up are not entitled to two council flats (or cannot afford two flats on the open market). The local authority usually transfers the tenancy to the one with custody and evicts the other. Nine times out of ten, the father is kicked out. The same is true of low-income housing in the U.S.

Consider the case of Mr Edwards, one of Nicky Hart's most

harrowing tales. Mr Edwards, in his early fifties, had a safe job as a mechanic, a wife who worked part-time, two adult sons at home, and a house free of debt upon which 'he had lavished decades of do-it-yourself improvements'. One evening he returned home drunk and was flung out of the house by his angry wife. He spent the night in the local doss house. Next day he returned, but there were police to stop him getting in. The doss house became his more or less permanent home. Now his life became like a nightmare. His wife obtained court orders for legal separation and banning him from the house (he assumed 'she'd made up a cock and bull story about me for the police'). Mr Edwards shared a room with three other men, usually tramps. His clothes were stolen as he slept. He was soon reduced to one jumper and one pair of socks which he had to wash repeatedly in a cleaner's bucket. There was nowhere to sit. The meals were terrible—'Two fish fingers, six chips, eight peas!' The price for this farcical domestic life was £9 ($21.60) per week. He had to pay £3 ($7.20) a week to his wife, plus all her fuel bills, rate bills, light bills. He worked as a decorator in his spare time to meet these endless costs. Friends said go to the law, but Mr Edwards felt hopeless and also felt a sense of poverty and weakness in the face of the bureaucratic machine. He had plunged in a year from comfort to the depths of the transient homeless and most poverty-stricken of all, with nothing to look forward to but a life of endless work to support a wife who had secured all the marriage assets, including the car. There remained only beer, which understandably had become a source of comfort.

In America there are state pockets of injustice, usually biased against women. In New York, for instance, a wife guilty of a 'fault'—even if her husband is too—can be denied all support. The New York property situation is unjust.

It does seem quite absurd that in England a man should have to continue supporting an ex-wife *for life* unless she remarries. Men feel, with justice, that it's like compelling an ex-wife, by law, to cook, shop and love him years and years after the marriage is dead.

There should be reform here. Personal maintenance to wives under a certain age—say forty—should be reduced after a certain time—say four years—to an agreed minimum; perhaps to the difference between a woman's average salary or pay packet and a man's in the husband's or wife's profession. That is, Britain should adopt the same flexibility as America.

Actually, these inequities amount to a very small proportion of the mass of divorces, and in any case most of them get sorted out. Money—due to simple and obvious association and observation from childhood up—means love. But as we have seen, it is the storms of love and hate which dominate the first period of divorce. As these tempests die away it becomes possible to behave fairly. Many people can from the start. A survey by Mervyn Merch of Bristol University, showed that most divorces were settled amicably at the beginning. And most people remarry—something like 80 per cent in the end, and of the remainder an unknown proportion set up in liaisons of one sort or another. In the end the financial burdens of an ex-husband, or financial exigences of an ex-wife, are relieved by a new husband, and though both husbands may be supporting absent children slightly more expensively than they would if they had them under their own roof, they won't have more children than they would have done anyway. For most people, the crash in the standard of living does not last for ever.

There are always cases of financial unfairness, and they will usually be unfair to women. Since men have the money, it could hardly be the other way round. But women have the children. People who complain that the major unfairness in divorce is the number of women who don't get enough money, or, conversely, the appalling amount of money men have to shell out, simply reveal their scale of values. The central and most biting injustice in divorce today over all the West, from Oslo to Los Angeles, from Edinburgh to Sydney—and one about which, for some extraordinary reason, absolutely nothing is done—concerns children. And since it is the children who suffer as much as anyone, it is worth approaching the problem through them.

6   *'Oh my son Absalom, my son, my son Absalom! Would God I*
     had died for thee, O Absalom, my son, my son!'
                         David's lament for his son Absalom
                         who had rebelled against him and been
                         executed contrary to his wishes

There is a myth that we are a child-centred society. There is
truth in it, of course, but it is really based on the hope of realising
something which is seen as valuable, but which cannot be sustained because it conflicts with something now seen as more valuable—the self-realisation of the parents. Society often says it is
doing one thing to hide from itself the fact it is doing the opposite.
It will come as no surprise to learn that people no longer stay together, as they did at one time, because they have children. Indeed, in America and Britain far more divorces involve children
than don't. (See Appendix G.) The same pattern is found in Australia, West Germany, France, Austria, Scandinavia and Japan.

It is not all that easy to find out about the effect divorce has on
children. Because the phenomenon on this scale is relatively new,
there are not many really long-term studies. Hunt quotes a disturbing study by R. E. Baber in 1956 which showed that far more
delinquents—80 per cent—came from broken homes. And this
was confirmed by a very long-term study of 1,333 such children in
Sweden from 1921 to 1949. This found that four times as many
boys and three times as many girls had to go to reform schools; 20
per cent of the men would have been convicted of a felony by the
age of fifty (compared to 9.9 per cent in the rest of the population); and alcoholism was three times higher among women than
in the rest of Sweden.

In America, though, it was felt that poverty was to blame for
delinquency almost as much as divorce, which it probably caused
as well. American sociologists Eleanor and Sheldon Glueck compared delinquency rates from broken homes with those from intact homes at the same economic level. They found it was true
that a slightly larger proportion of delinquents came from broken
homes, but that, on a closer look, even within the same economic

group these homes were poorer. They also found it impossible to isolate the various factors. The tensions, rows and instability which led to divorce may have caused the delinquent reaction, not the physical break itself (indeed the break may have lessened these effects). Hunt also quotes a massive survey in 1964 by Professor Burchinal of Iowa State University comparing seventh grade and eleventh grade students, half from divorced and half from intact homes. He could find virtually no difference between them.

The most interesting study comes from Sweden. G. Jonsson, studying a large group of boys from divorced homes with those from intact homes in 1967, also found that delinquent children were more likely to come from the divorced homes (42 per cent compared with 13 per cent). However, when he compared the later adjustment of children from divorced homes who were not delinquent to those from intact homes, he found no difference at all. Jonsson now looked closely at his sample and was able to isolate a convincing crucial factor. He found that what counted was the stability and care devoted to reconstruction after the divorce. In particular it was continual visiting by the father and good relations with the stepfather that were important. Where there were no visits, or few from the father, and if, where there was a stepfather, relations with him were bad, then, if either of these situations existed, there was a high incidence of upset and delinquent children.

Research seems quite unequivocal, also, that a tense intact home with conflict between the parents is worse for children than one where the parents are divorced. Hunt quotes studies by Dr Louise Despart, the distinguished American psychiatrist, and F. Iran Nye, author of *Family Relationships and Delinquent Behaviour*, in 1960. Professor W. J. Goode, of the Department of Sociology of Columbia University, found the same thing.

I would conclude, therefore, three things: (1) A 'bad' after-divorce is severely upsetting. (2) A 'good' after-divorce has no serious long-term effects. (3) The effects of a conflict-filled home are worse than a good divorce. Now this is reassuring. No doubt many, probably most divorces are, after initial difficulties, 'good' ones.

Unfortunately, there are bleaker sides to the picture. It is not easy to organise a 'good' divorce. It requires tolerant and co-operative ex-wives and, where these exist, stepparents. Above all, it throws burdens on fathers, burdens of physical and emotional stamina which are often very large indeed. Some men don't bother. Statistics on this situation don't exist, but a number of men simply clear off out of indifference or for reasons of pain and rage. They may pay for, but they rarely see and offer no support for their children. There are many more who, in the ordinary course of events, would be perfectly adequate, even good fathers, but who cannot cope in what are supposed at the moment to be reasonable circumstances. There are other fathers in whose way, however great their stamina, are placed by wives or the law or both, intolerable obstacles.

There is no knowing how many divorces are not 'good'. It seems likely, though direct links would be hard to establish, that the general rise in juvenile delinquency all over the West has something to do with the general rise in divorce. We have seen that most studies find a connection between divorce and delinquency—the suggestion being it is 'bad' divorces that do harm. But of course delinquency is only an extreme expression of unhappiness, insecurity, resentment and lack of control. For every delinquent child there are probably many more suffering in a similar way who react differently or whose unhappiness is less intense. It is clearly often very difficult indeed for mothers in one-parent families. One researcher, D. Marsden, found that in one-third of one-parent families total anarchy reigned. One of the most horrifying figures from Britain—for children in care from these families—is the estimate from the National Council for One-Parent Families that anything from 50–75 per cent of children from these families are in care.

One thing is quite clear. In the initial stages, very many children, 'either witnesses', in the words of Dr Jack Dominian, of the Middlesex Hospital, London, 'or participants in some of the bitterest manifestations of human intolerance, anger, antagonism and hatred', suffer acutely. Symptoms of crying, tantrums, loss of school interest, regression, and bed-wetting are common. The parents may feel their home had been hate-filled and unhappy during marriage—and it may have been, for them. Not for the children. Research has shown that large numbers of them consider their homes were happy or very happy before divorce. In fact, children hate divorce. 'They simply yearn for their mother and father to get back together,' said a probation officer. 'And you have to tell them that it will never happen.' This painful longing lasts for years, for ever perhaps at some level, affecting rich and poor alike. *The Times* obituary of Alexander Onassis said that he and his sister Christina had 'always entertained hopes for a reunion between their parents, especially after their mother and her second husband were divorced last year'. Hunt is full—and here we approach the central injustice—of pathetic stories of children trying to draw their parents together. The five-year-old girl, whose father used to drop in on his way to work: 'Why do you have to go Daddy? To make money? I have money for you, from my savings bank.' And I noticed a phenomenon which I'd last discovered researching a book on nannies. There, the untimely ripping apart from much-loved figures often fixed the face of the nanny with great vividness at an extraordinarily early age. Here, it was details of the father's life with them before he left. A little boy, three at the time, remembered his father's breakfasts—always grapefruit. A little girl, four-and-a-half at the break, could still, six years later, remember each detail of the morning routine: 'First he'd shave, then he'd give me breakfast, then he'd have breakfast, then he'd clean his teeth, then I'd clean my teeth, then he'd take me to nursery school, then he'd go to work.'

The great area of family change, a change reflected in the research, lies in the father looking after the children, and this increased desire to care is based on very powerful feelings. Parental love—mothers' and fathers'—is an *instinct*, triggered off by having physical contact with the helpless child *from the start*, an instinct which has an automatic and quite uncontrollable force and which brings into play every fibre of the being. Furthermore, it is one which elicits an equally profound instinctive response. The more and earlier a child is loved the more it loves; and in small children love means need. The few deeply loved figures in its life become the essential base and environment for growth and development.

How can a father who may have watched his child being born, who has shared with his wife the rising throughout the night to change and feed and quiet a crying baby, who has lived for some years the continuously active life of father-in-the-home, possibly transform, on the instant, into a visitor, seeing a son or daughter for a short time each week? What are children to make of it when this solid, loved figure—part of the air they breathed—vanishes, to reappear at infrequent, irrelevant intervals? The fact is, often neither can cope. What results are situations too well known to describe: fathers desperately spoiling their children with gifts, or awkward, the children shy, those uneasy knots in museums, zoos and parks—the most boring places in the world.

Here the law is not only no good, it often makes a concept, already inadequate, virtually unworkable. The 1973 Guardianship of Minors Act in Britain gave mothers and fathers equal rights over their children. But judges in Britain and all over the West, have at last, years late, become steeped in the wisdom of the 1950s, Bowlby *et al*: so far, nothing else has penetrated. Practically always, mothers are awarded custody. In Britain, in 1974, according to a study by Wolfson College, Oxford, fathers were given custody in 7 per cent of the cases, joint custody was awarded in 3 per cent, mothers gained custody in 76 per cent of the cases. The father's solicitors usually—and quite wrongly—advise him to accept this. Fathers are allowed 'access'. This is normally small, and differs widely depending on the judge. An example might be visits on alternate weekends, and three single weeks during the school holidays each year. This is quite good. Not unusual is two hours on alternate Saturdays, often on 'neutral' territory (like a police station. That is in case there is 'the other woman'; this frightful creature might be seen). The playwright

Terence Frisby went to the High Court to ask that his access—
one *afternoon* a fortnight—should be extended to one a week. The
judge turned the application down flat on the grounds, some mad
fragment of uncomprehended jargon floating into his head, that
he was 'in grave danger of becoming too possessive'. There are
cases of fathers being jailed for trying to see their children more
often than the pathetic allotment given by the Court. Custody to
the wife is often assumed to mean that the father is a 'bad' father.
Schools won't allow him any say and give no information. There
are cases where the wife has fallen ill and the children were
slapped into care without the local authorities even bothering to
inform the father, or seek his help—because he must be a 'bad' father.

This ludicrous situation is much exacerbated because, just as
men use maintenance to vent their rage and hate, women use
their children.

Here, the wife's technique on the telephone (the telephone is
the medium of middle-class divorce) is faultless:

> SHE: Well, I'd think you'd want your children to go to
> camp this summer for their health, if for no other
> reason.
> HE: But I can't afford it. I'm supporting all of you,
> and also living in a place of my own, and—
> SHE: Whose fault is that?
> HE: Look, let's not start that again. I—
> SHE: But you want to penalise your children for some-
> thing that isn't their fault.
> HE: I'm not penalising them, I just can't afford it!
> SHE: If you shout, I'm afraid I'll have to hang up. Can't
> you just talk calmly about this?
> HE: Oh God . . .

Far more terrible victories are won—terrible, because in the
end it is not just fathers who suffer, but the mothers as well, and
most of all the children. Some mothers cannot resist making their
children hate their father.

'By now my older boy—he's fifteen—won't talk to me at all,' says a forty-nine-year-old man. 'She's convinced him over the past five years that I am a thoroughly bad and selfish man. He feels I did her a rotten trick leaving her. He has no idea of my side of things, and I can't tell him because he just looks through me when I go there, and never talks to me. He hasn't even said hullo to me for the past year. I recently yelled at him and said he couldn't behave like that to his father, and he just walked out and slammed the door. I've pleaded with her to do something, but she just gives me that thin little puritan smile and says that if you sow the wind you reap the whirlwind.'

'Access' is most vulnerable to these expressions of rage. A man who lived in Exeter, his wife in Bromley, would drive 200 miles for his two hours every alternate Saturday, and his wife would say the children were out. She'd sent them to play with neighbours. There are wives who ring up half an hour before the visit and say the children are ill. Or else they just refuse to let the father in and flout the court order directly. The courts do not help. 'In the last resort,' says Sir George Baker, 'you can't enforce access. Prison does infinite harm.'

There is, perhaps inevitably, an added dimension to the loneliness of men who are separated and do not have their children—they are often *completely* alone. Women nearly always comment that their children, however exhausting, are a comfort. In this area of particular injustice, the reactions are far more desperate. In their rage and misery (apart from cutting off maintenance—their sole weapon) Western fathers are often reduced to kidnapping their children. In Denmark they often do this to look after them in secret just to force Bowlby-stuck judges to realise that fathers *can* look after children. In America the problem is made worse because states won't enforce custody, and there are a lot of successful interstate kidnappings. Children vanish from their mothers for ever—as Yoko Ono's child has done, sunk into the marsh of some hippy commune. This is simply the same injustice in reverse. Finally, fathers despair and are driven to suicide. (*Families Need Fathers*, a society in Britain, was founded especially to deal with this whole problem.) Where married men have the lowest rates of suicide, divorced men are at or near the highest. It is reasonable to suppose children are the significant differential factor.

Wives suffer. Children remain curious about their parents for ever, for they are a part of themselves. If they are made to hate one parent, they will frequently seek that parent later on, and discovering at times the complete falsity of the position they were trapped into adopting (because no divorce is black and white) will often abandon the one who forced them into it.

But above all it is the children who suffer. Babies and little children use their parents, of course, for a number of main developments: for the confidence and security to grow, for the love which leads to self-love and the future ability to love, for the construction of their own identity, for the way they will respond to the two sexes in later life. Two parents are not essential for these developments (mothers caring for children on their own are perfectly viable); but once the process has been started with two parents, then both are necessary—and necessary precisely to the degree they have become involved from the start and the length they have been engaged in it. If a father doesn't visit (or is not allowed to by a furious wife) there are various inevitable reactions. Either, 'I was so awful I drove Daddy away', or 'Daddy is so rich and grand he can't be bothered with the likes of me.' The construction of the self-image (and this applies to girls too—we are amalgams of both sexes), the view of future relationships with men and with authority figures—all this will be damaged and distorted. And children are torn beyond endurance by the conflicts and rows in the divorce (for which they may subconsciously well blame themselves) which are often behind the father's absence.

We have seen that the 'bad' divorce is the crucial issue in terms of children. This situation with the father—these distortions, this damage, these conflicts—*are* the bad divorce. That is why Dr Alick Elisthorne, head of psychological medicine at the Royal Free Hospital, can confirm the Swedish findings by evidence from British clinical experience: 'The destruction of the child's relationship with the father is the single most important cause of teenage delinquency.' And as this book goes to press a massive new survey by American social psychologists Judith S. Wallerstein and Joan Berlin Kelly, who traced the mangled lives of sixty-eight divorcing couples over five years, underlines exactly the same factor.

This is a fraught area. It is important to be absolutely clear. We are not concerned here with 'good' divorces—most of which have initiated their own version of the necessary reforms and behaviour. Nor do I deny that father deprivation is, in an unknown but not negligible number of cases, the fault of the father. Unfortunately, you cannot legislate for love (though personally I wouldn't be averse to penalties against fathers who wilfully neglect their children). Nor is the poverty and resulting distress of the lone mother on inadequate and irregular maintenance unimportant. But the proportion of poverty caused by divorce is an inevitable economic consequence. It is not, in *general*, due to the malice of fathers. Its only practical solution is increased, if temporary, state support. And the pain of poverty is not so profound or important as the pain of destroying the instinctive love of parent and child. That is why the central injustice in divorce today is that of depriving fathers and their children of each other.

This is an area where men should help themselves, and in fact in all the countries involved organisations have appeared that try and do this. On the whole, they seem, like *Families Need Fathers*, the main one in Britain, to be small and unable to do much more than give advice and moral support. Men seem to find it much harder to achieve things in these role-changing areas than women. They are seeking to take on tasks which convention says are 'feminine' and this inhibits concerted and effective male effort. People often see fathers engaged on such a task as virtually homosexual. Sheila Burns, who helps run *Families Need Fathers* with her husband in London, was lecturing about it. A young student got up, rather awkward, and asked 'Are these fathers—well—all right?' The same inhibition often seems to castrate the solutions they put forward.

In fact, it is quite clear what should be done. The law, or practice of the law, should be changed. The principle underlying the change should be that a child has an inalienable right to two parents, and that each parent has an equal right to see and have its child. Except in exceptional circumstances (violent father, baby-battering mother), custody, care and control should both be joint—each parent having and looking after their child for the same amount of time. That is the principle; the practical working out will have to be extremely flexible. There is no evidence at all, as Martin Richards of the Medical Psychology Unit at Cambridge University has pointed out, that a 'main home' is either necessary or best. It is just assumed. In fact, American experience shows that alternating custody is perfectly viable. But in practice the arrangements will be very varied. Clearly, small babies will have to be with their mothers far more. There will be mothers who want to work and let their ex-husbands bear the brunt of the children. Any combination conceivable. Once the *principle* of real equal rights is established, the injustices would disappear (and much reverse injustice—nonpayment of maintenance is often the result of fathers' rage at not seeing their children). 'Access' would no longer be the pitiful two-hour-a-fortnight often awarded now. It would be given automatically to either parent in order to preserve contact and reassurance when the other had the child for any considerable length of time. Finally, both access and custody/care-and-control would be enforceable at law. There is absolutely no reason why women should not be punished in exactly the same way as men. Even as the law stands now, the situation would be immediately and immeasurably transformed for the better if a few mothers were sent to prison for denying children and fathers access to each other.

These common-sense, indeed obvious, reforms may not be easy to accomplish. Apart from the inhibitions of men themselves, and the suspicions these arouse—are such men 'all right'?—violent attack will come from what one might call the Left, and from feminists. Sheila Burns works in a left-wing North London Poly, seething, as she put it, with women's liberation. Regarding Families Need Fathers as virtually a fascist organization, they seem quite unable to see it is the same struggle. It is not understood that both are trying to alter role attitudes—and therefore exploitation— from extremes towards a common centre, where men and women should be allowed equal rights. (In fact, I suspect that modern feminism is split between two positions. The first is that of role-swapping—sharing of household duties, both working. The second is that everything—custody, family allowances, legal rights—should be swung towards women. These can be held together technically, but they are really different. The first leads ultimately to improving marriage; the second to abolishing it.)

The position here is clear. You cannot compel love, and there will always be selfish men; but as well as being wantonly cruel and unjust, it also seems absurd not to give scope to love's fullest expression when women, especially in one-parent families, are desperate for help, children desperate to the point of delinquency for love, and hundreds of thousands of fathers desperate to give it.

6   '*If she's bossy, I'll divorce her.*'
                    Prep. school boy, aged eleven, to his mother

I remember, when I was twenty-five, an acquaintance Martha S. getting divorced. Her friend Sally W. was furious. 'She has no right to do that. It's quite monstrous.' I was astonished. 'Why shouldn't she? They don't get on at all, etc.' 'That's not the point. She's rocking the boat.' Sure enough, within the year, three more of that group—comprising what, twelve to fifteen couples—had started divorcing.

Divorce breeds divorce. Statistics make this quite clear. In Nicky Hart's sample of divorced couples, 13 per cent of their parents and parents-in-law had been divorced, as compared to a national average in 1950 of 7 per cent; 19 per cent of their brothers and sisters had been divorced, nearly double the crude national rate in 1960. National studies support this. In America the parents of nearly 2,000 students were studied by Judson T. Landis, of the University of California. If neither of the grandparents had divorced, the ratio of divorce to marriage was 1 to 6.8; if one set of grandparents had, the ratio was 1 to 4.8; while if both had, the ratio was only 1 to 2.6.

As Dr Gordon Ambrose's polymorph perverse showed, people repeat patterns that invite the very thing they fear. This begins in the cradle. A baby cries when its nappy is wet, not to be changed, but because it remembers and dreads the change. It would rather remain soggy and warm. It is crying because it knows that the terrible cold drying will soon happen—and, crying, brings about the very state it dreads. It will come as no surprise to learn that many children of divorced parents grow up dreading divorce, and are determined not to go through it themselves or inflict it on their children. This fear can be repressed and become the unconscious force which guides a person into the very situation he or she most wants to avoid.

All social movements are to some extent self-fuelling because children tend to imitate their parents and use them as models. This is particularly marked where the movement is concerned with anything that was once a taboo, or at least very strongly disapproved of. The disapproval of divorce—the stigma—was for years a major barrier. But it is not possible to disapprove of something all that strongly if your parents or brothers or sisters have done it. The family has in any case been tainted. And there are people near you who are able to give sympathetic and educated help in divorce.

You find the same sort of thing among certain criminals and suicides. The distinguished British historian, Peter Laslett, has put it forward with scholarly tentativeness as a way of explaining the bastardy figures in the seventeenth and eighteenth centuries—a whore-behaving, bastard-producing subculture, with identifiable members.

Indeed, the current situation is often referred to in terms of a subculture. 'Our divorce rate,' wrote the American Dr T. P. Monahan of the University of California, in 1962, 'is being compounded by the repetitiousness of divorce among a divorce-prone population group and there seems to exist in our American system a dual pattern of marriage with "sequential polygamy" being the practise of a substantial minority of the population.'

This is certainly one way of looking at it. But in fact I think something much more substantial is now happening. The stigma of divorce still exists though it is often ignored or repressed. At the same time, compared even to ten years ago, it has enormously diminished. It diminishes every year. If a subculture becomes large enough (as happened in Rome among the upper middle class in the second century A.D.) its canons become first tolerated, finally accepted. This process is accelerated by all the attention paid to divorce today by the articles and documentaries and statistics, by the nearly endless if sometimes quite specialised studies, and still more by books like this one which have, at least which are hoped to have, a slightly more popular sale. It is not just the families of the divorced; we are all one great family in that respect now. As once with death, so now with divorce; '. . . And therefore never send to know for whom the bell tolls; it tolls for thee.'

The Second World War played a crucial role here. The stresses this war put on marriage burst like a shock wave through the fabric of social disapproval. Divorce, both in America and in Britain shot up from about 1943 to 1947, it then sank until the mid-1950s, and after that steadily rose until, by the mid- to late-1960s, when the children of those divorced 1940s marriages themselves started divorcing, it reached the immediate postwar levels again. Since then, the statistics speak for themselves. But it is arguable that it was parental divorce on this scale that really introduced—following the law that divorce breeds divorce—the pattern we have since followed.

That structure of pain and suffering which, though of course not unmitigated, forms the core of what one might call the first wave of reaction after divorce, also underlies and dictates the second wave. One might suppose it would inhibit second or third divorces. In fact, second marriages are more prone to divorce than first marriages. One study found them twice as likely to break up. Something like a third to a half of second marriages end in divorce. Either (as sometimes seems to happen after childbirth) the pain is forgotten or, more likely, those who have been through it once realise it can be endured and surmounted.

Nevertheless, the pain is nearly always very considerable. It might be wondered what alternatives there are, what other ways to live that might avoid them. Divorce may be the largest, but it is by no means the only response by society as it seethes under the intense laser beam of change. There have been others—of which the total effect may, as we shall eventually discover, be very significant indeed.

10

AFFAIRS, COMMUNES, PROMISCUITY, GAY LOVE ... THE WAYS WE LIVE AND LOVE NOW

I need and want two wives ... I wish years ago I had found that I was polygamous ... [I] could be passionately married to several women and be sincere and wholehearted in each case.

STANLEY SPENCER

NELL DUNN begins her book *Living Like I Do* with a brief vignette:

> About a year ago I became involved with a man called Dan, who had four children. He lived alone in a ground floor flat, with his wife living in the same house. In some way this seemed far-out and ideal; in another, de-energised and static. We spent a Christmas together in the country—Dan, my husband, my husband's girlfriend, Dan's wife, his wife's boyfriend and the kids. We had kippers for Christmas dinner and lots of wine—it should have been fun and yet it wasn't.

Repressing the frivolous feeling that it could have been the kippers, one is led into a fascinating world of alternative ways of

195

life and love. It is not a small world. That is to say, the family pattern most people assume is usual—married parents plus their own
children—is no longer, in America at least, the normal one. That
is not to say it is not the most important, or the one people aim at
and judge themselves against; simply that it is not the situation
most people find themselves in. In 1972, 56 per cent did not.
Today, it is certainly a great deal more. (See Appendix H.) For a
lot of people monogamous life-time marriage has broken down.
The more we know, therefore, about the more alternatives to
this—about the strains, the satisfactions, the advantages and disadvantages, the more general effects—the wider becomes the
range of choice and the greater the possibility of finding a suitable
new style.

The first is that indicated by Nell Dunn's 'involved with' (highly
revealing and absolutely typical post-crack-up phrase)—the
world of the affair.

1   *'O.K.—so one is vaguely available.'*
                  Girl overheard talking to a man in a restaurant

There are affairs which, it has been argued, will significantly
reduce divorce. They are the two, three or four-year affairs which
either precede marriage to someone else or become a form of
marriage.

Acceptance of an affair can depend on area. Britain is, to some
extent, still in a state of transition. Someone I talked to said girls
or young women in the south part of Fulham in London can't; in
the north part of Fulham 'we *all* have lovers'. Or, an example
from another category, there was a woman whose husband hadn't
made love to her for eight years. While he was in the country, she
found a young lover and had him every night. When the sons
(aged fourteen and fifteen) came back, she said to the lover 'of
course' you can't stay every night now, it would have to be after-
noons. He was furious. He felt he was being used, a service—and
left. She was devastated. The point is, she was still at a period

when affairs should be secret; he, when they were accepted and open. Nevertheless, there is evidence that they are becoming a 'conventional' pattern to large numbers of people.

Certainly this is so in Europe, particularly in Denmark and Sweden. In Denmark about one quarter of *all* women eighteen to twenty-five are living with a man thcy are not married to; in Sweden 12 per cent of all couples living together (ages sixteen to seventy) are not married. What the Continental and Russian evidence suggests (I have put it in Appendix H) is partly a formalising of the experimental marriage stage; partly the evolution of a form of marriage without vows, both on a large scale. There is less research in America and even less in Britain, but the likelihood and such indications as there are suggest that 'consensual unions' are now something like 2 per cent of the population and that this proportion is rising. (See Appendix H.)

All divorce studies show that the later couples marry the less likely they are to divorce; and it is true that the figures for age at marriage have been rising. But in my view, the figures (see Appendix H) show that these changes, so far, have been far too small, the trends too weak, to provide the comfort as regards divorce which some commentators derive from them. They also show that the number of consensual unions is not yet large enough to have had a profound effect.

Even if they had, or have in the future, I do not see how the effect would be to reduce divorce—or, to phrase it more broadly, reduce the numbers of committed couples splitting up. The argument here (particularly popular in Sweden) is that a major cause of early divorce is the 'shock of intimacy' (that is why so many marriages break down in the first year). The difficulty of living all the time with someone, the revelations about their character and yours, the contradictory and conflicting desires, all often prove overwhelming. The practise and wisdom gained in an affair or affairs will remove this. While there is certainly truth in this, at the same time, there are powerful reasons to think the opposite—that 'serious' affairs generate forces which will increase divorce.

A fair proportion of these affairs seem to be marriages without vows. I see no reason to doubt those people today who say they do not require vows to feel as committed as their married counterparts. The fact that, in Sweden especially, unmarried couples have children is convincing (in America in 1975, 14.2 per cent of births were illegitimate, of which an unknown proportion would have been among such couples). But you could not say that they were in general *more* committed than married people. These unions are subject to the same stresses, expectations, demands, and interpersonal conflicts which cause divorce. One must assume they split up in roughly the same proportions. Indeed, since they are by definition not 'conventional' and therefore less subject to the restraints of the remaining stigma of divorce they probably break up more often. Just as divorce breeds divorce, so the breaking of these consensual unions will become part of the same social self-fuelling process.

I think the same is true to a quite unrealised if lesser degree with many other affairs—though no doubt some sort of rough sliding scale of effect exists, depending on length and depth of association. How long, do you suppose, these 'less serious' affairs last—nine months? A year? Often as long as three or four years. Yet, though the commitment may be felt as less, many of the processes of living together take place without our knowing it. The entwining of lives happens as automatically as that of limbs, the long thick roots of habit, of answered need, of reliance gradually growing deeper; the tendrils of shared feeling and thought higher, forming that same (if metaphorical) 'structure in the head' whose smashing is seen in divorce. The ending of an affair of one and one-half or two or three years is often in almost every respect as painful as many divorces. And it is this pain in all its ramifications which is one of the main reasons divorce breeds divorce.

To the degree an affair has come close to a marriage, so that the pains of its dissolution equal those felt at divorce, to that degree and in that area will it have the same effect later on. I suspect that this is the reason divorce has not declined but risen in Sweden, though the numbers of affairs of every sort have grown enormously over nineteen years.

2   *The world of the one-parent family*

With one-parent families we are dealing with a new norm. In 1961 in Britain there were 474,000 single-parent families. By 1976 the figure was 750,000—a rise of over 60 per cent—or 11 per cent of all families with children. In fact about half of these families had two or more children—a total of 1.25 million children. The picture is the same in America, and in Europe (10 per cent of all families). But since the one-parent family is fairly transient (not very), the total who have been in this situation is enormous; in Britain one child in three will spend formative years like this, in America two out of every five—20 or 30 *million* children during the 1970s, probably more in the 1980s.

It is essential to discover as much as we can about these families—to see what they are like, what effects they are having, suggest remedies. And to look at them in all their variety—because they are by no means one uniform clump.

Confirmed bachelors are, where not homosexual, usually somewhat odd; the same is true of elderly spinsters. You agree? The fact is, we force marriage on people. And in this respect we are no better than the Russians, who claim that anyone who goes against what the state (i.e., society) thinks, is mad. We think, or at least *feel* even if we don't admit it, that someone who rejects marriage is, if not mad, certainly abnormal. This is quite wrong.

In the Middle Ages, the single state was prized. A function, usually as a monk or nun, was found for those with a gift for it. There are many women with a gift for children, who want them, but who don't want a man. 'It is a tragedy,' wrote the Swiss Jungian psychiatrist Guygenbühl-Craig, 'that they should have to drag a man around with them for a whole lifetime when he does not interest them in the least.' (Yes—bad luck for him, too.) There are now numbers of brave women who are freeing themselves from the (to them) terrifying need to marry, and who are having children on their own. Often they find support in the women's movement or set up as part of a lesbian couple. Society also imposes the anxiety that children brought up in this way won't be 'normal'—which means they won't learn normal sex-orientation. It is possible some mothers of this sort would not mind if they didn't, but a recent paper in the *American Journal of Psychiatry* proves that children brought up in sexually atypical households develop in exactly the same way as children in normal households. Professor Richard Green of New York State University studied thirty-seven children raised from one year or earlier by lesbian couples. They ranged in age from three to twenty. Professor Green found that all but one of the thirty-seven children had conventional heterosexual orientation, to toys, in sexual fantasy and practice, and in role. The 'exception' also seems normal enough—a sensitive boy who disliked rough games, but who had a girlfriend and played father in games with her. 'Children do not live in a universe composed entirely of their home environment,' wrote Green. School, television, their friends, books are quite enough to give them normal role orientation.

This form of one-parent family is, in a practical sense, the easiest, since it is chosen. The vast majority of such families have their circumstances thrust upon them—and fairly difficult they are too. The principal difficulties are the children themselves, money and loneliness. Three-quarters of one-parent families live alone, with no other adult. The single fathers suffer the most. Although numerically now quite large, at about 10 per cent of the whole, they find it hard to find people in the same situation and become very isolated. In London many of them ring up The National Council for One-Parent Families and ask desperately for addresses of men like them, so they can go out and discuss it all in a pub. Women have centuries of gossip-and-support traditions to call on.

All share equally in poverty. The complexities of welfare, of how and when and how much supplementary benefit you can draw are so baffling to understand and humiliating to extract if you depend on it (here the full force of the stigma strikes home), that I think the best thing to hold in the mind is a single stark figure. Of all the poor families so poor that they have to receive state benefits of one sort or another, *over half* are one-parent families.

Even without poverty, social attitudes exacerbate the one-parent difficulties. They feel they cannot alone provide the full emotional spectrum. Says David, a single father: 'I feel one effect of him not having had a mother is that it's made him frightened of women . . . He's only spoken about his own mother a couple of times and that in a very cagey way, as if he were in No-man's Land.' It is these sex-role attitudes which make mothers find it hard to discipline their children and lead to the anarchy common in so many homes. Also since women are less powerful in society, so the family as a whole feels less powerful (credit is harder, dustmen ruder). No doubt it is hard to provide the full emotional spectrum (we are not in the situation of the one-sexed parent *from birth*, as with the lesbians above), but the more you move to real sex equality, the easier these problems become.

But it is poverty which makes all problems difficult and sometimes intolerable. It is poverty which causes the incessant anxiety, overwork, exhaustion, and neglect, so that the sociologist Robert Chester found that many of these families suffered, paradoxically, from *maternal* deprivation. And it is poverty which brings about one of the most tragic of the one-parent situations—that of children in care. Between 50 and 75 per cent of all children (often very small) taken from their parents and put into homes or farmed out to foster parents come from one-parent families. Something like 60,000 in Britain in 1976. Nor are they separated briefly: local authorities are too embarrassed to give figures, but The National Council For One-Parent Families estimate the average stay is one year, which means a fair number will be gone for several years.

This is the situation with the one-parent family as a whole. Society's reluctance is based on a number of prejudices, unthought-out assumptions and ignorance. Ignorance is shown in the idea that, though it may be unpleasant, it is a transient state and therefore soon rights itself. Transient is a relative term. In America the period is estimated as at least five years: in England at about six or seven years. And this, usually, when the children are most vulnerable. Just about as long, that is, as the average divorced *marriage* in America.

The solution seems quite clear, and was first put forward in essence by the Finer Report on the situation in Britain years ago. Divorce is the modern death, and it should be treated like that. Widows in Britain today receive £17.50 ($42) a week plus £8.40 ($20.16) for each child. An equivalent sum should be given automatically to one-parent families. It should be moderately means-tested, so that a single parent can work or not, to suit the family's needs. (I say moderately because I do not see why those well provided for should get it. A cut-off might come when the income is three or four times the single-parent allowance.) It should be non-contributory, to avoid excluding those least likely to have paid their contributions to the National Insurance Scheme. In America, where the social and welfare system is on the whole derived from an automatic contributory base, the principle would be the same—the poor single-parent family would be treated like a widowed family. The central government would probably have to produce a larger proportion of the cost. This scheme would at least remove the stigma still imposed by the state. It would reduce the number of parents who have to let their children go into care. Other countries do this sort of thing. In France, it was estimated recently, the average wage to all families with children from the state in 1976, from birth to the third year was £35.56 ($85.35) a week. There is also an automatic means-tested allowance to all one-parent families. There is no reason why Britain and America should not do the same.

Perhaps that is optimistic. There would certainly be strong objections. The first would be that one-parent families don't deserve it; a version of the idea that people divorce for fun—which it must be clear now is not true. There is also no doubt that despite the £17.50 plus £8.40 (which is not exactly *wealth*), the loneliness and difficulty of one-parent life will mean some form of couple-dom will be preferred.

The second objection is that society can't afford it. In some ways a straight payment saves money—a foster mother gets twice as much to foster as a real mother; one child in care can cost four times as much to keep as a whole family spends at home. But ob-

viously it would cost money. David Ennals in the last British Labour Government estimated it would cost £550 million ($1.32 bil-
lion) to pay all one-parent families enough for them not to need
the various benefits. £500 million ($1.2 billion) is more accurate
because Mr Ennals did not include the money the government would get back in tax from the large number of women and
men who would then work. This sounds like a lot. In fact it is
not a great deal in the total Social Security budget of *£11,000*
million ($26.4 billion). But these things are not really weigh-
able. To have 75,000 children in care, probably for a year,
sometimes for years—and the number constantly increasing—
is shocking. There is no way of estimating what it will ultimately
cost the country; in crime, in psychiatrists' fees, and mainly in
plain suffering.

The idea that these sorts of proposals would increase the number of divorces, and increase them in the area where the potential
damage is greatest—parents with young children—is perfectly
true. But it is far too late to consider that now. Society has long
since taken a whole series of steps to facilitate divorce. It can
either go into reverse and repeal the legislation of the last thirty
years, or face the consequences. As regards parents with young
children, it has been shown that the children's presence does not
stop divorce. It is clear that welfare and the tangle of supplementary benefits do now allow poor couples to split up, but they simply place the mother in a position where she cannot do her vital
job adequately. Society insures against the consequences of death,
of old age, of ill-health, of car accidents and other inevitabilities.
It should insure against divorce.

There remains, finally, the question of when this help should
end. The answer surely must be, when it is clearly no longer necessary: when, I suggested, the single parent is receiving four times
the given allowance, or is being adequately supported by someone
else. At the moment, in Britain, widows and single mothers lose
their benefits if they appear to be living with a man. People object
to this: if a woman sleeps with a man it doesn't mean she is kept
by him, on the contrary quite often. Why should it only apply to

women? If a man lives with a woman who is keeping him *he* doesn't lose his state benefits. Then, there is the prurient snooping that goes on, inspectors up drain pipes at night with torches and so on.

I can understand these objections. But there is force on the other side—why should the state support people who can support themselves or are being supported by someone else? Although there are a lot of past and present one-parent families, most people *have* not been and *are* not in that position. That society (which is themselves) should shell out unnecessarily is maddening, and there is no reason they should allow it. The criterion, however, must be that word 'necessary'. Sleeping with someone is an absurd criterion. Local inspectors can challenge this on whatever evidence they think is convincing. If it transpires that a man is being adequately supported by a working woman, then he doesn't need state money. If a woman has chosen to share her one-parent allowance with a man, then she does need it. As for climbing drainpipes, that is unlikely to stop. Local authority inspectors lead dull lives and one of their few excitements is climbing drainpipes.

3 Sex—and living in communes

> *'I moved up north and ended in Leeds living with a lot of people in the drug scene . . . They were passive, quiet people, a lot of semi-musicians.'*
>
> Annie, aged 25

The more unconventional a form of group behavior is, the more intolerant and aggressive the group tends to be towards outsiders, and the more strictly they erect and live by their 'new orthodoxy'. All rebel groups have to respond like this: feminists, gay liberationists, black power groups, nudists on beaches—and communes.

DAVID: 'I feel very alienated if I go into an ordinary straight pub, with straight people drinking their beer, sometimes I actually feel horror.'

ROSE: 'It was as if our friends couldn't accept that John's relationship with both Nicole and me was serious. They can accept screwing around if it's not serious but they couldn't quite take our living together.'

JOHN: 'I resented any implication that I was exploiting the girls—I had no magic power over them, they were both free.'

This means that it can be quite difficult finding out about communes. Luckily there is Nell Dunn's brilliant book, *Living Like I Do*, as well as some seven other studies which go into the subject in considerable detail.

Of course, commune ideals are not new. Shelley was passionate about them at the age of twenty, and planned one of ideological radicals, believers like him in liberty and egalitarianism. In practice, it seemed more to involve Shelley shutting himself away with two young girls. It seems that what Shelley really wanted was two wives. It bored him to be alone for too long with one woman. His honeymoon with Harriet, aged sixteen, was for the first seven days spent almost entirely in a coach, with his friend Hogg—whom in an ambiguous way he was later to encourage to sleep with Harriet. After Hogg, a Miss Hitchener came to join them. But when he later eloped with Mary Godwin, he took with them her stepsister, Claire Clairmont, and they lived together for the next eight years. Actually, it was not so much two wives, as a wife, and then a mistress who could embody his fantasies of romantic love. When Claire finally left, he at once began a series of falling-in-love relationships with other girls, ending with Jane Williamson. He also wanted everyone to sleep with everyone, and does seem to have got Hogg into bed once with Harriet and perhaps twice with Mary. Hogg always obediently fell in love with Shelley's girls, and ended by marrying Jane Williamson.

In so many ways communes seem an answer to life's difficulties: children and household problems shared, economies, and even possessions pooled; all better off and not possession-clogged, the too-much-togetherness of marriage alleviated by like-minded friends, yet a closeness and privacy possible. One would think the conflict between sexual adventure and stability might be easier to resolve in a commune. In fact, the practical difficulties of living in a commune seem a great deal more difficult and complicated than one might have supposed, though the dream has led a good many people to try and live in them.

Numbers with minority groups are always a bit foggy. Cogswell gives a figure of 6 per cent of all family groups in America in 1970. There are no figures for Britain, but the commune movement in 1971 had a membership of 300, and the magazine *Commune* came out bi-monthly and had a subscription of 3,000.

In two areas communes can work. If you are very poor, then a number of very poor people live better than just two. The second area is very young children—where mothers often talk of the help and support, and the pleasure the children get from each other. The sense of communal family is warming—one of Nell Dunn's gave themselves a name, Wild. In another, there was a crèche meeting each week to discuss the children. Those in communes don't really see them as permanent; they talk vaguely of three or four years. Sometimes it seemed to depend on how long they'd need help with the children—and I'm not sure that that isn't really their most valid function, to help one-parent families through the most difficult years with their children. The Rapoports said there was evidence that some commune children grew up with rather diffuse emotional attachments. In a divorce-prone society this may not be a disadvantage. In a Leeds collective, which formed because its members didn't like couple situations, '. . . you weren't meant to mind whom you slept with, or who was in the room'—this was done deliberately.

Even in these areas there are more serious difficulties. Financial arrangements can cause resentment: someone contributes too little, the house belongs to one of them, or to an ex. The advantages have their reverse sides—the short-term element means instability, for the children, and also for the nonbiologically related adults who had come to love them. Albert, in one, felt the whole thing 'might blow up'. He loved the collective children, especially one, Jan, whom the mother was planning to take away (although to do this, to break with the commune, made her feel guilty). In another commune, Commune X, one man loved his three 'nonbiological' children. He'd been present at the birth of one. Then he had a biological child with a woman in Commune Y. At once there rose a terrible decision—should he leave his 'children' to be with his biological child or not? He agonised for weeks. Finally he stayed in Commune X, but made regular visits—had 'access' as it were—to Commune Y. Again, that shared support also means an audience for parent-child relationships, or jealousies between biological and 'nonbiological' parents.

It isn't necessarily easier to live with several people than with one. As time passes, many people in communes begin to long for privacy. Sometimes they have joined communes bruised after divorce, only wanting shallow relationships—'to relate to others in a lower key', as one said—but then, growing stronger, they want to return to something closer. They miss the intensity. This can destroy a commune. Nell Dunn describes one consisting of seven people, which suddenly, like crystalline structures forming in a liquid, split into three couples who shot off in different directions. The seventh, Mary, said, '. . . it's happened so suddenly—one minute everyone is generating a family feeling round the supper table, and the next minute everyone can desert you. The most important thing in their lives is the other half of the couple . . .'

And the difficulties, the decisions, the conflicts can be multiplied in communal life. 'Now I can settle something with one person rather than having to discuss it with seven others,' said Maureen, having left a commune again to become part of a couple. Complications can increase at a sort of compound rate. Shelley, with Claire and Mary together in Italy, Mary's child, his children by Harriet in London, trying to arrange for Harriet to come and make it a *ménage à quatre* (*sept* if you count the children), until, as his biographer Holmes says, 'He was hemmed in on all sides by personal responsibilities. It was ironic that the results of all his efforts to liberate himself and those around him from the trammels of morality and society seemed so far to be an almost total entrapment in the complications of his daily existence.'

What then of sex? Can at least this dream be realised? Here again there has been a good deal of experimenting. A newspaper survey, reported by Morton Hunt, found that out of 2,000 communes in America in 1970, group marriage was common among a great many. Yet even here—or especially here—it doesn't seem much easier. Albert again (uphill in Albert's Commune)—'I have multiple sexual relationships, two in this house and two out of the house, and it gets very tense and neurotic for me at times. I have big heavy freak-outs . . .' However difficult, those involved often think that it is 'better than the emancipated middle-class position—which is characterised by the marital structure where the husband and wife screw around with lots of dishonesty and argument and bitchiness'. But the difficulty encountered is the same in both cases and so are the reactions. They can be summed up in one word which, since it derives to a considerable extent from romantic love, could have been foreseen—jealousy.

In a Ramsgate commune there was completely open, shared sex. But there were two problems. The first was straight jealousy. Said one member called Peter: 'My theoretical platform would still be for openness sexually but I have learnt that my actual capacity to cope with it is much more limited than I thought.' In fact, he had devastating rows with Christine and Martine, who were furious at being shared. While '. . . me [Christine speaking] being angry . . . exploded . . . Martine being in tears for days and me feeling guilty.' In the end, the jealous rows brought sharing to an end.

Jealousy can arise in group sex if everyone doesn't get roughly the same amount. With Nicole and Rose, for instance, the aim was to share John sexually. Nicole had moved in on the other two. 'We decided to sleep alternate nights with John and that went O.K. till we had some terrific bust up. Rose had been away for the weekend, to give me time on my own with John as she'd been with him three or four years and knew him much better. Anyway, when she came back, he let slip to her that we had screwed four times one afternoon and she got very jealous and resentful that I was, as it were, taking it all and that, when he came to sleep with her he would be sated. So we decided it should be two nights each, so that when he'd had this tremendous amount of screwing with me, he could then get over it on the first night and have a good night on the second night.'

Any form of polygamy is always hard work on the man, incidentally. His women often become competitive as to who can get the most out of him. John: 'I went down to see my parents once and it struck me that it was the first night I'd had on my own, without sexual expectations for four months, and how nice it was.' In the end Nicole walked out. She felt too jealous of the bond between Rose and John which even the tremendous amount of screwing couldn't get her into.

These examples could be extended indefinitely. I came across no *long-term* examples of successful group marriage, either in the literature or in life. Communes are certainly viable and are particularly helpful as regards support with very young children and when people are broke. But they are not easier than marriage. The difficulties may be different, but they are as intractable and in a good many respects more intractable.

4   *Open Marriage*

When one of the partners in a marriage reproaches the other for concealing things from him or even for lying, he has as a rule only himself to blame. He had allowed himself to become a person to whom it was not easy to confide or speak the truth.

GERALD BRENAN,
*Thoughts in a
Dry Season*

I remember when I first heard of open marriage. It was at a party given by my sister. I was told about it by a slightly drunk, fairly overexcited psychiatrist of about fifty who worked in Ipswich, whom I'll call Derek. Derek and his wife had just got deeply into open marriage. At least Derek had, because it seemed to consist in his having mistresses and telling his wife. He was having two at the moment. He called over his wife—it took rather a lot of shouting—and said didn't she agree how marvellous it was, how free they were? His wife seemed to me a bit tense and, while not disagreeing precisely, was rather silent, and not exactly bubbling over with the same red-wine-quaffing enthusiasm.

Because, sexually speaking, open marriage doesn't work for the vast majority of people, that does not mean it is absolutely *impossible*. The O'Neills based their book, *Open Marriage*, on sixteen ('very strong') couples who did make it work. I interviewed two such couples, and I was interested to find that on the whole they agreed with the general guidelines laid down by the O'Neills. Here is a summary: you must be secure, and to some degree independent. If you depend on your mate for all your needs, then you will feel insecure if he/she gives to someone else. Choose others who are also secure. Don't, for instance, start with someone in a rocky marriage. You and the third person must know that your marriage is the primary relationship; other ones must be in addition. Finally, as well as increased gratitude, love and trust, an open-marriage couple will find they relax. The forbidding of affairs in a closed marriage is what makes them so desirable. Once allowed, the whole strain evaporates—just as cows cease to lean towards the grass in the other field once the fence between them is pulled down.

Take Philip Moore-Cudley, whom I had gone to talk to about other matters and only discovered he was engaged in an 'open marriage' towards the end of our discussion. He was almost offhand about it. Yes, there were various rules. The primary one—the O'Neills were quite right—was that no second partner should be as or more important. It was also true that, once free, you wanted affairs far less. You don't thrust it at each other; you do it with tact: 'Got to go and see about X or Y; I won't be back till about one.' Or go to New York for a week. 'Actually we do talk about it sometimes. It turns Jane on to hear me describe it.' He said they 'got off together' on his descriptions. I asked about the dangers of falling in love. Philip agreed, but said wasn't that danger universal even—or especially—in marriage? Open marriage, like all marriages, was a question of temperament. In his early thirties, he had a broad strong face, with white, almost translucent skin. I felt he was a very controlled person, unlikely to lose his head.

Jane, his wife, told me more later. They were one of the rather few couples, incidentally, who did not mind their names being mentioned. She'd been married before, for ten years. Towards the end of that time, she'd started an affair with Philip, who worked in the same office. It had got out of hand and she'd gone to live with him. Then, for nine months, she had both men equally: husband and children at the weekends, Philip during the week. 'I liked that,' said Jane. 'I could detach myself from one when with the other. I was happy—provided they were.' But they weren't. Or rather, Philip wasn't. He didn't want to share. So they embarked on their open marriage, which seemed to have lasted four or five years.

'The first year I think we had about eight or nine other partners,' said Jane. 'Since then we've simmered down. Also I noticed that subconsciously we competed, if he got a lover, so did I. Now we're relaxed. This year I've had two. With Philip it's libido; he has greater need. He finds that sexual relationships are a way of finding out about himself. Mine last longer. I definitely love two of them. One was my first lover when I was eighteen—he lives in New York—it's far more than simple sexuality. In fact, many sexual experiences can become loving ones.'

That, of course, is what makes this system of freedom the most difficult to operate. Though secondary, some of the relationships are expected to go quite deep. Whenever Philip started an affair, Jane always had a fleeting moment of insecurity—what is she like? Is she prettier?—which is why she got him to talk about them. I mentioned that Philip said she enjoyed hearing about them. 'Did he? Yes—he probably thinks that. Actually, they don't turn me on particularly. I like him to talk about them to reassure me they are not more serious than I am.'

Four years ago she'd become pregnant (when trying to conceive they don't sleep with other people). After she had miscarried (in the seventh month) she was unstable and the open marriage came unstuck. Philip slept with someone else three weeks after the miscarriage. She was very upset. He hadn't realised. They got over it. When I saw her, she was pregnant again. She was worried, felt low and unconfident. 'If Philip gets into a relationship [and he has] then—well, I've reacted very badly—I don't know how to resolve it, but we will. I'm at a difficult stage (first three months). We'll have to slow down on these relationships. That's how it works. We adapt.'

The unfinished dramas of research—are they still together? What of Albert and his 'big heavy freak-outs', or the woman looking after her children in the Jaguar? But, a rare occurrence, I heard of the euphoric Ipswich psychiatrist, Derek, twice more. I asked my sister how his open marriage was going. 'Badly. His wife has left him. He's been absolutely shattered, but he's sticking to his open marriage guns.'

Most people find open marriage impossible—though I suspect this is an old form in a new guise. I don't just mean condoned adultery on Edwardian-European mistress lines, but also normal marriages where the husband is absent for months or even years—traveling salesmen marriages, service marriages, especially naval ones. These marriages can last happily for years, and are only revealed as forms of open marriage when, on the husband's retirement, they become closed and collapse.

This type of freedom seems easier to manage if it is *exclusively* sexual. The most successful and common examples of this are male homosexual marriages (using the term loosely, though there are priests both in America and Sweden who will bless such unions). These are intense for two or three years, then gradually there is a cooling off sexually, but the couple live together and lead separate sex lives—'going our separate ways'. Jeremy Seaforth, author of *A Lasting Relationship*, suggests that it is the prevalence and possibility of total promiscuity in homosexual life, the threat of boundless appetite which holds these marriages together. There are many embalmed relationships, shallow but serving a function—a protective base, a port within and a rampart against the chaos of desire and promiscuity. Many go deeper. He describes Charles and Tim, in their thirties, together nine years, living in a maisonette in West London. They have an intense emotional life with occasional sex, but mostly get their sex from outside. They value their love far too much to give it up for some sexual encounter—but the possibility of this, especially at the start of some strong sexual passion, gives an edge, a tension, to their relationship.

Seaforth may be right about the ramparts against unbounded appetite (though homosexuals tend to boast about this), but I think there is a more significant factor. What gives romantic love its power is that it gathers to itself a great many different desires and emotions—love, sex, longevity, exclusivity of association—which don't necessarily belong together. If you can split off the ingredients, then romantic love as a total concept loses some of its power. These homosexual marriages reserve love and longevity for their marriage, and sex for casual or fairly casual contacts, where friendship may occur but is incidental. Something of the same sort occurs in wife-swapping—a fairly rare phenomenon in percentage terms (2 per cent in the *Redbook* survey) but the actual numbers must be quite high.

More interesting are intimate networks, where different elements are split off from romantic love. Studied by Dr James Ramey, visiting Professor at the Bowman May School of Medicine, North Carolina, and Dr Robert T. Francoeur, Professor of Human Sexuality, Fairleigh Dickinson University, Madison, N.J., these are often quite extensive groups of friends, all either married or in analogous long term associations. Here, sex, love and longevity are reserved for the marriage, but new friendship is encouraged among the network. Sex may take place, but it is not the main aim—it is, as it were, incidental. Ramey found there were groups which had been in existence twenty or thirty years (average age, forty-two), which had allowed sexual escapades and especially new friendships, without causing divorce or forcing people to marry someone they didn't want to. Francoeur, a Catholic priest (ex-priest, surely?) saw this 'pleasure bond' being the basis for a new society, which would be held together, not by family groups, but by friendship and copulation which was roughly what Noyes planned and later practised in his Oneida community.

This sort of system, especially in homosexual marriage, starts to impinge on the most extreme area of freedom—total promiscuity.

5 Promiscuity as a way of life

> *Our next subject was promiscuity—in my opinion a natural state of youth, exciting and stimulating without being a great source of happiness. To prolong it often comes from timidity, the fear of risking too much in a more solid relationship.*
>
> FRANCES PARTRIDGE,
> *A Pacifist's War*

The faery power of unreflecting fucking—product of youth experiment and high libido—to which Frances Partridge refers is certainly a pattern, but it is usually short-lived. Promiscuity as a way of life is completely different.

It, too, is rare, and the surveys show it is not increasing. Among the variety of ways of living these sexually free ones are in a single respect not the most difficult, since they do not involve the hardest changes, those of role patterns. It seems clear that in an unknown, but probably high, proportion of cases, lifelong promiscuity is the product of neurotic conflict. Often love and sex are not so much separate as antithetical. The classic situations are oedipal: the man who loves his mother, so has prostitutes; the man who has a deep fear of his homosexual elements (which may be stronger in fact) and has endless women to prove himself; the woman who loves her father and has dozens of different men, either to punish herself or so as not to interfere with the secret central love. Finally, one should not underestimate the force of feeling. The most 'passionate' loves are usually the most neurotic—since in them individuals will attempt to satisfy or to atone for powerful and unreasonable desires. People who prefer promiscuity are not necessarily immature. If they are, they often are in no other way and many great poets, painters and distinguished men and women in every field have been immature too, and the word loses much of its force. In so far as it is an expression of emotional difficulty it is among the most harmless, and no guilt should arise. It is far less unpleasant and damaging than many other expressions, such as aggression or acquisitiveness or the lust for power. The only dangers are pregnancy (negligible now) and of hurting yourself or others. But since promiscuity by definition needs a steady stream of new, almost unknown and transient partners, the promiscuous are usually only so with each other.

There are men and women who find that the casual, shallow relationship is all they need. They have three or four going, in a random way, all at once. If one starts to get serious, they move on; they often disguise the pattern—especially from their married friends, but feel nothing but satisfaction. Hunt quotes a managing editor of a large newspaper, aged fifty: 'For about five years after my divorce I thought I wanted to remarry. But slowly I realised that in truth I didn't want it at all. I'm very much my own man, the way I live. I love the peace and privacy of my apartment after the day at the paper, but whenever I want company or an overnight partner I have three or four girls I can get in touch with . . . It's my nature. Having tried marriage for almost ten years, I know now that I could never be this happy married again or trying to be true to just one.'

The pattern is usually much more extreme. It involves the endless, almost frenzied search for partners, two nights, three, four, every night of the week—in bars, discos, clubs and other 'market places', with sex the same night. After two or three meetings, disenchantment sets in and the search is on again. It was partly for people like this that places like Plato's Retreat in New York were started where you can go (with a partner of the opposite sex), pick up, fornicate in public or watch others do so (about 50 per cent are voyeurs) and leave with a (different) partner of the opposite sex, all for $25 (£10.42). The most common and extreme examples of this as a permanent way of life, however, are found among male homosexuals.

Why is this? Leaving aside psychological factors for the moment (in many cases probably overwhelming) gays themselves say that if heterosexuals had their opportunity they too would be as promiscuous. They 'really' want it as much. Perhaps. But, since some do follow the same pattern, this begs the question why do more of them not want to create equal opportunity? There is a suggestion that homosexuals are more highly sexed; author Jeremy Seaforth thinks it is in some way a manifestation of the consumer society—gays consuming each other. I always suspect such conjunctions—people are not goods or food, they cannot therefore be 'consumed'. Nor are the promiscuous necessarily highly sexed. A married man who sleeps with his wife 2.8 times a week will have the same person for five years. An equally (that is averagely) sexed homosexual will have 2.8 men a week. Say two. That is a potential 540 in five years. Now 540 men sounds like a great many; but the drive is the same.

I think that, historically, high libido may have played a part. For several centuries homosexuality was a crime, involving vicious punishments, shame and secrecy. It is still not all that easy. This had three results. Particular mannerisms and inflexions evolved to allow those in the subculture to signal their orientation. 'Feminine' mannerisms, obviously, since the desire was to attract men. Only the most determined could enter it and this was likely to mean the highly sexed whose needs were imperative. Homosexuals therefore became socially upwardly mobile—since they were brave and determined. In our context a pattern of promiscuity developed, partly because the taboo made a settled partner difficult, partly because a varied sex-life can be particularly congenial to the highly sexed. None of these patterns developed where homosexuality was accepted, in ancient Greece for instance.

You might suppose that romantic love would be entirely absent in the lives of the permanently promiscuous; in fact the opposite is true. There is romantic love of the utmost, almost feverish intensity—but romantic love of a rather bizarre kind. One of Jeremy Seaforth's characters is Leo, 'flamboyant, loquacious and theatrical'. He had recently been devastated by an enormous passion for Jean-Paul, whom he met in the summer of 1972.

> The moment I saw him, I thought of some archetypal myth about the god sent down in disguise, you know, Philemon or something like that, where nobody recognised him and all turned away . . . Like Jesus Christ, I suppose, it's only a recrudescence of the same myth . . . Anyway, when I saw him, I said that boy is a god! He was dreadfully scruffy . . . his face was dusty, his hair tangled and looked about ten shades darker than it was—which turned out to be the colour of corn of a ripeness you don't see in England, a kind of auburn rust-colour . . . the moment I saw him, I think I was aware of a peculiar kind of magnetism . . .

For thirty-two days they had an idyllic relationship. They didn't sleep together. Jean-Paul wouldn't. Then, after a perfect evening, Leo tip-toes in to look at the sleeping god.

> And what I saw is what makes me believe that he is the most corrupt and depraved person I have ever met. On the pillow two heads. He must have gone out and picked somebody up, in a bar, in the street . . . The most degenerate scugnizzo would have shown more sensitivity . . . The next morning, I tried to indicate the shock which the delicacy of my nature had undergone, but I don't think he understood. All lost on him, I suppose. He

wept. But as I then realised, tears were only part of the extensive armoury with which he laid seige to people.

Leo sent him packing, swearing he would never love again—or forget this wound—not to his vanity, but to his *pride.*

'However,' writes Seaforth, 'I met him a few months afterwards and he had almost forgotten Jean-Paul.' 'Oh don't mention that wretched creature's name to me.' He had met someone else. *'Al cor gentil ripara sempre amore.'*

Promiscuous romantic love flares up, burns and dies all in a few sex-filled days. It is set off instantly by the sight of a neck, a profile in the street. Endlessly vanishing, it leads to considerable emotional vulnerability. There is a curious, haphazard, bitter-sweet quality to this life, also something childish and schoolgirl. Seaforth describes in his book a gay evening at which they'd played Shirley Bassey and agreed she had a special heart-on-sleeve emotional appeal to the gay which went:

> My heart is broken, but I'll put on a happy face and the world will never know the hurt inside; I shall never find another love like this, but I'm going to sing and have myself a really good time, and then, who knows maybe across a crowded room one day I'll start all over again, dust myself down, and when I find myself a new love that is impossible to find I'll die for it, I'd go to the ends of the earth, climb the highest mountain, there's never been another love like this mythic impossible love I feel for you and if you should ever leave me I'd die, or alternatively start all over again, the first time I looked at you I just knew, I saw stars and you are my world, I've given you my heart and what have you done with it; but I have my pride, I'll start all over again.

This gay love has as its obverse a mythology of amazing events—police say 'come with me' then a wild time in the back of the police car—and of disaster. Promiscuous encounters *can* be both dangerous and extraordinary and these myths keep alive and exaggerate the drama: 'This boy met this leather guy and went back with him, and his room was in the basement, done out like a torture chamber, and he tied him in chains and kept him there for three days, and it was sound-proofed and he gave him nothing to eat, and the only way this guy could come was by hanging him upside down from the ceiling and beating him with a chain. At the end of it he had two broken fingers and a fractured skull. It damaged his brain, he's just a vegetable now.'

Sadly, the promiscuous often long for the calm, the stability, the love that lasts which they affect to despise. Hence the poignancy of those endless columns and appeals in the gay publications, where individuals of flawless beauty and goodness seek their counterparts, laying down conditions—'no one-night stands', 'sincere and genuine friendship', 'meaningful lasting relationship'— which are the precise opposite of those which have given rise to their state of mind.

The promiscuous of this pattern have concentrated on the intensity, idealisation and sex elements in romantic love and removed affection and longevity (marriage). It is a pattern predominantly homosexual probably, in part, because children/marriage and therefore longevity of relationship are not an integral part of their lives. You occasionally get the same frenzied search, the same romantic flare, among heterosexuals. You find it to an extent in Byron—though he did not have to search much, at least for women, since they flung themselves at him. He was very quickly in and out of love; and by the end of his life he'd completely lost count of how many people he'd slept with, except that it was well over a thousand.

6   *Nonmarriage, arranged marriage*

Marriages would in general be as happy, and often more so, if they were all made by the Lord Chancellor, upon due consideration of the characters and circumstances without the parties having any choice in the matter.
                                        Dr Johnson

A strong case can be made that far fewer women should have children. Many career/working women go through severe crises when their 'need' to have children conflicts (and usually overwhelms) other needs. Their need for children is certainly in part a cultural imposition; if that were to weaken, so would the need, and society would see more clearly, as would women themselves, that there can be other priorities.

In general terms, the sustained *effort* of children is colossal. A great many young women can hardly take it and certainly their marriages can't. Fewer children to those who find them very difficult would mean that one area of harm in divorce—hurt to children—would diminish. The ideal would be that women who are good with children (to an extent this is an alternative to that shared life I sketched earlier) should have several children; other women should feel no guilt about having none and having other pursuits. This may seem odd to you, or impossibly utopian. In fact it was the system in ancient Greece and probably in large measure accounted for their extraordinary balance.

There is some evidence this is taking place. There are organisations like The National Organization of Nonparents (*NON*) in America whose aims are to persuade women that not to have children is not appalling. Books, like Ellen Peck's *The Baby Trap*, have the same message (Ellen Peck started *NON*). One or two small surveys show pockets of determination. A study of 232 women by the Institute of Planning Studies at Nottingham University found that 64 per cent said *at the time questioned* they had decided never to have children.

There is certainly considerable economic pressure not to have children in the West (see Appendix H), and in general, people are having fewer children. In Britain, Austria and East and West Germany there are already more deaths than births. Although such prognostications are notoriously difficult, it is now believed that the same will have happened to most of Europe by 1990, all of it by 2000 and to America by about 2020.

The drive to have children has lessened, but only slightly. Society's aim is still overwhelmingly to have children, albeit fewer. The significant statistic, the number of couples who have (voluntarily or otherwise) no children remains the same—in both America and Britain around 15 per cent. There is evidence that women are postponing families; none that numbers of women are opting out. The church, the state, the media, the health industry, the adoption societies, grandparents, parents, friends—the whole of society is still overwhelmingly in favour of women having children in marriage. Most of them do, and those who can't still feel it is a disaster.

Contract marriage as envisaged by Locke was one that would be terminated after a period of time according to mutual agreements (in Locke's case the purpose of marriage was to rear children and the marriage could be terminated when this was completed). What you find today are couples who are not formally married, but who live together having legally drawn up and signed a contract. These can be quite simple—joint wills, mortgage in common; or very elaborate—mutual insurances, detailed responsibilities to each other and any children in case of a split, division of property, even contractual agreements as to rights during their association (all much more elaborately binding than a conventional marriage). They see themselves as permanent couples, who have sensibly made provision in case they cease to be together. Certainly, if they do so cease, such arrangements make things much simpler. It might be argued that since the bulk of their arrangements are to do with the end, their association is, as it were, founded with that in mind and there is an inherent lack of commitment. Such couples would not agree. Unfortunately, you can't measure commitment, nor is there research to say whether they stay together longer than divorcing couples.

In America, marriage bureaux really seem places to find people to sleep with. This is a perfectly laudable function, but it is not as fundamental as in Britain, where people marry through them. In the 1970 survey by the sociologist and anthropologist Geoffrey Gorer, 3 per cent used these and similar means. Some of them are very successful—Heather Jenner's agency has arranged 15,000 marriages, and follow-up studies seem to show that they do well—though her book, *Men and Marriage*, is not very precise about this. The secret of a good marriage bureau is clear. It needs the age-old talents of the match-maker: an eye as to who will suit whom, and the skills of a confidential go-between, patching up quarrels, explaining misunderstandings.

Other forms of arranged marriage today take place among small minorities and they will not spread. I was, however, rather fascinated by one case I heard of from an informant. She knew, slightly, a thrusting member of Hare Krishna who was sent out, fundless, from America to Hong Kong to get it all going. Single-handed he raised money, recruited, set up a temple, started a candle factory (one of their staples apparently) and finally felt he should get married. He sent back to base in the U.S. and in due course a wife arrived. 'It worked,' said my informant, 'perfectly. They had ordered roles, the same background, the same views. He found her, for this reason, extremely attractive and they fell in love more or less on the spot.'

7   The great loosening of monogamous marriage

No one has suggested any viable alternative to mar-
riage—not Laing or Cage or anyone. One-parent is hell,
to put your children into care is ridiculous, commune
life is just as hard; there is left only coupledoms—which
are usually just forms of marriage, with or without the
vows.

NELL DUNN,
interview, May 1978

As the Rapoports point out, many people pass through several of these different ways of living. Some only pass through two. I saw Derek, the Ipswich psychiatrist trying to practise open marriage, once more, again at a party of my sister's. He looked frightful—lined and about seventy. His wife was also there. 'Yes, they're together again,' said my sister. 'Poor Derek—it's a very closed marriage *indeed.*' But the Rapoports cite an interesting case of a woman, now in her late thirties, who had four affairs when she was seventeen, had an illegitimate child and for a while lived alone as a one-parent family. She finally settled in with a man who looked after the child while she worked. After this broke up she married a man and had another child; they divorced and she eventually married a man who had two children by a previous marriage. Her second marriage was an open marriage and soon led to a free-sex commune, where she found she was quite strongly lesbian, and left to set up home with a girl who also had two children. This lasted two years and then they broke up and now she's on her own—one-parenting again.

I say the Rapoports cite this case, and it is true they give the example up to her remarriage. But while copying it out, I suddenly found the whole thing had begun to take wing. I felt she must now be growing a little wild, *into* one or two things . . . but the point is, you may have blinked, but did it strike you as quite impossible? Extreme perhaps—but not inconceivable.

I doubt you could have glided so easily over it forty years ago. Whatever is going on, we are only at the start of it. These developments, products of the forces we looked at earlier, have only appeared since those forces began to operate as what I metaphorically described as a laser beam. Another sign that we are at the start of something is that, though often the developments— communes, open marriage, couples without children—are numerically small, the books about them are numerous, the articles and media attention large. They arouse enormous interest. Consciousness-raising groups, discussion—there is a feeling of society trying to organise itself for a change. We don't know how some of these things could develop. We clearly don't know how to handle communes yet; but if children who have been brought up for five early years in communes decide to bring their children up in the same way, and so do their grandchildren—it is possible we may be seeing the start of a series of different upbringing and behavioural traditions. Heather Jenner noted that several of her ex-couples said they would send their children to find partners at a marriage bureau. It took over 1,000 years to embed monogamous marriage in Western consciousness and Western behaviour. There is no particular reason it should be dug out much faster.

What we are seeing is a great loosening of monogamous marriage. It is clear that there have always been people to whom it wasn't very suitable—those too neurotic, disorganised or inadequate; others too finicky or highly sexed; or dedicated people, artists, scientists, politicians, who can't compromise. These numbers have been augmented by the laser beam creating new (or allowing expression to hitherto smothered) demands: women who want children without men, for example, or old people who want sex. Society is slowly allowing them to find different ways of living, of satisfying themselves.

This leads to the question of form. The value of the marriage ceremony, it is argued, is twofold: first, couples want to state publicly the uniquely important quality of their love. Then there are the religious vows, long dead in objective reality, which distil a subtle psychological and primitive magic; the witnessing by family and friends confers a deep feeling of security and belonging, to society, to the community. Some sort of 'step' seems necessary to cement the commitment: and human beings have always created forms and institutions to symbolise and structure such great steps—they give peace of mind, make the step 'real' because visible. (In the pagan country of Britain, a nationwide poll done for the B.B.C. in 1978 found that 80 per cent of marriages had been celebrated in church and 70 per cent were about to be so celebrated.)

Yet I wonder how absolutely necessary these forms are? The institution of monogamous marriage has gone against almost as many fundamental drives and expectations as those it has provided expression to. To what extent was the bulwark of the institution a necessary defence against powerful desires and hopes which sought to destroy it? And if you start to allow different modes of expression for those drives, then does the bulwark, the institution become less necessary?

To the married, an affair seems obviously 'less committed'. But one could argue that the vast practice of divorce means that those marriages—and in some sense all marriages—are less committed, in that the vital element, till death do us part, has been eroded or has vanished. Both views ignore the profound capacity people have to believe and not believe at the same time. Children do this when they read fairy stories. It is an absolutely necessary power. I could sometimes hardly get through my life did I not believe I was going to win £50,000 ($120,000) on a premium bond; at another level, of course, I am aware the odds are nine billion to one. It is the capacity to behave *as if* something were true. It is the power which allows nations or people to win against hopeless odds. It is this same capacity which operates in marriage and often in serious affairs today. People don't enter them thinking they will end; they know that they *can*, but they enter them thinking they will last forever.

However much it is loosening and cracking, marriage remains overwhelmingly the central institution in the West today. Affairs, a couple arrangement, judge themselves against it; a very large number of affairs are directly part of the second wave reaction to divorce. Far the largest variant—the one-parent family—is almost always a direct result of marriage breakdown; the aim (usually achieved) both of one-parent and second wave reaction affairs is remarriage.

It is time to return to the point reached at the end of chapter 9, to look again at those millions as they pass through the last stages of the terrible fires of divorce, until the flames die down and from the ashes, groggy at first, lumbering a good deal, they start to rise and—with very variable success—soar into the high blue sky of their future.

11

INTO THE FIRE AGAIN—DIVORCE AND THE SECOND WAVE REACTION

People are laughed at when they have too many shots at marriage, failing and trying again. But they shouldn't be, for they are after the best thing.

FRANCES PARTRIDGE, *A Pacifist's War*

MANY WRITERS (many of them sociologists) seem to see the desire to remarry as an almost artificial reaction to social forces. With a sense approaching wonderment they note how people feel odd going to restaurants or theatres alone, the pressure of friends—'Met anyone nice yet?'

Being a couple is naturally nicer. We are formed so that we can only listen to one person at a time, only (on the whole) love or make love to one person at a time. No matter that it be in series—or one in the morning and another in the afternoon—it is a series of couple reactions. And human beings are so constructed that for their pleasures to bring happiness they must contain a feeling of permanence, the greater the better. Society's attitudes and pressures are secondary to this and the result of it; they are, as explanations, unnecessary and obvious. What would need explaining is a situation where people stopped forming into couples.

There is one rider to this—an observation of Margaret Mead's among others—which may possibly be true. Americans take very seriously the obligations imposed by a situation—and require people to be in a situation. They are usually tolerant about what it is, but they must know it. Europeans always note with interest the series of direct questions and equally direct information by which Americans elicit your position and define their own; and also note the stylised warmth, the instant and, it seems, shallow emotion with which they respond to the 'right' situations. This is a development to impose forms and structures, to 'place' and accept people, in a still fairly formless, improvising society, with varied cultural backgrounds and still dominated by immigrant-derived reactions. It does, if true, help to explain some extreme remarriage frenzy Americans sometimes exhibit.

The physical facts of the situation—how many people remarry, at what age, how long it takes after divorce—are in Appendix I. There are considerable differences in all of these and they make the charting of this period hard, but there are a number of patterns, some or all of which most people follow, which help impose the structure on divorce that at first seems the element most lacking.

These are difficult years; they are not sterile. They are often years of increasing self-knowledge. They can also be creative. Bertrand Russell produced during the harrowing period after his first marriage broke up the work for which he will always be remembered: the *Principia Mathematica*.

1 The market place

The last fifteen or twenty years have seen an enormous growth in the number of clubs and societies whose aim (overt or covert) is to help divorced people find new partners—though of course they provide moral support, give advice and supply entertainment. In Britain the National Federation of Clubs for the Divorced and

Separated (now over 100 branches) was started in 1966 partly to encourage these clubs, which have names like The Lone Parent Association, Phoenix Club, Solo. They are now to be found in nearly every large town and city in the country. There are thousands, even hundreds of thousands, of similar clubs and societies all over America, with the same aims and the same sort of names—Parents without Partners (166 chapters, 18,500 members in 1966), Second Time Round, Get Up and Go. They hold meetings, functions, dances, weekend outings, or 'singles' cruises.

Although there are a great many of these clubs, they are not particularly numerous compared to the enormous numbers of divorced and separated, and on the whole they sound fairly grim. Partly it is the overt, desperate quality. 'I do it,' said a woman of thirty-four, speaking about a 'singles' outing at a resort, 'because how many legitimate ways are there to meet men anyway? You have to try. But I hate being on the open market. It isn't fear of competition—I think I'm more attractive than most of the women at these places—but the men are so awful in their manner. They're all looking for something quick and easy, and they think all the women are too. It's really disgusting.' Hunt describes a meeting with the same atmosphere—the eager searching, the daring women giving open smiles to men they wish to attract, daring men cutting across the room to speak to some woman they've spotted. Dances have the forced gaiety and desperate courage of a high school disco where everyone has inexplicably grown twenty years older. Also, there is often a *petit bourgeois* feeling—salesmen, lower-echelon executives. Hart, whose sample seemed to come from a particularly gloomy and depressed end of the market (one of her interviewees described them as 'a bunch of social cripples'), met in a drab room, its ceiling stained with 'decades' of cigarette smoke. She pin-pointed one danger. The middle-aged, single again, feel they have somehow returned to the age they were when first single. 'In magazines the divorced woman is always the "femme fatale" with men wanting to jump into their arms,' said a woman of fifty-two with two dependent teenagers. 'Well, no one seems keen to jump into mine.'

These places are sad because the people who go to them *are* sad. (I suspect a good deal of the disgust is transferred stigma.) But on the whole they work—they wouldn't continue otherwise—and they proliferate: '. . . when I finally tried, in a desperate period of my life, I found it very unpleasant,' said a fifty-three-year-old man. 'The congregation of women—the hungry, eager, slightly shopworn women—at those places seem terribly sad.' However—'It was a freak bit of luck that I found my Audrey there.'

Smarter, younger, richer divorced do tend to shun the clubs as too depressing and down market. There are of course all sorts of other societies and clubs whose real aim is one thing, but who perform the same service and thrive for this reason (sociologists talk of 'manifest function' and 'latent function'). These can be anything: bridge clubs, tennis groups, night classes, university extra-mural classes, art classes, health classes, dance classes, weekends in Wales to discuss psychic phenomena. I think this may be one of the forces behind the enormous increase in consciousness-expanding and 'growth' groups generally over the last fifteen years.

Among what one might call the impersonal sources of new mates, there are the marriage bureaux, the computer-dating organisations, the small ads. One study revealed that 3 per cent found partners through these means in Britain in 1969 (this was total couples, but the majority would come from the divorced); Hunt has a similar figure for 1967 in America. Both predicted large increases. I can find no more recent research, but my clear impression is that these have taken place. Heather Jenner, for instance, finding that country men would as soon think of going to the North Pole as to London to seek a wife, has branches all over England. In general terms, surveys by Professors Goode and Hollingshead, quoted by Hunt, suggest that 50 per cent of remarriages in America take place from these impersonal sources.

The other 50 per cent find their partners through friends and relations. Here certain patterns begin to emerge. There is some antagonism between divorced and widowed. The latter feel, 'How could you be mad enough to choose what cruel fate slung at me?'

Also widows and widowers are usually older, over sixty, and their pain, as great or greater, does not have elements (rage, rejection, guilt, the stigma and so on) which give peculiar twists to the second wave reaction pattern.

The divorced and separated drop away from their married friends (in particular those who have never been divorced) and start to find their contacts among themselves, or among those who have been in the same situation for some time. 'You see other people on their own,' said Jackie, twenty-six. 'You don't see couples much.' Married people feel threatened in various obvious ways. They turn out to be hopeless at finding new partners for their divorced friends. Leafing through their address books, they usually seem to choose people more as a punishment. Those divorced for seven or eight years who find it satisfactory are obviously the most dangerous. Hunt describes one such man getting rather drunk with two old married friends, and saying how pointless marriage was, how happy he was. Suddenly the wife began to yell at him: 'We're like two little people who have been struggling fourteen hours a day for years to make this corner candy store pay off, and get rid of the mortgage and you come along and tell me capitalism stinks. Well, that stinks.' The man realised, on reflection, that he had spoken to the couple on the phone, but not seen them since.

The presence of a divorced or separated person (aside from the temptations to the sexually restless) suggests that any difficulties of the marriage might be similarly solved—*even though that could well be the wrong solution.* One marriage guidance counsellor, recently divorced, told me she discovered that she was suggesting divorce to every single one of her clients; as a result she was temporarily giving up her work. The distance between the married and divorced is sensible and necessary.

Sensible for both. They have quite different aims. The O'Neills quote a study made by Nicholas Babchuk of 116 married couples. He made each partner compile a list of the pair's closest friends. There was an odd result. When compared, only six couples had produced the same list. If they can't agree on who their close friends are, do they in fact have any close friends at all? Couples gain their closeness, their intimacy from each other. It is, besides, much harder to be intimate in groups of four to six. Couples meet to discuss mutual interests, mutual friends; their meetings are amusing, even brilliant; not usually deep. But the divorced meet to interact, to reveal and discover themselves, to pursue. Married people find their sparkle isn't listened to. The divorced find their married friends aren't revealing themselves—or indeed anything at all.

Thus drawing apart, once the initial shocks are over, they set out upon a new, shifting, tentative, temporary but quite numerous society, creating what does now begin to resemble, no matter that some of its *mores* may affect the whole, a definite subculture.

2   *Sex and the divorced—the pattern of affairs*

He that woes a maid must come seldom in her sight.
But he that woes a widow must woe her day and night.
He that woes a maid must fain, lie and flatter;
But he that woes a widow, must down with his breeches
and at her.

> J. RAY, *A Collection of*
> *English Proverbs*, 1678

It is sex that drives us from the nest. And so it is often with the divorced. After some unspecified time that very common cessation or disturbance of the libido starts to end. Hunt, who sometimes writes with a slight gulp in the throat, invented an imaginary figure to illustrate this, who returns from a party full of plans 'to read the current important books, take French lessons . . . she lies in bed and finds herself strangely desirous, though not of anyone in particular . . . she is half-ashamed to be directing on such thoughts, astonished at the signs of readiness in her loins . . . sleep will not come easily this night . . .'. No, especially if she dwells on those French lessons; but at some point the decision to return is made, frequently sparked or signalled by such awakening.

That inner decision to return is crucial. Heather Jenner found that the very act of handing over to a marriage bureau often led to marriage to someone who had nothing to do with the bureau. Just as adoption often leads to pregnancy (psychosomatic relaxing of the fallopian tubes) so the fact of deciding to get married, to face up to loneliness and do something about it, meant starting to see people, making an effort.

The sexual lives of the divorced are obviously enormously varied. Some deliberately abstain for neurotic reasons, or religious ones. Or else they disapprove of sex outside marriage and have a rather wretched, frustrated time. Said a thirty-six-year-old schoolteacher (woman): 'But I had no idea that the sexual urge, when unsatisfied, could make me so restless, irritable, and upset that I just want to scream. Sometimes I have to work in the yard, raking or digging or pulling weeds, or paint the house, or go swimming, until I'm too exhausted to even move my arms or legs.' There are those who masturbate. There are those who abstain because they so strongly associate romantic love and sex that they get no pleasure if the two are separated. Hunt found that these people (more women than men) find love partners rather quickly. They seem to imagine love where they feel desire, 'a phenomenon', he notes drily, 'not unheard of in the history of love'.

The married, and other outsiders, imagine the divorced to be having the most enormous quantity of sex. Kinsey in fact found that the 'previously married' had less sex than married men and women of the same age (only 36 per cent of women under fifty-six were having an active sex life, for instance). Kinsey included widowed in this category, who are, a study by Professor Ira L. Reiss of Iowa found, much less free in their behaviour. In any event, today there is probably little difference. A *PlayBoy* survey found 91 per cent of divorced women had active sex lives. But Hunt makes a shrewd point. The divorced and separated expend great effort and psychic energy in their search for sexual satisfaction. Their entire lives are coloured by it and revolve round it, which is why, even when their actual 'count' is lower, fewer 'outlets', their way of life is by comparison far more perfused by it.

One category is indeed so perfused as to consist of almost nothing else. The 'erotomania of the newly divorced', noted in the 1930s, is in fact an historical phenomenon, as the quotation at the head of this section shows. There was an Elizabethan proverb, 'He that wooeth a widow must go stiff before'. Sexual excitement, release, discovery, can sometimes for a while get out of hand. There is a promiscuous search very similar to much homosexual behaviour: the endless cruising of singles bars, the three-night stands, then someone new. And this can ally itself to a more general frenzy—the terror of being alone, of being 'unmarried', the desperate search, not for anything real, but an impossible dream mate, the devouring of *Self-help* books—a frenzy which does seem more common in America.

> 'I've done everything to get myself in circulation and meet new men,' said a woman of thirty-five. 'I've learned how to swim, play tennis, make cocktails, bowl and ski. I've learned how to really make love—I never knew while I was married. I've joined or visited the International League of New York, The Bon Vivants in Westchester, the City of Hope, Parents Without Partners, The Minus Ones of Great Neck, the Suburbanites of Westport, a Mr. Sword party; I've taken graduate courses at the New School—I've gone to dozens of weekends at the Concord, Grossingers and Griswold; I've been to Europe; I took a course in French at Hunter College; I tried a matrimonial agency, tried a year of psychotherapy, had plastic surgery. I've been to scores of cocktail parties and dances. I've gone out with at least 100 different men, from a fellow two years younger than myself to a man of sixty-three. I try anything and anyone. But I'm frightened—so many places, so many men, and I can't find it. Where is it? Have I lost the way?'

There is what one might call a stable promiscuous group of those who find it suits them, a pattern which may develop out of the frenzy as it calms down. Erich Fromm gives a possible analysis of some of these: 'Often psychoanalysts see patients whose ability to love and be close to others is damaged and yet who function very well sexually and indeed make sexual satisfaction a substitute for love because their sexual potency is their only power in which they have confidence. Their inability to be productive in all other spheres of life and the resulting unhappiness is counterbalanced and veiled by their sexual activities.'

The divorced and separated have been wounded in their love and sex. The pattern of their return is dictated by the healing of that wound, the restoring of confidence, the tremulous testing, the highly complicated interaction between wanting love and intimacy and dreading it, a slow and devious return to commitment, learning to love again. That is why there is often a good deal of what looks like casual and meaningless sleeping around. Sex is chosen because (aside from the fact it is an urgent instinct that needs satisfying) it allows some of the feelings of love without total commitment. It is intimately bound up with identity—with maleness and femaleness—so is a good method to rebuild that. It is basically soothing and reassuring.

Three, four, five or fifteen affairs may take place over the first few years. Hunt estimates anything between six to twelve dates before meeting someone with whom this is possible (Heather Jenner found an average of eight introductions—though twenty or thirty was not unusual). They usually know very quickly if it is going to work. 'If it isn't there in a few minutes,' said an experienced young woman, 'you might as well forget it.' Now it becomes clear why the divorced infinitely prefer someone in the same position or at least someone who has been through the same experience. It is then as though they were veterans of some tremendous mutual suffering—survivors of Dunkirk, say, or Vietnam. Intimacy is almost instantaneous in such circumstances, frequently fuelled by discussions of their marriage, their divorce, their pain. To some, this mutual confession pattern can become boring, an act. But most remain endlessly fascinated by their autobiography. And it has a function. The retelling of the pain exorcises it; at each telling some new facet is discovered. The subculture works as a vast mutual therapy group. The retelling boosts the teller, arouses sympathy, gives the other a chance to talk too, and allows them both to reveal what they want, and what they want to avoid in future relationships.

It is far less satisfactory meeting people who have never married or who have been widowed. The divorced find they are no more stable emotionally than these others but they are emotionally more aware. Also, marriage or a deep long-term relationship is so much the norm that those who have had neither by their thirties are probably at variance with the culture in some way. That is not to say they are necessarily worse, but they are different and therefore not much good as a future partner. The widowed are as bad in this respect. As well as their hostility, they carry the love of their dead partner as a sign of loyalty, of the marvel they have lost. This antipathy is not superficial and shows up strikingly in the later remarriage patterns of both divorced and widow/widower.

These early affairs are not easy. The old marriage still hangs over them. 'I even have problems about a double bed,' said one woman. 'I suppose because it smacks of marriage—we couldn't sleep in a double bed for ages—it really freaked me out.' Their tentative nature is revealed in the language of love—the language, that is, of *not* being in love: they are having a *relationship*, an *attachment*, an *involvement*. They are not 'in love', but are *involved with, tied up with, going with,* very much *interested* in someone. If they are involved, they may not be *committed*. They seek and need love strongly, they also dread and reject it strongly—and so they will find someone they *cannot* love. Here is another common reason for the long gap between separation and divorce—to make it impossible to become committed. Difficulties may also arise because, as marriage is so implicit a goal, anything that goes wrong, temperamental differences, loom huge in the eye of eternity. For all these reasons, these affairs during the first five years or so *do* end. The result is a brief flare up of old reactions—depression, insomnia, loneliness. But these people now

know they can survive. There are irritating elements, like telling
friends and hearing them say, 'What—not again!' But most recu-
perate quite fast.

There is also what one might call the 'sham love affair'. This is a
relationship which does not involve deep love and commitment,
which both in varying degrees dread. They seem in love, act much
of it, but it is a simulacrum of love, an imitation. It is quite a difficult relationship, which threatens all the time to wither away or
become more involving than one partner can endure. The tension
between the more loving/less loving is greater than in most marriages or long relationships. Classic differences show up: men
being more likely to want the comforts of counterfeit intimacy
and being untroubled by shallowness; women frightened of being
thought casual, and desiring (for her children often) permanence.
It is the shallowness which maintains the balance, and often these
sham love affairs—more friendly than loving, more comfortable
than compelling (yet how many marriages are as much?)—can
last for several years.

There is, finally, in this series of patterns, the long affair, in
which there is real love and emotional commitment—but where
both (one more than the other usually) continue to need a certain
amount of independence, the right to spend time apart with
friends, or to be alone. Token freedoms which reduce the sense of
enclosure, the degree of commitment. You will remember Nell
Dunn was not living with but was 'involved with' Dan. When I
spoke to her it was certainly a close relationship. It was totally
binding as regards fidelity. 'It wouldn't hold if we had affairs—
and I feel that. It wouldn't last five minutes if we were unfaithful.'
She'd said to him the other day, 'I'm only with you because I can't
find anyone better,' and felt a bit dismissive. Then realised it was
the nicest thing she could have said: 'You're the best person I can
find.' But they had separate economies. And Dan was buying a
flat just down the road to which he could retire from time to time.

These relationships often presage remarriage, showing that the
recovery is almost complete; or else, they themselves become the
marriage. 'I never flitted from one relationship to another, and

each one felt sound to me in its day,' said a woman researcher, aged fifty-nine. 'The last one before my present marriage continued for over five years and I believe that it prepared me for my present marriage in a number of ways, including a final break emotionally with my first marriage, and some learning about how to appreciate a relationship fairly far short of perfection. The five-year relationship was ended by my decision to start having an affair with the man who is now my husband ... My ex-lover thought he wanted to marry me but I'm not sure he really did, and I certainly never wanted to marry him or I would have done so. Yet he gave me the stepping stone to my present marriage.'

There is a problem about children that is particularly relevant in this kind of second wave reaction to divorce. D. H. Lawrence showed the pain of it in *The Rainbow*.

> 'Why do you sleep with my mother? My mother sleeps with me,' her voice quivering.
> 'You come as well, and sleep with both of us,' he coaxed.
> 'Mother!' she cried, turning, appealing against him.
> 'But I must have a husband, darling. All women must have a husband.'
> 'And you like to have a father with your mother, don't you?' said Brangwen.
> Anna glowered at him. She seemed to cogitate.
> 'No,' she cried fiercely at length. 'No, I don't *want.*' And slowly her face puckered, she sobbed bitterly.
> He stood and watched her, sorry. But there could be no altering it.

Yet the difficulties become far more acute, apparently, when children reach adolescence. The British journalist and author Brenda Maddox found a child psychiatrist, a woman, in Manhattan who was 'frequently' faced with this problem. Her advice was dazzling in its unhelpfulness. 'I tell them, "Do what you feel is right".'

What do most people feel is right? The study by Ira Reiss

showed that the divorced are more permissive towards their children's sexual behaviour, but they fuss. Though sexual rebelliousness (if it can still be called that) suits them, they wonder if it will suit their children. They also wonder what their children will think when the full scope of the rebellion dawns on them (all those partners!). Hunt found that most people conceal their sex-lives from their children. He recounted two good lines. A woman asked by her fourteen-year-old son whether she kissed her dates or what, said it was her business, and that everyone—child or parent—had a right to areas of privacy in their life. A man told his eleven-year-old son that he only slept with a woman if he liked her well enough to think he might marry her (number could vitiate this a bit). My own feeling is that lies probably do more harm in the end than teaching children the realities of adult sexual behaviour, particularly when in many instances the realities of adolescent sexual behaviour are not strikingly different. But it is not easy, and certainly not for those trying to bring up their children to be chaste. No doubt they will continue to tiptoe about.

The final pattern in the second wave reactions is one which emerges over ten years or so. There are certain widows and divorced women who often have something archetypal about them. They are independent, the man is absent and one gets the impression of 'thank God!' Martha Gelhorne, one of Hemingway's wives, is one of these. Lauren Bacall is another. Fifty-four, still beautiful, she has lived alone in her New York apartment for the last ten years.

> I like living alone. I like it a lot. It's selfish and dangerous in a way. But if I don't want to talk to someone, I don't have to. If I'm feeling sulky, I can be. There used to be children always in the house, but Sam [her sixteen-year-old son] is away at boarding school now. I don't lead a quiet and peaceful life. Sometimes it's as if everyone wants a piece of me—the wrong piece. But I don't want to live with a man unless he's terrific. There's 'companionship' I guess. But I'm not ready for a kind of

retirement village. I'll live alone till someone makes me not want to. Hopefully there'll be someone I'll meet. But there's not much around, I can tell you *that*.

It takes some people fourteen or fifteen years to get over, sometimes by some complex combination of these patterns, the devastating effects of divorce and separation. Upon which they join the vast six-sevenths majority—some of whom get over the whole thing with no trouble at all.

3 *How successful is remarriage?*

The divorced and separated mostly marry other people who have been divorced and separated; 60 per cent find their partners here. When you look closer at the statistics this preference is even greater. Divorced women make up a quarter of the unmarried women among whom divorced men could choose a mate. One would therefore expect them to choose a quarter divorced women and three-quarters widows or single women. In fact they choose divorced women *two and a half times* as often as chance or random choice would dictate.

It is this above all which makes those who have been divorced a subculture in society, since the patterns and experiences become concentrated. At the same time, when they remarry they are like prodigals returning to the fold. They cease to move in the intense world of single people, gradually dropping the divorced and separated they had been seeing and start to see their married friends again. This complex process can often happen once they have set up in one of the semi-stable couple situations.

What are the chances of success? One view, the extreme psychoanalytic one, is that there is really no chance of success. The extreme exponent of this was the late Dr Edmund Bergler. The divorced think they have learnt a lot because they have been through a lot, but this is an illusion. They are usually completely unaware of the real reason for their choice of the wrong partner, and the significant part of their behaviour in marriage is their decision to flee via divorce. These reasons are part of their neuroses and neuroses are hidden in the unconscious. Since personality traits at this depth are not modified by experience but only by extensive analysis and psychotherapy, divorced people are bound to fall in love unwisely again and fail in marriage again. 'Since the neurotic is unconsciously always on the lookout for his complementary neurotic type,' wrote Dr Bergler, 'the chances of finding conscious happiness in the next marriage are exactly zero.' There are some disturbing statistics. All surveys show that second marriages divorce more easily than first ones. One survey in Iowa found that if both partners had been married twice before the chances of a later marriage failing were five times as great as for the first.

However, Bergler was always rather extreme and not all psychiatrists agree with him (we shall soon see Bergler running his head slap into the female orgasm). For one thing, the figures are considerably biased by chronic repeaters—that is, those who divorce and remarry again and again. These are often neurotic but not necessarily so, nor are they necessarily immoral—they may even be overscrupulously moral. For many years, so her charming biographer told me, Elizabeth Taylor could only sleep with someone if she was married to them (she eventually managed to overcome this). Furthermore, as opposed to neurotic repetition, one of the main reasons those divorced once can more easily divorce again is precisely because they have been through the experience—they know what it is like and that they can take it. As was shown previously, it is this which means a long affair or affairs before marriage do not necessarily mean a later marriage will last longer. Paradoxically, the mini-divorces which take place during the second wave reaction—the break-up of shallow affairs with the short flare-up of old pain—while they are part of the recovery process are also a way of practising further, as it were, for a future divorce.

There is a much stronger tendency today to understand that fundamental modification can take place continually through life.

Certainly, Berkowitz and Newman have evidence that while two or three divorces can show a pattern, they can equally well show a progression—each one an improvement, the final one stable. Dr Jessie Barnard found that many first marriages failed through an incompatibility which was accidental and due to misjudgment that had nothing to do with neuroses.

Studies of these marriages which do last show they stand up well. Barnard looked at 2,000 marriages, of which two-thirds were remarriages. She found seven-eighths were satisfactory to extremely satisfactory, with one-eighth unsatisfactory to extremely unsatisfactory. Another researcher found that 90 per cent of his sample thought that their second marriage was better than the first. An understandable response, perhaps, but the latest figures from America are that about 50 per cent of remarriages will last for life. This is 10 per cent fewer than when Hunt was writing, but it is still, as he said then, a qualified success, a human situation—certainly not the disaster, the 'zero' predicted by Dr Bergler.

4   The step-situation—other people's children

> *There was once a man whose wife died and left him to*
> *bring up their only child, a little daughter, who was*
> *sweet and gentle by nature and as pretty as a girl could*
> *be. Father and daughter lived happily enough together*
> *until the man married again. His new wife was a proud*
> *and masterful woman, with two plain daughters who*
> *were as arrogant and disagreeable as she was herself.*
> PERRAULT, *Cinderella*, 1697

Brenda Maddox asks at the start of her book, *The Half-Parent*, why the stepchild/stepfamily situation has not been adequately researched. Her answer is that people go into a second marriage with huge hopes and are then appalled to find that the usually difficult and often hostile situation aroused by the partner's children threatens the marriage. A good many marriages break for this reason and people don't want to discuss it. These children often pose a threat long before—during the second wave reaction affairs. 'Phil was good with Matthew,' said twenty-six-year-old Jean, 'but he really just wanted that central exclusive boy-girl thing of being with me.' Everyone hopes the new family will succeed and therefore they don't probe into it. As a result, people think they know what is involved, what they will meet and how they should cope, but they don't.

I can see this might be a reason the parents themselves shy away from it but researchers and sociologists are not usually put off because an area is a sensitive one. The fact remains there *is* very little research.

It is the most confusing of the post-divorce-remarriage fields. There are no clear patterns—just a mass of individual difficult situations. Brenda Maddox sometimes makes it seem even harder than it is. Her book is fired by the very tough time her two stepchildren gave her—it's clear she did a very good job. 'But,' she writes, 'I was not a good step-mother. I simply mean that we, the three of us, never got it right during a decade of family life together. The arguments never went away; only the subjects changed. I was too inexperienced and inflexible to enjoy the job I was doing. They never fell into the rhythm of the home I was trying to establish. They fought it all the way even when they were benefiting from it.' Her old feelings jet out sometimes in quick stabs. Hamlet, she notes, 'A classic stepson, given to muttering to himself . . .' (This on his aside, 'A little more than kin and less than kind'.) She observes, irritably, of the *Cinderella* quotation above, how it takes a kick at the stepmother in the very opening lines.

A stepfamily can be defined as a household unit, with a married couple at the head, where a child or children from a previous marriage either lives or is a regular visitor. Because well over half of divorces involve children and most people remarry, there are a great many stepchildren (some 20–30 *million* in America during the 1970s).

There are two main roots from which the difficulties of the situation spring. The first of these is basically one of confusion, and in

Adoption	Step- parenthood
Adoption involves a change in legal status	The stepparent has no legal rights over the stepchild
It is permanent	The relationship usually dissolves with the marriage creating it
The adopting couple have a marriage of proven stability	Stepparenthood is simultaneous with the new marriage
They both want a child	The fertility of the new marriage is usually untested (or they don't want children)
They stand at the same distance from the child (unless they are adopting a child who is a relative)	The stepparent stands in opposite relation to the child and spouse as one is the biological parent and the other a stranger
They acquire an infant or young child with little memory of its parents	The stepchild usually knows or remembers the parent whom the stepparent replaces
They receive professional guidance on possible emotional problems ahead	There is virtually no professional guidance offered to the stepparent
Their act is seen by society as kind and generous	The stepparent is burdened with an ancient and unflattering myth

this it is compared to adoption. In fact, in many crucial respects it is directly opposite. (See table.)

A child sits at table with the 'bread-winner', but is probably being supported by an absent father. Different children in the same family have different hopes, expectations and claims—which they learn, and learn about each other, and this causes envy and jealousy. A crucial difficulty (for stepchildren and stepparent alike) is one of identity. *Who* we are dictates how we behave and 'who we are depends entirely on two families—our family of origin and our family of procreation; we are the children of our parents and the parents of our children. But we are not told how to preserve our sense of identity, if we have a mother in one family, a father in another, a son in a third, and a daughter in a fourth.' The difficulty becomes concrete over names. Are the parents to be Mummy and Daddy or Christian names? Do you say, this is my son, my daughter, or this is my stepson, my stepdaughter? Brenda Maddox describes her acute embarrassment when she rushed her new six-year-old 'daughter' to hospital in America for a tetanus injection only to reveal that she didn't know whether she'd had one before. 'What kind of mother *are* you?' said the head nurse. 'A step-mother.' Since then, she's always referred to her daughter as her stepdaughter. Her daughter sees it as rejection: 'Why tell everyone?'

An interesting example of the enormous need children have to sort out this problem—and the power it can generate—is Jesus Christ. As opposed to Joseph, his stepfather, he created another father—his father 'which art in Heaven'. (There is expressed here a second unconscious fantasy, the desire to be the son of someone great.) But in order to make his basically confusing position not confusing but absolutely normal, Jesus went a step further—he made his father, *everyone's* 'Father which art in Heaven'. In the eyes of Jesus and the Christian religion we are, in this respect, all stepchildren.

Since something like 80 per cent of custody cases go to the mother, the most usual pattern is the confusion between the new father with his new stepchildren. A main difficulty here is rivalry with other boys in the family—Heather Jenner found that if there was a child already men preferred it to be a girl. In the same way some couples wish that the stepchildren had been of different sexes so that they wouldn't have been rivals. (Other couples are glad when both are the same sex since they can play together.)

The normal role of the modern stepmother is that of 'weekend stepmother'. It is not an easy one. Brenda Maddox points out that it is very hard work and should be called part-time, not weekend. She quotes the husband: 'You know that old Helen Hokinson cartoon where the woman is packing the car when the husband comes home and she announces, "I can go to the country for the weekend or I can get ready to go to the country for the weekend but I can't do both"? Well that's how [my wife] felt.'

Brenda Maddox suggests that the central role of women in family life means that men, since less is demanded of them, find it easier to love their stepchildren. There is also a sort of reverse childbirth. A stepmother can't lose the feeling that 'she's not had this child in her body'. This may be true where the stepmother is in the role of permanent mother (Brenda Maddox's own position); but since this is unusual, I would have thought, despite their lack of centrality in most family situations, in this particular one more was demanded of men than women.

Even more important than the essential confusion, and underlying all the other difficulties, is the fundamental issue of love.

5 *Can you love your stepchildren?*

'Put another man's child in your bosom, and he'll creep out at your elbow'—that is, cherish or love him, he'll never be naturally affected towards you.

> J. RAY, *A Collection of English Proverbs*

The central fact about the step-situation is that both stepparents and stepchild are frequently in a position where they both want love and want to feel love. Yet they find they can't give love, or they are not getting love, or they don't want the love they are offered.

Professor Goode of Columbia University, found that most remarrying couples, even if they don't admit it, want their partner

to 'love' their children. This is particularly true of women, and as
a result 'loving' the children becomes part of the wooing, even if
the intention may be quite different. Many people marry to get 'a
father' or 'a mother'—at least it is a strong element, one which
they don't admit. They think they are marrying because they are
'in love'. But it is as well to face up to it, because though step-love
may grow, the likelihood is that it will not.

Usually there seems to be a simple lack of involvement. 'Now
you mention it,' said one of the fathers in Brenda Maddox's book,
'I think I always refer to them as "our children", or "the children"
but never as "my children". If it is something that just involves me
and them like if I was telling a colleague that I was taking them to
visit their grandmother, then I call them "my kids".' This can hide
stronger feelings. 'He sat up,' said Brenda Maddox, 'and said
fiercely, "Because I do not feel they are my children. They don't
look like me. My sister's children look more like me. They could
be my children." ' A wealthy man, he'd left all his money to his
sister's children.

It is quite possible for stepparents to hate their stepchildren.
Here is an Irish writer married to an American:

> I cannot bear to touch my step-son. If we sit beside each
> other on the sofa, my flesh pulls away. I cringe. With my
> own children I'm positively incestuous. I'm always
> touching them, rumpling their hair, pulling them on to
> my lap. I've never gone in for any of the American senti-
> mentality of pretending that there must be absolutely
> no difference between my wife's children and our own
> together. Her parents insisted on that from the start:
> 'There must be *no differences*'. Of course there's a differ-
> ence, and I'm afraid I haven't concealed it. One can't
> hide one's feelings. It shows in matters of fairness. One
> would like to be fair and I'm just not. The two boys row
> all the time, and again and again I find myself coming in
> to protect Oliver (my own) . . . Actually my step-son is
> brighter and better-looking than my own son. Speaking

objectively, I can admit that. But I cannot tell you how
that boy irritates me. Friends tell me, 'Richard is aw-
fully fond of you', and I just don't believe it. I found his
diary the other day. He had written 'I think Daddy' (yes,
he calls me Daddy, always has) 'hates me more and
more'.

One reason for these feelings is that the stepchild reminds the
stepparent of the last wife or husband—and causes retrospective
jealousy. With natural children, anger and even temporary hatred
is allowed to be directed against them because it is part of love, is
combined with it. Here, love absent, you get terrible tales of rage,
and then guilt and desperate attempts to repress and hide. Stepparents overcompensate, putting up sometimes with situations
which freeze the blood—the sheer exhaustion and nightmare of
family life naked in their accounts. Winifred, who had married a
widower: 'When we got married about a year after their mother
died, we had the youngest, Robert, in bed with us for the first six
months (six months!). He couldn't sleep. He thought crocodiles
were nibbling his toes. The next oldest, James, wandered through
the house in his sleep. And the girl—she was ten—had to wear
protective pads to bed because she wet the bed. And as soon as
she stopped wetting the bed, she started to menstruate.'

What often makes it worse is that the stepparent may never
have had any children before—or know what it's like. They come,
as Brenda Maddox puts it, from a land of white rugs and glass objects on low shelves into their new world—where crocodiles nib-
ble toes and the house is in *chaos*.

Of course it does happen in reverse. People don't just marry to
get a mother or a father for their own children, they marry to become a parent of someone else's family. One man married a
woman with three children to compensate for three children lost
at his divorce. He longed to be a 'father' and was devastated when
he found the three had not the faintest interest in being his children. Stepchildren react with indifference or hostility and hatred
even more than stepparents. They struggle, often quite uncon-

sciously, to break up the marriage—and succeed. This is perhaps so well known that it is unnecessary to illustrate it. But difficulties have always intensified love. Children today have become like parents in the past; their opposition to the love shows the couple how much they themselves want it, and united, they will survive. The fatal move is for one parent to side with their own child against the other parent.

The reasons stepchildren feel strong negative feelings are clear. Practically all children hate divorce; the new parent, symbol (and often apparent 'cause') of that divorce can become the recipient of that hatred. There is straightforward jealousy. Quite often stepchildren feel for their stepparent emotions they have had about their own parents but repressed. This is helped by what psychoanalytic theory calls 'splitting', when love and hate, felt contradictorily about one person, are divided and projected on to two people—one seen as entirely good, the other as entirely bad. Clearly, the stepchild is in an ideal position to do this. Unlike the ordinary child who has to live with the fact that the good mother or father who comforts him is also the wicked mother or father who punishes or angers him, the stepchild can assign all the good qualities to the 'real' parent, all the bad to the stepparent.

Lack of love, low voltage involvement, hatred—where there are stepfamily difficulties, some or all of these confusedly together are of their essence. This shows up in research. Charles Bowerman and Donald Irish studied 2,145 stepchildren in Ohio and Washington in 1962. They found the cultural hope that the stepparent be like a 'real' parent was not often achieved. Children believed a stepparent was less fair than a real one; stepmothers less satisfactory 'mothers' than stepfathers 'fathers'; and stepchildren felt more distant from both their parents—real and false—than did children living with two real parents. There is some slightly more optimistic research, but that of Bowerman and Irish is the most comprehensive.

6   *The problem of incest*

'I'm going to tell you something very strange; it was she
who seduced me.'

VLADIMIR NABOKOV, *Lolita*

Incest is sexual intercourse with a close relative. In most U.S.
states and Europe it is as in Britain, where 'A man may not have
sexual intercourse with a woman he knows to be his mother, sister, grandmother or daughter.' A woman, of course, is correspondingly bound. Close blood relationship suggests strong instinctive feelings. The step-relationship is not a blood one; but the
emotional confusion just discussed underpins incest too and is reflected in the law. In Alabama, Georgia and Mississippi, and in
France, sexual relations between stepparent and stepchild are
considered incestuous. In England and Wales, Sweden and most
of the rest of the U.S. and Europe this is not so.

Most places ban marriage to people so related, but not all. And
this confusion is cross-cultural: both to the primitive and sophisticated mind the love is less strong and so is the incest taboo. In the
1930s the anthropologist A. L. Kroeber investigated what he
called 'stepdaughter marriage' in all the Indian tribes of the
American Northwest. He found that 5 per cent encouraged it, 25
per cent tolerated it, the rest banned it. This picture, with no particular geographic pattern, had the same patchwork quality of the
then forty-eight states of the U.S.—where twenty-four allowed it,
twenty-two forbade it and two allowed marriage but not intercourse outside marriage.

Since a man can't marry his stepdaughter while he is still married to his wife, one might ask how these laws can exist at all. But
if the wife dies or they divorce, then her daughter is no longer a
stepdaughter and it is then the difficulty arises. It is in fact to this
problem of whether the step-relationship ends on death or divorce that the laws, and the confusion, relate. It is a confusion
which, as well as spreading across cultures, goes back deep into
the past. The plot of *Phèdre* hinges on it, as Racine makes so
agonisingly clear. Phèdre felt terrible guilt because of her pas-

sionate desire for her husband's handsome son. About to die from suppressed agonies of lust, she confesses to her maid, who is properly horrified at what she realises is incest. Then the maid hears that Thesius, the husband, is dead. At once, all is changed. Now, of course, the maid announces delightedly it is no longer incest.

> Live then, no longer tortured by reproach.
> Your love becomes like any other love.
> Thesius, in dying, has dissolved the bonds
> Which made your love a crime to be abhorred.

Unfortunately, gloomy news follows swiftly. 'The King we thought was dead will soon be here.' Once more it's incest. Phèdre, consumed and transformed by self-hate, arranges the death of Hippolytus and takes a slow-acting poison, to give time to confess to her husband:

> Each moment's precious. Listen. It was I
> Theseus, who on your virtuous, filial son
> Made bold to cast a lewd, incestuous eye.
>   (John Cairncross's translation, 1963)

Incest can be a major problem in stepfamilies. It is not talked about. Psychiatrists and sociologists either evade it or say it does not exist.

It does exist. It exists, says Brenda Maddox forcibly, to the extent that stepparent-stepchild love is one of the world's great dramatic plots: we have seen it in Racine, which of course derived from the *Phaedra* of Euripides. It is in Verdi's *Don Carlos*, Eugene O'Neill's *Desire Under the Elms*, and Nabokov's *Lolita*.

It can be difficult and sad. Brenda Maddox describes 'Mary, an open agreeable young woman', who had married a man of forty-five before she was twenty-one. 'Conrad was forty-five when I met him,' said Mary. 'Two of his sons were older than I was. The youngest boy was, then, thirteen. In all of them I saw flashbacks of Conrad, what he must have been like at the different stages of his life before I knew him. They were all great companions for me when I married. We went swimming and mountain climbing. Conrad doesn't like those things. Oh, we all kiss each other. My oldest step-son—if I were alone with him for a week I'd be crazy about him. And my second step-son is very dashing, very tall. As for the youngest boy . . . well, I became very attached to him. He opened out to me in a marvellous way. When he was sixteen or seventeen, I was his confidante.'

Mary then admitted to Brenda Maddox that she was 'most sexually attracted to him, the youngest one, of all. I've travelled with him. I've swum naked with him. To tell the truth, I was quite in love with him about three years ago. I think Conrad knew, but we didn't talk about it. When they went off to college, I was low. Very low.'

The love was contained. She got over it. But the aspect of seeing her husband in his son is common; as is the husband seeing a young fresh version of his wife in some teenage moppet. In Racine's *Phèdre* the same phenomenon inflames the stepmother. When she becomes aware of her lust for Hippolytus she demands that he be banished. But

> I shunned him everywhere. O crowning woe!
> I found him mirrored in his father's face.

Ordinary parents have sexual fantasies about their children. In stepparents—no matter how sexually satisfied they are—these fantasies are much nearer the surface.

The same is true for stepfathers about their stepdaughters. In West Germany this was once classed as incest and prosecuted. Dr Herbert Maisch, analysing seventy-eight cases in a book called *Incest*, found that thirty-two of them were step-incest. It is interesting, incidentally, how accurate *Lolita* proves to be from his study. For instance, most of the girls were not mid to late teens as you'd suppose, but averaged 12.3 years (a few months younger than Lolita). Also, frequently it was the girl who seduced. He also noted the connivance of the mother—putting them in the same room or staying away from home.

Brenda Maddox goes into a long, inconclusive but fascinating discussion about why the incest taboo exists. One of the psychoanalytic bugbears is the *primal scene;* sexual intercourse between the parents which if witnessed by a small child has serious psychological effects. Freud believed this, and therefore many analysts today do so.

Ninety per cent of humanity still lives in housing conditions which make it impossible small children won't accidentally witness the sexual activities of their parents. A few thousand years ago—and during the millennia our instincts evolved—this would have been 100 per cent. This means that an experience which belongs unavoidably to the childhood of most people, and once always belonged to the childhood of everyone, creates serious neurotic damage. Odd.

The same sort of argument applies to incest. I suspect this was once very common. Usually supposed to be biologically disadvantageous, if everyone practised it, the reverse would be true. Where a whole people practised incest they would have increased the unfavourable hereditary factors among themselves. The children with such factors would have died off and then the people would have had fewer unfavourable factors in their gene pool. That is why animals have no inhibitions in this field and it may help to explain our own evolutionary emergence. It is also interesting that in the very earliest Oedipus myths he felt no guilt for sleeping with his mother and was not punished. London psychiatrist Dr Gordon Ambrose told me that the daughter who'd actually *had* her father was usually better than the other in the family who hadn't. What has happened is that sophisticated socialisation has imposed guilt on a deep and powerful desire which *in general terms* was evolutionarily advantageous. (By this I do not mean the incest taboo should be abandoned. The socialisation, the guilt, are with us; the taboo protects us from the guilt. The dilemma of the stepparent is acute because the taboo is weak.)

Another important aspect of the step-situation is the difference between replacing a dead parent or a divorced one. One group of people is quite sure that stepparenthood by death is easier—and that is stepparents by divorce. Probably all partners to a divorce wish frequently that their opposite numbers would silently, suddenly and painlessly dissolve—taking with them all traces of their past and present existence. This is particularly true of the step-situation. 'If only Kathryn would die and I had them all to myself then I could get their loyalty'—a typical remark.

In fact, as Bowerman and Irish and other researchers found, the opposite seems to be the case. The interval between death and remarriage is longer than between divorce and remarriage, so the child has become used to living with the single parent. The dead parent is idealised, and therefore the new parent suffers by comparison. Conversely, where the old parent is still alive he or she often shares some, or indeed a lot, of the parenting burdens. The children of a marriage ended by death are older than those from divorced homes, and it has been shown that teenage children, less able to adjust than small ones, are a greater difficulty in the step-situation. A widowed family can present a solid wall of two or three teenagers allied against the intruder. (The novelist Ivy Compton-Burnett was good on this.) And the difficulty in adjusting works the other way. People who divorce want to improve their lives and are therefore flexible; widows and widowers cling to the past.

The greater difficulty of the step-situation after death helps to explain the myth of the evil stepmother (in particular) and evil stepfather. This myth is found all over the world: in every culture from Celtic and Mediterranean to Zuni Indian; and in every age, from myths like that of Ino and Athanias in remote classical Greece, to more recognisable ones like *Hansel and Gretel* or *Snow-White* as we move through the centuries. Even these are very old. *Cinderella* was first written down by Perrault in 1697, but it certainly existed in China in the ninth century A.D. and probably much earlier than that.

During those many centuries when it was believed good for children to discipline them harshly, stepmothers had far greater temptations than ordinary ones to become savage. They did not resist them. Many, probably most, were unkind or brutal. It was because this fact was so universal and so true that it could become a myth—and at once, like other myths, be able to express other unconscious needs as well. No doubt the first stepmother tales were told by people who hated their cruel stepmothers and for whom the first and main need was to express the hatred.

Today is the first time—with our terrible new knowledge—that stepmothers and stepfathers heroically repress natural angers and hatreds, sinking back at the end of each day nearly worn out with frustration and effort. In their fifties, some of these will take to writing fairy stories (probably the stepfather—the new central step-figure). Thus will be born the first of the cruel stepchildren tales—which will gradually assume the stature of myths. How the evil taunting stepson and the seductive shameless stepdaughter wrecked the marriage and therefore the lives of the kind, conscientious stepfather and his sweet new wife.

7   The rewards of the stepfamily

The central step-figure today, the most common, may be the stepfather by divorce; the one with the hardest task is undoubtedly the stepmother looking after her new husband's children. They do it primarily because they love their husbands. A second husband means security. He's been through, or thinks he's been through, hell. He is struggling to support two homes and won't bolt again. There are rewards—the gratitude and perhaps love of the children. The gratitude of the husband which, even if it is the gratitude of a man thankful to have found someone to do what he couldn't, or wouldn't, is very strong and real.

What can be done to make the step-situation easier? In America, the law increasingly takes the view that the best policy is adoption of the stepchildren. This does have advantages. It is permanent, and therefore spells the security of the stepfamily to everyone in it. It gives the stepchild the same status and rights as any natural child; and since the stepchild is under the stepparent anyway, it is just fitting the legal position to the actual one. Something like 50 per cent of American adoptions are by stepparents.

This all sounds sensible, but there are drawbacks. For one thing, the motives prompting adoption may not be particularly pure. Couples do it simply to change the child's name and hide the fact of a divorce. The wife may urge it as a way of forcing the father to demonstrate his commitment to her and her children. Or the couple may be trying to take revenge on the ex-husband, trying to obliterate his love for and tie with his children. And what of the real father? In America, courts quite often force adoption against his furious protests. Apart from the basic and cruel injustice of this, it leaves the stepfamily with the problem of explaining what has happened to him. Many lie. A British study in 1966 found that 50 per cent of adoptive stepparents lied in this situation. Also, adoption cuts a child off, not just from one of his natural parents, but from half his family—aunts and uncles, cousins, grandparents—from whom children create their own identity. Adoption studies show that children who have lost this often suffer in adolescence from a sense of genealogical bewilderment and identity anxiety. In Britain, since the Children Act of 1975, the adoption of stepchildren has become virtually impossible. The stepparent can take legal custody of the child using guardianship, but the child keeps its family ties, though the name may be changed in a separate action. This is seen as a move towards greater honesty in family relations.

As regards the daily battle of step-life Brenda Maddox gives some sound advice. If possible, have another child. It is as profound a sign that the union is permanent as adoption. And it strikes at the fundamental difficulty, the lack of blood-love. The new arrival is a half-brother or sister, linking the stepchildren with the parents and each other. Research done by Dr Lucile Duberman of New Jersey State University in Newark in 1972 confirmed this. This research also found that step-sibling relationships were best if they all lived together.

But her main plea is for more honesty and less pretending. Don't expect to love or be loved. If love grows, fine. If not, that is fine too. The problems—the possible hatred, the lack of involvement, all we have discussed—should be known about and tackled as they arise; all that should be demanded from both sides is consideration.

And love *does* grow. Oddly enough, this is the clue to Marabel

Morgan—the Total Woman. Her mother married three times, and her third husband adopted Marabel when she was three. He loved her and she him. And she loved him all the more because he didn't *need* to love her. This is the emotional base, I suspect, for her willingness to please men.

But there are many perfectly amiable and relaxed relationships without love. The Duberman research found most thought theirs were 'reasonably good', while if another child had been born 78 per cent reported their relationship 'excellent' (53 per cent 'excellent' without a new child). This can often be the advantage of the stepfamily. It is frequently easier to have a calm, supporting, friendly relationship with children who are not your own. (Brenda Maddox makes the sensible suggestion that to start this process the stepparent should teach the new stepchild something. This allows close contact and the display of good qualities without involving the artificial assumption of parental behaviour.) There is even a suggestion that divorce has created a new, looser, freer form of extended family. Paul Bohannan calls it a 'divorce chain'. I remember a man I met in New York who was planning to move to Los Angeles to a new job. Fifteen people met to discuss it: he and his second wife and their two psychiatrists, his ex-wife and her husband, his new wife's ex-husband and his wife and her psychiatrist, and five teenage children from these marriages, one of whom brought a psychiatrist.

I don't think this very often takes place—the co-operation is so often uneasy and nearly hostile, the interests conflict. Or if it is a new form of extended family, it is not at all efficient (yet how efficient is the ordinary family? Not very). But there is truth here, and it is on this note that Brenda Maddox ends her book.

Stepfamilies have special and real tensions and difficulties. Yet the strange child taken in, the absent parent often sharing the burden, dispersing the loyalties, creates a lightness. There is a lifting of that claustrophobic lid that clamped down on the old closed nuclear family 'with its narrow privacies and tawdry secrets', as Professor Edmund Leach put it. The stepfamily is open and tough and, if the difficulties are faced honestly and clearly, can be a good place to live.

12

SOME SOLUTIONS TO THE PROBLEMS OF MARRIAGE, DIVORCE AND SEX

More longs to marriage, than four bare legs in a bed.
English proverb, 1678

THE STUDY *Who Divorces?* found that couples in difficulties often wanted help, but were too embarrassed to go for it. Besides, they didn't know where to turn for guidance. This may be strictly true—but in practice it isn't exactly like that. People are very reluctant to face marital problems; at the same time these are often acute and pervade most of a couple's life. As a result they turn to their doctor, lawyer, gynaecologist, solicitors, local social service office or priest (especially in America) with problems that are really marital.

A striking instance of this is that the very large amount of money granted for marital separation cases in legal aid in Britain does not even nearly correspond to the actual number of separations and divorces. That is, people are using the law to solve their marital difficulties—by bringing matters to a head, by compelling climbdowns. So little is this realised, that a recent three and one-half-year research into the social services in Britain found that some social workers would go so far as to say—though 90 per cent

257

of their clients were married—that *they had no married people coming to them at all.*

Clearly, all these people would benefit from knowing something about marital therapy. Lawyers, for example, would become much less exasperated if they could discern the true cause of their clients' cases. The Institute of Marital Studies, a branch of the Tavistock Institute in London, which carried out the social worker study, and which was set up in 1948 as a research and training centre, focuses on the concept of crisis points. These are moments of high stress—first child, children reaching adolescence, child leaving home, parents having been married twenty years and so on—which impose sudden stress on a marriage. It has been found it often only requires a little help, a slight push in the right direction, and the couple can solve the problems themselves. An American project found that after four therapy sessions a couple in difficulty after their first child were four times less likely to divorce than untreated couples.

People like solicitors and welfare workers don't have to take up marital therapy professionally themselves. That would be absurd. Often all they need is something a bit more elaborate than the facts above—enough to know when to make sensible referrals. (Probably some helping figures—doctors, priests—should know more.) But if all the professional people upon whom married couples call in difficulty with disguised marital problems had a grounding in marital therapy, a lot of trouble would be saved.

It is sometimes suggested that young people should have 'lessons in life', classes in how difficult babies are, in the less romantic aspects of marriage, in the fact that a mother (or father) may not like children of all age groups. American universities went in for this quite a lot in the 1950s. Their success can be gauged by the booming divorce figures of the 1960s. They still have them in high schools and colleges but, according to Dr Ellis, they are feeble and fairly useless. My own feeling is that you can only learn about life from living it.

There are a number of practical ways in which divorce could be made better. As long ago as 1974 the Finer Committee suggested Britain set up family courts, which would take all family business except juvenile crime out of the judicial system: adoption, wardship, divorce, matrimonial upsets. The staff would include specialists in dealing with broken families, marital therapy and the whole spectrum of the social services.

It is sometimes assumed that family courts would automatically smooth the process of divorce. But there have been family courts in America for years and divorce there is not noticeably more amiable than it is in Britain. (In fact a tentative start has been made in Britain too.) The core of the matter is the adversary system, which both countries share. Eleanor Alter, a divorce lawyer in New York, said that lawyers were necessary because they were trained in the elucidation of facts. No. Lawyers are trained to elucidate facts and then marshal them in favour of their client, and it is this that intensifies a situation already fraught with fury. I would suggest that into family courts should come a totally new type of family lawyer—trained in law and the elucidation of facts, but whose skills are not adversarial but rather directed to lessening aggression, to conciliation.

Governments, of course, object on the grounds of cost. The cost of new buildings alone, said Barbara Castle when she was British Social Services Secretary, meant it was out of the question. That is to miss the point. New buildings are not needed. Broken marriage is no longer a crime. Divorce proceedings should be conducted in surroundings as unlike a court as possible—a room in the town hall or local school. Those involved, including the children if they are old enough, should sit round a table and discuss things and draw up a reasonable agreement. People are much easier with things they have helped arrange. Which is not to say family courts should not be courts. They should have sanctions and should enforce them. But they should be courts to enforce, in this respect, the fair sharing among its split members of the rights each held as one of the family; the right of a child to be seen by its father, the right of a mother for adequate support, the right of a father to see his child.

A completely new court set-up, a whole new class of lawyers

with a new and quite different training won't come free. The underlying principle of solving divorce problems is that society has willed divorce and is now accepting, and must increasingly accept, the fact and consequences of divorce. As this happens, so money will be spent, so people will learn more and more of the problems of divorce itself, of one-parent families, of stepfamilies, so they will accept the need for counselling—step-counselling, marital counselling and, above all, post-divorce counselling.

This is the most urgent area. America is in advance of Britain here. In the mid-1960s, according to Hunt, one-fifth of the men, two-fifths of the women divorcing sought some form of help. I can find no precise figures, but the consensus is that closer to half now sought help (men especially ask more freely than before). In America you have to look for organisations or people to help—but you can find them. A book by Joanne and Lew Koch, *The Marriage Savers*, which came out in 1976, had an appendix of thirty closely printed pages with lists of people and organisations, under sixteen general headings, who would help. In Britain, although more numerous than they were ten years ago, you could look for such help and find nothing.

The Marriage Guidance Council is the largest single free therapy organisation in Britain. There are currently 155 councils, with about 1,800 counsellors (close to their aim of one for every 25,000 of the population). They accept anyone who comes, no matter what their problem: anxious homosexuals, couples for couple-counselling, people who are single—'I can't seem to get married'. Plainly, from their name, their problems are mostly marital. Already this involves them in post-divorce counselling— sometimes for people who have already been for advice, then have returned after the marriage breaks up, for therapy and advice, sometimes for those who break up while being counselled (the 'successful' outcome to counselling can well be divorce) and who continue being treated. I would say the Marriage Guidance Council is the obvious base for a nationwide organisation for divorce counseling and that it would be a logical extension to its current work. David Barkla and Nicholas Tyndale, officials at the

Council's headquarters in Rugby, to whom I talked about this and many other matters, were appalled. They saw an endless extension—family, sex, children, 'The National Council for *everything*'. Yet they are already that to an extent (they now include counselling on sexual dysfunction at nine centres and are training more people). None of the centres does enough follow-up work, but when Barkla and Tyndale did some recently their first response was from a lone homosexual who'd found counselling a help.

Their clients are on the whole representative of the population (in so far as this is possible. All social organisations find the lower social categories are slightly reluctant to take up any service). Their treatment methods are analytically derived and the kernel is to get people to understand, to work out for themselves, the real, often unconscious, causes of their actions, and to realise the consequences. As regards divorce—aside from the immediate support they could give—this approach, used in retrospect, is highly relevant: to find out really why the marriage took place and why it broke up is of the essence; particularly as regards any future remarriage.

The proposals in this section might mean more 'good' divorces; but they would not necessarily mean fewer divorces. New courts, a new style of lawyer, greater facilities for divorce counselling and greater acceptance of it—so that divorce counselling became as inevitable as a visit to the doctor if you broke your leg—all this would have the effect of institutionalising divorce, giving it an institutional structure which would complement that rough psychological structure it already has. This would make divorce easier and therefore increase it.

1 *The psychological causes of marital breakdown*

Since personal fulfilment is the main goal and focus of marriage, it goes without saying the problems (and pleasures) when they arise, will do so in the personalities of the partners and in their interaction. When there were other goals, there were other problems. (Henry VIII divorced or executed his wives because they couldn't give him a son, not because they were stopping his 'growth'.) But there are particular reasons why marriage is likely to bring neurotic elements into play. Many neuroses are the result of unresolved emotional difficulties and conflicts with parents. The emotional closeness of marriage revives the buried love/hate of childhood, and with it the difficulties. Marriage is the place where the past is most active in the present. A peculiarity of this is that this development sometimes depends on the first child. Dr Pines has written: 'Pregnancy and parenthood produce an irrevocable change and a major landmark in the life cycle . . . there is an accompanying revival of earlier conflicts dealing with love and hate and a revival of the struggle to solve them and integrate them.' The full import of marriage as a love relationship may well not arise until a child is born, or even a child of the appropriate sex. The therapeutic—and so dangerous—exchange may then be with that child, the nonparticipant wife or husband a helpless spectator.

There is some objective proof that neurotic difficulty is a major cause (many people would say the major cause) of marital breakdown, even when it does not seem to be. Mixed religious marriages are at greater risk than same religion ones. This seems a clear case where external factors are paramount. One study showed this was not so. Many mixed marriages do very well. In comparing the two, it was found that those that went wrong were those where the couple had bad relations with their parents or where the home had been full of strife. These are exactly the home characteristics of those who have personality difficulties in later life. The couples' personality difficulties had expressed themselves through mixed religion difficulties but had not been caused by them. Where the difficulties and bad backgrounds did not exist, the mixed religious marriages were as smooth as any other. In the same way, mixed class or colour marriages are often ways of rebelling against parents. Once that battle is won, the partners start to rebel against each other. The breakdown of the marriage results from personality difficulties for which class or colour is wrongly blamed.

The processes at work in a difficult marriage are the same as those at work in all marriages, only more extreme. 'Neurotic' has become a vague word; we are all to some extent neurotic. Looking at extremely neurotic marriages makes clear stresses we all experience because they become exaggerated. It takes two to make what one might call a true neurotic marriage. A wife with a severely disturbed husband can soon see his hostility is neurotic. She can then accept it, or see he gets treatment, or decide she doesn't want to live with someone so neurotic and leave. It is when she is severely neurotic too that you get trouble.

For a marriage to work it is usually necessary for the partners to have reached a sufficient degree of independence, trust, and flexibility to accept each other, and give of themselves. Attaining these conditions should be the result of passing through various phases of growth as a child. Where this hasn't happened, writes Dr Jack Dominian, in his book *Marital Breakdown,* using italics to emphasise the principle upon which the book rests, *'the spouse is chosen as a means to complete growth which should have been completed prior to marriage or to supply vital personal needs missing during that period of development'.* This means that needs, characteristics and conflicts which really belong to childhood seek satisfaction or expression in the marriage—and much marital failure is due to one or both of the couple having personality defects because of this.

One major trait is overdependence due either to continually overprotective, overanxious parents, or else strict and authoritarian parents who take all decisions and allow no independent action—both are versions of dominance. If both partners are overdependent, there can be several results. They may both continue to return to their parents, caught in an endless yo-yo: desire to be home, desire to escape. Parents play a vital role here, and should help them escape. If both sets of parents are determined to reclaim their children, the marriage is doomed.

More usually, one partner will try and find the strength they need in, and become dependent on, the other. This is often shown in a dread of being alone. The spouse is desperately needed. A wife will sit at home all day, having rung her husband numerous times. Finally, when he returns, he is attacked. Often now the partner who pretended to be strong—he may hold a dominant social position such as a soldier or policeman or schoolteacher—reveals his weakness and panics. He can't take it, and stays at work doing hours of overtime or goes out with friends. His partner feels a deep bitterness and rage at being cheated. Anger is a keynote of these relationships. The overdependent child feels anger and hostility, his parents trapping him with love or crushing him with their authority. Those rebel mixed class/colour/religious marriages I mentioned are therefore often of this sort.

Or one partner is dependent and the other not. These marriages can last for some years, the dominant one taking the decisions and burdens. But obvious dangers lurk. The dependent husband might find his latent hostility toward the parental situation easier to express on a wife than on father or mother. This will increasingly emerge in sniping, taking the children's side against her, blaming her for the futility of their life. The wife stops sleeping with him.

Two other reactions are more common. Gradually the husband matures, until after years of harmony he has grown enough to want a new relationship. His attempts to take decisions, get out more, perhaps have more sex, are attacked and put down. The wife may have been dominated as a child and chose a submissive husband to be safe for ever. The worm turns and fears of her aggressive mother revive. He sees his wife as a jailer. Having outgrown the need for her presence, he 'falls out of love with her' and leaves.

Or else it is the dominant wife who changes and begins to grow. This can often be when she is forty-five, fifty. For years she has been nurturing; now, suddenly, she becomes aware of passing time, an urgency to be fulfilled as a woman seizes her. The inadequacies of her husband become intolerable. All at once decisions about house and children are hurled at him; immediate and enormous sexual demands explode beneath him. *For Christ's sake be a man.* If by some remote chance he has been maturing too, he may be able to respond. If not, the urgency and magnitude of her requirements precipitate a crisis beyond his comprehension or con-

trol. Desperately trying to cope with terrible and totally unfamil-
iar responsibilities, the husband scuttles helplessly about the
house, submerged in huge waves of anxiety. The tremendous sexual demands have already precipitated complete impotence. Not
that this makes the wife sympathetic. Her husband's response—
scuttling, impotence—further enrage and frustrate her. Streams
of criticism and abuse pour from her, combined now with sexual
taunts. Soon, the marriage collapses.

The varieties of personality immaturity resulting from unresolved childhood dependencies and conflicts, the modes of their
expression, are fascinating, usually tragic, and almost endless.
They can derive from emotional deprivation in childhood, lack of
love, lack of contact. Two people are drawn to each other by their
desperate hunger for love—and find they are asking it from the
one person who can't give it because that person is seeking it too.
Lack of love can result in extreme insecurity which generates a
deep mistrust of intimate figures nearby, often furious and quite
irrational jealousy. I knew a man whose wife upbraided him
wildly with having just slept with the Matron of a hospital while
he was coming round from the anaesthetic after a serious operation. She'd seen toothpaste stains on his pyjamas. The hospital was
staffed by nuns. Lack of love can result in lack of self-esteem, the
presence of self-hate and guilt. 'I am surrounded by a husband
who adores me, two lovely affectionate children and yet I can
enjoy neither because I don't feel I deserve it,' said one wife. Several personality difficulties can exist together, interacting and
confusing each other, and combining with those of the partner, in
highly complex and baffling patterns.

Some general observations can be made. Neurotic interactions
can break marriages; but neuroses can bind, if uneasily. The domi-
nant-submissive partnerships, the woman married to an alcoholic
because she's afraid of male sexuality, such marriages can last for
life. Almost as many marriages are founded on mutual inhibition
and fear, probably, as are founded on freedom and strength.
There is a further reason 'neurotic marriages' do not necessarily
end in divorce. With the help of therapy one or both of the part-

ners can change, can resolve those early conflicts. But that help is essential—the conflicts are profound and intractable, buried deep in the past and, because painful, deep in the subconscious. It is very rarely possible to deal with them oneself (again we see how fatuous are the *Self-help* books). Because the psyche wants to resolve those painful conflicts—to escape that smothering mother, that buried autocratic father, even if both are dead—they continue to act if not resolved, the second marriage repeating the first. Ideally, nearly all the divorced should have some form of therapy.

Finally, marriages, love relationships, are above all about feelings and emotions. An analysis of great social movements, however profound, and however illuminating, does not seem quite real. It is the sudden spurt of panic or anger as the woman we are with starts to assert herself, or the sense of threat, of being rendered useless as the man appears to take on more and more of the children—that particular, individual instant that counts, not the 'feminist movement' or the 'new role of the father'.

Paradoxically, it is precisely because the difficulties so often lie in the intractable area of neurotic conflict that the future of modern marriage is hopeful. As Dr Jack Dominian points out in his book, anxiety about marriage breakdown and attempts to prevent it are quite new. It didn't really begin in Britain until 1936, with the founding of Marriage Guidance. It is virtually a new science. Dr Albert Ellis thinks it is among the hardest of all therapies. As it develops and progresses, it should become easier, more successful; more therapists and counsellors will become available, more people will go to them. In the abstract, and in general terms, this is probably true. Certainly there are steadily rising numbers of therapists and more people do go. Hunt notes that in 1965 Wayne County, Michigan, offered marriage counselling to all people filing for divorce. Out of 11,000, 401 accepted. By 1968 something like 6 per cent were seeking it in Los Angeles County. When Dr Dominian was writing in 1968, 57,040 people sought interviews with Marriage Guidance in Britain; by 1970 this was 87,640, by 1973, 116,510. One might refine the observation. Since neurotic difficulties often do not appear until a couple get married, and because the 'successful' outcome of counselling can well be divorce, we might expect to see the most impressive result of more and improved counselling and therapy in more stable second marriages.

It is very hard to evaluate accurately how much difference it would make. I cannot help a feeling of doubt. The whole practice of what one might loosely call modern mental medicine—psychoanalytical, behavioural, physical, and the rest—has been in existence, its numerous branches for differing lengths of time, about seventy years. It would be a bold man who'd say we were *for that reason* in general more content and better able to lead our lives, and to what degree. The fundamental solution to marriage breakdown in this area is better child-parent relationships, better upbringing. You'll get stronger marriages when you get less disturbed individuals. Is this happening? It's impossible to say, but it certainly doesn't feel like it. I think we probably do know more about child-upbringing, but actual practice changes very slowly. You can postulate X million more enlightened parents, but suddenly huge impersonal factors intervene: a war, poverty or even economic collapse, the ever-rising divorce rate.

There is, however, one avenue through which marriages are and will increasingly be helped. That avenue is sex. Although sexual lives will also be improved, that is not what we are initially concerned with. Sexual difficulty may be a problem on its own, innumerable studies show that it is almost invariably a symptom of a much more general marital distress with different causes. It follows that if the very large number of marriages which suffer from sexual difficulty could go and be treated successfully for this the likelihood is they would also find themselves being treated for their marriage troubles generally. It is here that the last twenty years have seen some absolutely fundamental and fascinating advances.

2   *Sexual function and dysfunction—the Masters and Johnson revolution*

Since copulation is the most important act in the lives of living creatures because it perpetuates the species, it seems odd that nature should not have arranged for it to happen more simply.

GERALD BRENAN, *Thoughts in a Dry Season*

In England, incompetence is the same thing as sincerity.

QUENTIN CRISP

The rising orgasm ('outlet') obsession of America during the 1950s and 1960s brought into the open the enormous amount of sexual 'dysfunction' which impelled the researches and solutions of Masters and Johnson. Because it began in America, and because America is far less obscurantist than Britain in these matters, it is much easier to receive treatment for sexual dysfunction in America than in Britain. There are a great many therapists and clinics; most medical schools have courses on sexual function. In Britain, it is on the curriculum of not one single medical school (though in some teaching hospitals, concerned individuals have set up courses—Guy's, St George's and the Central Middlesex in London, for instance). In the last five years, at last, something has been done. Marriage Guidance has trained, as I write, twenty-eight counsellors on M. & J. lines. The British National Health Service has set up some self-counselling groups. The March 1978 issue of *Forum* listed eighteen major cities, excluding London, where you could get free sex therapy. Lone pioneers, Dr Prudence Tunadine and the Institute of Psychosexual Medicine have trained 700 therapists over the last twenty years. This may sound like progress. It is as nothing compared to the need. Masters and Johnson wrote, 'A conservative estimate would indicate half the marriages [in America] as either presently sexually dysfunctional or imminently so in the future.' A psychiatrist I talked to in London about impotence spoke of 'a hidden army'. It is revealing, too, that though of the popularisers of Masters and Johnson, *An Analysis of Human Sexual Response* is in many ways the most interesting, it sold only some 15,000 copies in Britain, while the book on sexual inadequacy has sold 90,000 to date, is continually reprinted and sells steadily.

It was in response to the hundreds of letters about sexual distress he received as Director of the Reproductive Biology Research Foundation in St Louis, that William H. Masters embarked on fifteen years' work—four of straight sex research, eleven with sexually inadequate clients—out of which the treatment evolved.

It is based on three principles. First, sex is a natural function. 'Nobody really appreciated that sex is a natural function until we went into the laboratory and found it out,' wrote Masters. 'We had no concept of this either. We always thought we should be teaching something. It just isn't so. A man is born with the ability to achieve an erection. The first time he had one he didn't think about it. He just found himself with it.' It is, however, one of the very few instinctive physiological functions which man can quite easily interfere with, which can become blocked—not by psychiatric illness, but by social and cultural pressures (guilts, anxieties, ignorance) and by past patterns, and associations (often frightening or unpleasant) which have been caused by these pressures. The dysfunction caused by these things is the problem which must be cured. Second, new patterns must be set up, ignorance and anxiety removed, in the sensate focus sessions, which do this by a series of simple physical behavioural steps.

Third, the re-education and anxiety-lifting are carried on simultaneously in the dual couple therapy sessions. Masters appears to have begun the basic research by himself, using prostitutes, since he did not think ordinary people would co-operate (he couldn't have been more wrong; later on, ordinary people *flocked*). One of these had a Ph.D. in sociology and was supplementing her income working as a call girl. Masters: 'I had been talking with this girl for about an hour and a half listening to her attempt to tell me something about female sexual functioning, and it wasn't getting through at all. I didn't know what the woman was talking about. Finally, in utter frustration, she said, "Doctor, what you need is an interpreter because you are never going to know anything about women!" ' Masters agreed. He sought an assistant. The criteria were stringent. She had to be in her late twenties or early thirties; had to have at least one child; had to be divorced (to work his long hours. He works about eighty hours a week). Virginia E. Johnson got the job.

They found the dual therapist treatment necessary for several reasons. Each patient has a 'friend in court'. This is often necessary just to explain: a strong silent man needs a mouthpiece; a tense excitable woman needs another woman to put clearly and logically what she is pouring out. There is no feeling of 'ganging up'—as there might be for a woman if the couple see only a male therapist. This is necessary because the dysfunction will almost certainly have damaged and tangled up the marriage. This will need sorting out, and on the whole (first interviews are single, therapist to one partner) people can explain what's wrong more easily to someone of the same sex (though sometimes the reverse is true).

Dual therapy also helps with the transference. 'Transference' means putting strong negative or positive feelings (usually to do with the father or mother—and from there husband or wife) on to the therapist. That is, someone will actually feel towards the therapist what he feels for these people. This, if the feelings are positive sexual or loving feelings, can lead to a great increase in communication between therapist and patient; by the same token it closes communication between the patient and the spouse. This opening of communication between the spouses is the essential element in unravelling the marriage tangle. Dual therapy is ideal for cutting off transference. If, say, the wife starts to pay exclusive attention to the male therapist, then the therapist will address all his remarks and questions to the husband, while the female therapist tackles the wife. She soon learns she can't develop a special relationship with the male therapist.

Masters and Johnson stress the dual role in their treatment of marriage therapy combined with simple behavioural dysfunction techniques, the one reinforcing and benefitting the other. But I think they probably underestimate the role of the transference. I suspect that what they do is to raise old and deep feelings—highly intimate transfer-type material—by creating a measure of transference. This is partly how they get the material up again (not wholly), how they get the discussion going so that the couple can face the whole situation of the marriage and work it out with the therapist's help. The transference is then redirected back on to the spouse.

The couple must both come for treatment together and they must both *want* treatment. It takes place over just two weeks (not the least astonishing aspect) at the Foundation, which is at 4910 Forest Park Boulevard, St Louis, Missouri, where other doctors have offices so patients don't feel conspicuous. They all have vastly different reactions, 'Except,' says Dr Masters, 'every married couple, if they are speaking at all, will try and have intercourse the night before they see us if they can. They get here and invariably go to bed together.'

The first few days are taken up entirely with searching in-depth interviews, exploring the personalities of the partners, their marriage, their attitudes to sensuality. Day 1—same sex interviews; Day 2—opposite sex. By the third and fourth day they are moving into four-way talk in which, guided by the therapists with their now intimate knowledge and, in my view, ability to redirect transference, the couple start to communicate. 'After a decade or so of being room-mates,' write Masters and Johnson, 'they've talked a lot, but they've never really said anything to each other.' Suddenly, the accumulated past pours out. It is allowed to do so for forty-eight hours and then the couple move to the sensate focus sessions, the second pillar of the treatment.

The skin is the largest organ of the body—and the sensation of touch is the most important physical element of sex. One partner is chosen and directed (authority) to 'trace, massage or fondle' the other and discover which parts the other least likes to be stroked, and which best. The one 'getting' has only to stop the strokes which do anything irritating or distracting. The couple must learn to regain (or perhaps experience for the first time) the response to touching—how it can convey tenderness, affection, comfort, finally desire and passion.

One of the most destructive myths of male dominance—and one that has put quite unfair pressure on men and lifted it from women—is that men automatically know all there is to know about sex and that they can divine and satisfy a woman's needs. They don't and they can't. Usually women don't know what they like until they experiment. They must then teach men, guiding their hand, where and how and when they like to be caressed. Exactly the same is true in reverse.

This becomes particularly true as the sensate focus sessions inch towards the genitals. This takes time. At first the genitals are directly forbidden. The goal is not to arouse desire. This, of course, is to remove the most intense dysfunction-inducer—the pressure to perform, produce, achieve. The impotent man becomes more impotent each time he approaches a woman; he is obsessed by anxiety about whether he'll have an erection, or if it will stay hard enough to insert, or if it will collapse inside. The woman who can't reach orgasm will wonder if something is wrong with her. Her partner will feel he must 'do something'—remember the Hite quote: 'Feels like he's trying to *erase* my clitoris.'

Masters and Johnson lift this pressure in all sorts of ways. Authority figures (no Christian names), they direct each step. The therapy lifts the pressure off the sensate focus sessions; the dysfunction here is treated as part of the married relationship. And the sensate focus reinforces and informs the therapy. The early sessions are exploratory and almost objective—and so can allow a nonorgasmic woman, for example, to discuss without 'anger, fear or frustration' what she dislikes about her husband's way of stroking her back or her legs. The early sessions have no sexual goal, but are meant rather for giving and receiving stroking pleasure. But the goal is such a simple one that nearly everyone can achieve it. Thus emboldened they move to the genital areas, but again, no sexual response is required. That is not yet the point. It is just to learn what it feels like, to explore and discuss. Now myths and fallacies come up, and now the years of experiment bear fruit. The years of experiment . . . these do, for an instant, give one pause. *Understanding Human Sexual Inadequacy* is not a humourless book quite, but the setting, even in the very bare catalogue they present, is a strange one. A plain room, windowless, with light green walls. The temperature and humidity were controllable, there was a bed, and absolutely masses of equipment: 220 volt outlets were spaced round the entire room with a few inches between; there was elaborate lighting—but the pride was a splendid artificial phallus, plastic, which could be controlled for length and breadth and depth of penetration and rapidity of thrust. Here 694 men and women aged eighteen to eighty-nine, 276 of them married couples, performed 2,500 male 'cycles', and 7,500 female 'responses'. First they were encouraged to have intercourse alone in the pale green room. Then they were told they would be watched—not just by the therapists, but often by assistants, cameramen (miles of film were shot) and artists (*artists!*). They must have, at times, been festooned with wires and tabs and instruments. Yet there were astonishingly few failures—only 220 male failures out of 2,500, only 118 female out of 7,500.

3   *How the Masters and Johnson treatment works*

The results of this research are fundamental to the Masters and Johnson treatment sessions. The underlying discovery was that the basic sexual responses of men and women during intercourse are the same, and that these can be roughly divided into three: excitement phase, plateau phase and orgasmic phase, followed by resolution and return to normal.

The excitement phase is initiated by anything that excites sexually, and is followed within thirty seconds by an erection in man, and vaginal lubrication in women. This seems to follow the general engorgement (filling of blood vessels) all round the vagina, which forces fluid through the vaginal walls. Various changes of colour and temperature take place. But it was around the clitoris that Masters and Johnson made major discoveries. Marriage manuals had been vaguely centring on the clitoris for decades. Masters and Johnson were precise. In the past size was said to be important (related to size of penis myths), as was anatomic position (which might bring it into better contact with the penis; Margaret Mead constructed a whole theory on this); it was also thought that the clitoris *had* to swell (it often does in this phase). Masters and Johnson showed all these variables were irrelevant. With regard to clitoral foreplay, none of the manuals said how to do it, or how much. Masters and Johnson found that when, how and how much were so variable that it was essential women learnt themselves and then indicated it to their partner. They noted two related things: women masturbating usually stimulate the whole general area and not simply the clitoris; very few women manipulate the extremely sensitive top of the clitoris directly or for long (they did so only during the excitement phase, and then most often stimulated one side of the shaft).

The plateau phase is the stage of continuing excitement at 'a high level of pleasurable tension' and two interesting discoveries were made about it. The outer third of the vagina now becomes so engorged with blood that it swells up until it has decreased in size by a third or more. This is *why* penis size is irrelevant to a man's virility or his ability to give pleasure. Any penis *feels* large, since the vagina, swelling round it, is filled; at least this was so down to the smallest erect penis Masters and Johnson observed, under two-and-a-half inches, belonging to a man nearly six foot tall. The second thing that happens during the plateau phase is that the clitoris retracts to a relatively inaccessible spot under the clitoral hood. At this stage the clitoris is automatically stimulated because each thrust causes traction on the clitoral hood, which in turn strokes the clitoris itself (the *Hite Report* suggests reservations here).

Finally, *orgasm.* In both sexes, this is physiologically the same: breathing becomes rapid, heart rate, blood pressure double or treble, both may become covered in a light film of sweat. With men sperm and seminal and prostatic fluid are forced out in a series of contractions, beginning at 0.8 second intervals. With women, contractions, also at 0.8 second intervals, take place in the outer third of the vagina and recur from three to fifteen times. Along with this, the uterus also contracts rhythmically, in wavelike movements, starting from the top and flowing to the lower end. The more intense the orgasm the stronger the waves, similar to those in childbirth, though not as strong. So Masters and Johnson removed for ever the conflict between vaginal or clitoral orgasm. From an anatomic point of view there is no difference in response, and the response occurs whether clitoris or breasts are stimulated, indeed with any effective stimulation which can, though this is fairly rare, be simply imaginative. But from a physiological point of view there is only *sexual* orgasm. And during it women prefer the man to continue thrusting (just as they continue masturbating during orgasm). Most men at the final phase thrust in and clutch rigid—the thrusting becoming internal as it were with the contracting of the urethral canal.

Eighty per cent of women were most responsive sexually in the second and third months of pregnancy; suckling often leads to 'plateau phase' pleasure levels and sometimes to orgasm (why isn't this put in the propaganda to stop Third World mothers feeding with powdered milk?): but for the full rich range I refer you to Masters and Johnson themselves and in particular their popularisers.

Many of their discoveries emerged from their practical treatment of dysfunction, and to appreciate the significance of Masters and Johnson it is necessary, quite aside from the inherent interest, to have some knowledge of their technique. The most common dysfunctions are impotence and premature ejaculation in men; orgasm difficulty or absence and painful intercourse in women. Female orgasm difficulties are quite often caused by premature ejaculation, itself the most common male dysfunction.

Masters and Johnson define it as the inability to delay ejaculation long enough for the woman to have an orgasm 50 per cent of the time (unless she can't for some other reason). Other therapists define it as the inability to delay for thirty seconds or a minute; Masters and Johnson's definition has the advantage that its criterion is the pleasure of the partner.

Treatment begins about the sixth day of sensate focus. Previous therapists suggested the man concentrate on business problems or count backwards (and men do go to great lengths to distract themselves—sometimes pulling out their hair while making love): also they warned against touching the explosive genitals till the last possible second. The Masters and Johnson treatment is an ideal example of how practical their method is. It in fact focuses *on* the genitals, the source of the trouble.

The woman sits up leaning against the back of the bed, the man lies on his back facing her (that is, with his genitals nearest her). The wife now caresses his genitals and encourages an erection. Once achieved, she employs a simple manoeuvre called the squeeze technique. With her hand (if I follow aright) outstretched but bent at 90° so the palm is facing her she takes the penis between the thumb and first two fingers. The thumb is placed on the frenulum (where shaft ends and head of penis begins) and the first two fingers are placed round the other side—top finger on the glans, just by the ridge or edge which separates it from the shaft, the second finger just below this ridge. The woman then squeezes fairly hard for two or three seconds—even fairly hard squeezing does not hurt an erect penis.

Apparently, this at once makes the man lose his desire to ejaculate. Why this is so is not known—but it is so. After twenty seconds or so, the process starts again. The wife manipulates her partner to full erection (which may have been lost) and again uses the squeeze technique to prevent ejaculation. Quite soon, by repeating this, it is possible to have fifteen to twenty minutes' continuous sex play without ejaculation.

Masters and Johnson say—and one can understand it—that it is marvellous for the couple to find they can do this, on their own, after years of instant ejaculation. It usually takes only two or three days to establish ejaculatory control in this way.

Next, once they have achieved some control, they learn to put the penis in the vagina without thrusting (there is a rather moving line drawing of the man and wife. She, despite no eyes or real features, I thought looked particularly concerned). The man lies down and the woman straddles him in the woman-on-top position. A few squeeze techniques then she inserts the penis and both remain motionless, while the husband gets used to the strange new feeling of his penis in the vagina with no urge to ejaculate immediately. Should he feel he may, the woman merely raises herself, employs the squeeze technique, and after a while reinserts the penis.

Before this, the usual method was for the man to stimulate the woman almost to orgasm and then enter. The wildly excited woman would thrust frantically in an effort to reach orgasm before him, but would only succeed in making him come at once, while he tore out his hair and imagined he was at a board meeting.

After a few days, continually using the squeeze technique, the husband is allowed a single thrust or two, not to ejaculate but to maintain his erection. The couple can usually remain like this for twenty minutes.

So, by simple steps, each stayed with till achieved, the couple moves forward. Now a new position is adopted, 'lateral coital', the wife on top, with one leg outside her husband's, one inside—the easiest position for ejaculatory control (man-on-top is hardest). Still eyeless and almost featureless, I think I can detect a subliminal look of eagerness on the line drawing Masters and Johnson use of the female partner's face—and rightly. As the treatment allows orgasm, many women who have never been able to achieve it before because of their husband's speedy ejaculation now find they are completely responsive, and this usually takes place during the two-week period. If not, it will certainly be reached once home, where simple squeeze technique sessions continue for six months. It usually takes up to a year to establish full ejaculatory control.

This is the standard of all Masters and Johnson treatment: talk, step-by-step relearning, the partner who is not dysfunctional to-

tally at the service of the other, pressure to perform almost completely removed. Considering most of these dysfunctions were
previously considered 'incurable'—or to require years of psychotherapy—their success is phenomenal. Premature ejaculation is
the easiest to cure. They have a success rate of virtually 100 per
cent and feel that, like some sexual smallpox, it could be completely eliminated in ten years if their technique was applied
generally. With primary impotence, someone who has never had
intercourse with an erection, 59.4 per cent were successfully
treated. With secondary impotence, those who have at some time,
even if only once, had successful vaginal intercourse, 73.8 per
cent were cured. There was an 81.7 per cent success rate for orgasm dysfunction in women.

The Masters and Johnson sample is not in the least representative, as they fully admit, of those suffering from these dysfunctions. Those coming to St Louis are extremely highly motivated
and from a high socio-economic level (apart from other considerations, the expense ensures both). There is a sliding scale for two
weeks at St Louis—but it always includes all living expenses and
the top fee, quite usual, is $3,000 (or something under £1,500).
They screen out all those whose relationship has completely collapsed. Both these factors mean they don't get drop-outs, which
can be as high as 50 per cent at ordinary clinics. They also probably don't get the most severe cases. At the Institute of Marital
Studies in London they had couples who couldn't bear to touch
one another; 'couldn't', as Janet Mattinson of the Tavistock Institute put it graphically, 'even get on the Masters and Johnson's ski
slope'. Thus where Masters and Johnson have a 73.8 per cent success with secondary impotence, other therapists will range from
22 per cent to 55 per cent.

Masters and Johnson do stress the role of the marriage therapy
in their treatment, but there is evidence it is of absolutely fundamental importance. *A priori*, it is likely. If dysfunction is overwhelmingly a symptom of marital discord, as it is (no matter that
it finally becomes a cause), then its successful treatment must
strike at the main cause. Masters and Johnson seem to have dis-

covered two things. First, you can sometimes cure the soul through the senses. There is some power in touch (a lot of recent research supports this) that occasionally allows physical treatment alone to clear up deep-seated distress. More significant and of more general use, just as marital discord manifests itself in this highly sensitive area, so this area provides one of the most direct routes back into that discord and method whereby it can be resolved in an astonishingly short period of time. In fact, this route—literally in a physical sense—was discovered independently some twenty years ago by the Institute of Psychosexual Medicine in London, and is described by a leading member, Dr Prudence Tunadine.

Doctors working on contraception through family planning clinics found that women coming to discuss methods of birth control, to get fitted with coils and caps, were often really coming about sexual dysfunction. They then discovered that the mutual exploration of the patient's vagina was a swift route into the patient's fears, fantasies and guilts about sex. Not only that, but the doctor's reactions to the patient, the relationships that developed, were a crucial key to the marriage. From this they evolved a simple, nonbehavioural therapy which Dr Tunadine describes in her book *Contraception and Sexual Life.* It would take too long to describe, but only one doctor sees the patient, and often only one partner attends. The method certainly stands comparison with Masters and Johnson. Indeed, though such comparisons are tricky, one study found the Institute nearly twice as successful in treating the whole range of dysfunctions as a clinic in Oxford using Masters and Johnson methods—50 per cent successfully treated compared to 26 per cent. With premature ejaculation (they work more and more with men now) they have 67 per cent success; with orgasmic dysfunction in women, 62 per cent. With an average time per case of two-and-a-half hours, they are also quite astonishingly swift.

It has not been possible to do anything like justice to Masters and Johnson in this short space. I would refer you to their books except that, terrified of the furore over Kinsey, they deliberately wrote them in a style to discourage mass success. Certainly, I found *Human Sexual Responses* a tough read. But the two popularising books, *An Analysis of Human Sexual Response* and *Understanding Human Sexual Inadequacy,* are excellent.

Masters and Johnson's attempts to avoid best-sellerdom, incidentally, were a hopeless failure. *Human Sexual Response* sold thousands and thousands. A major Hollywood film company rushed in with offers to buy the film rights. Asked if he had read it, the chief executive said no, but he understood it was a very good story. A New York theatre agent asked if the musical comedy rights for the book were still available. I must confess I can't think why, in these liberal times, neither of these schemes has been taken up. Though probably opera—the medium above all for exalted sexual passion—would really be the best vehicle.

4   *The female orgasm—and multiple orgasm*

> *I masturbate with my middle finger rubbing around my clitoris very fast until I come again and again. I rarely fantasize during masturbation. I simply want the sensation.*
>
> Respondent in
> *The Hite Report*

> *Every woman is at heart a rake.*
>
> ALEXANDER POPE

It is widely known that women can experience multiple orgasm, but it was Masters and Johnson who revealed the extent and potential of this.

The outer areas of the vagina, and the last third, remain sensitive after orgasm, and if restimulated lead to continual orgasm, a woman being capable in most instances, reported Masters and Johnson, 'of having a second, third, fourth or even fifth and sixth

orgasm before she is fully satiated . . . within a matter of minutes.'
Each multiple orgasm is physiologically the same in all respects as
a single orgasm. They reported that multiple orgasm occurred
more frequently with masturbatory techniques than with intercourse. When allowed to masturbate 'a woman may experience
from five to twenty recurrent orgasms with sexual tension never
allowed to drop below plateau phase level . . . '.

It is not just a masturbating response. Five men came to the
Foundation for infertility. They were sexually potent but could
not ejaculate into a vagina. As a result they could maintain an
erection for thirty to sixty minutes at any given opportunity.
Three of the wives achieved rates of orgasm comparable to those
in masturbation. Nevertheless, it was these which showed how far
the process can go:

> The average female with optimal arousal will usually be
> satisfied with three to five manually induced orgasms;
> whereas mechanical stimulation, as with the electric vi-
> brator, is less tiring and induced her to go on to long
> stimulative sessions of an hour or more during which she
> may have 20–50 consecutive orgasms. She will stop only
> when totally exhausted.

Masters and Johnson tentatively advance historical speculation
based on this apparently infinitely greater orgasmic potential in
women than in men (I say apparently because they may be
wrong). The 'double standard' meant that women could only give
rein to their sexuality under very specific canons of 'love', 'marriage' and so on. Men had these too—but it was also taken for
granted that male sexuality could function separately. Girls before, and to a considerable extent still, require society's permission to be sexual beings (I remember talking to a girl who couldn't
have an orgasm unless she had a quick fantasy of her nanny saying
'yes'): romantic dreams are allowed—the actual sensation, the desire, the masturbating repressed.

Amazed at the orgasmic power revealed as their research volunteers trembled into ecstasy minute after minute, finally flopping back after an hour or more, the vibrator falling from limp hands, Masters and Johnson wrote this:

> Yet woman's conscious denial of biophysical capacity for sexual response infinitely surpasses that of man. Indeed her significantly greater susceptibility to negatively based psychosocial influences may simply be the existence of a natural state of psychosexual-social balance between the sexes that has been culturally established to neutralize woman's biophysical superiority.

That is to say men, with the connivance of women, imposed brakes on female sexuality in order to remain confident enough to get erections.

A number of things seem wrong about that conclusion. For one thing, it is to an extent anachronistic. The *extreme* potentiality (fifty orgasms) was really only revealed by the vibrator. But in fact the capacity for multiple orgasms considerably in excess of the male has been known for centuries (in twelfth-century Japan for instance). As Thomas Wythorne, the Elizabethan musician said, 'Though they be weaker vessels, yet they will overcome two, three or four men in the satisfying of their carnal appetites.'

In 1621 Robert Burton asked 'of woman's unnatural insatiable lust what country, what village does not complain?' Behind the apparent disapproval—due to the prohibitions of a religious age—one senses not fear but desire; just as the much more overtly fear-filled descriptions of male libido in the nineteenth century, at the height of upper-class female repression, were really expressions of the desire to be raped—sex without responsibility or guilt. In liberal ages, female sexuality was openly delighted in. It was a common belief among sixteenth-century doctors that a woman had to have orgasms to conceive.

Why should men not delight in women's orgasms? It is, surely, not so difficult for most men to satisfy most women? Masters and Johnson note that women usually report the second or third orgasmic episode as the most satisfying—and that this could occur in a matter of seconds. Five manual orgasms were sufficient—and multiple orgasms occur something like once a minute. It could be argued that many men—especially those in the Privilege Bulge with their new nonorgasmic skills—should be well capable of giving their women as many orgasms as they need. Surveys bear this out. In the *Redbook* survey, for example, the vast majority of both sexes said their sex lives were satisfactory or very satisfactory. Eighty per cent of the men said that the most exciting thing about sex was women's sexuality; and a good many men fantasised about being set on by sexually voracious women. Clitoris/orgasm fear or envy would seem to be a myth.

There are social, economic and religious reasons which explain the periodic male dominance and repression of female sexuality, but I don't think the power of female sexuality is one of them. One might speculate about the separating of sex and love. A Freudian would say that, since women and usually mothers have brought up children, the oedipal situation brings particular pressure to bear on men in this direction. There has not been the same necessity for women. It is at any rate interesting, even if it is only a coincidence, that as women are more and more learning to separate their sexuality from emotion, husbands should be becoming ever more intimately involved in rearing children.

I said that most men should be capable of giving sufficient orgasms; but, without thinking, I was really repeating the old imposition—that men somehow automatically know how to and are able to satisfy women. It is not so simple. There are large numbers of women, particularly young women, who don't find it easy to achieve orgasm through intercourse. This is the central preoccupation of *The Hite Report*.

This is a very odd book. It is more or less entirely about the female orgasm (the 100,000 questionnaires on the 3,000 answers to which the book is based, were printed by the Come Press). It consists of vast numbers of quotes—90 per cent of the 638-page book, forty-six pages of masturbation quotes alone—and these are no doubt why the book sold so well. Two samples: 'It is fastest lying

on my stomach with both hands under me, thumbs inside, next to
one another, rubbing myself in a circular motion or up and down.'
'I feel it at the base of the vagina—a burning, tingling, feeling,
then I feel like jumping and screaming.'

Shere Hite's book is polemical and it is tempting to argue with
her. The book is strongly anti-male. Male intercourse is referred
to at first as 'male thrusting' (in parentheses); finally, coldly, simply as 'thrusting'. Indeed, intercourse at all often seems to be condemned. 'If orgasm during intercourse is vague . . . how can you
be sure you have orgasmed at all?' 'To assume that intercourse is
the basic expression of female sexuality . . . is to look at the issue
backwards.' The real expression, it follows, is masturbation—
since it is this women do first and do most easily. There is a long
biological discussion which finally proves 'Intercourse was never
meant to stimulate women to orgasm', and the replacement of intercourse by masturbation recurs again and again, if only in the
energy of her language.

It is tempting in the first place to speculate why the book is so
violently anti-men. One of the women sexologists I spoke to said
Shere Hite was a lesbian. Well, I don't know about that, and certainly it doesn't matter. Popular writers about sex get accused of
more or less anything (as did Kinsey). Lesbian bias certainly
doesn't appear in her book. I was surprised, however, to see in it
evidence of an old psychoanalytic idea which I thought had been
exposed as a myth.

Since the book is almost entirely about the female orgasm, the
clitoris is central. Shere Hite takes as her launching pad, discoveries (recounted by Masters and Johnson populariser, Edward
Brecher) of the American sex researcher Dr Mary Jane Sherfey:
'The truth is . . . that the glans and shaft of the human clitoris are
merely the superficially visible or palpable manifestations of an
underlying *clitoral system* which is at least as large, as impressive,
and as functionally responsive as the penis—and which responds
as a unit to sexual stimulation in much the same way that the
penis does.'

Hite elaborates: 'Our sex organs . . . expand during arousal to approximately the same volume as an erect penis . . . the only real difference between men's and women's erections is that men's are on the outside . . . Think of your clitoris as just the *top* of your 'penis' . . . or think of a penis as just the externalization of a woman's interior bulbs and clitoral network.' In fact, the clitoris is really just the tip of a huge iceberg. And unlike the now rapidly dwindling penis—just an attempt, one begins to feel and not a very good one, to externalise vestibular bulbs and so on—which gets slower and feebler with age—this network gets better and bigger still. 'Mary Jane Sherfey has also pointed out that female sexual capacity increases as women get older, because they develop a larger and more complex system of veins (varicosities) in the genital area.' Finally, the summing up. 'When fully engaged the clitoral system as a whole overshadows the clitoral glans and shaft *in the ratio of almost thirty to one.* The total blood-vessel engorgement of the clitoral system during sexual excitation may actually exceed the more obvious engorgement of the male.'

What enrages Shere Hite, what absolutely infuriates her, is that this 'vast anatomical array', these networks, systems, shafts and bulbs, these veins and varicosities, this colossal complex of tissue—*can't be seen.* It is, to all intents and purposes, invisible.

It is tempting to engage in polemics because the argument is often weak. In the long section proving that 'intercourse was never meant to stimulate women to orgasm', many of her reasons are irrelevant since they did not exist, could not even have been imagined, during the millennia that our instincts and responses were evolving. When she deals with those millennia her grasp of evolutionary forces is extremely hazy. It would be as easy to prove that 'intercourse *was* meant to stimulate women to orgasm'.

Her book is muddled because the overwhelming majority of her respondents preferred intercourse to masturbation. Hite assumes women prefer intercourse to masturbation because sex is only legitimate if it means giving enjoyment to men. There is truth here, but that is not something you can deduce from her material. Nor is it borne out by other studies. Masters and Johnson showed that masturbation is physiologically more intense for most people,

whether male or female; but it is not psychologically the most satisfying. Dr Prudence Tunadine of the Institute of Psychosexual
Medicine in London found that there was a deep psychical difference between orgasm from self or mutual stimulation of the clitoris, and intercourse. 'The togetherness, mutual abandonment of
control systems,' she wrote, 'the emotional acceptance of the
penis and all it implies in terms of the man, and of the vagina and
all it implies in terms of the woman, make this a unique experience that is not mimicked emotionally by mutual masturbation
however loving.' Surveys which can be expected to include a far
higher proportion than the Hite sample of women who don't regard the object of sex as pleasure for men, still more strikingly
prefer intercourse to masturbation. In the *Redbook* survey only
half of those who had masturbated since marriage found it satisfactory, and two out of ten did not find it at all satisfying.

Masters and Johnson said that the penis moving over the 'hood'
of the clitoris was sufficient stimulation for orgasm. Hite says that
quite often it is *not* sufficient, that in many cases, particularly
among younger women, it does not lead to orgasm. (Her conclu-
sions are borne out by other studies—one by the American sex
therapist and psychoanalyst Dr Helen Kaplan for example. *Honey*
magazine in Britain recently found that only 29 per cent of their
seventeen to twenty-eight-year-old readers had regular orgasm in
intercourse.) Since women can have orgasm easily when their clitorises are stimulated, especially by themselves, it is the *method* of
stimulation which both have to learn. Hite gives a great many examples (fourteen pages of them) including this: 'I lie on the bottom with my legs around him, then grind my pelvis and pubic
area against his.' There are five pages of various intercourses plus
manual methods. 'I am on top, sitting up during intercourse. He
touches my clitoris lightly with his finger, hand or both hands, in a
way that I can move against it as I want to.' Women should become much more conscious of their own pleasure, their clitorises,
their breasts; they should centre their attention on them as well as
on the man. Hite puts it in a way which may sound rather depressing but will no longer surprise us. In intercourse, a man is

really masturbating against the inside of a woman. 'This clitoral stimulation during intercourse could be thought of, then, as basically stimulating yourself while intercourse is in progress.'

This 'learning' is of course at the heart of the behavioural treatment of orgasmic dysfunction. Many therapists find that once orgasm has been experienced *at all*, it can be transferred to intercourse (and often this alone will by-pass, as it were, deep-seated fears and inhibitions). Since 95 per cent of women experience it with the vibrator, this is frequently recommended. (The vibrator industry owes a very deep debt to sex therapy.) The Masters and Johnson treatment is the same in essence as those we've looked at, only now it is the woman who controls the man—showing him how she wants to be stroked and when and where. Only slowly is she allowed to direct him to the clitoral area. And when excitement is felt there, it is carried over into the experience of feeling a penis in her vagina—but motionless, so that she feels dilation but with no demand to orgasm. When she wants to move she is told to think of the penis as hers to play with, to feel and to enjoy. For an account of the full gradual, skilful process I would refer you to the books.

The learning is partly necessary because whereas with men the most distinctive social pressure is the need to perform and anxiety about this, with women it is guilt and ignorance about their own sexuality. The extent of this, still, today, would take pages to demonstrate. It can be illustrated by a case of Dr Tunadine's, of a highly intelligent biologist who 'knew' the physiology of her body perfectly but who had a fantasy that the vagina and rectum were the same. The idea that intercourse was 'dirty' made her incapable of allowing it until this guilty fear had been uncovered. What is moving about books like *The Hite Report*, however bizarre aspects of them are (or still more extreme ones like Betty Dodson's *Liberating Masturbation—A Meditation on Self Love*) is that they can be seen as great cries of relief and delight as vast numbers of a whole sex, half of humanity, find that they are important and that what they feel is right and good.

This instruction (self-taught or otherwise) is also necessary because it seems that orgasm in women is a behavioural response which *has* to be learnt. Margaret Mead suggested this from anthropological evidence. In some societies women are actively sexed, recognise orgasms and seek them with the same freedom and eagerness as men. The Mundugumer is a society of this sort. There are other societies in which the phenomenon is not recognised and does not have a name. The Arapesh are one such. But even among the Arapesh there are some women who feel very active sexual desire which can only be satisfied by orgasm. Margaret Mead deduced that orgasm is a potentiality which has to be learned through practise, and in a society like the Arapesh the highly sexed are likely, for that reason, to learn it easily—probably through some accident of childhood experience. The potentiality to orgasm is present in different degrees (as it is in men) and is differently led to in all women. It therefore requires a society like the Mundugumer or Samoan, or as ours is becoming—which emphasises varied male approach, and encourages full expression in women, especially from the earliest age they show interest—for women to realise their full potential.

Women are sometimes irritated by this. 'Learnt' behaviour somehow seems less natural, feeble. This is not so. Many, perhaps most behaviour patterns vital to the species are learnt. Walking has to be learnt, and the evidence of children brought up by animals is that if it isn't taught or there are no models to imitate it won't be learnt. Animals learn to orgasm. Kinsey (initially a zoologist) had a film of a chimpanzee masturbating to orgasm by clitoral manipulation. He noted that rabbits and cats have orgasms.

This isn't all that different from men. There is some evidence that to experience the full potential of their orgasmic capability men have some learning to do too.

5   *Male multiple orgasm*

I remember Betty Friedan describing to me (a story she also tells in *It Changed My Life*) how in the early days of the feminist

movement Dr Masters was giving a conference on the female orgasm. They felt 'one of them' should go. So Betty went. There
were hundreds of grey men, and one or two tired and elderly
women doctors. But as the conference reached the films of multiple orgasm (its climax no doubt) these old hacks gradually went
wild. Cries, questions, counter cries filled the air. But suddenly
one of the very grey doctors silenced them. This was dangerous
stuff. They should consider whether to allow these revelations out.
'It could be a grave threat to the penis.'

Well, we've seen that the penis survived, but that doesn't mean
some people didn't feel threatened. The whole thing made Dr
D. E. Bergler ('Zero remarriage success' Bergler) absolutely furious. He devoted almost his entire life to the fight, in books like
Kinsey's Myth of Female Sexuality. Multiple orgasm wasn't sexuality at all; it was actually a form of frigidity.

Yet, what man (as indeed many women) can't help feeling some
slight envy? Not that young men can't have several orgasms fairly
close together. Here are three cases reported by the psychothera-
pist and author Dr Robert Chartham: 'Four or five years ago I was
making some investigations into sexual capacity and performance.
Among those who helped me were three young men aged 19 (A),
22 (B) and 23 (C). Under controlled conditions and with the help
of two partners, in one session (A) had seven orgasms in 55 minutes (with the same erection) and in a session some four hours
later had 13 orgasms in roughly two and a half hours by masturbation.' (B) by various means had 8 orgasms in 2½ hours; (C) 10 in
1 hour 20 minutes.

These must be very exceptional. Certainly they exceed anything reported either by Masters and Johnson or Kinsey. Even
then they are as nothing compared to the great female flows reported and filmed by Masters and Johnson—fifty to sixty orgasms
in an hour or so.

Recently, however, there has come evidence—reported in
Forum and as far as I know reliable—that man can also achieve
multiple orgasm. The pioneer was a Californian sexologist called
Stan Dale. He discovered that though they are usually found to-

gether, there is in fact a physiological difference between ejaculation and orgasm—and that *'orgasm can take place without ejaculation'*. It is certainly true that pre-adolescent boys can masturbate to orgasmic climax without there being any ejaculation. Dale found that it was a question of learning to control what are usually involuntary sexual reactions; to train and control the ejaculatory response, while giving rein to the orgasmic one. The learning took some time, but gradually his reactions began to respond automatically to these learned instructions. He then found enormously enhanced sensation—'intense, almost electric excitation flowing not only through the penis, perineum and testicles, but also through the entire body, including the skin'. He began at first rarely, then frequently, to experience multiple orgasm.

His work has been corroborated by research conducted by Dr Gordon Jensen, Professor of Psychiatry and Paediatrics at the University of California at Davis, and Dr Mina Robbins, at California State University, Sacramento. 'In a three year study of male orgasms conducted at their Sacramento laboratory they report that, of fifteen men aged 22 to 26, *all* had from three to ten orgasms per sexual session, with one man experiencing thirty. Erections varied from slight lessening between orgasms to constant erection throughout. All multiple orgasms occurred *before ejaculation.'*

Dale gives instructions on how to achieve these delicious feats.

1 Learn to control the anal sphincter muscle by holding back your stool when you defecate and then letting it out.
2 To strengthen the urinary muscles start to urinate then stop; repeat several times. Repeat frequently.
3 When about to ejaculate, attempt to hold back. This may cause some pain at first, but soon you will be able to delay ejaculation for amazingly long periods.

Once these exercises have been thoroughly practised, you have to internalise them to allow them to operate automatically. (Dale compares it to learning to drive a car.)

I discussed this with Dr Albert Ellis. He thought it was suspect, a product of female orgasm-envy. There was a sort of convulsive feeling—he got it after fucking, if someone stroked his thigh. 'I get a sort of little convulsive twitch if a woman strokes my thigh after fucking.' It was pleasant, and Dr Ellis thought this was what they were talking about.

It doesn't seem to me that this *is* quite what the Californian sex researchers have in mind; nor do I see any reason to suppose they are mistaken or playing some sort of joke. Nevertheless, what they advocate—this learned behavioural response—if it is possible, requires considerable dedication. I tried to follow Dale's instructions, but didn't really achieve anything. After a week of pinching and squeezing and delaying I'm afraid I grew bored and slumped coarsely back into the old common-or-garden ejaculatory orgasm—perfectly content with one or so a night.

13

THE FUTURE OF MARRIAGE, LOVE, SEX AND DIVORCE IN THE WEST

THE QUESTION to answer first is the one with which I began: does the 'breakdown' of marriage inevitably mean the 'breakdown' of society? Anxiety of this sort arises because the situation is now assumed to be different from some much more stable society in the past. The vision I evoked was of some rural community in seventeenth-century Stuart England: 'A cottage, a village of cottages, smoke curling in the spring air; a calm, traditional, settled community where marriages too were settled and enduring.'

The extraordinary thing is, if we actually look at those Stuart villages in detail the picture is completely different. So far from stable, the family was in a state of 'collapse' which it has not yet reached even in America. At Clayworth (one of the parishes where evidence over time exists) in 1688, 39 per cent of marriages were with a partner married before; 13 per cent were second marriages, 3 per cent were third marriages, 4 per cent were fourth and one person had had five previous partners. From other sources one can gauge that approximately one-third of all marriages in Stuart England were second marriages or more. And the inference must be that it was the same or more in the yet further distant past.

Death played the part then that divorce does now. In some respects, marriage was not more stable than now. And here we have the explanation of the stepmother myths—myths only arise when there is a near universal situation to contend with. (It also explains the prevalence of the orphanage in pre-twentieth-century literature.) And people were aware of this instability. This knowledge, this possibility, must have done something to alleviate the pain of a bad marriage. One can speculate that, if the same conditions existed today and if death struck by chance as often, then one-third of the marriages which today solve their difficulties by divorce would have them solved by death.

This picture does need a serious qualification. Today families split when the children are young (often under five); in that idyllic past it was the other way round. (To show this exactly, I have put some figures in Appendix J.) But calculations (based on French figures from the 1750s but roughly applicable) illustrate it strikingly: in their first year 2 per cent of children born had lost one parent; second year, 4.6 per cent; fifth year, 3.46 per cent—not until the fifteenth year were 32.6 per cent of preindustrial children in a 'divorced' family. Figures don't exist for a precise parallel to be drawn with today, but they would once again roughly be reversed.

The process of 'socialisation', of becoming a person, learning to love and acquiring identity, takes place especially over the first three to five years; the process of transmitting the culture, those 'learnt patterns' is more extensive, continuing into adolescence. It is clear both could be carried out in the preindustrial family—particularly the first, with only 13.46 per cent losing one parent by five years old. As for 'socialisation' today, it has already been shown that 'bad' divorces did upset socialisation, but that probably the majority of divorces were 'good' ones; and that more 'bad' divorces would become 'good' as the principal areas causing 'bad' divorce—poor father and child contact, one-parent families and poverty—were alleviated. I would conclude that divorce is certainly a disruptive factor here, but it is not overwhelmingly so and certainly not enough to bring about the breakdown of society. As regards transmitting the culture, we have some slight advantages over the past, in that as time passes marriages become more likely to survive. Where they do not, the stepfamily, schools, and the environment generally are quite sufficient to pass on cultural values and *mores*.

So different in other respects are the two situations that it is not really possible to say if one is 'easier' than the other. The step-situation today is hardest where the absent parent is dead—the dead parent is idealised, the phalanx of hostile teenage children face the new spouse. You could argue this was much more common in the past. But much of our difficulty today is due to what I described as our 'terrible new knowledge'—our knowledge of the effects of upbringing. There may have been phalanxes of teenage stepchildren idealising dead mothers or fathers but they were simply thrashed into submission (hence the virulence of the myth). There are all sorts of other differences—the former spouse still being alive today makes the role of the stepparent difficult; there is alimony and the exacerbating of tensions this brings; divorce does not end marriage—which make exact comparison impossible.

The idea that the instability of modern Western marriage, all the divorcing and splitting and affairs, somehow means that society is actually less stable, is not true. The institutions in the old world were expedients to provide an illusion of permanence in a world which was impermanent and insecure. They were therefore talked and written about as permanent to such an extent that we have come to believe it. The evidence, however, is that they were not. That is not to say that divorce today doesn't introduce a strong feeling of insecurity. Only that in this respect we are no different in broad terms from the past. But all the commentators who assume without argument that society will break down because marriage is breaking down, can derive some comfort here.

In fact, looked at in another way, we are just as stable as the past. That social stability rests on the fact that socialisation and cultural transmission can continue despite death or divorce. It is therefore theoretically possible to envisage a stable society evolving over the next forty to a hundred years, where, say, 85 per cent of marriages end in divorce. Indeed, a good many people do envisage it. Albert Ellis does: 'Life-long marriage will become a minority cult.' There is a particular view of monogamous marriage which explains why this might (indeed should) be so, and also throws light on this central institution in a way which I think illuminates the vast field we have now nearly finished traversing.

1   *The granite of love—monogamous marriage for life*

> *It's not too bad a thing to marry your problem. Containing it keeps you in touch with it, gives you a chance to solve it.*
>
>> DOUGLAS WOODHOUSE of
>> the Tavistock Institute,
>> London, in an interview

The most neurotic, the most difficult marriages, those with a lot of anger and frustration, are not those that dissolve most easily. In fact, outwardly bad marriages often last till death. It is the easy marriages, those with less pathology, that often separate so smoothly they scarcely seem to have been joined.

In fact, marriage until death seems an absurd route to choose for an easy life. An absurd route to choose for other goals—not necessary for sex, indeed in the long term inimical to it; very difficult for equal and mutual growth; deep relationships are quite possible outside it (one of the messages of Ingmar Bergman's *Scenes from a Marriage* was that the couple could only be genuine friends once they were apart. Only then did they understand each other). Indeed, one quite possible explanation of the state of marriage today is that a great many people are entering it who are quite unsuitable to something so strenuous. A hundred years ago far fewer people were able to marry, largely because of their financial situation. About one-third of adult women under forty-four, for example, were not married in the Victorian era. Today about 95 per cent of males and females have been married by the time they reach forty-five.

What then is the point of monogamous marriage till death? Guygenbühl-Craig, the Swiss Jungian psychiatrist who made all these observations, derived the facts from the married people he treated in his practice. In his book *Marriage—Dead or Alive*, he looks at an archetypal marriage, that of Hera and Zeus. To the Greeks, this *was* marriage. It was extremely stormy—usually about Zeus's incessant infidelity (though Hera was by no means faithful herself). At one time Hera tied Zeus up so completely that helpers from Tartarus had to free him. At another, he had her hung from the rafters of heaven. She was furiously jealous and would exact appalling revenge against his lovers. When he seduced Io, Hera turned her into a cow. This wasn't enough, so she loosed upon Io a gadfly, a gigantic insect whose stings drove her mad. In complete panic, raving with fear, Io as cow raced through large parts of the world. Many wives must have longed for such powers.

This myth holds a clue to what marriage is about. It is about the Jungian view of salvation.

Salvation is distinct from well-being. Well-being means comfort, freedom from anxiety, sexual relief, companionship. Salvation has to do with the meaning of life far beyond comfort. It is about facing up to suffering and death. Jungians have a word to describe the search for salvation—'individuation'. Guygenbühl-Craig says that individuation can be described *exactly*, in detail. This is not true. It is a mystical concept which is rather fuzzy and that is its strength. It can only be described in terms of the kind of things it involves, and by reference to myth and metaphor. It means not just finding out about, but working through, the forces in our subconscious: in a man, the powerful aspects of the feminine which are part of him; in a woman, the active masculine aspects; dark forces of destruction and cruelty which are also part of our natures. This last is particularly difficult, and all ages try and avoid it (putting it on to the devil, for instance, or, like us, on upbringing or social forces or 'capitalism', 'communism'). This process is, in fairy stories, a journey. But individuation is both the journey *and* the goal—the process of working through the self and the achieved reconciliation. It is like the life of Christ, where the life and its end were together the message.

Marriage till death is a pathway to salvation, a process of individuation. Because there is no avenue of escape it is an extremely unusual path. Here it resembles the strictest of enclosed mediaeval orders, or the vocation of a hermit. 'In this partially uplifting, partially tormenting evasionlessness lies the specific character of this path.' It is absurd to expect that marriage should be 'happy'. It is the way of salvation, and in myth the road to heaven leads through hell. Because it is a way of salvation marriage is an endless series of exalted high feelings and deep low ones, a continuous belt of ups and downs. It has happy moments of course, many of them, but also suffering and sacrifices.

Sacrifice always plays a major role in the myths of salvation. It is true that with Abraham and Isaac, God accepted a goat, but many myths have a tendency to comfort. The point was that Abraham had to be *ready* to sacrifice. In Christianity, the central myth of the last 2,000 years, sacrifice is cardinal. In any road to salvation there is a profound need to sacrifice oneself, a feeling *one should pay the price*. It goes without saying—you have only to look—that great sacrifices are demanded by marriage. The long-term confrontation of marriage is only possible if one or both partners renounce something important. This sacrifice is necessary to the personality. It is quite wrong for friends or therapists to say no one should have to go on giving affection to someone cold, no one should have to make such sacrifices. That situation *is* the marriage. Their sympathy is misplaced. Dante crossed hell, but he reached heaven. The successful marriage, the endured marriage, leads to the deepest kind of existential satisfaction.

Within this view of marriage a crucial Jungian concept, the archetype, plays a vital part. An archetype is a form existing in so-

ciety—in the past or present—which embodies a particular potential of the human psyche. The archetype 'war captain' or 'sci-
entist' gives the form which these particular talents can take.
Those talents cannot be exercised without the archetype. No
doubt there were 'scientists' among Neanderthal man, but not till
science and scientists had evolved could their skills find full expression.

Women today are leaving a small group of archetypes
('mother', 'sex goddess') and approaching a much larger group.
But society has not yet fully crystallised this new group. That is
why women are confused; why so many want to 'find' themselves,
lead their 'own lives'. Magazines are filled with 'find yourself' articles for women over forty. In fact this is a meaningless phrase.
To say 'I want to be myself' makes as much sense as saying 'I want
to speak my own language'. You can only speak the language you
have grown up with, or one you have learnt later. If you did speak
your 'own' language, no one would understand you. As more archetypal roles exist, become possible in the culture, women will
increasingly become able to express themselves. Here is another
reason why women in recent films have often been photogra-
phers—they are recording the outside world to catch the image,
the answer, which will eventually emerge there (sometimes, as in
Manhattan, they are journalists—observers again).

One archetype which is emerging is the aggressive, destructive
anti-male archetype. The figure of the dominant destructive husband crushing the wife is familiar and has always been a male archetype. But now we begin to recognise the murderously aggressive woman, the Amazon, the fanatical feminist.

Marriage is not necessarily harmonious. People can come together for mutual strife, for mutual rejection. They come to fight.
It is only in the context of a marriage that they can become aware
of their archetype, since it involves, on one side or on both, destructive hostility to the opposite sex. So it is only in this context
that they can gradually make it real, live it and so learn to control
it and live with it. These are not neurotic relationships, though
they will be violent, difficult, complicated and often painful. They
will also be vital, alive and have marvellous moments.

The fact that marriages last till death despite their pain-inflicting structure can *only* be explained if they are seen as something not to do with welfare. Marriage is to do with salvation, it is a way of life, a religion. It is a place of discovery, where someone rubs, grates against themselves and their partner; where they bump together in love and rejection, and so learn to know themselves, the world, good and evil, the heights and depths. It is a fairly tough picture.

It is also a profound one, whose truth raises echoes. Some marriages we all know become clear. Behind the deep angers or bleak despairs which only close, locked-in relationships can produce, you are also, sometimes, aware that you are finding out, living out, parts of yourself, often parts, forces, which are deep and painful. There is, besides, something cleansing in the grim, granite monogamy till death—standing out against the swirling but somehow softening tides of present-day morality. Yet I wonder—is there a great deal to be gained by standing against the tides? Should you not move inshore? Or, if that is not possible, alter your dwelling—take to rafts or a house on stilts?

Certainly it is relevant to some, and throws light on all; but I remember discussing it with David Barcla of British Marriage Guidance. 'It doesn't relate to most of what I do in my practise,' he said. 'They are mostly just quarrelling in a thoroughly messy way, which is of no benefit to anyone. And what do violent marriages do to those around them, to their children or friends or themselves—what is the *point* of spending forty years fighting?' I think of a couple who did quarrel for thirty years, not in the way of individuation but simply because they were not suited: she was witty (finally sarcastic), light, subtle; he was pugnacious, obsessed with boring pursuits, rural. They quarrelled—and led very separate lives. Until, by the time he was sixty-six, his aggression died away and he became dependent on her; she had grown to love the country, interested in his pursuits; and he found he could appreciate her wit when it was exercised around the dogs and the grandchildren. The last calm, companionable twelve years were the happiest of the marriage—indeed, it seemed as if it were the first time they'd really been together.

In fact people seek satisfaction for all sorts of different things in marriage—intellectual, spiritual, sexual, simple things to do with work, children, health and so on—and to label some of these 'welfare' isn't going to stop people seeking them as three-quarters still do—in marriages which last for life.

2   Guessing the future

The causes of the present situation in the West lie in a vast complex of social, historical, physical, legal, psychological and technological forces—some recent, some very ancient—which have all come together in a peculiarly intense way over the last thirty years. To guess at the future it is necessary to determine what is going to happen to these forces.

Some of them will stay the same, or will continue with increased strength. The onset of puberty has stabilised. Birth control will continue to get more efficient (as I write, not only does sterilisation increase, but a reliable male contraceptive looks likely). There seems no likelihood of a mass return to the country, which means that privacy from neighbours' scrutiny for the mass of people—a fundamental development—will continue. People will continue to live longer and therefore have (potentially) a longer time together and a longer period after children leave. The Privilege Bulge will grow and become more powerful as the century progresses, remaining particularly susceptible to 'growth' propaganda and 'growth is a new person' temptation. There is no evidence that romantic love is losing its power. People will have fewer children—the effects of which are imponderable. The number of analysts, therapists, counsellors and so on, that great 'life-support system' round the structure of marriage, shows no sign of diminishing.

As far as legal aids to divorce go, we have nearly reached the end. I rather doubt we shall ever reach the Roman position— 'Take your goods and go'. As far as the law goes, I expect (I certainly hope) the central injustice to fathers will soon be rectified.

The stigma of divorce will diminish. The pattern of divorce breeding divorce will continue: my own feeling is that affairs, consensual unions, will also grow and augment this pattern. But divorce not only fuels itself, it fuels that role change which underlies so much of our changed behaviour, and fuels it in the simplest way: fathers see and look after their children; mothers, for a while, become heads of households (and often *have* to work). As divorce becomes more accepted, and understood, the trend toward seeking help about it will become quite common. Thus will grow the institutional structure to complement the already existing behavioural structure. It is also possible that as people continue to lead the variety of lives we looked at, they will become more adept at them. In a sense, variety breeds variety. Those brought up in communes may be better adapted to living in that style and will bring up their own children in the same way.

The very large and measurable change to accepting premarital sex and allowing adolescent sex makes it likely that orgasm obsession will diminish. Sex will clearly always be central, and I would expect the 'flood' of literature, films and so on to continue (just as, since servants are not going to return, people have to cook for themselves, and the 'flood' of cook books and cooking articles will continue).

As for the role of women, the 'feminist movement', the crucial area here is women working. It is very difficult to see what will happen. One view is that though it is of course *possible* to change the economic base of society back (clearly, since it has been changed forward), it is much harder if the change has been economically beneficial. This view was easier to hold before the possible implications of the microelectronic revolution had been appreciated, which complicates the issue. It may facilitate women working, since it will increase pressure towards part-time labour—and this always favours women. Indeed this seems to be happening. In Britain, part-time labour is by far the fastest growing sector in the labour market (a 30 per cent rise between 1971 and 1976) and by far the largest proportion is women. This will probably mean more intersex friction initially as men are compelled to role-change further, but ultimately that would bring us closer to that equality which would benefit both sexes.

However, it could produce the opposite reaction. If the microelectronic revolution produces large-scale part-time work (two and one-half days a week and so on) men will fight to keep the work for themselves. The future, then, is that either women will get work, and there will be role-change trouble; or they will not, and the frustrated housewife figure will continue. Either way women working will continue to be a source of contention for the next twenty to thirty years and a factor causing divorce. (After that, I think equality will begin to prevail.)

On the whole, all these factors suggest current trends will continue and divorce rates continue to rise. What will slow them down or set them in reverse?

Guessing somewhat wildly, I think it will be the end of the century before the energy problems behind our economic difficulties will be solved. Economic reaction is not nearly so significant as a moral and intellectual reaction—since it is not a conscious and deliberate attempt to change the goals and patterns of social behaviour; but it is sometimes confused with it and can have some of the same effects. For example, I don't see the plight of the poor one-parent family being effectively mitigated in the near future. Nor do I see the special non-adversary lawyer system being set up in a hurry.

Divorce is not at all pleasant, nor do people do it for fun. I was at pains to emphasise this earlier, to emphasise the suffering which we wish on each other and our children by this unique form of behaviour in the West, this self-inflicted death. It is the extreme feature of the current trend that will, as divorce becomes still more widely known, as the children of divorce become more numerous, either slow it down or provoke the reaction.

For this reason (and others) I do not see the economic reaction affecting measures which will bring beneficial results far in excess of their relatively small cost: some training to lawyers, doctors, gynaecologists, social workers, priests and so on in marital therapy theory; and the growth in post-divorce therapy and sex therapy (particularly in Britain—a desert as far as such things are concerned).

Finally, there is what you might call the momentum of marriage-for-life. This has been the standard in the West for many hundreds of years. What we are seeing is something analogous to the break-up of a great empire. At first the central core remains very large, the breaking pieces only fragments. As time passes the fragments become larger (attracting others by a sort of gravitational force) and more numerous as the power of the central body wanes. Eventually the old 'empire' is simply a single territory again—one among many. But this is a very slow process indeed. The Roman Empire at the end frequently regained lost territories in sudden triumphant campaigns. And it was still, as Gibbon showed, detectable 1,000 years after its final collapse.

My own opinion is that over the next thirty to forty years three things will take place: affairs and consensual unions will become more common, amounting to perhaps 10–15 per cent of the whole, but marriage will remain overwhelmingly the central institution. Divorce will continue to increase and something approaching 50 per cent of all marriages will end in divorce. Within that pattern, second marriages will become more stable.

3   Reaction—the fallacy of the rigid swing

All movements of social change are accompanied by pauses and reactions—and each time these are heralded as the end. It is quite clear we are in one of those periods now. There is a right-wing Tory government in Britain, right-wing movements across Europe, a new middle-class white conservative resurgence in America. The spirit expresses itself in such things as strengthening the police, anti-abortion and anti-porn crusades, male-backlash, 'tightening up' of educational standards, anti-homosexual moves, hold-ups to the Equal Rights Amendment bill in America, some legislation against pregnant women working in Britain.

How serious is this? Some of it is economic reaction; this is true of the concern students in Britain and America now show with exams and jobs and standards; it is the reason for the legislation which makes it harder for pregnant women to work in Britain. Some of it—the anti-homosexual moves for instance—has failed. Nor is anti-porn always anti-liberal; in America it is a feminist cause (the proposal in Britain at the moment is that porn sellers should be licensed). Abortion has always raised strong passions, and it is uncertain how the campaigns in both countries will end. But that is the point—they are *campaigns*. The supporters are as numerous and vociferous as their opponents. There is no sense of a right-wing reaction sweeping all before it with overwhelming force.

What is noticeable, what is in fact *measurable*, is not so much reaction over the last few years, but rather a pause, a consolidation. (See Appendix J.) Nor is there any significant change in two absolutely fundamental areas. There has perhaps been some very mild reiteration that children benefit from firm guidelines, but the *goals* of child-upbringing—free and guiltless sexuality, secure, loved, self-regulating, unrepressed children and so on—remain exactly the same. Nor has there been any lessening of books and studies which go to make up what one could loosely call the ideology of the last thirty years—feminist books, studies on the role of the father, 'growth' books, consciousness-raising books, sexual engineering books, books on relaxed birth and child-upbringing. Certainly there has been no counter-flow. When Steven (*Inevitability of Patriarchy*) Goldberg cries in the wilderness, he cries alone.

There is also a firm restatement of old opinion by certain groups who have felt swamped during the last twenty years: women who don't want to work but only to look after home and children, men who think they should be dominant and don't want to change role. Along with these, there are minute pockets of anti-liberal sentiment remaining from the 1950s.

Of course I could be wrong. These—in the context—rather piddling demonstrations, the ridiculous Festivals of Light in Britain, and the like, might be the *start*, the first quivers of the pendulum prior to its downward swoop. Which takes us to the eighteenth century again.

The *idée reçue* is that these social revolutions seem to last from 80 to 120 years. They always generate extreme features, whether they be liberal or puritan, which provoke the reaction. Our current liberal movement began in the 1880s and is therefore near its end. But the actual *experience* of the present liberal movement (and so of any 'extreme features' it may have generated) among the mass, has only lasted thirty years. If there is any validity in the pendulum theory, then we have a further fifty to ninety years to go.

But evidence for 'extreme features' provoking a reaction in the eighteenth century is not very convincing: V.D. and drink among the upper classes, illegitimate births and prostitution among the lower classes. This leaves out most of the population. The extreme features played no part except in so far as they fuelled religious revival. It was *religion*—the rise of the Puritans at the start of the seventeenth century, the rise of evangelical fervour from the middle of the eighteenth century—which was the decisive force in the pendulum swing.

What evidence have we that a religious revival is on the way today? I think virtually none, as far as Britain goes. (See Appendix J.) In America, the Bible Belt retains most of its traditional strength, but this is not the same as a national revival. 'Religious type' movements—astrology, ecology, psychiatry—although highly significant, do not constitute a religious revival. And in America, as in Britain, there are fringe cults, Moonies, Bagwams, middle-aged Indian men with large breasts nearly naked on the walls of subway and underground; but they are precisely that—fringe.

It is likely that even if there were to be a religious revival it would no longer concern itself with certain vital areas. Kinsey found that strong religious belief made no difference to the number or ease of orgasms among women. Since then an interesting and unexpected change has taken place. The *Redbook* survey found that strong religious belief had a decisive effect in improving sexual life, and the stronger the religious belief the greater the improvement, the more women enjoyed it. In the thirty-five to thirty-nine age group, for instance, 73 per cent of strongly religious women were orgasmic all the time; while only 61 per cent of nonreligious women were. Religious women, no matter what their age, were more likely to be active in love-making than nonreligious ones. Similar developments have taken place in Britain.

What seems to have happened is that over the last twenty years a complete change has come over the attitude of great numbers of religious leaders, leaders in *all* religions as regards sex. Rabbis, ministers, priests, Imams have been teaching that not only is sex for pleasure, but that it must also be actively learnt and enjoyed. That tremendous power which for centuries repressed, now, and with equal success, releases the sexual instinct. Indeed it seems clear that far more than sex has been released. (See Appendix J.)

The fact is, there is something rather parochial about these 80–120-year swings. European and American history over the last 400 years has been studied by more people for longer than any other area or time in the whole world. Yet why should the pendulum swing to the metronome of those few centuries just because we know them so well? Why not different more ambitious swings—or no swings at all? We saw, for instance, that our sexual behaviour now resembles that in the Saxon period as much as anything else. Why, religion declining or acquiescing, should the pendulum not have swung back that far? And why should it not stay there?

I said that we all knew approximately what was happening to us because it stared us in the face; but that precisely because it was so obvious, the significance had not been completely grasped. To understand fully what is happening it is necessary to pull back still further, back until we can see once again into that distant period where we looked at the very start of the book, where we looked correctly but in the wrong place—that turbulent period just before the collapse of the Roman Empire.

14

THE GREAT CHANGE

*But if they cannot contain, let them marry: for it is better to
marry than to burn.*

ST PAUL

EVERY SO often there take place profound changes in human
consciousness—great alterations which affect the course of
human feeling, behaviour and thought for the next 500, 1,000,
even 2,000 years. It is my belief that we are at the start of one of
these massive shifts at the moment—that it is indeed the reactions
to this that we have been studying. Before beginning the speculative flight that will make clear what I mean, I want to look at similar movements in the past, since they are all linked.

1   The birth of guilt

The very early Greeks led full and easy lives, almost untroubled by scruples. Karl Jaspers says their lives were characterised
by an animal-like acceptance. But it was not so much animal-like,
as that they had discovered an ingenious device—they projected
their feelings on to gods, making them responsible for human behaviour. Anger, murder, love, lust—all were ascribed to possession by the appropriate god, or by a particular god in the appropriate mood. Anxiety over behaviour was only caused by the
sanction of losing the good opinion of their fellows.

Gradually, in that springtime of the Western world, there began to dawn on those early Greeks—'the men who invented names', as Plato called them—the extraordinary power of the human mind. As more and more of the natural and philosophic world came under their control, there seemed no end to it. They would understand, and so control, everything. But that which you can control, you are responsible for. At the same time, the sanctions of the outside world appear to have become internalised, probably as social life became more complex and social conventions therefore more important. In any event, men came to fear the rebuke of their own consciences; guilt had arrived.

The progress is nicely illustrated in the myth of Oedipus. By the time of Sophocles, in 500 B.C., Oedipus is overcome by guilt at sleeping with his mother and killing his father, and puts out his eyes in atonement. Freud said the myth reflects the universal guilt of the son wishing to sleep with the mother (blinding is a symbol of castration). But if we go back to the period when the Homeric myths probably originated, around 1200 B.C., Oedipus couldn't care less about sleeping with his mother. He feels no guilt, suffers no penalty and reigns in honour for many years. The guilt which had emerged by 500 B.C. was fairly rudimentary—it had less to do with direct personal responsibility than with an often accidental offending of a god or gods, leading to a state of impurity which had to be purged. It was an emotion, a passion almost, which was to become ever sharper, loom ever larger and plague the West for 2,500 years.

During the next six or seven hundred years the implications of this change became steadily more acute, the search for a solution more and more desperate and confused until around A.D. 1, when it is clear the ancient world was approaching crisis. That it was a crisis concerning moral behaviour and responsibility, about guilt, is shown by the solutions sought. There was a general and enormous upsurge of speculative enquiry which chiefly found expression in a great number of oriental religions and mysteries, a whole series of movements one could loosely label Orphic, and whose attraction to the Romans and Greeks was exactly that: concern with the moral and spiritual values of life on earth. The oppression caused by a sense of guilt, and the isolation of guilt, also found relief in the idea of a life after death where you would be at one with the gods (or God).

There had long been a tradition in Greek religion, the Dionysiac tradition, of seeking direct contact with the gods through ecstasy—a state of mania, of self-escape, induced by wild ceremonies involving drinking, dancing and sex. By the time those Orphic religions had begun to take hold, the Dionysiac rites, seeking a spiritual ecstasy, had on their own begun to abandon earthly desires. Rites of this sort had a tendency to degenerate; it was clear to initiates that gross and sensual men did not usually attain a high level of experience. Eroticism gave way to asceticism. Orphic religions much reinforced this Dionysiac development, since their goal was a still greater spiritual ecstasy leading to a spiritual afterlife. They rooted the source of evil in men's carnal appetites. For the first time, repression comes on the scene as a solution.

At this stage, these religions were quite easy on unbelievers. They demanded sexual continence as part of their programme to detach the mind from earthly matters, to lead to the spiritual revelation. But they didn't try to enforce it on others. Their religion *was* that experience; to enforce an outward conformity where there was no desire to have the experience, and so no chance of having it, would have been quite pointless.

Despite the ever-increasing number of religions, cults, mysteries and the like, there was no satisfactory solution to the problem of guilt. Indeed, the very number of competing leaders and gods increased the confusion. Social and economic factors now intervened as well, as Roman civilisation gradually collapsed with frightful spectacles of blood and sadism and the disintegration of values. The widespread nature of the phenomena—Palestine preaching a repressive patriarchal morality, Greece more and more dominated by destructive magical techniques, Egypt and Babylon also affected—argues something far greater than the collapse of the Roman Empire, tremendous as that was. In increasing distress, the ancient world was approaching some great crisis in the human psyche—and the second profound movement in human consciousness which would attempt to solve it.

It was in fact at this precise point that two 'new' religions emerged, both very alike, one of which was to triumph. The first was brought by Roman soldiers returning from Persia about 60 B.C. It was a mystery religion, practised in secret conventicles, its members calling each other brethren. They believed in baptism, confirmation, resurrection of the dead, and celebrated a Eucharist of bread and wine in memory of their Mediator's last meal. They believed in heaven and hell, the immortality of the soul and the last judgment. They also believed that immortality could only be obtained through the exercise of asceticism and self-control in this life. It was different from other mystery religions in that the central figure was a god and not a goddess, there were priests and not priestesses, and the chief priest was the deputy of god. His role was that of a divine being who was to be a mediator between man and god.

This religion was Mithraism. It was carried by the Roman legions the length and breadth of the Empire, until it even leapt the Channel and temples were created to the new god at Chester, York and London, as there were already in Cologne, Bonn and hundreds of other places. Mithraism swept and nearly conquered the Roman world. Yet in fifty years it had collapsed—ousted by a rival creed that was essentially the same, except in one single, but absolutely crucial respect.

The other religion was Christianity. Jesus cut to the heart of the problem with a simplicity that is almost staggering (the essence of these great movements is always simple; the working out anything but). Jesus said he came 'to take away the sins of the world'. The cardinal sentence in the New Testament, the one that sets it aside from all the other religions of the time and which led to its victory is: 'Thy sins are forgiven thee.'

St Paul grasped the significance of this. It was St Paul who, by involving the Jewish version of sin—an offence against a far more directly concerned and therefore offended God—further sharpened and focused the vague Greek feelings of guilt, and by doing this made them resolvable. St Paul has been credited with the fierce sexual repression that finally evolved. I am not sure if this is so. Well known as the quotation is, since it is arguable that the whole of Western morality for 1,000 years is built on this minuscule foundation stone, this foundation *pebble*, it should be looked at here:

> It is good for a man not to touch a woman. Nevertheless to avoid fornication, let every man have his own wife, and every woman have her own husband. For I would that all men were even as myself. But every man has his proper gift of God. I say therefore to the unmarried and widowed, it is good for them if they abide even as I. But if they cannot contain, let them marry: for it is better to marry than to burn. Now concerning virgins, I have no commandment of the Lord: yet I give my judgment. If thou marry thou hast not sinned; and if a virgin marry she hath not sinned . . .

From this we gather: (1) It is best if fornication does not take place. Not everyone is capable of this restraint; indeed the impression is that *most* are not. Therefore, marriage is for intercourse (and not, it can be noted, to produce children). (2) It was not the official teaching of Christ, but simply St Paul's opinion in response to questions from the Church in Corinth. (3) The final sentences are really a justification for premarital intercourse.

In fact, repression was a later growth. It has no foundation in the Bible. The picture that has emerged from the great deal of biblical research in the last seventy years is clear. Here were numerous small groups, held together by a joint, vivid and *felt* religious experience, preserving the essential view that sins were forgiven and the afterlife was assured by belief. There was no doctrine at all. They did not celebrate the birth or death of Christ. They did not claim he was divine. The divinity of Christ was not official doctrine until A.D. 269, when the Patriarchs of Samosata

protested it was nonsense. It depended on an electrifying experience of the divinity, in which dancing played a major part, and in
which chastity was a rule to enhance receptivity. But, like the
Orphic religions, it was an asceticism gladly embraced, it was not
imposed on others. That would have been pointless.

But the growth of repression over the next 400 years certainly
came from within Christianity. Unfortunately, this new and gentle religion contained a rogue gene.

2   *Christianity and the rogue gene*

Extreme chastity, continued over years and years, is virtually
impossible without considerable neurotic reaction. Even the
saints failed to transcend the body, despite terrible torture. And
some of the early Christians did seem to embrace their asceticism
with a violence you do not find in the Orphic religions. Nacarius
went naked into a mosquito-ridden swamp and let himself be
stung until he was unrecognisable. Burning, freezing, whipping—
still lust tortured their quivering flesh. St Jerome: 'How often
when I was living in the desert which affords to hermits a savage
dwelling place, parched by burning sun ... that prison where
scorpions and wild beasts were my companions, how often I fan-
cied myself among bevies of young girls. My face was pale and my
frame chilled from fasting, yet my soul was burning with the
cravings of desire, and the fires of lust flared up from flesh which
was that of a corpse.'

It would not perhaps have mattered if a few hundred or thousand demented saints had driven themselves barmy over the centuries. The trouble was that, in those early communities, since
sexual restraint was a goal, clearly the earlier you taught it the
better. It is likely that all sexually ascetic religions, if universally
applied, have this tendency to impose their rule on babies and
children. Certainly we find masturbation prohibition central to
Jewish post-captivity law. Jews were not allowed to lie in certain
positions, not allowed to wear tight trousers, not allowed to touch

the penis when urinating. One authority called it a crime worse than death. Exactly the same intense focus on the infant hand took place in Christianity.

This, then, is the *accidental* effect, the rogue gene attached to the good one of uplifting religious experience. We now know that doing this to tiny children has a catastrophic effect. It leads to a general feeling of guilt and worthlessness which can only be assuaged by the application of authority-given punishment and forgiveness, which soon—since the temptation and the fall are inevitable—becomes a pattern. The fever produced in childhood is imposed when adult. The process becomes unstoppable. So we see the group system giving way to the authority of the priest to administer the punishment; since that was his function, the more he punished the better, so we see the proliferation of doctrine and sin; since sex was bad, and sex required women, women were downgraded. The religion which came to remove guilt found itself, paradoxically, creating it. Or perhaps it isn't a paradox. You can't forgive if there is nothing to forgive.

The mediaeval Church became completely obsessed with sex, and with stopping sex. It barely allowed enough to continue the species. Sex outside marriage was of course forbidden. Within marriage it was allowed only in one position—there were penances for experiment. From behind, for instance, was especially bad and got seven years' penance. The Church continually whittled away at sex. First, it was made illegal on Sundays, Wednesdays and Fridays—effectively removing five months of the year. Then it was illegal forty days before Easter and forty days before Christmas—another two-and-a-half months gone. It was forbidden for three days before communion, and there were regulations enforcing frequent attendance at communion. It was also forbidden from the moment of conception till forty days after birth. Since wives became pregnant at least once a year, though quite how I don't know, the ideal was clearly really no sex at all.

As a result, in historian Rattray Taylor's words, 'It is hardly too much to say that mediaeval Europe came to resemble a vast insane asylum . . .' It also resembled, *was*, a slaughterhouse. Since punishment demanded an all-powerful central priestly authority any disagreement with the central authority was a sin. From A.D. 385 the punishment for heresy and many other offences was death. The executions were horrifying. 'A Bishop of Geneva is said to have burned 500 persons within three months . . . A Bishop of Bamberg 600, a Bishop of Wurzburg 900. Eight hundred were condemned, apparently in one body, by the Senate of Savoy.' In Spain, Torquemada personally sent 10,220 persons to the stake and 97,371 to the galleys. Heretical persecutions were responsible for reducing the population of Spain from 20 million to 6 million over 200 years. More people were put to death in Europe by this means and for these reasons than were killed in all the wars fought up to 1914—and many of those wars themselves, particularly the early ones, had strong religious elements.

Very gradually Western man gave up the hopeless battle to supervise how men thought and what they believed as regards religion; though it was not until the eighteenth century that toleration became widespread. The fight to control behaviour, however, to dictate morality, continued unremittingly. Although it was, of course, sex-obsessed, it also reached into every corner of every activity. This was because the mediaeval mind saw man as part of a vast interlocked system set up and moving according to God's laws. The movements of the stars were an expression of these laws and astrology was a respectable science, a way of finding out what they were. Since the system was locked together, the stars influenced human beings, crops, wars, tides, the weather, indeed everything. Conversely, human beings influenced the stars. So if humans misbehaved, disobeying God's laws, the stars would alter and so would events. To sin was therefore dangerously anti-social, causing plague, wars, crop failure.

All communities impose their morality with some vigour on their members. However, this mediaeval concept and above all the sex-obsession, although it steadily declined, lent for many centuries a ferocity, an interference as to detail in personal morality all over the West to which, at its most extreme, it is difficult to find equals. In sixteenth- and seventeenth-century England, the seduction of maidens was reported on hearsay. People objected if a boy of seventeen still slept in his mother's bed. They knew and complained about over-enthusiastic sex in marriage. They objected to a nagging wife. They objected to an overbrutal husband. As well as ecclesiastical courts, they had their own punishments—the 'rough music' or charivari, when the community would go howling round the wrongdoer banging pots and pans. These charivari could reach nightmare proportions, going on night and day for weeks or even months in France. They were common all over Europe and the United States—from Puritan New England to the mountains of upper Bavaria. This went on in England until well into the nineteenth century; indeed, the nineteenth century marked a particular height in that long attempt at repression and control. There was even a return of the mediaeval 'interlocked' idea. 'To the decline of religion and morality our national difficulties must both directly and indirectly be chiefly ascribed,' wrote Wilberforce in 1797.

Then, during the last quarter of the nineteenth century and the first twenty years of this, there began to be definite signs over the whole of Western Europe and America that we were once again on the point of a new and profound movement in human consciousness—the third which Western civilisation has so far undergone in 3,200 years.

3 *Conclusion*

A good many people are aware of this movement, of course. In a recent article the novelist Nicholas Mosley saw it as something both profound and exceedingly complex. He described it as a development in which men, from being capable of seeing themselves, had evolved the ability to *see* themselves see themselves. This has an interesting feeling about it, but I don't really understand what it means.

I think that what is happening is in essence extraordinarily simple (though the working out will be difficult, dangerous and complicated). And like the last great change it is concerned with the central issue of guilt and morality. The clue is found in some of the most interesting manifestations as the movement began to surface.

The early years of this century were characterised by religions founded by women, for example, Christian Science by Mary Baker Eddy, the Theosophists by Madame Blavatsky, the Maria-vites in Poland by Maria Kozlowski, and Miss Ellen G. White with the Seventh-Day Adventists. This was accompanied by a revival among Catholics of Mariology generally, and, in France, of an interest among French intellectuals in Catharism. Perhaps even more interesting, since it presaged these 'religions', was the way the Virgin kept on appearing. In 1896 she was seen at Tilly-sur-Seine and other Normandy villages. In this century, she appeared at La Salette, Lourdes, Fatima. The point is not that she appears, but that people want her to appear. That is why—responsive to the telepathic pressure of the community—it is frequently girls at the age of puberty who first see her.

This is sometimes explained as a sign that feminine qualities were trying to replace masculine ones. This is not actually true in a literal sense (because I think women are probably less tolerant than men as regards society *in general*) but it is true in a figurative one. The West was expressing a deep desire for the historically feminine—it was, in Jungian terms, a profound upsurge of the collective anima. Woman, in these terms, represents tolerance, gentleness, love, sex as opposed to the strict, authoritarian, repressive male. A very sensitive prophet might just have guessed what would follow from those early manifestations of the feminine alone.

In the same way that it gradually allowed religious toleration, Western society and the major religion which permeates it are finally becoming tolerant of how people behave. Personal morality is slowly moving away from the organised supervision and direction of society itself and, particularly as regards sexual repression, from the control of that central religion. We now have relative freedom to believe and behave and live as we like provided it does not, with obvious provisos, damage others.

How simple and obvious it sounds. How simple and obvious the solution—'Thy sins are forgiven thee'. Yet the working out of the second solution to the problem of guilt was difficult, unforeseen, frequently disastrous and has finally been abandoned.

The Christian view that the individual was supremely important has survived the demise of the myth. It was therefore likely—at least it was logically possible—that humanity might experiment with realising all the potentialities of that individual, no matter what. At the very base, Christ is more important to what is happening now than Freud. And we are only at the start. Over vast stretches of Catholic Europe, down that 3,000 by 3,000-mile intercrossing Main Street which is America, in rural areas everywhere, the changes have often been relatively small and sometimes nonexistent. Nor do the changes mean there is *no* morality—on the contrary, there are a great many different and sometimes conflicting moralities. But where, when the Roman Empire collapsed, the confusion of religions was a sign the ancient world was looking for a solution, here the confusion *is* the solution. I say 'solution'—but it is a solution at the start of its unfolding. The problems of guilt, of goal, of responsibility, are still with us. That is why one of the most prominent of the religious-type developments—the psychoanalytical one—is centrally concerned with these great questions. But it means that the burden is slowly being lifted from society.

Margaret Mead had an interesting idea about feminism (which at bottom is clearly a manifestation of this toleration—to allow women to be what they want). Limiting any activity to one sex diminishes the other sex and also limits the potentiality of the activity. For example, there are societies in which only women sing, except for men who learn to sing falsetto. There are, or were, societies which wanted to achieve the full range of the human voice but which, having limited singing to religion, and having banned women from the Church, used boys and eunuchs. In the end they had music which approached perfect orchestration at the price of excluding women and castrating men.

Approached perfect orchestration. Probably *all* complex civilised activities are limited if confined to one sex. Woman cannot only sing treble and alto as well or better than boy or eunuch, she brings a different quality and range of skills—the art is enriched, its full potential realised.

Conversely, it is likely that an activity which is restricted to one sex sooner or later exhausts its developmental possibilities; the rigid one-sex patterns which grow up finally stop progress. This may be one explanation behind the decline of great civilisations—that there has been too rigid adherence to the views and insights of one sex. The Roman equality of the sexes can be viewed as a last instinctive and desperate attempt to ward off the collapse of that so male-orientated society.

There is a sense here of a civilisation unconsciously gathering itself to meet some tremendous crisis. Today, for the first time, mankind—with its pollution, its weapons, its population growth, its gobbling of natural resources—can destroy the species. Allied to this is the fact it took the most enormous amount of energy on the part of society and each individual to impose rigid beliefs and moralities. This energy, released, will partly (increasingly) go into the complexities of different ways of life, has partly gone into the artistic explosion of the last eighty years—but is still a great potential store at the service of humanity.

But number alone would have made some such development likely. It is difficult, but possible at least, to think of imposing a uniform morality and way of life on a single small population of one fairly isolated national culture. The problem becomes too large when vast populations (single countries now comprising more people than the whole world once contained), huge international markets, different cultures all interlock and interact. Uniformity becomes impossible. It seems clear there must be dozens, hundreds, of schools of painting in such a context, or people who follow no school; different types of books read and written. The same is true of private morality. Just as rival moralities have often existed at peace in the world so now they do in single countries.

Or it is possible Western civilisation took a different sort of wrong turn when it repressed Eros 1,500 years ago—and used reason, rational rules and strictures to do so. Not only was Eros repressed (then to run amok) but it meant repressing the whole unconscious, and this meant repressing the powers of the unconscious—telepathy and other forms of extra-sensory perception. Humanity therefore missed or ignored the existence of forces which reason can't really detect—or will reject. It is these forces and unconscious potentialities we are examining or reaching for now—but to carry this out needs the removal of the whole edifice which buried them.

I can think of quite a number of qualifications which might be made about these speculations. But I don't want to argue here. I want only to indicate the dim, submerged outline of what I think one can sense is going on. So great a movement will embrace practically all areas of the human condition; it will be many-sided. I think it probably contains elements of all these ideas. But though the detailed survey in this book helped explain why the change became evident when it did and the forms it is taking at the moment, it is quite simply not possible to grasp the significance of what is happening unless it is appreciated that some vast reorganisation of the modern psyche is actually in progress and that what we have been exploring is one of the most important and revealing manifestations of this great change.

As to how we should view it, we can only feel what men and women feel before all great human enterprises. Certainly, fear. There is no guarantee we shall succeed. Freedoms of this sort are very difficult; they have never been attempted on this scale in this sphere before. I do not for a moment think we are happier. Human societies seem to have something akin to the ecological fabric found in animals and plants. You cannot, therefore, 'solve' anything without creating a new balance of problems and solutions which involves the same elements (people, families, the society itself). People today are able to commit the most appalling mistakes; we are making ourselves and our children suffer in ways which are every bit as bad, though different, as in the past.

But is happiness the point? The essence of all life—its 'task'—is to survive and adapt, and that means experiment. We marvel at the prodigality of experiment; as it becomes conscious, marvel at the courage. We are all engaged in the first confused moves in an experiment to let people live and love and explore as they think fit, however bold or foolish or dangerous; to explore as far as they like into powers which may or may not exist; to try and lead the huge variety of lives of which they are capable or of which they dream; to let them change and suffer and explore as far as it is humanly possible. And from this can come a profound and exhilarating sense of power, of lifting vision, of release.

APPENDICES

The figures in the appendices which follow are given only to illustrate, support, and sometimes elaborate statements in the text. They do not necessarily provide full statistical or research proof. For full details I would refer you in all cases to the sources given in the References.

APPENDIX A—REALITY OF THE SEXUAL REVOLUTION

1 *Sources*

To save continually referring you to sources in appendices A and B, they are as follows:

BRITAIN: Margaret Bone, *The Family Planning Services—Changes and Effects*, HMSO, 1978; Family Planning Association, *Fact Sheet* 7, April 1978, FPA, *Inform*, no. 1, July 1973, *Inform*, no. 8, March 1977; Christine Farrell, Leonie Kellaber, *My Mother Said . . .*, Routledge & Kegan Paul, 1978; Geoffrey Gorer, *Sex and Marriage in England Today—a study of the views and experiences of the under 45s*, Nelson, 1971; Dr. A. B. Hewitt, *British Journal of Venereal Diseases*, 46, 106, 1970; M. Schofield, *The Sexual Behaviour of Young People*, Longmans, 1965.

AMERICA: Morton Hunt, *Sexual Behaviour in the 1970s*, New York, Playboy Press, 1974; Alfred C. Kinsey *et al.*, *Sexual Behaviour in the Human Male*, and *Sexual Behaviour in the Human Female*, Philadelphia, W. B. Saunders, 1948 and 1953; *McCalls* Readership Survey, April 1976; *Redbook: A Study of Female Sexuality*, June, Sept., Oct., 1975; *Redbook: A Study of Male Sexual Behaviour*, Feb., 1978; Robert C. Sorenson, *Adolescent Sexuality in Contemporary America*, World Publishers, 1973.

GENERAL AND OTHER COUNTRIES: Harold T. Christensen and Christina F. Gregg, 'Changing sex norms in America and Scandinavia,' *Journal of Marriage and the Family*, 32, 1970; *People*, vol. 4, no. 3, 1977; Edward Shorter, *The Making of the Modern Family*, Collins, 1976; Pierre Simon

321

et al., Rapport sur le comportement sexuel des francais, Paris, 1972. Some comment is necessary on the surveys done by American maga-zines—*Redbook, McCalls, Playboy* (this last the foundation of the book by Morton Hunt). The first two are questionnaires answered by readers and one must wonder how representative they are. *Redbook* is different from the national sample in that its readers are more likely to be mar-ried (9:10 as opposed to 7:10); more likely to be white, younger, better educated and better off. *Redbook* claims that since this is much the same bias, excepting being married, that Kinsey admitted to, its sur-veys provide, where the questions are similar, a good index of change over the last 25–35 years. I doubt this is true in any precise way. It does not say if the *answering* sample conforms to the *readership* profile. I suspect that, as it notes, the 100,000 women who voluntarily answered the questionnaire were on the whole as *Redbook* puts it (typical phrase) 'comfortable with their own sexuality'; as were the 40,000 men. (It is true Kinsey's sample was also voluntary; but it was so in much the same way as fish caught in a net are 'voluntarily' in that part of the sea as it sweeps through). I think that *Redbook* exaggerates liberal attitudes and behaviour, and this sometimes shows up in comparison with other data. At the same time, the *Playboy* survey, which on the whole corroborates *Redbook*, was done independently among 2,026 people in 24 cities weighted demographically to duplicate Kinsey. Even here I am suspi-cious. Reading for this book I was repeatedly struck by how many soci-ological studies and apparently objective surveys mirrored the opinions of those writing or conducting them. *Playboy*'s object is to promote sexual freedom, and four out of five people approached by the organi-zation conducting the survey for Hunt and *Playboy* refused to answer. It seems likely that the one out of five remaining were sexual liberals.

Nevertheless, these surveys represent very large sections of America. The changes they found, even if exaggerated, clearly reflect the various trends—since they are supported by other more sober studies. And these in turn are supported in a general way by similar surveys in England, Norway, Denmark, Sweden, France and Russia.

2 *Premarital pregnancy*

Pre-1950: From 1900 to 1950, few chances. In America between 1900 and 1909 a 7 per cent chance; 1945–49 a 10 per cent chance. In Swe-den in 1911 a 1 in 3 chance; 1948, the same. In Germany, the same be-fore the Second World War as before the First.

Post-1950: Sweden, 1950, 20 per 1,000; 1970, 28 per 1,000. Britain doubled in the same period, 32.8 per 1,000 to 65.7. America tripled.

The greatest increases were among teenagers—in England from 14.7 per cent in 1971 to 35.6 per cent in 1973. Peter Laslett has shown that the use of illegitimacy figures in the past to prove increased sexual activity is mistaken. But there is no other conceivable explanation than that for these figures. This is borne out by the figures below.

3 *Premarital sex*

This showed very large increases, especially among the young. In England, in 1964, 16 per cent of 15–19 year olds were sexually experienced; by 1974, 48 per cent were. If you include married teenagers, in 1974, by 19, 77 per cent of boys and 73 per cent of girls were experienced. And the trend is towards earlier experience—thus in 1964, 6 per cent of boys and 2 per cent of girls who had sex were 15; by 1974 this was 26 per cent and 12 per cent. It is not, noted Farrell, a question of why did some have sex before marriage and some not, but why did any of them wait for marriage? The likelihood is that in the end hardly any will wait. In all cases, attitudes are still more liberal than behaviour. Only 8 per cent of Farrell's sample disapproved of sex before marriage.

In America there is the same pattern, only more so. Shorter quotes a survey of adolescent girls in 1971, where 50 per cent of 25-year-old women had premarital sex. *Redbook* found for those married between 1964–69, it was 81 per cent; between 1970–73—89 per cent; after 1973—93 per cent. There is the same trend to earlier sex.

Now a good deal of this is sleeping together before eventual marriage (probably around 50 per cent). This has often been a norm. It was so on both sides of the Atlantic in the eighteenth century—where premarital pregnancy was often over 40 per cent.

But all these surveys show that it is now becoming accepted that young people should sleep together in the ordinary course of events, whether they are going to marry or not. Margaret Bone found that in England those not engaged were more likely to advocate sex with a boyfriend than those engaged. Hunt's survey found that 50 per cent of men had had between 1 and 5 premarital partners. Sorenson's survey of teenagers in 1972 found that 50 per cent of the sexually active had slept with more than one partner. Among those 16–19, over 50 per cent had slept with several partners. 'Just imagine,' cries Shorter, doing so, 'how high these scores may be by the time these women marry.'

4 *Increased sexual activity generally*

Shorter finds more intercourse, more masturbation, more orgasms, more time spent on sex, more people having more people. In 1940,

Kinsey found 40 per cent of married men masturbated; in 1972 Hunt found 70 per cent. For married women it rose from one-third to two-thirds. In Kinsey, the median time for love-making was 2 minutes; 10 in Hunt. There were three times the number of orgasms among the young. Fifty-three per cent of the wives in Hunt's survey had orgasms 90 per cent of the time after fifteen years of marriage, while it was only 45 per cent of the time in Kinsey.

Marital coitus in the United States, frequency per week, 1938–49 (Kinsey); and 1972 (Hunt)

1938–49		1972	
Age	Median	Age	Median
16–25	2.45	18–24	3.25
26–35	1.95	25–34	2.55
36–45	1.40	35–44	2.00
46–55	0.85	45–54	1.00
56–60	0.50	55 over	1.00

Marital coitus in Britain 1970 (Gorer)

Times per week	% Married population
3 or over	24
1–3	36
1 or less	37

The tables given here provide only the roughest of comparisons. Hunt probably found a slightly overliberal, overactive sample. Nothing is known about Britain nationally before Gorer, nor after him (a survey is in progress from Glasgow but not available as I write). Gorer says that his is in fact the only survey of intercourse rates which conforms to a national configuration—which is still technically true. He implies that other surveys are biased by boasting. The criteria he chooses to validate his figures is that intercourse requires two people and the rates given by men are the same as those given independently by the women. They are unlikely to boast by precisely the same amount. But *Redbook* validates its own 1977 figures by the same consideration, though they are concerned with (revealingly) orgasms. The *Redbook* sample, incidentally, had more sex than anyone else, again suggesting it was not really representative: 5 per cent of respondents once a day, 20 per cent 4–6 times a week, 39 per cent 2–5 times a week.

In America, love-making became more 'inventive'. In the 1940s only a third of couples experimented with woman on top; while by the 1970s (Hunt) three-quarters did so. All surveys report colossal increases in oral sex (also in France, though to a lesser extent).

5 *Adultery*

There does not seem to have been a great deal of change in incidence of this since Kinsey—except that American surveys show that the figures among women are catching up with men. Everywhere attitudes are more relaxed—discussion not divorce. *Redbook* found a small correlation between premarital and extra-marital sex, which some people have made something of. But, clearly, as more and more men and women have premarital sex, then more and more people having premarital sex will show up in whatever activity you report on. When premarital sex equals 100 per cent, as it nearly does in some groups and probably will in all, then premarital sex will be a prerequisite of every other behaviour pattern.

6 *Universality of the sexual revolution*

Premarital sex became all but universal in Scandinavia. In Sweden, between 1960–65 the figures increased by 5 per cent a year, to reach 65 per cent. At church-related schools these increases were particularly large—from 38 per cent to 78 per cent at one, 80 per cent to 87 per cent at another (Shorter is 'stunned' by these figures). In 1959, 40 per cent of women at Danish universities were still virginal; by 1968 only 3 per cent were. And the trend was again to several partners and not just sleeping with the person you'd eventually marry. In Denmark, 43 per cent had more than one man in 1958; in 1968 it was 75 per cent. In France, in 1970, 9 per cent of women aged between 30–49 had had several partners, 16 per cent of those between 20 and 29.

All the same patterns are found in Russia. In 1965, 65 per cent of men and 28 per cent of women had premarital intercourse. Now, according to *People*, it is 'much higher'. In 1966, 32.1 per cent of all legitimate babies were conceived before marriage; 12 per cent were illegitimate. Contraception is increasing. The pill is imported from Hungary and can be bought over the counter, though it has had little publicity; but they have the interuterine device and import spermicidal jelly in tons. Sixty per cent of all married women have an abortion between their first and second child. Recently, advertising for partners, computer dating and singles clubs for the over-thirties have become common. Erotic literature is banned, but that there is an increased interest in sex generally is suggested by the sales of sex manuals. These are translated from German and Polish, published locally in editions of several hundred thousand and vanish overnight.

APPENDIX B—ATTITUDES TO SEX

1 Calm of English sex lives

Seventy-five per cent of Gorer's informants thought their sexual performance was 'about average'. What they actually did made no difference. The wife of a bus conductor, aged 20, married for two years, who had intercourse two or three times a day thought she was average, so did many others with similar rates; but so did a 30-year-old upholsterer, who did not have sex before his marriage at 36 and now had it 3 times a month, as did the 27-year-old wife (virgin at marriage) who had it once a month. Nor was there any consistency between those who thought they were not average. Eight per cent of those who had intercourse 4 times or less a month thought they were above average; 10 per cent of those with more than 3 times a week thought they were below average.

2 Importance of love in contemporary adolescent sexual life

Three-quarters of girls in Sorenson's study said, 'I wouldn't have sex with a boy unless he loved me.' In Schofield's survey both boys and girls agreed that emotion was extremely important. But, much more convincing, the fact that the experiences were long-lasting and in *series* confirms this. Three-quarters of the English girls had had the same partner for the past 12 months and only him. And the importance attached to these experiments in grand passion is shown by the attitude to contraception. This too is responsible. Christine Farrell found that only 8 per cent never used any method. Abortion was not seen as a form of contraception. It is clear, incidentally, that from this point of view the age of consent in England should be lowered or better still abolished. Girls who do not use any method are often under 16; they turn up promptly at birth control clinics on their 16th birthday. They are being exposed to the risk of pregnancy through shame and fear.

3 *Greater expectation of successful sex in marriage*

Gorer found that there was 50 per cent greater expectation of successful sex in British marriages in 1970 than 1950. The *Redbook* surveys found the same thing in American marriages.

APPENDIX C—SOCIO-ECONOMIC FACTORS

1 *Boredom of housework*

The experience of monotony, fragmentation and speed; housewives and factory workers compared

Workers	Monotony (%)	Fragmentation (%)	Speed (%)
Housewives	75	90	50
Assembly line workers	67	86	36
Factory workers	41	70	31

Fragmentation = pointless, disconnected tasks
Speed = stress, time pressure

2 *Increased longevity*

In America in 1920 women could expect to live to 54.6 years. By 1960 this had increased to 73.1; in 1975, 76.5. In Britain the figures are: 1931, 51.8; 1961, 73.8; 1975, 75.6

3 *More and more women working but in lower paid jobs*

In America and Britain women are now about 40 per cent of the labour force; in 1911 10 per cent of married women worked in Britain, today it is 50 per cent; in 1971 among those aged 40–44 it was 62 per cent,

45–49 it was 63 per cent; in America in 1950, 26 per cent of women with children worked, in 1970 it was 46.6 per cent.

In Britain (but the situation is comparable at all points in America) 1.7 per cent of university professors are women, less than 2 per cent of The Institute of Directors, 6 per cent of the legal profession—as opposed to 90 per cent of typists, 75 per cent of cleaners and shop staff and 60 per cent cooks, clerks, packers. Women dominate the part-time sector—7,287 million out of 13,942 million in America in 1976; in England in 1978 women's wages were 73.9 per cent of men's for the same job, a fall from 75.1 per cent in 1976.

4   'Diffuse' reaction: deep contradiction in Western upbringing

Genital indulgence when small, the freeing to an increasing extent of adolescent sexuality, are both clear responses to, and causes of a fuller and freer sex life. At the same time, this is wished for in the context of a stable marriage. This in itself is not contradictory. The Samoans have an extremely vigorous and free sex life. Adolescents sleep together before marriage; and after marriage infidelity and affairs are quite common. But on the whole marriages remain stable. The reason is that babies in Samoa never form strong relationships with either parent, they are brought up in common, passed from hand to hand among dozens of relations. Emotion is warm but diffuse. As a result, adulteries are settled by an exchange of mats. 'Love and hate, jealousy and revenge, sorrow and bereavement, are all a matter of weeks,' writes Margaret Mead. Even break-up of marriage, which does come sometimes, does not cause much pain—either to the couple or their children.

The Western contradiction arises because we value deep and intense relationships. There are several reasons for this, but a major one is because we are dominated by the tenets of romantic love. We value intense relationships in love and with our children, and we bring them about by forging single and powerful bonds with our children which they repeat as adults. Thus on the one hand we encourage a relaxed and easy sexuality; in several respects we encourage divorce; on the other hand we create conditions where the fullest expression of the first, and recourse to the second, cause the maximum pain to everyone involved. Society could make a decision: to trade intense feeling for a freer sex life and stable marriage. There are few signs this is happening, though the reaction to nursery care, and also a similar effect of commune upbringing could be construed as signs—so far on a very small scale.

5   Unemployment

Unemployment figures are extremely difficult to estimate. Professor Wiles, of the London School of Economics, tells me that no one really knows how many people are unemployed. It is complicated by Russia, which has 'abolished' unemployment. They have no dole or unemployment Social Security. Instead, many Soviet workers earn a full-time wage for doing practically nothing at all. But the figures I have used and their sources are as follows:

EEC, 16 million	Speech to the House of Commons, Denis Healey, April 3, 1979
America, 7.520 million	Statistical Abstract, 1978
Canada, 946,000	Statistics Canada, Daily List, Feb. 12, 1980
Australia, 395,000	Year Book Australia, 1979
New Zealand, 52,537	Monthly Abstract of Statistics, November 1979
Russia, 1 million	P. J. D. Wiles, 'A Note on Soviet Unemployment by US Definitions,' *Soviet Studies*, vol. XXIII, University of Glasgow, 1972

This gives us 25,903,837; or for the approximate figure that is all we need for our purposes—26 million.

6   The inevitability of patriarchy

One of the most important pillars upon which the feminist case rests is that it can be shown anthropologically that there is virtually no non-maternal role or occupation which women cannot or have not successfully filled. Margaret Mead was the most influential figure here, citing (names frequently copied) the Mundugumor, the Tchambuli and the Arepesh. The Mbuti are often quoted too. Goldberg takes these examples and others and shows that the significant factors are the importance given to the roles and male dominance. The point about the non-maternal roles the women took in the cultures cited was that *the societies did not think they were the most important.* Goldberg, indeed, takes all the societies, out of the 4,000 or so that have been studied, which have been quoted as proof that women can take on male roles, and shows that this is always so. The male always has been and always is dominant over three spheres: he *invariably* attains high status in all the important non-maternal roles; he is overwhelmingly top of the political and very important social hierarchies; in all male-female encounters (e.g., marriage) the male expects to dominate and is expected to.

Societies differ as to what they think important. But whatever they think is important—there males dominate. It does not mean what they decide is important really *is* so—that plucking humming birds, say, is more important than agriculture. But once they have decided it is, males do it. Nor is it important *because* males do it. If women have done it, and it is then upgraded, men take over. Second, in the political and most important hierarchies, women have sometimes held some of the high positions—but never more than about 6 per cent of them. Third, in the male-female encounters it does not mean women don't get their own way. Often, perhaps nearly always, they do. But it is always from the standpoint of getting round the men. Of being allowed. Lastly, and perhaps most tellingly, he shows that Margaret Mead herself did not think her studies proved anything else: 'Those,' he writes, 'who so frequently invoke the Tchambuli (and occasionally the Mundugumor, also studied by Dr Mead) as societies that do not exhibit the institutions under discussion must explain why the ethnographer who studied them does not consider them to be exceptions.'

This is the first stage of his argument. He says that it does not prove that any other sort of society is impossible, but the fact that none has ever existed is at least highly suggestive. Next he goes on to prove that in fact any other sort of society *is* impossible. The reason is that male dominance is the result of physiological differences between male and female which are ineradicable and inevitably lead, and will always lead, to male dominance. (It follows that, if even one society can be found where there is not male dominance in the three spheres I outlined, his theory collapses.)

The evidence is this. The process of masculinization begins in the foetus. At one point androgens (male sex hormones—of which testosterone is the most powerful) are released into the blood and cause the differentiation of the sex organs—but also sensitize certain areas of the brain which will make it later respond to social situations in a 'dominating' way. Androgen continues to be released in small quantities after birth, but at puberty this is greatly accelerated and causes the full emergence of male characteristics, including dominance.

But it is the prenatal androgen work that is vital, and it is here that

Goldberg 'proves' his case with some fascinating work done on human hermaphrodites by Dr John Money at Johns Hopkins University. There are certain rare cases in which genetic females produce large quantities of androgens, are hormonally masculinized at foetal stage, thus altering the central nervous system, but whose anatomy is not altered. They are identified and brought up as females. And indeed *think* of themselves as females (Goldberg is not concerned with gender identification). But what the 25 females, as quoted by Goldberg, showed were marked dominance characteristics—called 'tomboyism' by Dr Money. They preferred rough-and-tumble games, and male toys, they had less enthusiasm for motherhood, they planned to work and have careers. And this can only be explained by the foetal hormonisation—since all socializing was to make them female, which indeed it had done.

This is Goldberg's case in a nutshell. I have had to leave out much powerful argument and telling illustration. He quotes animal studies which show the same effects—but without the hermaphrodites his argument would be much weaker. You cannot base an entire social and psychological theory on mice.

There are weaknesses to the first part of what Goldberg calls 'The Theory'. The fact that something has not been done before is not an argument that it cannot ever be done. That way, humanity would not have advanced at all, in any sphere, in any direction. Second, Goldberg admits that environmental influences (not hormonal ones) can produce some women who are more dominant than some men—or any man. He puts the figure at 6 per cent—but why 6 per cent? In chapter 5, I referred to the Rapoports 'exceptional' women who were estimated at 10 per cent of any population, and it is significant that the influences on them (being considered their family's 'sons', having a career mother) are just the ones that the feminists would argue so favour men. One can easily envisage another 10 per cent or 20 per cent below that, not so exceptional, but who in the altered circumstances we discussed would be just as able to compete with men on equal terms as the exceptional 10 per cent. This of course does not affect Goldberg's theory, but a society in which 20 per cent or 30 per cent of the leading pursuits are successfully followed by women is quite different from the bleak picture presented by him. Third, to the most obvious argument against him, that male dominance is a cultural imposition, or overwhelmingly cultural—Goldberg answers, why should the cultural imposition *always* be towards male dominance? I don't see that this is a question that has to be answered. The prime fact to establish empirically is whether or not it is the cultural imposition which is decisive. (It is then easy enough to speculate why and how it has evolved.) It is because Goldberg believes he has empirically *proved* that hormonal masculinisation in the foetus and not cultural socialisation is the cause of male dominance, that he does not waste time speculating why that has evolved. These are facts. No more need be said.

But it is when one actually reads Dr Money (and in particular Money and Erhardt—the fullest exposition of his views) that Goldberg's facts start to become distinctly fuzzy. In the first place one can legitimately throw in his face the same argument he used with Margaret Mead. It is true Dr Money's work was not primarily concerned with dominance (he was interested in whether we 'learn' our roles of male and female or if they are genetic), but he considered dominance, and with care, and he does not come to the same conclusion as Goldberg. Dominance, says Money, 'might conceivably be subject to prenatal hormonal influence on the brain,' but is 'equally well' likely to be caused by 'social contingency learning'. Goldberg must explain why, if he places such weight on Money's findings, Money does not place the same weight on them himself. I suspect those mice are going to have to take a much heavier load than hitherto—and heavier than they can stand.

In fact, I think Money's findings point, if anything, in the opposite direction. Goldberg says that the genital equipment of the vital 25 female hermaphrodites had not been altered. But this is not so. To speak frankly, their genital equipment was more usually a disaster. Vestigial testes had to be removed, over-large clitorises reduced. Few of them could have children of their own. Many had to have false wombs 'constructed' at adolescence. They all, from birth, had to take continual doses of cortisone to counteract the androgens. That is to say, they did not have a normal socialisation at all. By the time they were born, much was known of the condition. The likelihood is their parents expected them to be 'tomboys' and were ready to encourage it (an inference supported by the fact they were all 'proud' of being so described). It is hardly worth over-encouraging someone to concentrate on motherhood if they can't have children; it is equally sensible to encourage a career. (You don't need a mass of androgen to bring this about. In a recent survey by *Glamour* magazine, 94 per cent of their women readers worked full time; 75 per cent worked for 'fulfillment', 65 per cent said they'd work all their lives—and only 32 per cent said they'd give up work for marriage and children.)

That these hermaphrodites were to some extent socialised to their strange half-way house is borne out by a study of another group. These were born before nearly so much was known (the use of cortisone was only discovered in 1950). Consequently, it is likely they were brought up with no expectation of 'tomboyism.' It is quite true that some of them showed some of the 'tomboy' effects; but some (the number is not specified) showed none of them. That is, foetal masculinisation does not inevitably and irresistibly produce these results. But the most extreme and poignant example comes from the most effective androgenisation of a foetus. A little baby boy, not a hermaphrodite at all, was being electrically circumcised when there was a flash, and his little penis vanished—burnt flush to the skin. But cavities were bored, and cortisone and hormones administered, active socialising with dolls commenced, and he showed, again, none of the attributes Goldberg predicts.

But the clincher comes from Dr Money, commenting on his own material. 'Though the variable was not identified in advance,' he writes, concerning the vital dominance factor in the group that is of most, indeed of total significance to Goldberg, 'so that specific data pertaining to it were not collected, in retrospect it appears that the *girls of the diagnostic groups did not strive for dominance in competition with boys*, and were not interested in the rivalries of the girls.' The italics are mine. Dr Money concluded they did not strive because of social convention and fear of rejection. That is—the cultural imposition is more decisive than the hormonal one, not less.

I do not think this necessarily destroys Goldberg's case—but at least it does very seriously reduce it. It is no longer nearly so clear cut. And even if there is still a good deal of truth in the theory, though it will affect what happens, what you or I feel about male and female roles, it does not affect the position reached in chapter 5. The economic arguments, the benefits to men, women and children, all remain. If Goldberg is right, though, we shall still have male dominance: with some unknown per centage (6 per cent? 10 per cent?) of women in top jobs and pursuits; a far larger number in special 'feminine' tasks or working under men—but content since their hormonalisation makes them *want* that. And they will do it without the hassle they have now.

But if, as I suspect, Goldberg has been led by a lack of logic that is, in his own terms, almost feminine, into a serious misreading of the evidence available from this tiny band of pathetic natural mutilates—a misreading carefully not made by its originator—and as a result has grossly underestimated the effect of the cultural imposition, then we will see the much wider opening up of society suggested in chapter 5, with 20 per cent, 30 per cent or 40 per cent of the top jobs and pursuits open to women. The moment it reaches 51 per cent, of course, the theory, and Goldberg with it, at once collapse.

APPENDIX D—THE 'PRIVILEGE BULGE'

1 *'Privilege Bulge' political and economic power growing in future*
In America in 1975, 22.4 million people were 65 plus. By the year 2000
it will be 31 million; by 2030, 55 million. If you took those between 45
and 65 the figures would be much higher. In Britain this group com-
prised 13.2 per cent of the population in 1972. It will be 18 per cent by
1991 and 21 per cent by 2011.

APPENDIX E—ADULTERY AND ROMANTIC LOVE

1 *Evidence of a tradition of adultery in America*
The recent *Redbook* surveys suggest that a segment of America is developing a tradition of adultery. Hitherto this has really only existed
among *macho* business men. *Redbook* found that out of the 38 per cent
who had extra-marital sex, 20 per cent of the women and 27 per cent of
the men had highly satisfactory marriages, including 'very good' sex.
That is, one could deduce, they saw romantic love affairs as something
they *should* have as well. A neat example of this was the film *Same
Time Next Year*. Although on the whole frankness, honesty, and communication, even if difficult, are best in relationships, dishonesty and
secrecy are also essential at times. Romantic love has long dictated that
to be so in this area. And if *Redbook* shows an evolving of an adulterous
pattern, then it is well in this ancient tradition—a tradition which was
once common among the British upper classes and is still not completely dead. Of the *Redbook* readers, only 4 per cent had tried the
open/honest/swinging/wife swapping methods of adultery, and over
half of these only once.

2 *Social and anthropological necessity for romantic love*
William J. Goode, in an article 'The Theoretical Importance of Love',
recently reprinted, said that romantic love, far from being a rare ingredient in marriage until recently, as anthropologists, historians and
sociologists have said, is and has long been an almost universal presence. This is shown by the fact that societies recognise that their continuity depends on a general continuity of values, ideas, aims, of family
lives, and often of property and material possessions. This in turn de-

pends on keeping marriage within certain cultural and social peer-group limits. Romantic love is the one force that can compel mate choice outside these limits. Therefore, to guard against this, the choice is taken away from the children and controlled by the parents. Wherever you find mate choice not left to children—something which is and has been very common—you can infer the presence of love as an ingredient of marriage.

I think Professor Goode has gone slightly astray. In general, all you might infer logically is the *danger* of love being an ingredient in choice, not its actual presence in marriage. Also, this could apply to ordinary sexual attraction; but romantic love is a particular form of love, with its own peculiarities—intensity, exclusivity and jealousy, with many other accretions, and we *know* this to be a fairly recent and geographically circumscribed development. Finally, romantic or any other love *can* remove mate choice from accepted lines; but the fact is it very rarely does. On the contrary.

It seems to me that while money, property, family improvement and so on were the prime objects of marriage, then the parents were involved as those best able to understand such matters, and because they were the ones to whom the property belonged. As these considerations dropped away owing, among much else, to the spread of wealth, so there was left—in anthropological terms—only the continuity of cultural aims and values; these above all require intermarriage among a peer group sharing the same ideals. But romantic love, with its emphasis on intense feeling, deep personal involvement, its psychological ingredient of self-love, is the emotion above all which leads into a peer group as similar as possible to that of the partner. That is why all studies of marriage show that couples marry into the same class, religion, race, educational and social group. And that is why romantic love became general precisely during those years—from 1850 on—when consideration of property and lineage were dying. (The control of the elders remains strong, as Goode notes, since they dictate where the family lives and therefore the composition of the peer group. But romantic love alone can be relied on to make sure a similar group will be chosen.) That is to say, romantic love is the most powerful of all forces ensuring cultural continuity now that those hitherto powerful considerations—material prosperity and lineage—have vanished.

APPENDIX F—MARRIAGE DURATION

1   *Length of marriage in the past*

For the years 1599 to 1811 in England, Laslett gives a figure of about 20 years for most couples. Stone gives a variety of figures: 17 to 20 for the lower classes, 22 years among the squirarchy in the early seventeenth century, with a median of 17–20 for the whole period 1500–1800. At Senely-sur-Sologne, in France, during a period of just over 100 years (1675–1779) the average marriage lasted 6 years.

2   *Evidence of increased length of marriage*

The length of marriage increased rapidly during the nineteenth and first half of the twentieth centuries. Thus a study over time of American Quakers has these marriage lengths: 18th century, 30.4 years; by the 1880s, 35.4 years; by the 1920s, 43.6 years. In New Zealand, marriages were already lasting 41 years by 1900, and had reached 48 years by 1972. Contemporary figures for England don't exist (typically, more is known about that in the seventeenth century than is known today), but obviously the same development has taken place. The average age at marriage for men is 24.99 and for women 22.78; at these ages men can expect to live a further 46.6 years and women a further 52.4 years. Couples who don't divorce, therefore, can very roughly expect around 40–50 years of married life together.

APPENDIX G—ASPECTS OF DIVORCE

1   *Divorce law*

Between 1715 and 1852—nearly one and a half centuries—there were in England an average of two divorces a year. These required an Act of Parliament and cost, in today's terms, about £15,000 ($36,000). In 1857 the Matrimonial Causes Act created a new Civil Court in which husbands and wives could sue for divorce on the grounds of a *matrimonial offence,* a concept which was to dominate thinking for 110 years. The offence was usually adultery, but at first women had to prove something additional such as rape, desertion or cruelty. The next 100 years saw a series of legislative reforms which gradually eliminated the appalling sex-based inequalities discriminating against women. These culminated in a new Matrimonial Causes Act in 1950, which allowed equality of offence (both sexes could sue for adultery, cruelty and desertion; women were given a bonus of rape, sodomy and bestiality). Divorce was spread from the London High Courts to all the provincial assizes. But far more important in extending divorce was the Legal Aid and Advice Act of 1949, which assisted those too poor to afford solicitors and barristers. However, the central concept was still that of an 'offence' against the sanctity of marriage. The 1960s polished this off. By the 1971 Divorce Law Reform Act the grounds for divorce became 'irretrievable breakdown of marriage'; it can be agreed by both parties after two years' separation, and by one after five years. Moves are now afoot to allow divorce after one year's separation. The logic must be that they will be successful. (The concept of 'offence' remains, but usually only in battles over the children.)

The same sort of development has taken place in America since about 1966, though there are the usual differences between the states. Most states don't require a matrimonial 'fault', most allow divorce after a certain period, and quite often six months is enough—though some are more liberal than others (California compared to New York, for instance, which with its Catholic background is traditionally tough on divorce). Divorce in one state is usually recognised in another, though there are some very easy 'nonsignificant' divorces (that is, which don't sort out money or children) that can be challenged in the courts: Haiti, for example, where you can be divorced on consent in 48 hours.

If there is no viable escape, people stick together. Each extension or relaxation of divorce laws over the last 100 years has been instantly followed by an increase in the number of divorces; and with the exception of those following the post-1939 war divorce boom, each leap has been larger than the last. Obviously, the law is not the major cause. The law usually responds, considerably *en retard*, to movements of public opinion and public need, and these in turn arise through the interaction of social and historical forces. They are the major reason the divorce laws have changed; the reason they have changed the way they have; and the reason the changes have been made full use of.

If Western culture had not responded to the various social and historical pressures by divorce it would have responded in some other way—though how we can only guess. There might have been a vast increase in married neuroses—alcoholism, insomnia, and depression such as Betty Friedan detected in housewives during the 1950s. We do in fact have at hand an ideal model. Since the Revolution in 1917, Russia's divorce rate has always been some way above America's (last year, for instance, *Pravda* announced that one-third of first marriages ended in the first year; the total divorce figures are therefore much higher). In 1944 all this divorcing was abruptly stopped for several years. Stalin's aim was not moral; he simply thought this was the best way to increase the population. Unfortunately, as far as I can discover, no one has reported in the West the result of this clampdown. However, the most likely response in the West generally had divorce not started to become easier during the last 25 years would have been clandestine forms of escape, just as the Roman world took to adultery in the first and second centuries A.D. Italy, in 1967, had no divorce. But at the time there were some 2.5 million people living in illegal unions pursuing precisely those satisfactions—feminist, sexual, Privilege Bulge—discussed in this book.

2   *Increasing numbers of divorces*

In Britain, in 1965, there were 37,785 divorces; in 1970, 58,239; in 1975, 120,522. In America the increase in the same period was from 393,000 to 1,036,000. These rises continue: in America in 1976, 1,077,000 divorces; in 1979, 1,170,000. In Britain, in 1979, 138,700; in 1980 (provisional figures) 148,200.

3   *Young marriage means more divorce*

Divorces in any one year can take place among marriages of enormously different lengths. The figures can be rearranged so that one can isolate all the marriages that took place in any one year—groups of marriages called cohorts (the 1963 cohort, for example, being all those who married in 1963). Once isolated you can then watch each cohort as it careers through time. These cohorts can be again subdivided into age at marriage; so that you can follow all those who married when the bride was under 20, or between 20 and 25 and so on. If this is done it is clear that the steeply rising divorce figures affect all cohorts and all age subdivisions of cohorts.

But the cohorts of those marrying young divorce sooner and more of them divorce. For instance, 9 per cent of all marriages in Britain started in 1963 had ended in divorce after eleven years; where the bride was under 20, the figure was 16 per cent, compared with only 8 per cent if she was over 20. Hunt quotes studies showing that under-20 husbands are three times, and under-20 wives four times more likely to divorce than over-20.

4   Gap between separation and divorce

This gap is put at 4.6 years by Robert Chester; by Nicky Hart at 2.9. Say between two and five years.

5   First years the most difficult

The study *Who Divorces?* by Barbara Thornes and Jean Collard found that in 520 divorced couples in Britain, the problems that wrecked their marriage began in the first year for well over a third—though they frequently struggled to save it. I cannot find a comparable study for America, but I think it extremely likely that in both countries far the largest proportion of marriage breakdown takes place in the first few years.

UK: Percentage of divorces after years married

years	1–4	5–9	10–14	15–19
%	17.07	30.01	18.81	12.98

US: Percentage of divorce by age

Age	20–24	25–29	30–34	35–39
%	21.6	27.4	18.8	12.8

The statistics for each country are unfortunately not organised in the same way, but the sets above provide a rough comparison. It will be seen that most divorce *seems* to take place between the 5th and 9th years of marriage. But given the gap between separation and divorce it is clear that probably something like half of the 5–9th year *divorces*, should be referred back to 1–4th year *breakdowns*. If you apply this adjustment right through the table it looks different.

Adjusted UK

years	1–4	5–9	10–14	15–19
%	32.08	24.42	15.90	10.84

Adjusted US

Age	20–24	25–29	30–34	35–39
%	15.3	22.4	15.8	10.4

This second table gives a much clearer indication of the periods at which marriage breakdowns take place, and in particular of the importance of the first four years. In fact this is a fairly conservative adjustment and I suspect that something closer to 40 per cent of marriages break down during this period.

6 Divorce and socio-economic class

In America, there is a feeling that divorce is a lower-class habit that has been caught by the middle classes; in Britain that it is a middle-class habit that is spreading down. Both these assumptions are difficult to test, because none of the official census returns breaks divorce down into socio-economic groups; but the American assumption would seem to be more sensible, on the grounds that poverty leads to friction and conflict and this leads to divorce. There are studies in both countries which bear this out. Hunt quotes several analyses which show that low income and manual and blue-collar workers are twice as likely to get divorced as higher income and white-collar workers. A study by C. Gibson found the same was true in Britain. But a survey in Britain in 1959 showed that the composition of divorcing couples was exactly the same as the married population as a whole—that is, 70 per cent were manual workers. In Britain, at least, I suspect we may have something much closer to the picture we found with sexual customs: that is, the different classes now behave in much the same way. What is left behind (and it is still very strong) is prejudice.

7 Mid-life peak

The Rapoports, along with many others, find this, with more divorce after 15 or 20 years of marriage. Hunt confines himself to the middle classes, and because of the paucity of socio-economic analysis is therefore harder to check. This is particularly so, because he relies to some extent on a 'modest' survey of his own. As far as the general figures go, there is no evidence of a 'mid-life' peak whatsoever. In Britain, from the 5th year of marriage to the 19th, divorces decrease by an almost uniformly steady 0.5 per cent—9.3 per cent a year. The actual figures are the same as those in appendix G, section 5; the *apparent* peak years 5–9 we have already explained. The detailed graph of the American figures shows exactly the same gentle decline as in Britain—with the same explicable peak at the fifth year.

8 *Separations and 'hopeless' marriages*

Another factor which can be muddling is separations and marriages which, though together, are really hopeless 'open warfare' marriages. The Rapoports say that figures for both of these must be enormous and that therefore divorce figures are only the 'tip of an iceberg' in the real picture of broken marriages. Tip of an *iceberg*! If this is so the state of marriage is in a parlous state indeed. As regards separations, they are no doubt right—we saw there is a 2–5-year gap between complete marriage breakdown (which nearly always means separation) and the actual divorce. But these separated couples will show up in, will in fact *be*, the divorce figures of the next few years. That is to say, the divorce figures do give an accurate picture of the state of marriage, but slightly *en retard*.

As regards open warfare marriages, Rowntree did a study of 3,000 men and women between 16–59 in 1960 to find out this very thing— that is, how many couples were separated or living in near silence or open warfare at any one moment. He found you can add a rough 4 per cent at a given time. But since all divorces for varying periods are 'separations' it would be very generous to assume 2 per cent to be open warfare marriages.

That is to say, divorce has cut what was once no doubt a common feature—as it was in some of the Great Terrible Marriages of the nineteenth century—down to something very small. In the same way, though legal separations as such dropped by half in Britain between 1973 and 1976, they had not been a significant figure for some years.

9 *Length of marriage at divorce*

In America it has been around 6.5 years since 1970 (the lowest, oddly enough, not California or Hawaii, but Idaho and Wyoming, with 4.5 and 4.7 years. The states where people stick it out the longest are Maryland and Connecticut, with 8.3 and 8.2 years.) The British average has remained stable since 1965, at about 13 years. But Britain shouldn't be too complacent—the tendency seems to be towards shorter marriages. In 1964, 11 per cent of marriages ended under five years; in 1973, 15 per cent.

10 *International Divorce League*

Group One   USSR, USA, Hungary, Egypt, Denmark
Group Two   UK, E. Germany, Czechoslovakia, Sweden, Austria
Group Three   Portugal, Venezuela, Canada, Mexico
(In fact, the latest figures, as this book goes to press, show that England now leads Europe as regards divorce; followed by Denmark, the Netherlands, Belgium, France and W. Germany, in that order.)

11 *Divorce statistics a young science. Contradictory findings, e.g., effects of children on marriage*

The compilation and study of these figures is, like the phenomenon itself, a very young science. As a result the studies and analyses often contradict each other. For instance, people usually think that childless couples are far more likely to have a divorce. But many other studies have found that children make marriages less happy, while Burgess discovered that it is couples who are having difficulties, or fear they may have them, who put off having children, and it is these difficulties which lead to the divorce, not the lack of children.

12 *Effects of divorce compared to death*

Rates of Mortality per 1,000 Population (*Registrar General's Statistical Review 1967 Part III.*)

Status	Males Age 25–34	Age 35–44	Age 45–54
Married	0.8	2.1	6.6
Widowed	5.1	5.8	12.7
Divorced	1.4	3.8	9.7

	Females		
Married	0.6	1.6	4.0
Widowed	2.0	3.6	5.9
Divorced	1.2	2.3	4.9

In these figures the separated are added to the married. Since the period of separation is the time of greatest stress, if the separated were added to the divorced, where they clearly belong, then the similarity between the effects of divorce and death would be even more striking. The same applies to the Registrar General's figures for suicide in Britain. Once again if, as Hart argues, the separated are added to the divorced, where they belong, then at certain times the suicide rates for the divorced can be ten times those of the married. See Hart.

13 *Divorces involving children*
In America in 1948, 42 per cent of divorcing couples had children under 18. By 1955, it was 47 per cent; by 1962, 60 per cent—involving 537,000 children. In 1972, 1973, 1974, 1975 about a million children a year were involved in divorce. In Britain, 68.3 per cent of marriages involved children under 18 in 1961; by 1973 it was 75 per cent.

APPENDIX H—CONSENSUAL UNIONS AND THE FAMILY

1 *Conventional family not the normal one*
In 1972, in America, the family types were as follows: 15 per cent married couples without children; 13 per cent single-parent families; 15 per cent remarried; 8 per cent some other traditional form (such as extended family); 8 per cent experimental (communes, etc.).

That this situation is more advanced now is suggested by the figures for young people living alone—potential fuel for different unions and ways of living. In America there has been an increase of 134 per cent in this since 1970 among those under 35 (U.S. Bureau of Census). In Britain, 21 per cent now live alone, and the figure is expected to rise to 31 per cent. A proportion of these will be under 35. But, young or old, they show the degree to which the conventional family is no longer 'normal' (*Observer*, March 18, 1979).

2 *Increase and formalisation of consensual unions on the Continent*
That the pattern is of swift growth is shown by the fact that these unions increased by 50 per cent between 1974 and 1976 in Denmark; in Sweden, looking at it differently, the number of marriages fell by 30 per cent between 1966 and 1975. In Holland, they have fallen by 25 per cent.

These unions are partly a formalising of the experimental marriage stage—one third of the Danish couples said this. They are also in part a form of marriage without vows—a further quarter of the Danish couples said this. And in Sweden this element is borne out by the number of children born to such couples. A third of Swedish children are illegitimate and laws have been passed to make sure they are protected if the couple split. During the census in Russia in February 1979, a Moscow woman said, "Many people live together who are not married. But if they are asked the woman always claims that she is married while the man says no. I remember the last census—there was a big mystery afterwards because it showed so many more married women in the Soviet Union than married men."

The trend in these countries is interesting in itself, since we are concerned with the whole Western culture grouping. But our emphasis is on America and Britain, and for both, Sweden and Denmark are often precursors in these matters.

3   *Approximate figures for consensual unions in Britain and America*

Westoff, in the article I used above for the Danish figures, says that 2 per cent of all American couples (over one million) are estimated to be consensual. I think he must be referring to figures in the Statistical Abstract 1977. Some of these '2 person households sharing with an unrelated person of the opposite sex' will be ordinary nonsexual situations (friends, friends of relatives). But no doubt a high proportion are consensual. In the *Redbook* survey 3.2 per cent of the sample were living with a man. In Britain, Richard Leete has estimated that 50,000 out of 570,000 one-parent families were cohabiting in 1971. The bulk of these would probably fall into our Second Wave Divorce Reaction, but the figure of roughly 2 per cent of the married population approximates to the American figure. That it is rising is suggested by a BBC report that a girl's magazine survey in London found recently that 17 per cent of their readers were living with someone. This had never shown up before. They thought either their readers were becoming more honest or it was becoming more common. It was probably both—more honest because more common.

4   *Age at marriage rising*

In Britain, in 1973, 10.6 per cent of brides were under 20; in 1974, 10.5 per cent; in 1975, 10.1 per cent, in 1976, 9.8 per cent. In America, the movement has been a bit more, but not much. The median age at first marriage for women was 20.6 in 1970; 20.9 in 1972; 20.6 in 1973; 20.6 in 1974; 20.8 in 1975; 21.3 in 1976.

5   *The cost of children*

In America, in 1976, it cost $80,000 to rear a middle-class child from birth through college. By 1979 this had risen to $86,000. In Britain, married couples have been consistently and increasingly discriminated against as regards tax since 1945. In 1945 such a couple lost 6 per cent of their income. In 1977, 23 per cent (by contrast, single person's contribution had risen only 6.3 per cent). The same holds true of tax thresholds. No wonder consensual unions are increasing.

APPENDIX I—REMARRIAGE

1   *Remarriage after divorce*

Goode found in a 1962 analysis that within 26 months of divorce 53 per cent remarried, whereas census returns used by Glick show that 75 per cent had remarried by 5 years, and by 14 years 6 out of 7. The age at which people remarry varies greatly, but in America the typical ages for men are 25–34, and women 20–34. Heather Jenner found the average for men on her books was 34 and for women 27.

APPENDIX J—RELIGION AND OTHER FACTORS

1   *The different patterns of death equalling divorce*

Pre-industrial England and Today

Divorce/Death by 5-year intervals	Pre-industrial England	UK figures 1975 adjuster as per Appendix G5
years	%	%
0–5	9.57	32.08
5–10	10.63	24.42
10–15	12.12	15.90
15–20	13.88	10.85
20–25	15.89	7.39
25–30	19.56	6.23

2   *Consolidation not reaction*

Illegitimacy figures have been falling in America and Britain since 1974. In America, figures for gonorrhoea have started to level off (syphilis falling); in the UK gonorrhoea has been level since 1973. The same approximate picture is true of sex (extra-marital and premarital), drugs, and drink—except where in these spheres you get a pattern of women catching up on men.

3   *Decline of religion in Britain*

Gorer's 1970 survey showed that religion in England had reached rock bottom. Since 1950 there had been a 2 per cent increase in those saying they had no religion, and a decline in church attendance of 4 per cent. Only 6 per cent could be said to practise in any serious way.

4   *Slackening influence of religion over behaviour*

The readership of *McCalls* in America is far more religious than the rest of the country—73 per cent said it was important in their lives. Of these, 19 per cent had been divorced, 89 per cent approved of divorce. Only 17 per cent cited the Church as the chief moral influence on them, a fact amply proved by other replies. Thus 50 per cent of Christians and 84 per cent of Jews did not regard premarital sex as immoral; 60 per cent and 93 per cent respectively approved of abortion. In Britain in 1969, Gorer found that out of 26 per cent who used the sheath then, 10 per cent were Catholic; of the 13 per cent then on the pill, 10 per cent were Catholic. The most recent survey shows the position today among Catholics: 75 per cent approve of artificial birth control, a majority approve of divorce and nearly half see nothing wrong in premarital intercourse. One-fifth approved of abortion. In Russia between 30 and 50 million of all ages are believed to be seriously practising Christians; yet Russia probably has the highest divorce rate in the West today.

REFERENCES

CHAPTER 1—INTRODUCTION

p. 11, 'Depending on how . . . one-third will.'
Paul C. Glick, 'Updating the life cycle of the family', *Journal of Marriage and the Family*, vol. 39, Feb. 1977; Richard Leete, 'Marriage and divorce', Population Trends, 3, Office of Population Censuses and Surveys, 1976.
p. 11, 'In that respect . . . of my time.'
Statistical Abstract of the United States, 1977; *Social Trends*, 9, 1978, H.M.S.O., 1978.

CHAPTER 2—SAXON SEXUALITY AND THE RAGE TO DIVORCE IN ANCIENT ROME

p. 17, 'Princess Findahair mentions . . . with him tonight.'
Gordon Rattray Taylor, *Sex in History*, Thames & Hudson, 1953; R. Briffault, *The Mothers*, Allen & Unwin, 1927.
p. 17, 'In the mid-fifteenth . . . of mortal sin.'
Laurence Stone, *The Family, Sex and Marriage in England 1500–1800*, Weidenfeld & Nicolson, 1977.
p. 17, 'As in all . . . repression and control.'
Rattray Taylor, op. cit.
pp. 18–24, 'The only other . . . can barely envisage.'
Jerome Carcopino, *Daily Life in Ancient Rome*, Routledge, 1941.
p. 19, 'Experiments in love-making . . . became common.'
Alex Comfort, *Sex in Society*, Duckworth, 1963.
p. 20 'Ovid's *Ars Amatoria* . . . with romantic love.'
Ovid, *Ars Amatoria*, trans. B. P. Moore, Folio Society, 1967.
p. 21, 'O Caelus . . . lordly-minded Remus.'
Gerald Brenan, *Thoughts in a Dry Season*, C.U.P., 1979.
p. 22, 'Human societies . . . society collapses.'

Margaret Mead, *Male and Female*, Gollancz, 1950.
p. 22, 'The family . . . in grave danger.'
Ibid.
p. 23, 'Professor Edmund Leach . . . in grave danger.'
Edmund Leach, B.B.C. Reith Lecture, 1978.
p. 23, 'Dr Jack Dominian . . . marriage and family.'
Jack Dominian, *Marital Breakdown*, Penguin, 1978.
p. 26, 'Lynn Linton . . . in the world.'
A. O. J. Cockshut, *Man and Woman—a study of Love and the Novel 1740–1940*, Collins, 1977.
p. 27, 'Talk-show host . . . what went wrong?'
Time magazine, March 20, 1978.
p. 27, 'Even in 1970 . . . foreign-born parents.'
The Population of the United States, C.I.C.B.E.D., 1974.
p. 27, 'It was indeed . . . Alexander Cockburn.'
Alexander Cockburn, *Village Voice*, Oct. 1977.
p. 27, 'The volatility . . . do so too.'
Peter Laslett, *Family Life and Illicit Love in Earlier Generations*, C.U.P., 1977.
p. 28, 'Yet the curious . . . due to migration.'
Ibid.

CHAPTER 3—SEXUAL REVOLUTION

p. 31, 'Part of the . . . call it revolutionary.'
Peter Laslett, review in *American Journal of Sociology*, July 1978; review, 'Sexual revolutions', in *New Society*, June 10, 1976.
p. 32, 'Battered babies . . . *control themselves.*'
Jean Renvoize, *Web of Violence*, Routledge & Kegan Paul, 1978.
p. 32, 'Some long . . . strong disapproval.'
M. Wolfenstein and M. Mead, *Childhood in Contemporary Culture*, 'Fun Morality: an analysis of recent American child-training literature', University of Chicago Press, 1955; G. Thomson and M. Wolfenstein, eds., *Behaviour in Infancy and Early Childhood*, Collier-Macmillan, 1976.
p. 32, 'So argued . . . contemporary events.'
Nicky Hart, *When Marriage Ends—a study in status passage*, Tavistock Publications, 1978.
p. 32, 'The sales of . . . life-long marriage.'
Sociologist interviewed on B.B.C. Radio 4, October, 1978.

p. 32, 'Over the last . . . the same number.'
Interviews and correspondence with Philip Hodson and Anne Hooper, November, 1978.

p. 33, 'At some time . . . sexual dysfunction.'
London Sunday Times, October 15, 1978; William Masters and Virginia Johnson, *Human Sexual Inadequacy*, Little, Brown, 1970; George and Nena O'Neill, *Shifting Gears: Finding Security in a Changing World*, Avon Books, 1975.

p. 33, 'The distinguished . . . have always done.'
Geoffrey Gorer, *Sex and Marriage in England Today—a study of the views and experiences of the under 45s*, Nelson, 1971.

p. 34, 'Some attitudes . . . behaviour does.'
Study of Ira Reiss quoted in Morton Hunt, *Sexual Behaviour in the 1970s*, Playboy Press, 1974.

p. 35, 'The goal of . . . adult sexuality.'
There are innumerable studies. See P. H. Mussen, J. J. Conger and J. Kegan, *Child Development and Personality*, Harper & Row, 1974.

p. 35, 'In the 1970s . . . place with boys.'
Peter Laslett, *Family Life and Illicit Love in Earlier Generations*, C.U.P. 1977; J. M. Tanner, *Education and Physical Growth*, University of London Press, 1961; J. M. Tanner, *Growth at Adolescence*, Blackwell, 1962.

p. 35, 'It is a . . . fluctuations in population.'
E. A. Wrigley, 'Family limitations in pre-industrial England', *Economic History Review*, Blackwell, 1962.

p. 35, 'It is still . . . England in 1978.'
Family Planning Association, *Fact Sheet 7*, 1978.

p. 35, 'Syphilis may . . . sexual emancipation.'
Family Planning Information Sheet, *Inform* no. 8, March 1977; Laurence Stone, *The Family, Sex and Marriage in England 1500–1800*, Weidenfeld & Nicolson, 1977.

p. 38, 'Some writers . . . happened before.'
Edward Shorter, *The Making of the Modern Family*, Collins, 1976.

p. 39, 'No doubt some . . . less elaboration.'
Interview, December 1978.

p. 39, 'A study carried . . . described to them.'
William Davenport, *Sexual Patterns in a Southwest Pacific Society*, reprinted in Ruth and Edward Brecher, eds., *An Analysis of Human Sexual Response*, Panther, 1969.

p. 39, 'Men and women . . . on moral grounds.'
Stone, op. cit.

p. 40, 'Some historians . . . marriage are changing.'
Shorter, op. cit.
p. 40, 'Oddly enough . . . does neither.'
Laslett, op. cit.; P. Laslett and K. Oosterveen, 'Longterm trends in bastardy in England, 1561–1960,' Population Studies, 1973.
pp. 40–47, 'It is here . . . familiar development.'
Stone, op. cit.
p. 44, 'It has emerged . . . last few years.'
Brenda Maddox, The Half Parent—living with other people's children, Deutsch, 1975; Renvoize, op. cit.
p. 44, 'Suddenly becoming . . . anyone realised.'
Russell Middleton, 'A deviant case: brother-sister and father-daughter marriage in ancient Egypt', in Rose Lamb Coser, ed., The Family: its Structures and its Function, 2nd ed., Macmillan, 1974.
p. 44, 'Wardell Pomeroy . . . one involved objected.'
Forum, August 1977, vol. 10, no. 6.
p. 46, 'But this view . . . under some attack.'
Peter Laslett, review in American Journal of Sociology, July 1978.
p. 48, '1880 has been . . . liberal development.'
Stone, op. cit.
p. 48, 'In 1963 . . . lack of excitement.'
Betty Friedan, The Feminine Mystique, Dell Publishing, New York, 1977. See also Betty Friedan, It Changed My Life, Dell Publishing, 1977.
p. 48, 'Alex Comfort . . . for sex itself.'
Alex Comfort, Sex in Society, Duckworth, 1963.

CHAPTER 4—IDEOLOGY OF THE SEXUAL REVOLUTION AND THE GENESIS OF OBSESSION

p. 50, 'We see the . . . happen to him?'
A. O. J. Cockshut, Man and Woman—A Study of Love and the Novel 1740–1940, Collins, 1977.
pp. 52–59, 'Kinsey's influence . . . a mass movement.'
Wardell B. Pomeroy, Dr. Kinsey—and the Institute for Sex Research, Nelson, 1972.
p. 54, 'There is a . . . in the Reports.'
Alfred C. Kinsey et al., Sexual Behaviour in the Human Female, W. B. Sanders, 1953, and their Sexual Behaviour in the Human Male, Saunders, 1948.

p. 55, 'They observed . . . on Masters and Johnson.'
Ruth and Edward Brecher, eds., *An Analysis of Human Sexual Response*, Panther edition, 1969.

p. 55, 'Of one of . . . School attendants.'
Ibid.

p. 58, 'Mildred Newman . . . all the truth.'
Interview, December 1978.

p. 59, 'in our culture . . . symptom . . .'
Albert Ellis and Robert Harper, *A Guide to a Successful Marriage*, Wilshire Book Company, 1977.

p. 59, 'By the 1970s . . . several orgasms.'
Shere Hite, *The Hite Report*, Summit Books, Paul Hamlyn, 1977.

p. 59, 'This shows up . . . times a week.'
'A Study of Female Sexuality', *Redbook*, June, September, October 1975; 'A Study of Male Sexual Behaviour', *Redbook*, February, 1978.

p. 60, 'The editor of . . . we have orgasms?'
Betty Jerman, *Evening News*. Antia Bevan, the present editor of *Parents*, confirmed that this trend continues.

p. 61, '(Jake . . . by the locals.)'
Kingsley Amis, *Jake's Thing*, Hutchinson, 1978.

pp. 61–64, 'Here is an . . . *Forum* collection.'
The Best of Forum, Forum International, New York, 1978.

p. 66, 'Sexual objectifying . . . feminine fantasies.'
Nancy Friday, *My Secret Garden—Women's Sexual Fantasies*, Virago/Quartet, 1975.

p. 68, 'This is . . . Sociological model.'
Nicky Hart, *When Marriage Ends—A Study in Status Passage*, Tavistock Publications, 1978.

p. 69, 'Certainly Eleanor Alter . . . going to happen.'
Interview, December, 1978.

CHAPTER 5—FEMINISM: ASPECTS OF WOMEN'S POWER AND WOMEN'S FREEDOM

p. 71, 'The genesis of . . . *The Feminine Mystique.*'
Betty Friedan, *The Feminine Mystique*, Dell Publishing, New York, 1977.

p. 72, 'In a series . . . be as well.'
T. Parsons, 'Age and Sex in the Social Structure of the United States', *American Sociological Review*, October 1942; T. Parsons, 'The Social

Structure of the Family', in R. N. Anshen, ed., *The Family: Its Function and Destiny*, Harper & Row, New York, 1949; T. Parsons, *Social Structure and Personality*, Free Press, New York, 1964; T. Parsons and R. F. Bales, *Family, Socialization and Interaction Process*, Free Press, Chicago, 1955.

p. 73, 'The cardinal . . . popularisers and commentators.'

J. Bowlby, *Attachment and Loss*, vol. 1, *Attachment*, Hogarth Press, Penguin, 1969 and 1971; J. Bowlby, *Child Care and the Growth of Love*, Penguin, 1973; J. Bowlby, *Attachment and Loss*, vol. 2, *Separation*, Hogarth Press, 1973; B. Spock, *Baby and Child Care*, New English Library, 1973; D. W. Winnicott, *The Child, the Family and the Outside World*, Penguin, 1969.

p. 73, 'One boy had . . . would do so.'

David Levy, *Maternal Overprotection*, Columbia University Press, 1943.

p. 74, 'I used to . . . (U.S. mother).'

Friedan, op. cit.

p. 75, 'Specific studies . . . but individuals.'

Michael Rutter, *Maternal Deprivation Reassessed*, Penguin, 1974.

p. 76, 'The experience . . . organisation in 1973.'

Group for the Advancement of Psychiatry, *Joys and Sorrows of Parenthood*, New York, 1973.

p. 76, 'Books appeared . . . harming their children.'

P. Roby, ed., *Child Care: Who Cares*, Basic Books, New York, 1973; L. N. Hoffman and F. I. Nye, eds. *Working Mothers*, Jossey-Bass, New York, 1974.

p. 76, 'Behavioural scientists . . . especially with girls.'

W. J. Gadpaille, 'Research on the physiology of maleness and femaleness' in H. Grunebaum and J. Christ, eds., *Contemporary Marriage: Structure, Dynamics and Therapy*, Little, Brown, Boston, 1976.

p. 76, 'From 1963 . . . of the father.'

H. R. Schaffer and P. E. Emerson, 'The development of social attachments in infancy, *Monograths in Social Research & Child Development*, 29, 3, 94, 1964; B. Z. Friedland et al., 'Time sampling analysis of infants' natural language environment in the home,' *Child Development*, 43, 730–40, 1972; D. Burlingham, 'The pre-oedipal infant-father relationship' in A. Freud et al., eds., *The Psychoanalytic Study of the Child*, vol. 28, Imago, 1973.

p. 76, 'The sixth myth . . . or future mothers.'

M. Rutter, 'Dimensions of parenthood: some myths and some suggestions', *The Family in Society*, Dimensions of Parenthood, H.M.S.O., 1974.

p. 76, 'Children who . . . effect on boys.'

U. Bronfenbrenner, *Two Worlds of Childhood: U.S. and U.S.S.R.*, Allen & Unwin, 1971.

p. 77, 'It is hardly . . . to be gentle.'

A. Oakley, *The Sociology of Housework*, Martin Robertson, 1974; I. Kon, 'Women at work: equality with a difference?' *International Social Science Journal* 27, 4, 1975; Edward Westermarck, *The History of Human Marriage*, Macmillan, 1921; Margaret Mead, *Male and Female*, Gollancz, 1950.

p. 78, 'Dr Jessie Barnard . . . and so on.'

Jessie Barnard, *Women, Wives, Mothers: Values and Options*, Chicago, 1975.

p. 79, 'In France . . . round the house.'

Edward Shorter, *The Making of the Modern Family*, Collins, 1976.

p. 79, 'In the last . . . suicide rate.'

Report in the *Observer*, March 18, 1979.

p. 79, 'When Reza Shah . . . by their men.'

Report in the *Observer*, February 25, 1979.

p. 80, 'Perhaps the most . . . never set foot.'

John Weightman, review of Alex Madsen, *Hearts and Minds: The Common Journey of Simone de Beauvoir and Jean-Paul Sartre*, William Morrow, 1978 *Observer*, June 25, 1978.

p. 80, 'A recent . . . mother role.'

McCalls Readership Survey, April 1976.

p. 80, 'What might . . . refrigerator-freezer.'

Marabel Morgan, *The Total Woman*, Pocket Books, New York, 1973.

p. 81, 'Just how . . . Robert Rapoport.'

Rhona and Robert N. Rapoport, *Dual-career Families Re-examined—New Integration of Work and Family*, Martin Robinson, 1976.

p. 81, 'In reply . . . resourceful and energetic.'

L. Lein et al., *Final Report: Work and Family Life*, Center for a Study of Public Policy, National Institute of Education Project, no. 3–3094, Cambridge, Mass., 1974.

p. 82, '(Both these . . . and Norway.)'

M. Paloma and N. Garland, 'Role conflict and the married professional woman', in C. Safilios-Rothschild, ed., *Towards a Sociology of Women*, Lexington, Mass., 1970; E. Grönseth, 'Work-sharing families—adaptations of pioneering families with husband and wife in part-time employment,' *Acta Sociologica*, 18, 1975.

p. 83, 'A survey by . . . *at all.*'

Audrey Hunt, *Management Attitudes and Practices towards Women at Work*, H.M.S.O., 1975.

p. 83, 'Research in . . . in the home.'

E. Heavio-Marmila, 'Convergences between East and West; tradition and modernity in sex roles in Sweden, Finland and the Soviet Union', paper given at 12th International Family Research Seminar, Moscow, 1972.

p. 83, 'Finally—Total Men . . . liberation bullshit.'

Observer, August 27, 1978.

p. 84, 'In 1979 . . . must be eliminated.'

Observer, February 11, 1979.

p. 84, 'In 1978 . . . with the children.' *Evening Standard*, February 12, 1979.

p. 84, 'By the 1920s . . . many primitive cultures.'

Edward Westermarck, *The History of Human Marriage*, Macmillan, 1921.

p. 84, 'In fact . . . by modern research.'

M. Greenberg and W. Morris, 'Engrossment, the newborn's impact on the father,' *American Journal of Orthopsychiatry*, 44, 4, 1974.

p. 84, 'Since the end . . . conceived children.'

D. Barber, *Unmarried Fathers*, Hutchinson, 1975.

p. 84, 'While Dorothy . . . paternal feelings.'

D. Burlingham, 'The pre-oedipal infant-father relationship', in A. Freud et al., eds., *The Psychoanalytic Study of the Child*, vol. 28, International Universities Press, New York, Imago, London, 1973.

p. 85, 'But the most . . . important part.'

S. Kitzinger, *Giving Birth: The Parents' Emotions in Childbirth*, Gollancz; Taplinger, 1973.

p. 86, 'This is . . . this stopped.'

Jonathan Gathorne-Hardy, *The Rise and Fall of the British Nanny*, Hodder & Stoughton, 1972 (*The Unnatural History of the Nanny*, Dial Press, New York, 1973).

p. 86, 'One can see . . . do send them.'

Jonathan Gathorne-Hardy, *The Public School Phenomenon*, Hodder & Stoughton, London, 1977 (*The Old School Tie*, Viking, New York, 1978).

p. 87, 'If they have . . . significance to them.'

E. E. L. Masters, *Parents in Modern America: A Sociological Analysis*, Dorsey, Homewood, Ill., 1970 (rev. ed., 1974).

p. 87, 'In America . . . happening in Britain.'

Statistical Abstract of the United States, 1977; *Hansard*, 3 July 1976, vol. 916, no. 155, cols. 415–446.

p. 87, 'But the . . . and sleeplessness.'

M. Guttentag and S. Salasin, 'Women, men and mental health', in

L. A. Cater and A. F. Scott, eds., *Women and Men: Changing Roles and Perceptions*, Aspen Institute, Stanford, 1975; Rhona and Robert N. Rapoport, 'Work and family in contemporary society', *American Sociological Review*, 30, 1965.

p. 87, 'And there are . . . they dislike.'
'I Want to Work but What about the Kids?' Equal Opportunities Commission, 1978.

p. 87, 'Over the last . . . any major area.'
Lois Meek Stolz, 'Effects of maternal employment on children: evidence from research', *Child Development*, vol. 31, March 4, 1960; Rhona Rapoport, Robert N. Rapoport et al., *Fathers, Mothers and Others, Towards New Alliances*, Routledge & Kegan Paul, 1977.

p. 88, 'The Swede . . . drop-out children.'
Interview, *Guardian*, January, 1978.

p. 88, 'Another study . . . in attachment.'
J. and B. Tizard, 'The social development of two-year-old children in residential nurseries', in H. R. Schaffer, ed., *The Origins of Human Social Relations*, Academic Press, 1971.

p. 89, 'Basement spacious . . . staff of six.'
Benjamin DeMott, 'After the sexual revolution', *Atlantic Monthly*, November 1976.

p. 89, 'In England . . . are illegal.'
Rhona Rapoport, Robert N. Rapoport et al., op. cit.

p. 90, 'But in most . . . this way.'
Lyn Owen, in the *Observer*, October 15, 1978.

p. 90, 'The benefits . . . their sex lives.'
Gronseth, op. cit.

p. 91, 'For example . . . 68.7 to 76.5.'
Statistical Abstract of the United States, 1977.

p. 91, 'Where both . . . and both sexes.'
Susan Vogel et al., 'Maternal employment and perception of sexroles among college students', *Developmental Psychology*, November 1970, vol. 3.

p. 91, 'It was studies . . . *same* workforce.'
J. Kreps, 'The allocation of leisure to retirement', appendix in M. Kaplan and P. Bosserman, *Technology, Human Values and Leisure*, Abingdon Press, 1972; R. Theobold, *The Economics of Abundance*, Pitman, New York, 1970.

p. 92, 'Americans tend . . . cause unemployment.'
Nigel Hawkes, report in the *Observer*, October 1, 1978.

p. 92, 'So much so . . . do the housework.'
Adrian Berry, report in the *Daily Telegraph*, May 8, 1979.

p. 93, 'Professor Stonier ... 30 years.'

B.B.C. broadcast, September 24, 1978.

p. 93, 'The British ... general unemployment.'

Ray Curnow and Iann Barron, *The Future with Micro-electronics*, Francis Pinter, 1979.

p. 94, 'I was therefore ... by Steven Goldberg.'

Steven Goldberg, *The Inevitability of Patriarchy*, Temple Smith, 1977.

p. 96, 'There was a ... a new woman.'

Nicky Hart, *When Marriage Ends—a study in status passage*, Tavistock Publications, 1978.

CHAPTER 6—THE PRIVILEGE BULGE

p. 97, 'The Bryn Mawr ... done in 1938.'

Rhona and Robert N. Rapoport, *Dual-Career Families Re-examined—New Integrations of Work and Family*, Martin Robinson, 1976.

p. 97, 'The boy who ... a 1943 study.'

David Levy, *Maternal Overprotection*, Columbia University Press, 1943.

p. 98, 'A therapist during ... her own stealing?'

Betty Friedan, *The Feminine Mystique*, Dell Publishing, New York, 1977; see also Betty Friedan, *It Changed My Life*, Dell Publishing, 1977.

p. 99, 'The only really ... them to change.'

Jonathan Gathorne-Hardy, *The Public School Phenomenon*, Hodder & Stoughton, 1977 (*The Old School Tie*, Viking, New York, 1978).

p. 101, 'They look like ... when young.'

Rhona Rapoport, Robert N. Rapoport et al., *Fathers, Mothers and Others—towards New Alliances*, Routledge & Kegan Paul, 1977.

p. 102, 'After a month ... full blast.'

Albert Ellis and Robert Harper, *A Guide to a Successful Marriage*, Wilshire Book Company, 1977.

p. 105, 'The O'Neills ... in a job.'

Nena and George O'Neill, *Shifting Gears*, Avon Books, New York, 1974.

p. 108, 'Marabel Morgan ... tell the world.'

Telephone interview, December 1978.

p. 108, 'I think ... Brenda Maddox.'

Brenda Maddox, *The Half Parent—Living with Other People's Children*, Deutsch, 1975.

p. 108, '*The World of* . . . Morton Hunt.'
Morton M. Hunt, *The World of the Formerly Married*, Allen Lane, Penguin, 1968.

p. 112, 'The O'Neills . . . get divorced.'
Nena and George O'Neill, *Open Marriage—A New Life Style for Couples*, Peter Owen, 1973.

p. 112, 'An article . . . serious conflict.'
Psychology Today, March 1976.

p. 114, 'In their book . . . are not members.'
Joanne Koch and Lew Koch, *The Marriage Savers*, Coward, McCann & Geoghegan, 1976.

p. 114, 'Edna Barrabee . . . thing to do.'
Benjamin DeMott, 'After the sexual revolution', *Atlantic Monthly*, November 1976.

p. 116, 'A modern account . . . been published.'
Jolan Chang, *The Tao of Love and Sex*, Wildwood House, 1977.

p. 117, 'In 1864 . . . On the contrary.'
Aldous Huxley, *Adonis and the Alphabet*, Chatto & Windus, 1956.

p. 119, 'Several Indian . . . practice of Tantra.'
Sir John Woodroffe, *Shakti and Shakta—Essays etc., on the Shakta Trantrashatra*, Madras, 1920.

p. 119, 'It also seems . . . spiritual experiences.'
Huxley, op. cit.

p. 119, 'The most emphatic . . . teach such wisdom.'
Wilhelm Franger, trans. E. Wilkins and E. Kaiser, *The Millennium of Hieronymus Bosch*, Faber, 1952.

p. 120, 'Writing in 1977 . . . home administrator.'
Robert Chester and John Peel, eds., *Equalities and Inequalities in Family Life*, Academic Press, 1977.

p. 120, 'A survey of . . . over-90s masturbated.'
British Journal of Sexual Medicine, no. 32, vol. 5.

p. 121, 'Less spectacularly . . . with homosexuality.'
Bernard Berkowitz and Mildred Newman, interview, December 1979.

p. 121, 'According to . . . threaten the marriage.'
Observer, May 2, 1979.

CHAPTER 7—ROMANTIC LOVE

pp. 122–50. Much of the information in this chapter comes from Denis de Rougemont, *Passion and Society*, Faber, 1956 (*Love in the Western World*, Harcourt Brace, 1940).

p. 120, 'Even the . . . fall in love.'
Heather Jenner and Muriel Segal, *Men and Marriage*, Michael Joseph, 1970.
p. 123, 'It was anti-marriage . . . it was symbolic.'
A. J. Denomy, 'Fin Amors: the pure love of the Troubadours,' *Medieval Studies*, vol. 7, Toronto, 1945.
p. 125, 'Jealousy is . . . is punished savagely.'
Edward Westermarck, *The History of Human Marriage*, Macmillan, 1921.
pp. 128–30, 'From 1740 . . . but somewhat later.'
Laurence Stone, *The Family, Sex and Marriage in England 1500–1800*, Weidenfeld & Nicolson, 1977.
p. 130, 'This was partly . . . nearly so successful.'
Mirabel Cecil, *Heroines in Love 1750–1974*, Michael Joseph, 1970.
p. 132, 'A study published . . . marital happiness.'
Mary W. Hicks and Marilyn Platt, 'Marital happiness and stability: a review of the research in the 60's', *Journal of Marriage and the Family*, November 1970.
p. 133, *'On the edge* . . . Spanish Copla.'
Gerald Brenan, *Thoughts in a Dry Season*, Cambridge University Press, 1979.
p. 137, 'But there is . . . two should join.'
Gerald Brenan, *Literature of the Spanish People*, Cambridge University Press, 1951.
p. 138, 'This ambiguity . . . certain melancholy.'
Gerald Brenan, *Thoughts in a Dry Season*, Cambridge University Press, 1979.
p. 139, 'A survey of . . . income providers.'
Jenner and Segal, op. cit.
p. 140, 'In monogamous . . . as you want?'
Margaret Mead, *Male and Female*, Gollancz, 1950.
p. 141, 'The Angolans used . . . old anthropologists.' Westermarck, op. cit.; Mead, op. cit.
p. 141, '(even Greece . . . in marriage).'
Dr. N. J. Carrattas, interview, Athens, June 1978.
p. 142, 'At the moment . . . image anxiety.'
Benjamin DeMott, 'After the sexual revolution', *Atlantic Monthly*, November 1976.
p. 146, 'The *McCalls* survey . . . husband or lover.'
McCalls, readership survey, April 1976.
p. 147, 'This is related . . . heights of masochism.'

I am indebted for this material to conversations and correspondence with Dr. Gordon Ambrose. I would also recommend his book on an unrelated but equally fascinating field: *Handbook of Hypnosis*, Bailliere and Tindall, 1980 (4th ed.).

p. 148, 'The specificity . . . can be neurotic.'
Robert F. Winch, *Mate Selection*, Harper & Row, New York, 1958.

p. 148, 'There is a . . . stretch ahead.'
Morton M. Hunt, *The World of the Formerly Married*, Allen Lane, Penguin, 1968.

p. 149, 'We say . . . who cast it.'
Dr. Gordon Ambrose, conversation and correspondence.

p. 149, 'Sociologists have . . . what is attractive.'
Robert Chester and John Peel, *Equalities and Inequalities in Family Life*, Academic Press, 1977.

p. 150, 'People like . . . into his eighties.'
Ronald W. Clark, *The Life of Bertrand Russell*, Cape and Weidenfeld & Nicolson, 1975.

CHAPTER 8—THE LASER BEAM OF CHANGE

p. 152, 'You get to . . . but nothing happened.'
John Mogey, *Family Neighbourhood: Two Studies in Oxford*, Oxford University Press, 1956.

p. 152, 'The nuclear . . . community pressure.'
P. Laslett, 'The family as a public and private institution: a historical perspective', *Journal of Marriage and the Family*, August 1973.

p. 152, 'In fact . . . write to them.'
M. Young and P. Willmott, *Family and Kinship in East London*, Routledge & Kegan Paul, 1957.

p. 153, 'The Rapoports . . . with stress.'
Rhona Rapoport, Robert N. Rapoport et al., *Fathers, Mothers and Others—Towards New Alliances*, Routledge & Kegan Paul, London 1977.

p. 155, 'An American . . . the first time.'
Denis de Rougemont, *Passion and Society*, Faber, 1956. (*Love in the Western World*, Harcourt Brace, 1940.)

p. 156, 'Even in America . . . time for life.'
Paul C. Glick, 'Updating the life cycle of the family', *Journal of Marriage and the Family*, vol. 39, February 1977.

p. 157, 'the impression is . . . and character.'

Jeremy Seaforth, *A Lasting Relationship—Homosexuals and Society*, Allen Lane, 1976.

CHAPTER 9—DIVORCE—FIRST WAVE REACTION. THE PATTERN OF PAIN

p. 163, 'Mrs. June Croxley . . . we are divorced.'
Interview in the *Sun*, 2 September 1977.
p. 164, 'If something of . . . feminine appliances.'
Jessie Barnard, *Remarriage: a study of marriage*, Dryden, New York, 1956.
p. 164, 'As the . . . seeping out.'
Morton M. Hunt, *The World of the Formerly Married*, Allen Lane, Penguin, 1968.
p. 165, 'I felt worthless . . . up for months.'
Ibid.
p. 165, 'One showed that . . . was to come.'
W. Waller and R. Hill, *The Family: a dynamic interpretation*, Holt, Rinehart, Winston, New York, 1938, rev. ed. 1951.
p. 165, 'There are what . . . burst into tears.'
Nicky Hart, *When Marriage Ends—a Study in Status Passage*, Tavistock Publications, 1978.
p. 167, 'One study found . . . at certain periods.'
Ibid.
p. 168, 'The family does . . . anthropological rule.'
Margaret Mead, *Male and Female*, Gollancz, 1950.
p. 169, 'The *McCalls* . . . completely necessary.'
McCalls, readership survey, April 1976.
p. 170, 'I was shocked . . . I could get.'
Hunt, op. cit.
p. 171, 'One man after . . . vaguely hopeful.'
Hart, op. cit.
p. 171, 'Stanley Spencer's . . . years later.'
Richard Carline, *Stanley Spencer at War*, Faber, 1978.
p. 172, 'A note of . . . between us.'
Hunt, op. cit.
p. 173, 'Nell Dunn . . . split husbands.'
Nell Dunn, *Living Like I Do*, Lorrimer, 1976.
p. 173, 'It is interesting . . . married opposites.'
C. Murray Parkes, B. Benjamin and R. Fitzgerald, 'Broken heart: a

statistical study of increased mortality among widowers', *British Medical Journal* no. 1 (740–43).

p. 175, 'Here is a . . . my life miserable.'
Hunt, op. cit.

p. 178, 'In fact the . . . pay up.'
Sir Morris Finer et al., *Report of the Committee on One-Parent Families*, H.M.S.O., 1974.

p. 180, 'A survey by . . . at the beginning.'
Good Housekeeping, October 1977.

p. 180, 'And most people . . . sort or another.'
Paul C. Glick and Arthur J. Worton, 'Perspectives on the recent upturn in divorce and remarriage', *Demography*, vol. 10, no. 3, August 1973.

p. 180, 'In the end . . . have done anyway.'
Rhona Rapoport, Robert N. Rapoport et al., *Fathers, Mothers and Others—Towards New Alliances*, Routledge & Kegan Paul, 1977.

p. 181, 'Indeed, in . . . and Japan.'
Hugh Carter and Paul C. Glick, *Marriage and Divorce: A Social and Economic Study*, Harvard, 1970; Social Trends, no. 5, 1974; Hunt, op. cit.; Family Planning Association, *Fact Sheet*, October 1976; *Atlantic Monthly*, November 1976.

p. 181, 'And this was . . . rest of Sweden.'
E. Otterström, *Acta Genetica et Statistica Medica*, 3, 1952.

p. 181, 'American sociologists . . . these effects.'
Sheldon and Eleanor Glueck, *Unravelling Juvenile Delinquency*, Commonwealth, New York, 1950.

p. 182, 'The most interesting . . . delinquent children.'
G. Johnsson, *Acta Psychiatrica Scandinavia*, supplement 195, 1967.

p. 183, 'One researcher . . . anarchy reigned.'
D. Marsden, *Mothers Alone—poverty and the fatherless family*, Penguin, 1969.

p. 183, 'One of the . . . are in care.'
Interview, December, 1978.

p. 183, 'Research has shown . . . before divorce.'
Paul C. Glick and Arthur J. Norton, 'Frequency, duration and probability of marriage and divorce', *Journal of Marriage and the Family*, May 1971.

p. 185, 'In Britain . . . of the cases.'
Stanley Reynolds in the *Guardian*, September 27, 1979.

p. 185, 'The playwright Terence . . . by the Court.'
Brenda Maddox, *The Observer*, May 28, 1978.

p. 186, '*She:* Well, I'd . . . Oh God.'
Hunt, op. cit.
p. 187, 'By now my . . . reap the whirlwind.'
Ibid.
p. 187, 'In the last . . . infinite harm.'
Brenda Maddox, 'Fallout,' *Observer,* May 28, 1978; *Good Housekeeping,* October 1977.
p. 187, 'In Denmark . . . look after children.'
London Sunday Times, April 16, 1978.
p. 188, 'That is why . . . teenage delinquency.'
Dr Alick Elithorn in the *Guardian,* April 15, 1980; telephone interview, January 1980.
p. 189, 'And as this . . . the same factor.'
Judith S. Wallerstein, Joan Berlin and Kelly Grant, *Surviving the Breakup,* McIntyre, 1980.
p. 190, 'There is no . . . is perfectly viable.'
Martin Richards, *Families Need Fathers Newsletter,* Summer 1978.
p. 191, 'Sheila Burns . . . equal rights.'
Interview, September 1978.
p. 191, 'In America the . . . only 1 to 2.6.'
J. T. Landis, *Social Forces,* 34, 2.
p. 192, 'The distinguished British . . . identifiable members.'
P. Laslett and K. Oosterveen, 'Long-term trends in bastardy in England, 1561–1960', *Population Studies,* 1973.
p. 192, 'Our divorce rate . . . of the population.'
T. P. Monahan, 'The changing nature and instability of remarriage', in *Selected Studies in Marriage and the Family,* Holt, Rinehart & Winston, 1962.
p. 193, 'In fact . . . to break up.'
Ibid.
p. 193, 'Something like . . . end in divorce.'
Hart, op. cit.

CHAPTER 10—AFFAIRS, COMMUNES, PROMISCUITY, GAY LOVE . . . THE WAYS WE LIVE AND LOVE NOW

p. 195, '*I need and* . . . Stanley Spencer.'
Richard Carline, *Stanley Spencer at War,* Faber, 1978.
p. 195, 'About a year . . . yet it wasn't.'
Nell Dunn, *Living Like I Do,* Lorrimer, 1976.
p. 197, 'In Denmark . . . a large scale.'

Charles F. Westoff, *Family Planning Perspectives*, vol. 10, no. 2, April 1978.

p. 199, 'With one-parent . . . in the 1980s.'

Population Trends, 13, 1978; *Observer*, May 28, 1978; *Atlantic Monthly*, November 1976.

p. 199, 'It is a . . . in the least.'

Adolf Guygenbühl-Craig, *Marriage—Dead or Alive*, Spring Publications, Zurich, 1977.

p. 200, 'It is possible . . . role orientation.'

Report by Colin Brewer, *London Sunday Times*, October 1, 1978.

p. 200, 'Of all the . . . one-parent families.'

Paul Lewis, *Community Care*, February 15, 1978.

p. 201, 'Nor are they . . . for several years.'

Interview, December 1978.

p. 201, 'In America . . . seven years.'

U.S. figures: *Atlantic Monthly*, November 1976; U.K. estimate by National Council of One-Parent Families, based on one-seventh turnover of total every year.

p. 202, 'In France . . . do the same.'

One-Parent Families, Spring, 1977.

p. 205, 'Luckily there is . . . considerable detail.'

D. T. Joffe and R. M. Kanter, 'Couple strain in communal households: a fair-factor model of the separation process', *Journal of Social Issues*, 32, 1976; R. E. Roberts, *The New Communes: Coming Together in America*, Prentice-Hall, New Jersey, 1971; A. Rigby, *Alternative Realities*, Routledge & Kegan Paul, 1974; B. E. Cogswell and M. B. Sussman, 'Changing family marriage forms: complications for human service systems', in M. Sussman, ed., *Non-Traditional Family Forms in the 1970's*, Minneapolis National Council on Family Relations, 1972; C. Gorman, *Making Communes*, Cambo, Whole Earth Tools, 1972; P. Atrains and A. McCullock, *Communes, Sociology and Society*, Cambridge University Press, 1976.

p. 205, 'Shelley was passionate . . . Jane Williamson.'

Richard Holmes, *Shelley—The Pursuit*, Weidenfeld & Nicolson, 1974.

p. 206, 'Cogswell gives . . . America in 1970.'

Cogswell and Sussman, op. cit.

p. 206, 'The Rapoports . . . emotional attachments.'

Rhona and Robert N. Rapoport, interview, 1978.

p. 207, 'Shelley, with . . . daily existence.'

Holmes, op. cit.

p. 208, 'A newspaper . . . a great many.'

Morton Hunt, *Sexual Behaviour in the 1970's*, Playboy Press, New York, 1974.

p. 208, 'Albert again . . . get her into.'

Dunn, op. cit.

p. 210, 'The O'Neills . . . make it work.'

Nena and George O'Neill, *Open Marriage—A New Life Style for Couples*, Peter Owen, 1973.

p. 213, 'Jeremy Seaforth . . . to their relationship.'

Jeremy Seaforth, *A Lasting Relationship—Homosexuals and Society*, Allen Lane, 1976.

p. 213, 'More interesting . . . Oneida community.'

R. T. Francoeur and A. Francoeur, *Hot and Cool Sex: Cultures in Conflict*, Harcourt, Brace, Jovanovich, New York, 1974; J. Ramey, 'Emerging patterns of innovative behaviour in marriage', *Family Coordinator*, October 1972; J. Ramey, 'Intimate groups and networks: frequent consequences of sexually open marriages', *Family Coordinator*, October 1975.

pp. 217–19, 'The moment I . . . state of mind.'

Seaforth, op. cit.

p. 219, 'You find it . . . over a thousand.'

Bernard Grebanier, *The Uninhibited Byron*, Peter Owen, 1971.

p. 220, 'There are . . . *The Baby Trap*.'

E. Peck, *The Baby Trap*, Bernard Geis, New York, 1975.

p. 220, 'A study of . . . to have children.'

John Cunningham in the *Guardian*, December 7, 1977.

p. 220, 'In Britain . . . by about 2020.'

Westoff, op. cit.

p. 220, 'The significant . . . are opting out.'

Rhona Rapoport, Robert N. Rapoport et al., *Fathers, Mothers and Others—Towards New Alliances*, Routledge & Kegan Paul, 1977.

p. 221, 'Some of them . . . precise about this.'

Heather Jenner and Muriel Segal, *Men and Marriage*, Michael Joseph, 1970.

p. 224, 'In the pagan . . . be so celebrated.'

B.B.C. radio broadcast, July 9, 1978.

CHAPTER 11—INTO THE FIRE AGAIN—DIVORCE AND THE SECOND WAVE REACTION

p. 228, 'I do it . . . really disgusting.'

Morton Hunt, *The World of the Formerly Married*, Allen Lane, Penguin, 1968.

p. 229, 'When I finally . . . my Audrey there.'
Ibid.
p. 232, 'Kinsey included . . . in their behaviour.'
I. L. Reiss, *The Social Context of Sexual Permissiveness*, Holt, Rinehart & Winston, 1967.
p. 233, 'The erotomania of . . . in the 1930s.'
Philip Lehrinan, 'Psychopathological aspects of emotional divorce,' *The Psychoanalytic Review*, January 1939.
p. 233, 'I've done everything . . . lost the way?'
Hunt, op. cit.
p. 234, 'Erich Fromm . . . sexual activities.'
Erich Fromm, 'Sex and character: The Kinsey Report viewed from the standpoint of psychoanalysis', *Sexual Behaviour in American Society*,
p. 236, 'I never fretted . . . my present marriage.'
Hunt, op. cit.
p. 238, 'I like living . . . tell you *that.*'
John Heilpern, Interview in *Observer*, January 14, 1979.
p. 240, 'One survey in . . . for the first.'
Hunt, op. cit.
p. 240, 'For many years . . . to overcome this.'
Brenda Maddox, interview, June, 1978.
p. 241, 'Certainly, Berkowitz . . . final one stable.'
Interview, December 1978.
p. 241, 'Studies of . . . extremely unsatisfactory.'
Jessie Barnard, *Remarriage: A Study of Marriage*, Dryden, New York, 1956.
p. 241, 'Another researcher . . . than the first.'
W. J. Goode, *After Divorce*, Free Press, Chicago, 1956.
p. 241, 'An understandable . . . last for life.'
U.S. Bureau of the Census, 'Number, timing and duration of marriages and divorces in the United States: June 1975', *Current Population Reports*, series p-20, no. 297, Washington, 1976.
p. 241–56, 'Brenda Maddox . . . place to live.'
Brenda Maddox, *The Half-Parent—Living with Other People's Children*, Deutsch, 1975.
p. 244, '*Who* we are . . . in a fourth.'
Ibid.
p. 245, 'Professor Goode . . . quite different.'
W. J. Goode, *World Revolution and Family Patterns*, Free Press, New York, 1963.

p. 246, 'I cannot bear . . . more and more.'
Maddox, op. cit.
p. 247, 'Winifred, who had . . . started to menstruate.'
Ibid.
p. 255, 'A British study . . . in this situation.'
Iris Goodacre, *Adoption Policy and Practice*, Allen & Unwin, 1966.
p. 255, 'Research done by . . . all lived together.'
Lucile Duberman, 'Stepkin relationships', *Journal of Marriage and the Family*, 1973.
p. 255, 'Oddly enough . . . to please men.'
Telephone interview, December 1978.
p. 256, 'There is even . . . divorce chain.'
P. Bohannen, ed., *Divorce and After*, Doubleday, New York, 1970.

CHAPTER 12—SOME SOLUTIONS TO THE PROBLEMS OF MARRIAGE, DIVORCE AND SEX

p. 257, 'The study . . . turn for guidance.'
Barbara Thornes and Jean Collard, *Who Divorces?* Routledge & Kegan Paul, 1979.
p. 258, 'The Institute of . . . would be saved.'
Interview and correspondence with Douglas Woodhouse and Janet Mattinson, September-October 1978.
p. 260, 'A book by . . . general headings.'
Joanne Koch and Lew Koch, *The Marriage Savers*, Coward, McCann & Geoghegan, 1976.
p. 262, 'Dr. Pines has . . . integrate them.'
Dinora Pines, 'Full circle: pregnancy and motherhood', paper delivered at the winter lectures of the British Psychoanalytic Society, 1975, quoted in *New Society*, February 2, 1978.
p. 262, 'In the same . . . wrongly blamed.'
J. S. Heiss, 'Premarital characteristics of the religiously inter-married in an urban area', *American Sociological Review*, 25 (1) 1960.
p. 266, 'Dr Albert Ellis . . . of all therapies.'
Albert Ellis and Robert Harper, *A Guide to a Successful Marriage*, Wilshire Book Company, 1977.
p. 266, 'When Dr Dominian . . . by 1973 116,510.'
National Marriage Guidance Council, *Annual Report*, 1974.
p. 267, 'Sexual difficulty . . . different causes.'
For example, R. M. Pierce, *Sociological Review*, 11, 1963.

p. 269, 'It is revealing . . . sells steadily.'

Ruth and Edward Brecher, eds., *An Analysis of Human Sexual Response*, Panther 1969; Fred Belliveau and Lin Richter, *Understanding Human Sexual Inadequacy*, Coronet Books, 1977.

p. 279, 'More significant . . . Dr Prudence Tunadine.'

L. P. D. Tunadine, *Contraception and Sexual Life*, Tavistock Publications, 1970; telephone interview, December 1978.

p. 279, 'Indeed, through . . . astonishingly swift.'

Eleanor Mears, 'Sexual problem clinics. An assessment of the work of twenty-six doctors trained by the Institute of Psychosexual Medicine', *Public Health*, 92, London, 1978.

p. 280, 'But the two . . . are excellent.'

Brecher, op. cit.

p. 281, 'The average female . . . totally exhausted.'

Belliveau, Richter, op. cit.

p. 282, 'It was a . . . to conceive.'

Edward Shorter, *The Making of the Modern Family*, Collins, 1976.

p. 283, 'This is the . . . *The Hite Report*.'

Shere Hite, *The Hite Report*, Summit Books, Paul Hamlyn, 1977.

p. 284, 'The truth is . . . the penis does.'

Mary Jane Sherfey, *The Nature and Evolution of Female Sexuality*, Vintage Books, New York, 1973; Edward M. Brecher, *The Sex Researchers*, Signet Books, New York, 1969.

p. 287, 'What is moving . . . *Self Love*.'

Betty Dodson, *Liberating Masturbation—a meditation on self-love*, Betty Dodson, New York, 1978.

p. 288, 'Margaret Mead suggested . . . full potential.'

Margaret Mead, *Male and Female*, Gollancz, 1950.

p. 288, 'Walking has to . . . won't be learnt.'

Charles MacLean, *The Wolf Children*, Allen Lane, 1977.

p. 289, 'He devoted almost . . . form of frigidity.'

D. E. Bergler, *Kinsey's Myth of Female Sexuality*, Grune & Stratton, New York, 1954.

p. 289, 'Here are three . . . 20 minutes.'

Anne Hooper, ed., *More Sex Life Letters*, Mayflower Books, 1977.

p. 289, 'Recently, however . . . drive a car.'

Stan Dale, 'Multiple Orgasms for Men', *Forum*, vol. 11, no. 8.

CHAPTER 13—THE FUTURE OF MARRIAGE, LOVE, SEX AND DIVORCE IN THE WEST

p. 292, 'The extraordinary . . . distant past.'
Peter Laslett, *Family Life and Illicit Love in Earlier Generations*, Cambridge University Press, 1977.

p. 296, 'In his book . . . *or Alive.*'
Adolf Guygenbühl-Craig, *Marriage—Dead or Alive*, Spring Publications, Zurich, 1977.

p. 297, 'In this partially . . . of this path.'
Ibid.

p. 298, 'To say I . . . my own language.'
Ibid.

p. 301, 'In Britain . . . proportion is women.'
B.B.C., 'Danger—women at work', *The Risk Business*, November 14, 1979.

p. 305, 'The *idee reçue* . . . 80 to 100 years.'
Laurence Stone, *The Family, Sex and Marriage in England 1500–1800*, Weidenfeld & Nicolson, 1977.

CHAPTER 14—THE GREAT CHANGE

p. 307, 'Before beginning . . . are all linked.'
For the historical information in this chapter see Gordon Rattray Taylor, *Sex in History*, Thames & Hudson, 1953; E. R. Dodds, *The Greeks and the Irrational*, University of California Press, 1951. Karl Jaspers, the philosopher, has put forward similar ideas.

p. 308, 'There was a . . . life on earth.'
J. P. V. D. Balsdon, *Romans and Aliens*, Duckworth, 1979.

p. 314, 'A Bishop of Geneva . . . Senate of Savoy.'
H. C. Lea, *An Historical Sketch of Sacerdotal Celibacy in the Christian Church*, Lippincott, Philadelphia, 1867.

p. 314, 'In Spain . . . religious elements.'
Rattray Taylor, op. cit.; R. Briffault, *The Mothers*, Allen & Unwin, 1927.

p. 314, 'In sixteenth- . . . over-brutal husband.'
Laurence Stone, op. cit.

p. 315, 'As well as . . . upper Bavaria.'
Edward Shorter, *The Making of the Modern Family*, Collins, 1976.

p. 315, 'In a recent . . . see themselves.'

Nicholas Mosley in the *Spectator*, November 18, 1978.
p. 317, 'Margaret Mead had . . . male-oriented society.'
Margaret Mead, *Male and Female*, Gollancz, 1950.

APPENDIX C

p. 327, 'Boredom of housework.'
J. H. Goldthorpe et al., *The Affluent Worker—Political Attitudes and Behaviour*, Cambridge University Press, 1968.

p. 327, 'Increased longevity' and 'More and . . .'
Statistical Abstract of the United States, 1977; Social Trends, 98, H.M.S.O., 1978.

p. 328, 'The Samoans have . . . or their children.'
Margaret Mead, *Coming of Age in Samoa*, Cape, 1929.

pp. 329–33, 'The inevitability of patriarchy.'
Steven Goldberg, *The Inevitability of Patriarchy*, Temple Smith, 1977.

p. 332, 'Dr John Money . . . Hopkins University.'
John Money, 'Matched pairs of hermaphrodites: behavioural biology of sexual differentiation from chromosomes to gender identity', *Engineering and Science*, 33:34, special issue, *Biological Basics of Human Behaviour*, California Institute of Technology, 1970; John Money, 'Sexually dimorphic behaviour, normal and abnormal', *Environmental Influence on Genetic Expression: Biological and Behavioral Aspects of Sexual Differentiation*, Fogarty International Aspects of Sexual Differentiation, Fogarty International Centric Proceedings, no. 2, U.S. Government Printing Office, 1971; John Money and Anke Ehrhardt, *Man and Woman, Boy and Girl*, Johns Hopkins University Press, Baltimore, 1972.

p. 332, 'In a recent survey . . . marriage and children.'
Research report 7349, *Glamour* magazine, September, 1977.

APPENDIX D

p. 334, 'The "Privilege Bulge" '
Health, U.S., 1976–77.
p. 334, 'The "Privilege Bulge" '
Annual Almanack of Statistics, 1974.

APPENDIX E

p. 334, 'William J. Goode . . . have vanished.'
Rose Lamb Coser, ed., *The Family: Its Structures and Its Functions*,
Macmillan, 2nd ed., 1974.

APPENDIX F

p. 336, 'For the years . . . most couples.'
Peter Laslett, *Family Life and Illicit Love in Earlier Generations*,
Cambridge University Press, 1977.
    p. 336, 'Stone gives . . . 1500–1800.'
Laurence Stone, *The Family, Sex and Marriage in England
1500–1800*, Weidenfeld & Nicolson, 1977.
    p. 336, 'At Senely-sur-Sologne . . . lasted 6 years.'
Gerard Bouchard, *Un Village Immobile*, Plon 1972.
    p. 336, 'The length of . . . 43.6 years.'
Robert V. Wells, 'Demographic change and the life cycle of American families', *Journal of Interdisciplinary History*, vol. 4, no. 2, 1971.
    p. 336, 'In New Zealand . . . by 1972.'
Correspondence with Peter Laslett, May 1978.
    p. 336, 'Contemporary figures . . . 52.4 years.'
O.P.C.S. monitor, DAI 77/3.

APPENDIX G

p. 336, 'Between 1715 . . . after five years.'
Jack Dominian, *Marital Breakdown*, Penguin, 1978.
    p. 337, '. . . (last year . . . much higher) . . .'
Guardian, October 20, 1978.
    p. 338, 'Italy, in 1967 . . . in this book.'
Morton Hunt, *The World of the Formerly Married*, Allen and Lane,
Penguin, 1968.
    p. 338, 'Increasing numbers of divorces.'
Britain: O.P.C.S. Marriage and divorce statistics, 1975; O.P.C.S. Pop
Trends 24, Summer 1981. *A Statistical Abstract Supplement*, U.S. Department of Commerce, Bureau of the Census, 1977; and 1980.
    p. 338, 'Divorces in any . . . over 20.'
Richard Leete, 'Marriage and divorce', *Population Trends*, 3,
O.P.C.S., Spring 1976; U.S. Figures: 'Number, timing and duration of

marriages and divorces in the United States,' June, 1975, *Current Population Reports*, series P-20, no. 297, U.S. Bureau of the Census, Washington, 1976.

p. 338, 'Hunt quotes . . . than over-20.'
Hunt, op. cit.

p. 339, 'This gap is . . . Robert Chester.'
Robert Chester, 'Contemporary trends in the stability of English marriage', *Journal of Bio-Social Science*, 3, 1971.

p. 339, 'Nicky Hart . . . five years.'
Nicky Hart, *When Marriage Ends—a Study in Status Passage*, Tavistock Publications, 1978.

p. 339, 'The study . . . first few years.'
Barbara Thornes and Jean Collard, *Who Divorces?* Routledge & Kegan Paul, 1979.

p. 339, 'UK: Percentage of divorces after years married.'
O.P.C.S., Marriage and Divorce Statistics, 1978.

p. 339, 'US: Percentage of divorce by age.'
'Number, timing and duration of marriages and divorces in the United States, June 1975', *Current Population Reports*, series P-20, no. 297, U.S. Bureau of the Census, Washington, 1976.

p. 340, 'A study by . . . true in Britain.'
C. Gibson, *British Journal of Sociology*, 25, 1 (79–98), 1974.

p. 340, 'But a survey . . . manual workers.'
Rowntree and Carrier, *Population Studies*, 11 (3), 1959.

p. 340, 'The Rapoports . . . of marriage.'
Lois Meek Stolz, 'Effects of maternal employment on children: evidence from research', *Child Development*, vol. 31, March 4, 1960; Rhona Rapoport, Robert N. Rapoport et al., *Fathers, Mothers and Others—Towards New Alliances*, Routledge & Kegan Paul, 1977.

p. 341, 'The detailed graph . . . fifth year.'
Current Population Reports, op. cit.

p. 341, 'The Rapoports say . . . of broken marriages.'
Rapoport, op. cit.

p. 341, 'As regards open . . . for some years.'
G. Rowntree, *Population Studies*, 28, no. 2, 1964.

p. 341, 'In America . . . and 8.2 years).'
Paul C. Glick, 'Updating the life cycle of the family', *Journal of Marriage and the Family*, vol. 39, February 1977.

p. 341, 'The British average . . . 13 years.'
Population Trends, 3.

p. 342, 'International Divorce League.'

Rapoport, op. cit.

p. 342, '(In fact, the latest . . . in that order.)'

The Guardian, December 17, 1980.

p. 342, 'For instance . . . have a divorce.'

G. Rowntree, op. cit.

p. 342, 'But many other . . . less happy.'

Mary W. Hicks and Marilyn Platt, 'Marital happiness and stability: a review of the research in the 60's', *Journal of Marriage and the Family,* November 1970.

p. 342, '. . . while Burgess . . . lack of children.'

E. W. Burgess and P. Wallin, *Engagement and Marriage,* Lippincott, New York, 1953.

p. 343, 'See Hart'

Hart, op. cit.

APPENDIX H

p. 343, 'Consensual Union and the Family'

B. E. Cogswell and M. B. Sussman in M. B. Sussman, ed., *Non-Traditional Family Forms in the 1970s,* Minneapolis, National Council on Family Relations, 1972.

p. 343, 'In 1972 . . . communes, etc.'

Rhona Rapoport, Robert N. Rapoport et al., *Fathers, Mothers and Others,* Routledge & Kegan Paul, 1977.

p. 343, 'That the pattern . . . if the couple split.'

Charles F. Westoff, *Family Planning Perspectives,* vol. 10, no. 2, April 1978.

p. 344, 'During the census . . . than married men.'

Dan Fisher, *The Guardian,* Feb. 7, 1979.

p. 344, 'In the *Redbook* . . . with a man.'

'A study of female sexuality', *Redbook,* June, September, October 1975.

p. 344, 'In Britain . . . in 1971.'

Richard Leete, *Population Trends,* 13, 1978.

p. 344, 'That it is . . . with someone.'

B.B.C. Radio One, September 20, 1978.

p. 344, 'In Britain . . . 9.8 percent.'

O.P.C.S. publications; *Population Trends,* 3–12.

p. 344, 'In America . . . in 1976.'

Statistical Abstract of the United States, 1977; *Hansard,* vol. 916, no. 155, cols. 415–16, 3 July 1976.

p. 345, 'In America, in . . . to college.'
Marvin Harris, *Cannibals and Kings*, Random House, 1977.
p. 345, 'By 1979 . . . to $86,000.'
Daily Mail, January 12, 1979.
p. 345, 'In Britain, married . . . of tax thresholds.'
London Sunday Times, May 28, 1978.

APPENDIX I

p. 345, 'Goode found in . . . per cent remarried.'
William J. Goode, *International Social Science Journal*, vol. 14, no. 3, 1962.
p. 345, 'while census . . . out of 7.'
Morton Hunt, *The World of the Formerly Married*, Allen Lane, Penguin, 1968.
p. 345, 'The age at . . . for women 27.'
'Number, timing and duration of marriages and divorces in the United States: June 1975', *Current Population Reports*, series P-20, no. 297, U.S. Bureau of the Census, Washington, 1976.

APPENDIX J

p. 345, 'Pre-industrial England and Today'
Ansley J. Coale and Paul Demery, *Regional Model Life Tables and Stable Populations*, Model North, Level 9, Princeton University Press, 1966.
p. 346, 'Consolidation not reaction'
Family Planning Association Fact Sheet, 30 Oct. 1977, and Fact Sheet 7 August, 1978.
Health US 1976–77.
p. 346, 'Decline of religion in Britain'
Geoffrey Gorer, *Sex and Marriage in England Today—a study of the views and experiences of the under 45's*, Nelson, 1971.
p. 346, 'The readership of . . . approved of abortion.'
Readership survey, *McCalls*, April 1976.
p. 346, 'In Britain in . . . were Catholic.'
Gorer, op. cit.
p. 346, 'The most recent . . . of abortion.'
M. P. Hornby-Smith and Raymond M. Lee, *Roman Catholic Opinion*, David Wedgewood, 1980.

INDEX